International Conferences Interfaces and Human Computer Interaction (IHCI2024), Computer Graphics, Visualization, Computer Vision and Image Processing (CGVCVIP2024), and Game and Entertainment Technologies (GET2024)

Held at the Multi-Conference on Computer Science and Information Systems (MCCSIS 2024)

Budapest, Hungary
13-15 July 2024

ISBN: 979-8-3313-0305-1

Printed from e-media with permission by:

Curran Associates, Inc.
57 Morehouse Lane
Red Hook, NY 12571

Some format issues inherent in the e-media version may also appear in this print version.

International Association for Development of the Information Society (IADIS)
Rua Sao Sebastiao Da Pedreira
No. 100, 30, 1050-209
Lisbon, Portugal

Phone: 351 21 3151373
Fax: 351 21 3151244

secretariat@iadis.org

Additional copies of this publication are available from:

Curran Associates, Inc.
57 Morehouse Lane
Red Hook, NY 12571 USA
Phone: 845-758-0400
Fax: 845-758-2633
Email: curran@proceedings.com
Web: www.proceedings.com

PROCEEDINGS
OF THE
INTERNATIONAL CONFERENCES
ON

INTERFACES AND HUMAN COMPUTER INTERACTION 2024

GAME AND ENTERTAINMENT TECHNOLOGIES 2024

and

COMPUTER GRAPHICS, VISUALIZATION, COMPUTER VISION AND IMAGE PROCESSING 2024

Budapest, Hungary
JULY 13 - 15, 2024

Organised by

iadis

international association for development of the information society

As a member of Crossref (a non-profit membership organization for scholarly publishing working with the purpose to make content easy to find, link, cite and assess) each published paper in this book of proceedings will be allocated a DOI (Digital Object Identifier) number for its fast and easy citation and indexation.

Volume Editor:
Katherine Blashki and Yingcai Xiao

Computer Science and Information Systems Series Editors:
Piet Kommers and Pedro Isaías

Associate Editor: Luís Rodrigues

TABLE OF CONTENTS

FOREWORD ix

PROGRAM COMMITTEE xiii

FULL PAPERS

INTERFACES AND HUMAN COMPUTER INTERACTION

DO WE HAVE GESTURES IN OUR HANDS? - ON THE INFLUENCE OF HAND CHARACTERISTICS ON MID-AIR GESTURE RECOGNITION 3
Lisa Graichen and Matthias Graichen

A REVIEW OF THE APPLICATION OF TECHNOLOGY ACCEPTANCE MODELS IN THE HEALTHCARE 11
Sadjad Eskandari and Juan P. Valente

FOSTERING EMOTIONAL ATTACHMENTS TO CARS: INSIGHTS FROM A FOCUS GROUP STUDY 19
Mareike Grund, Ingo Totzke and Arnd Engeln

PREDICTING STEM LEARNERS' PERFORMANCE IN SERIOUS GAMES FOR COMPUTATIONAL THINKING USING GAME LEARNING ANALYTICS FRAMEWORK 31
Fatin Nasuha Abdul Razak, Amirrudin Kamsin and Hameedur Rahman

DESIGN GUIDELINES FOR PERSONALITY BASED INTERFACES 41
Dina A. Zekry, Khaled Nagaty and Gerard T. McKee

NATURAL INTERACTION FOR MUSEUM INSTALLATIONS DISPLAYING CULTURAL HERITAGE: A CASE STUDY OF THE RECREATION OF THE TORRE DE LA PARADA 49
Luis Antonio Hernández-Ibáñez, Viviana Barneche-Naya and Guillermo Franganillo-Parrado

AN ANALYSIS OF INTERACTION BEHAVIORS IN PERSONALIZED LEARNING 57
Emine Cabı and Hacer Türkoğlu

GAME AND ENTERTAINMENT TECHNOLOGIES

FROM A PARTICIPATORY CITY TO A COLLABORATIVE CITY: VIDEO GAMES AS AN EMERGENT TOOL FOR COLLABORATIVE DESIGN 64
Khalil Morad El Ghilali, Iman Meriem Benkirane, Vassilis Bourdakis and Giorgos Papakonstantinou

DOWNFALL SEED SPREAD. A STACK-BASED ALGORITHM FOR THE AUTONOMOUS GENERATION OF 2D MAPS IN VIDEOGAMES 73
Lenin Acosta-Guevara, Félix Fernández-Peña, Pilar Urrutia-Urrutia and Diana Coello-Fiallos

REHASHING STORYTELLING IN THE MOBILE GAME: 'WALKING DEAD MATCH 3 TALES' CASE — 81
JaeJun Lee and Soyoun Eom

USING GAMIFICATION FOR TEAMBUILDING, COMMUNICATION AND INNOVATION – RESULTS FROM A LEGO® SERIOUS PLAY® WORKSHOP — 89
Julia Thurner-Irmler and Marietta Menner

EXPLORATORY STUDY ON QUANTIFYING COMPLEXITY IN THE TEMPORAL STRUCTURE OF ELECTROACOUSTIC MUSIC — 97
Jumpei Hayata, Shingo Honda, Soma Arai, Hidefumi Ohmura and Takuro Shibayama

UNFOLDING EDUCATIONAL GAMES AS SOFTWARE: GAME DESIGNERS' PRACTICES AND PLAYERS' PSYCHOLOGY — 107
Mifrah Ahmad

A PLAYFUL APPROACH TO EXTENDED REALITY GAME DEVELOPMENT BY INTEGRATING TANGIBLE AND VIRTUAL INTERFACES — 116
Hengbin Zhang, Xinyi Wu, Xiaoyang Wu and Ruowei Xiao

COMPUTER GRAPHICS, VISUALIZATION, COMPUTER VISION AND IMAGE PROCESSING

A METHOD FOR EMBEDDING BIOMETRIC AND OTHER INFORMATION IN COLOR IMAGES OF FACES — 124
Nazym Kaziyeva, Georgy Kukharev and Kalybek Maulenov

TEXTILE PATTERN DESIGN GENERATION USING GENERATIVE ADVERSARIAL NETWORKS — 131
Diogo Araújo, Luís Romero and Pedro Miguel Faria

BIDIRECTIONAL FEATURE PYRAMID FOR FACE DETECTION IN DENSE CROWD SCENES — 139
Yajuan Wei, Zhiejie Xu, Chuan Dai and Wanju Zhang

MESH-POLYPDET: SURFACE MESHES BASED POLYP DETECTION IN VIRTUAL COLONOSCOPY — 147
Ming Ma, Chenyang Sun and Na Lei

SHORT PAPERS

INTERFACES AND HUMAN COMPUTER INTERACTION

NONINVASIVE VISUALIZATION OF MUSCLES DURING SWALLOWING USING A MUSCLE DEFORMATION SENSOR — 157
Satoshi Shimabukuro, Ryouta Arashiro and Emi Tamaki

EXPLORING THE BENEFITS OF PHYSICAL FEATURES IN VIRTUAL REALITY ON CUSTOMER EXPERIENCE — 162
Robin Cherix, Maud Julmy, Marine Capallera, Julien Roland and Elena Mugellini

GAME AND ENTERTAINMENT TECHNOLOGIES

USER-CENTERED DESIGN OF AN OMNIDIRECTIONAL TREADMILL VIRTUAL REALITY EXERGAME 166
Daniel Cliburn, Vijay Kumar and Ethan Perez

REINFORCEMENT LEARNING TO GENERATE LEVELS FOR DESIRED DIFFICULTY 171
Donghyun Lee and Kyoungsu Oh

SERIOUS GAME FOR ADHD DIAGNOSIS 175
Georgios Liapis, Kejsi Rrasa, Michael Roditis, Kostas Klimantakis and Ioannis Vlahavas

COMPUTER GRAPHICS, VISUALIZATION, COMPUTER VISION AND IMAGE PROCESSING

A DEFORMABLE 3D ZEBRAFISH MODEL FOR BRIGHT-FIELD MICROSCOPY IMAGE SIMULATION 180
Richárd Jámbor and Attila Tanács

A RECEPTIVE ENHANCED BASED MULTI-SCALE FEATURE FUSION NETWORK 185
Guojun Mao and Xinchao Zhang

WORK IN PROGRESS: PRINTED CIRCUIT BOARD DEFECT DETECTION WITH PHOTOMETRIC STEREO AND NEURAL INVERSE RENDERING METHOD 189
Angelika Hable and Dieter P. Gruber

VIDEO-BASED PIANO PERFORMANCE EVALUATION VIA DYNAMIC TIME WARPING (DTW) 195
Vincentius Marcell and Chuan-Kai Yang

BONE POROSITY AND THICKNESS EVALUATION BY ULTRASONIC SIGNALS USING PATTERN RECOGNITION 200
Maksims Mamontovs, Aleksandrs Sisojevs and Alexey Tatarinov

REFLECTION PAPERS

INTERFACES AND HUMAN COMPUTER INTERACTION

EXPLORING THE INCORPORATION OF ARTIFICIAL INTELLIGENCE INTO DIGITAL TECHNOLOGIES FOR ART THERAPY 207
Augustina Ao Liu and Yuxi Ethan Cui

CLARIFYING DEFINITIONS: A SCOPING REVIEW OF DATA PHYSICALIZATION IN HUMAN-COMPUTER INTERACTION 211
Giorgia Burzio and Venere Ferraro

GAME AND ENTERTAINMENT TECHNOLOGIES

TRANSDISCIPLINARY FUTURES: ENHANCING GAME DESIGN AND INTERACTIVE MEDIA EDUCATION IN THE HIGHER EDUCATION LANDSCAPE 216
Bradley Young

ACHIEVING MOTIVATION-PSYCHOLOGICAL IMMERSION IN TECHNOLOGY-ASSISTED LEARNING, CONSIDERING EMOTIONAL STATES 221
Ehm Kannegieser and Robert Külpmann

DEVELOPMENT OF A COMPETENCE MEASUREMENT TOOL WITHIN A CUSTOMIZABLE GAMIFICATION ENVIRONMENT 225
Manuela Sachse, Christoph Laroque and Lisa Strauch

FOREWORD

These proceedings contain the papers of the: 18th International Conference on Interfaces and Human Computer Interaction 2024 (IHCI 2024), the 17th International Conference on Game and Entertainment Technologies 2024 (GET 2024) and the 18th International Conference on Computer Graphics, Visualization, Computer Vision and Image Processing 2024 (CGVCVIP 2024), which were organised by the International Association for Development of the Information Society, from 13 - 15 July, 2024. These conferences are part of the 18th Multi Conference on Computer Science and Information Systems 2024, 13 - 15 July, which had a total of 603 submissions.

The Interfaces and Human Computer Interaction (IHCI) 2024 conference aims to address the main issues of concern within Interface Culture and Design with a particular emphasis on the affective aspects of design, development and implementation of interfaces and the generational implications for design of human and technology interaction. This conference aims to explore and discuss innovative studies of technology and its application in interfaces and welcomes research in progress, case studies, practical demonstrations and workshops in addition to the traditional submission categories.

This conference seeks to cover both technological as well as non-technological issues related to these developments.

Submissions were accepted under the following topics:

- Affective User-Centred Analysis, Design and Evaluation
- The Value of Affective Interfaces / Systems / Application / Interaction
- Generational differences and technology design
- Measurement of success of emotional technology / interfaces
- Supporting user populations from specific Generations
- Supporting user populations with Physical Disabilities
- Supporting user populations with Intellectual Disabilities
- Creativity Support Systems
- Emotional Design issues / methods / experiences for novel interfaces including tangible, Mobile and Ubiquitous computing, mixed reality interfaces and multi-modal interfaces
- Usability
- User studies and fieldwork
- Methodological implications of Emotional User Studies
- Participatory design and Cooperative design techniques
- Ethical issues in emotional design
- HCI and Design education
- Eliciting User Requirements

The Game and Entertainment Technologies (GET) 2024 conference aims to bring together research and practice from creative, social and business practitioners and researchers in this challenging field. The focus of this conference is on design, development and evaluation of games, entertainment technologies and the nature of play. Known to have been enjoyed since at least 30 BC, games and entertainment are a universal part of human experience and present in all cultures. Games and entertainment activities contribute to the social, emotional, psychological and physical well-being of human society. As game and entertainment technologies become increasingly more pervasive we are continually challenged in our work, learning and personal life by increased access to virtual spaces and communities that offer opportunities for everyday needs and aesthetic experiences. The 'Creative Industries' require design and development structures, techniques and methodologies that enrich, enhance and encourage new interaction modes, metaphors and in-depth co-creation.

Topics of interest include, but are not limited to the following areas:

- Development methodologies
- Design issues
- Controversial issues – we welcome debate and dissension, for example; games as art, entertainment as purely for monetary returns etc
- Special Effects
- Animation
- Mobile and ubiquitous games and entertainment
- Serious Games –applications, critiques
- Philosophical issues
- Prototypes
- Social and cultural uses of/for Play
- Tools and technologies
- Skills, strategy, rules and chance
- Genre
- Immersiveness and engagement
- Research methodologies in creative practice
- Usability and playability
- User/player centered design
- Psychological, social, and cultural differences in perception and participation
- Communities, networks, social interaction and social capital
- Cross-cultural and intercultural approaches
- Assessment of exploratory learning approaches
- Emerging practices

The Computer Graphics, Visualization, Computer Vision and Image Processing Conference (CGVCVIP 2024), intends to address the research issues in the closely related areas of Computer Graphics, Visualization, Computer Vision and Image Processing.

The conference encourages the interdisciplinary research and applications of these areas. Submissions were accepted under the following 5 main topics:

- Computer Graphics
- Visualization
- Computer Vision
- Image Processing
- Other Related Topics

These events received 116 submissions from more than 22 countries. Each submission has been anonymously reviewed by an average of five independent reviewers, to ensure that accepted submissions were of a high standard. Consequently, only 18 full papers were published. The overall acceptance rate corresponds to about 16%. A few more papers were accepted as short and reflection papers. An extended version of the best papers will be published in the IADIS International Journal on WWW/Internet (ISSN: 1645-7641), the IADIS International Journal on Computer Science and Information Systems (ISSN: 1646-3692), and also in other selected journals.

This volume has taken shape as a result of the contributions from a number of individuals. We are grateful to all authors who have submitted their papers to enrich these conferences proceedings. We wish to thank all members of the organizing committee, delegates, invitees and guests whose contribution and involvement are crucial for the success of the conference.

Last but not the least, we hope that everybody enjoyed the presentations, and we invite all participants for the next years´ edition of these conferences.

Katherine Blashki, Noroff University College, Norway
Interfaces and Human Computer Interaction 2024
& Game and Entertainment Technologies 2024 Program Chair

Yingcai Xiao, The University of Akron, USA
Computer Graphics, Visualization, Computer Vision and Image Processing 2024
Program Chair

Piet Kommers, University of Twente, The Netherlands
Pedro Isaias, Universidade Aberta (Portuguese Open University), Portugal and
The University of New South Wales (UNSW – Sydney), Australia
MCCSIS 2024 General Conference Co-Chairs

July 2024

PROGRAM COMMITTEE

INTERFACES AND HUMAN COMPUTER INTERACTION CONFERENCE 2024 & GAME AND ENTERTAINMENT TECHNOLOGIES CONFERENCE 2024 PROGRAM CHAIR

Katherine Blashki, Noroff University College, Norway

COMPUTER GRAPHICS, VISUALIZATION, COMPUTER VISION AND IMAGE PROCESSING 2024 PROGRAM CHAIR

Yingcai Xiao, The University of Akron, USA

MCCSIS 2024 GENERAL CONFERENCE CO-CHAIRS

Piet Kommers, University of Twente, The Netherlands
Pedro Isaias, Universidade Aberta (Portuguese Open University), Portugal and The University of New South Wales (UNSW – Sydney), Australia

INTERFACES AND HUMAN COMPUTER INTERACTION CONFERENCE 2024 COMMITTEE MEMBERS

Afra Pascual, Universat de Lleida, Spain
Alexander Kröner, Technische Hochschule Nürnberg Georg Simon Ohm, Germany
Anastasija Nikiforova, University of Tartu, Estonia & European Open Science, Estonia
Andre Constantino da Silva, Instituto Federal de São Paulo, Brazil
Arianna D' Ulizia, IRPPS-CNR, Italy
Asterios Leonidis, Foundation for Research & Technology - Hellas, Greece
Birgit Bachler, FH Joanneum University of Applied Sciences, Austria
Bridget Kane, 1954, Sweden
Bruna Carolina Rodrigues Cunha, Universidade de São Paulo, Brazil
C.M. Nadeem Faisal, National Textile University, Pakistan
Eduardo Tanaka, Eldorado Research Institute, Brazil
Eleni Mangina, University College Dublin (UCD), Ireland
Felix Albertos Marco, University of Castilla-la Mancha, Spain
Habib Fardoun, King Abdulaziz University, Saudi Arabia
Janet Wesson, Nelson Mandela Metropolitan University, South Africa
Jesuk Ko, Universidad Mayor de San Andres (UMSA), Bolivia
José Antonio Macías Iglesias, Universidad Autónoma de Madrid, Spain
Juan Enrique Garrido Navarro, Universidad de Castilla-la Mancha, Spain
Kal Dhou, Texas A&M University Central Texas, USA
Larbi Esmahi, Athabasca University, Canada
Lavanya Elluri, Texas A&m University-central Texas, USA
Linghan Zhang, Eindhoven University of Technology, Netherlands
Maki K. Habib, The American University in Cairo, Egypt
Marcelo Romero Huertas, Universidad Autónoma del Estado de Mexico, Mexico
Mark Apperley, University of Waikato, New Zealand
Mathieu Raynal, University of Toulouse, France
Michael HOHL, HS Anhalt/FB Design, Germany

GAME AND ENTERTAINMENT TECHNOLOGIES 2024 COMMITTEE MEMBERS

COMPUTER GRAPHICS, VISUALIZATION, COMPUTER VISION AND IMAGE PROCESSING 2024 COMMITTEE MEMBERS

Full Papers

DO WE HAVE GESTURES IN OUR HANDS? - ON THE INFLUENCE OF HAND CHARACTERISTICS ON MID-AIR GESTURE RECOGNITION

Lisa Graichen[1] and Matthias Graichen[2]
[1]*TU Berlin*
10587 Berlin, Germany
[2]*81377 München, Germany*

ABSTRACT

Together with new hardware solutions, such as virtual reality (VR) headsets, the use of innovative interaction modes, such as mid-air gestures, is increasing in various areas of research, industry, and everyday life. As such setups are complex and not as well established as traditional haptic or touch-based interfaces, there is a higher risk of users experiencing errors, failures, or technical malfunctions. As for why gesture recognition rates may not be as high as desired, it is not yet clear why this is the case. We conducted a study in a VR context, using an HTC Vive headset and the Leap Motion gesture recognition device. Participants performed basic tasks with a "blocks" application using a pre-defined set of gestures. Afterwards they were asked to rate their levels on trust and acceptance. We also measured basic hand parameters. We examined the correlation between hand size and observed detection errors of the gesture recognition device. We found no significant correlation between hand measurements and error rates. However, there is some evidence that hand length has some effect, which means smaller hands seem to slightly increase the errors rate in interactions using the gesture recognition device.

KEYWORDS

User Experience, Virtual Reality, Gestures, Malfunction

1. INTRODUCTION

In recent years, extended reality applications have emerged rapidly, finding their way into users' everyday lives as well as professional applications, science and research. The term "extended reality" (XR) comprises different levels of immersion, including virtual reality (VR), augmented reality (AR) and mixed reality (MR). Although XR systems have existed for decades, recent technological advances have catalyzed the development of various applications and research questions. Consequently, low-cost systems, such as Oculus Rift and HTC Vive, have entered the market, making the VR experience affordable and available to almost everyone.

Typically, XR applications are implemented using head-mounted displays (HMDs). HMD systems usually come with a set of controllers that users can hold in their hands in order to control or manipulate the virtual environment. However, using such additional devices to interact with the virtual environment may not be suitable for several reasons. For example, holding the controllers for an extended period may cause discomfort for the user, some applications require that the user's hands are free, and if the controllers are used by many users and/or frequently changing users, there are additional challenges from a hygiene perspective. As an alternative to these controllers, gesture and voice control be used. However, these interaction types are not yet often used in combination with VR (Rakkolainen et al. 2021). In addition, the use of gesture-based interaction may have some disadvantages in terms of accuracy and reliability of detection, depending on various circumstances, such as lighting conditions or physical characteristics of the user. Therefore, we built a prototype application that can operated using gesture-based interaction (GBI; see Graichen, Graichen & Nudzor 2023 for details) to investigate the effects of hand characteristics on mid-air gesture recognition.

2. THEORY

In the domain of human–machine interaction, there is a wide range of interaction activities that are referred to as "gestures," beginning with clicking, pointing and moving a traditional computer mouse. In this area, the term "gesture" is most frequently employed to refer to the use of touch screens, with their well-established set of gestures including swiping, zooming and tapping in different contexts and dimensions (Saffer 2008). However, bodily movements that are performed in the air without making contact with a surface and hence without haptic feedback are also considered as gestures. Such mid-air gestures have applications in vehicles, for interaction with in-vehicle information systems, as well as in smart homes and VR. Even systems that use gaze interaction (where gazes are defined as a directional movement that triggers a predefined action) are referred to as "gesture-based systems" (e.g. Rakkolainen et al. 2021). Finally, use of the classical controllers that usually accompany VR HMDs is referred to as a "gesture-based interaction". In this paper, we use the term "GBI" to denote mid-air gestures that do not require physical contact with a surface (Saffer 2008).

Currently, there are few related works that combine GBI and VR. Therefore, research in this field, especially with a focus on user interaction, seems to be relevant. Some studies have been conducted in which users were asked to interact with virtual avatars. In Narayana et al. (2019), the authors built a prototype using an avatar. Users were asked to perform a task with blocks, and it was found that they considered social, deictic and iconic gestures to be important to employ when they could not use speech as a mode of interaction. Furthermore, users considered iconic gestures less important for communication to solve the task when they could use speech interaction. A similar approach is VoxWorld by Pustejovksy et al. (2020) , which also used a virtual avatar. Deictic, action and affordance gestures were used together with facial expressions and could be detected and performed by the virtual agent. Rodriguez et al. (2017) implemented a VR system using data gloves for gesture detection. This study investigated how quickly users could adapt to this system. It was found that experienced users adapted quickly, but inexperienced users needed more time to learn.

With regard to technical failures and errors gesture recognition device, it is of particular interest how users react and how such situations affect acceptance and trust in the system. Without acceptance and trust, users will not be willing to use a system. It is known from human-robot interaction that trust is not very stable, but changes over time, and trust can be reduced after users experience system failures (Esterwood & Robert 2022). However, trust seems to somehow stabilize after longer periods of use (Tolmeijer et al. 2021; Yu et al. 2018) reaching a level that matches the capabilities of the system. Thus, high system performance leads to high trust, and if performance falls below a certain threshold, trust would also decrease. The level of this threshold seems to be individual (Yu et al. 2018). Dorton & Harper; Dorton, Harper & Neville(2022) found that when interacting with AI, users may increase or decrease their level of trust after certain experiences and make adaptations in their workflows based on that by adding or removing certain tasks. Studies show that when confronted with errors in an automated vehicle, users seem to decrease their level of trust, but this effect was of a temporal nature. After perceiving accurate system performance, trust would recover, which is called trust repair (Lee et al. 2021; Dorton & Harper 2022; Kraus et al. 2020). Mishler & Chen (2023) found similar results in a similar setup, but the results show that trust recovered after an experienced failure, but trust levels measured before the failure were not reached again.

Despite its simplicity and usefulness, it is still a challenge to implement gestures in a way that every potential user with differing hand sizes, muscle tones or movement habits would experience perfect gesture detection. This led us to the question if parameters moderating gesture detection rates can be identified with the goal to mitigate potential issues in the future. In this study, we examine how hand characteristics such as length from wrist to middle finger tip, length from thumb to little finger, and middle finger diameter affect error rates to get an idea of why system errors occur. In addition, we compare error rates between male and female participants to investigate other reasons, such as differences in myotonus. We used a virtual reality setup in which participants were asked to perform basic tasks using mid-air gestures. Although this is well established and works well, it can still lead to errors, either because the system does not detect the hand movement correctly, or the user performs an incorrect gesture or the correct gesture in an imprecise way. We defined an error as any malfunction that did not result in the desired outcome.

We documented errors for each participant in order to examine the following research questions:

1) How do hand measures affect error rates? Is there a correlation between hand size and the number of errors documented?

2) Is there a difference between male and female participants?

3. METHODS

3.1 Design and Independent Variables

We chose a one-way repeated measures design with interaction mode (controller vs. mid-air gestures) as the factor. The controller interaction mode was used because it is the standard device that comes with the HTC Vive to familiarize participants with the VR settings and practice performing tasks in the environment. Using the standard controllers would also be considered gesture-based interaction, but performing mid-air gestures feels more natural to users because no tool needs to be touched, as in human communication, therefore we refer to this interaction mode as "gesture-based interaction".

3.2 Participants

An opportunity sample of 35 participants (21 females and 14 males, mostly students) was selected. The participants' mean age was 25.97 years (SD = 7.41, min = 15, max = 48). Four of them had no prior experience with gesture-based interaction, 31 already had some experience. None reported low interest in gesture-based interaction, 18 reported medium interest, and 17 reported high interest. There were no restrictions regarding VR experience or visual aids, however, it was not possible to wear glasses during the study. This research complied with the tenets of the Declaration of Helsinki, such that informed consent was obtained from each participant.

3.3 Facilities and Apparatus

We used an HTC Vive headset equipped with standard controllers to create VR experience. To implement GBI, we used a Leap Motion controller (https://www.ultraleap.com) that was connected to the HTC Vive and mounted on the front of the HTC Vive (see Figure 1). We used a basic application that allows users to perform basic tasks such as creating 3D blocks, resizing them, and grabbing and moving the created objects (see Figure 2). We used Unity to implement the block application. For details on the technical implementation. The experimenter was able to follow all the participants' actions on the connected laptop. We used a video camera to record the performed gestures and the laptop screen to be able to analyze the gesturing behavior and the reactions of the system.

3.4 Interaction Tasks

Six tasks were designed for both interaction types using the controller and the gesture recognition device. These tasks were derived from basic tasks that have the potential to cover a wide range of possible tasks (see Table 1 for details). To ensure that the gesture was appropriate for the selected interaction tasks, a pre-test was conducted with 17 participants using an online questionnaire. Participants were presented with images of different gestures and asked to rate the appropriateness of each gesture for each task. In the present study, we selected six gestures that were rated as highly appropriate for the selected interaction tasks. Table 1 shows the task descriptions and the corresponding gestures/controller actions.

Table 1. Tasks with Corresponding Mid-Air and Controller Gestures

Task	**Gesture**	**Controller**
Create Object		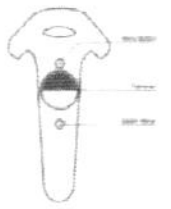
Change Object Size		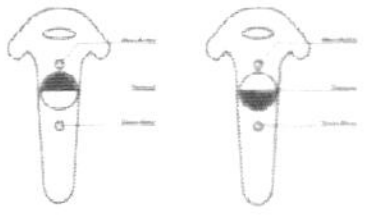
Rotate Object		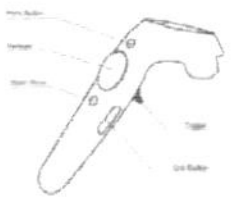
Move Object		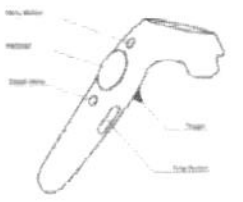
Toss Object		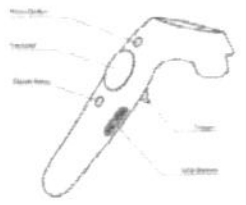
Remove Gravity		N/A

3.5 Procedure

Upon arrival, participants were introduced to the VR device and general usage of the system and devices (see Figure 1). Each participant was given as much time as necessary to learn and practice all interaction tasks. Participants were repeatedly tested on their interaction performance to reduce training effects during the experiment and to reduce the likelihood of making an incorrect gesture during an interaction task. The functionality of gesture recognition was demonstrated on-screen using an online visualization tool included with the gesture recognition device, which illustrated the device's tracking of the participant's fingers and palm. In the first phase, participants used a small application to familiarize themselves with the VR device. In the second phase, participants performed tasks using the controllers as a baseline or gestures using the gesture recognition device. In the third phase, participants used the other interaction mode to initiate tasks. See Table 1 for details on the tasks and gestures. Prior to each experimental trial, participants were instructed to perform the interaction task when they felt safe and comfortable doing so (see Figure 2).

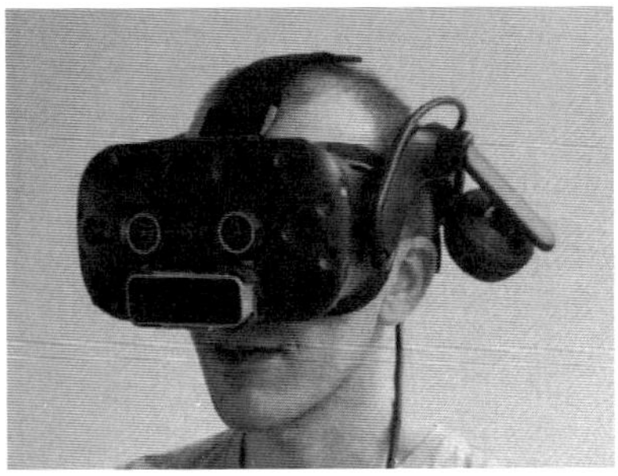

Figure 1. Setup of HTC Vive with Leap Motion mounted to the front

Figure 2. View of the participant in VR

After each phase, participants completed a questionnaire on their subjective impressions related to their most recent interaction. At the end of the experiment, participants completed additional demographic questionnaires, including hand measurements, sense of immersion, and simulator sickness. In total, the experiment took approximately 1.5 hours per participant.

3.6 Dependent Variables

Error rates were documented by the examiner during the study. A video recording was made in case an analysis was necessary after the study.

Hand measures have been documented by the participants with support of the examiner (see Figure 3).

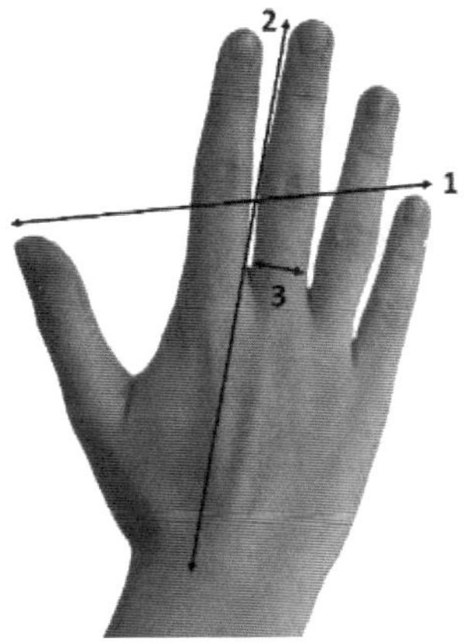

Figure 3. Hand measures used for the analysis: (1) Hand span, (2) hand length, (3) diameter of middle finger

4. RESULTS

One task from one participant had to be excluded from the analysis due to system crash. Since the data were not normally distributed, we calculated Spearman correlations. Correlations were interpreted according to (Cohen 1988).

For hand measures, we found that females generally had smaller hands than males, as expected. For female hand length $M = 17.7$ and $SD = 0.75$, for male hand length $M = 19.4$ and $SD = 1.2$. For female hand span $M = 18.9$ and $SD = 1.05$ and for male hand span $M = 21.1$ and $SD = 1.35$. For female middle finger diameter

M = 1.77 and SD = 0.12 and for male middle finger diameter M = 2.04 and SD = 0.23 (see Table 2 and Figures 4a-c).

Table 2. Hand measures for female and male participants.

Hand measure	Female		Male	
Hand length in cm	M = 17.7	SD = 0.75	M = 19.4	SD = 1.2
Hand span in cm	M = 18.9	SD = 1.05	M = 21.1	SD = 1.35
Middle finger diameter in cm	M = 1.77	SD = 0.12	M = 2.04	SD = 0.23

For documented errors, we found M = 0.82 and SD = 1.18 for female participants and M = 0.78 and SD = 1.28 for male participants. We conducted a t-test and found no significant difference, $t(33) = 0.29$, $p = .77$. This shows that there is almost no systematic difference between male and female participants in observed errors. However, it also shows that each participant experienced almost one error per task performed (see Table 3 and Figure 5).

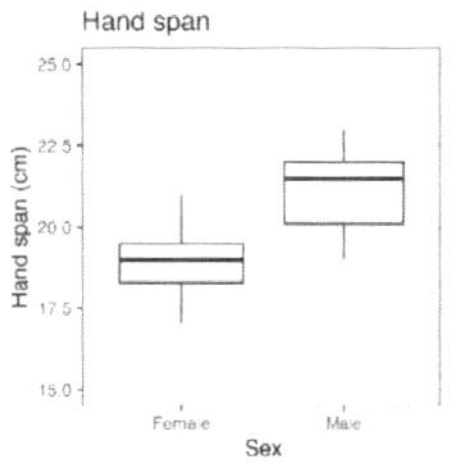

Figure 4a. Hand span for female and male participants

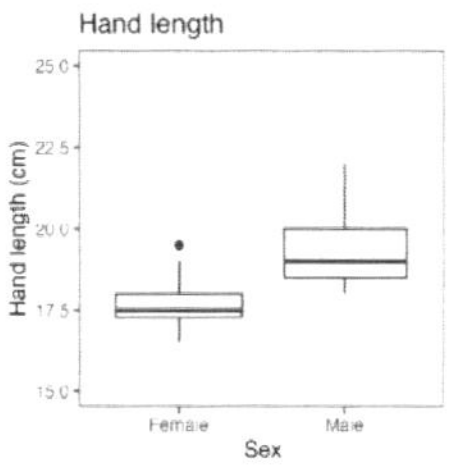

Figure 4b. Hand length for female and male participants

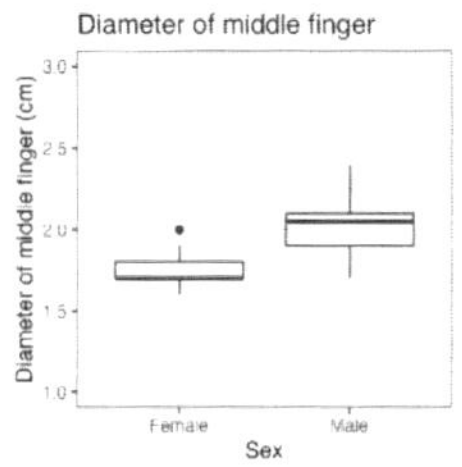

Figure 4c. Diameter of middle finger for female and male participants

Table 3. Error rates for female and male participants.

Hand measure	Female		Male	
Error rate	M = 0.82	SD = 1.18	M = 0.78	SD = 1.28

Spearman correlations for hand span and error rates reveal a small, non-significant effect of ρ = -0.17, p = .331, for hand length and errors also a small, non-significant effect of ρ = -0.2, p = .241 and for middle finger diameter no correlation with ρ = -0.04, p = .813.

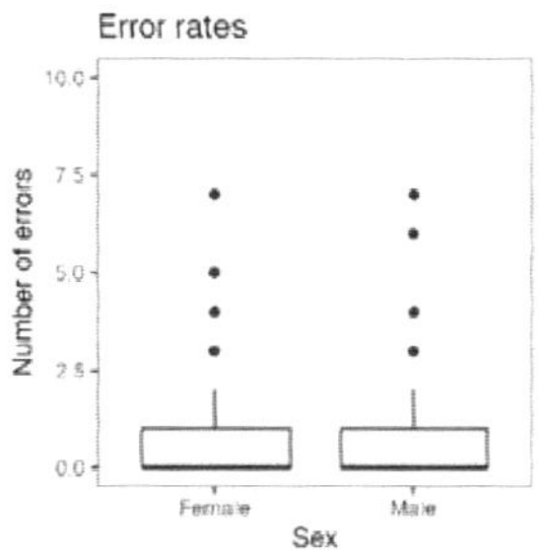

Figure 5. Error rates for female and male participants

5. DISCUSSION

In the presented study, we wanted to investigate whether we could identify systematic reasons for the errors in gesture recognition that we observed in previous studies. Therefore, we compared error rates between male and female participants to see if there were problems related to myotonus or similar anatomical characteristics. We also correlated various hand measures with observed error rates and subjective discomfort. As a result, we found that male participants had a significantly larger hand in all measures used. However, we did not find significant differences in error rates depending on the gender of the participants. We found a small to medium correlation between the size of the hand from the wrist to the middle finger and the error rates, but it was not significant. We found no correlation between hand size or middle finger diameter and error rates.

The use of gestures for human-computer interaction is a complicated issue. In previous studies, we found that gestures are attractive, stimulating, well accepted, and trusted by users (anonymized). However, large anatomical differences in hand size and shape, myotonus, and movement performance, can make it difficult to ensure robust gesture recognition. With regard to technological advances and availability of the necessary hardware and software, GBI devices can be easily implemented in different contexts by developers and researchers. Nevertheless, it can be seen that gesture recognition rates are significantly lower than when using more traditional interaction modes such as interfaces with haptic elements or touchscreens. Interestingly, participants do not seem to be too bothered by these errors and still have a positive subjective feeling about gestures. Nevertheless, gestures require a longer learning time for users, they might have to consult a user manual carefully, and they have to remember the gestures used by the system. Since there is not yet an established set of gestures similar to applied standards in touch-based systems, these gestures may also differ in different systems or applications. Developers must choose between two possible paths when implementing GBI. Either they design an interaction system with a small number of gestures that users can remember more easily, but which are limited in terms of their adaptability to different tasks. Or they implement a larger number of gestures, which are more difficult for users to remember, but which are more adaptable to different tasks.

With this study, we aimed to contribute to this discussion by investigating possible reason for relatively low recognition rates in GBI. We could observe that hand size seems to have some effect, meaning that participants with larger hands from wrist to middle finger experienced slightly lower error rates. This makes sense if you consider that the used gesture recognition device uses an infrared camera system and image processing algorithms to build a 3D model of the user's hand. This model includes the wrist, palm, and joints. The larger the hand, the more accurate might be the model as the discriminatory power changes relative to the distance of these anatomic characteristics. Therefore, more effort should be put into algorithms that work robustly for smaller hands as well.

The presented study is limited in scope due to its exploratory nature. Further research is needed to find the reasons why the gesture recognition rate is lower than desired and to find new technical ways to mitigate these problems. Since participants in such studies are often students, it would be interesting to see how attractive and acceptable gestures are to older potential users, and how gesture recognition works with these user groups. In addition, it would be interesting to gain insight into how hand muscle parameters affect gesture recognition and how gestures are generally performed by users, and how this compares to what is expected by gesture recognition developers, algorithms, and devices, and how improvements should be made based on these insights.

REFERENCES

Cohen, J. (1988). *Statistical Power Analysis for the Behavioral Sciences*, Taylor and Francis, Hoboken. Available from: http://gbv.eblib.com/patron/FullRecord.aspx?p=1192162.

Dorton, S.L. & Harper, S.B. (2022). 'Self-Repairing and/or Buoyant Trust in Artificial Intelligence', *Proceedings of the Human Factors and Ergonomics Society Annual Meeting*, vol. 66, no. 1, pp. 162–166.

Dorton, S.L., Harper, S.B. & Neville, K.J. (2022). 'Adaptations to Trust Incidents with Artificial Intelligence', *Proceedings of the Human Factors and Ergonomics Society Annual Meeting*, vol. 66, no. 1, pp. 95–99.

Esterwood, C. & Robert, L.P. (2022). 'A Literature Review of Trust Repair in HRI'. *2022 31st IEEE International Conference on Robot and Human Interactive Communication (RO-MAN)*, IEEE, pp. 1641–1646.

Graichen, L., Graichen, M. & Nudzor, J. (2023). 'Integrating Mid-Air Gestures into a Virtual Reality Application: A Methodological Approach'. *Proceedings of the International Conference on Virtual and Augmented Reality Simulations 2023*, ed M Kavakli.

Kraus, J., Scholz, D., Stiegemeier, D. & Baumann, M. (2020). 'The More You Know: Trust Dynamics and Calibration in Highly Automated Driving and the Effects of Take-Overs, System Malfunction, and System Transparency', Human Factors: *The Journal of the Human Factors and Ergonomics Society*, vol. 62, no. 5, pp. 718–736.

Lee, J., Abe, G., Sato, K. & Itoh, M. (2021). 'Developing human-machine trust: Impacts of prior instruction and automation failure on driver trust in partially automated vehicles', *Transportation Research Part F: Traffic Psychology and Behaviour*,
vol. 81, pp. 384–395.

Mishler, S. & Chen, J. (2023). 'Effect of automation failure type on trust development in driving automation systems', *Applied ergonomics*, vol. 106, p. 103913.

Narayana, P., Krishnaswamy, N., Wang, I., Bangar, R., Patil, D., Mulay, G., Rim, K., Beveridge, R, Ruiz, J., Pustejovsky, J.
& Draper, B. (2019). 'Cooperating with avatars through gesture, language and action' in *Intelligent Systems and Applications*, eds K Arai, S Kapoor & R Bhatia, Springer International Publishing, Cham, pp. 272–293.

Pustejovksy, J., Krishnaswamy, N., Beveridge, R., Ortega, F.R., Patil, D., Wang, H. & McNeely-White, D.G. (2020). *Interpreting and generating gestures with embodied human computer interactions*, Zenodo.

Rakkolainen, I., Farooq, A., Kangas, J., Hakulinen, J., Rantala, J., Turunen, M. & Raisamo, R. (2021). 'Technologies for multimodal interaction in extended reality - A scoping review', *Multimodal Technologies and Interaction*, vol. 5, no. 12, p. 81.

Rodriguez, G., Jofre, N., Alvarado, Y., Fernández, J. & Guerrero, R. (2017). 'Gestural interaction for virtual reality environments through data gloves', *Advances in Science, Technology and Engineering Systems Journal*, vol. 2, no. 3, pp. 284–290.

Saffer, D. (2008). *Designing gestural interfaces*, O'Reilly Media, Inc., Sebastopol, CA.

Tolmeijer, S., Gadiraju, U., Ghantasala, R., Gupta, A. & Bernstein, A. (2021). 'Second Chance for a First Impression? Trust Development in Intelligent System Interaction'. *Proceedings of the 29th ACM Conference on User Modeling, Adaptation and Personalization*, eds J Masthoff, E Herder, N Tintarev & M Tkalčič, ACM, New York, NY, USA, pp. 77–87.

Yu, K., Berkovsky, S., Conway, D., Taib, R., Zhou, J. & Chen, F. (2018). 'Do I Trust a Machine? Differences in User Trust Based on System Performance' in *Human and Machine Learning*, eds J Zhou & F Chen, Springer International Publishing, Cham, pp. 245–264.

A REVIEW OF THE APPLICATION OF TECHNOLOGY ACCEPTANCE MODELS IN THE HEALTHCARE

Sadjad Eskandari and Juan P. Valente
Department of Languages, Information Systems and Software Engineering
Universidad Politécnica de Madrid, Madrid 28660, Spain

ABSTRACT

In the present paper, a comprehensive review was performed on the application of technology acceptance models (TAM) in the healthcare sector. The important post-2019 published papers were searched and extracted by the Google Scholar search engine and important papers were taken into consideration for further analysis related to the use of recently utilized models on the final results of TAM based on different case studies. Although TAM has shown to have an outstanding role in predicting clinician acceptance and health information technology (IT) usage, there is still a need for improvement in cases of standardization, further relationship testing, better data reporting, and the exploration of new variables. In this regard, one can prioritize identifying clinicians' specific beliefs about health IT, enhancing the applicability of TAM in healthcare by evaluating contextual factors, barriers, facilitators, and social norms impacting IT adoption. In addition, based on the classification of recent studies into general variables and results, usefulness, ease of use, trust, and privacy concerns were determined as important factors in patients' acceptance of technology in healthcare services, and related recommendations were provided in this work. TAM-based models offer valuable insights into the adoption and acceptance of healthcare technologies and researchers and healthcare organizations should be mindful of their limitations and consider future research directions to enhance their applicability in an ever-evolving healthcare landscape.

KEYWORDS

Technology Acceptance Models, Health Information Technology, UTAUT, TTF

1. INTRODUCTION

In recent years, with the rapid development of information systems and the advancement of healthcare technologies, nurses are often required to learn how to operate relevant care assistance types of equipment while providing clinical care for patients. As the severity of patients' illnesses increases, nurses must spend more time taking care of them, therefore, lots of scholars assert that how to apply current information technology in assisting healthcare to effectively improve the quality of healthcare service and promote electronic case history has currently become an important subject in healthcare information management (Pai & Huang, 2011).

By developing technology especially information and communication technologies (ICT) integrated with people's private and professional lives, there remains an open question in the case of the acceptance or rejection of ICT still (Gupta & Yadav, 2022). Recently, the research community has intersected concerns about this issue leading to the development of many models of technology acceptance (TA) and its effective usage. The technology acceptance model (TAM), was first suggested by Fred Davis as a dominant model for evaluating the parameters affecting users' TA (Hariyanti, Sanjaya, Sutawinaya, & Sudhana, 2021; Purwanto, Hartini, Premananto, & Finance, 2020). Based on this approach a mediating role, two different variables namely perceived use and usefulness are assumed considering a complex relation among system attributes as external factors and potential system applications (Marangunić & Granić, 2015).

To determine the emergence of TAM and its developments, we first need to provide a short explanation of models affecting its appearance. As the early stages of technology have become an integral section of people, there is an important need to comprehend why technology is either embraced or rejected. In the first stages, many theories have been suggested to evaluate and predict these decisions which are rooted in the psychology field. In (Ajzen, 1980), scholars considered a hypothesis in which individuals tend to be rational and make systematic use of available information. They also formulated a theory capable of forecasting behavior and attitudes. In addition, they suggested that the actual behavior of an individual could be determined by considering their prior intention in conjunction with the beliefs they hold regarding the given behavior (Davis, 1985). Based on this theory, the main predictor of behavior is behavioral intention, with the effect of attitude on behavior being channeled through this intention. In this approach, one can classify different stages of this method as perceived usefulness (PU), perceived ease of use (PEOU), behavioral intention (BI), and actual use (AU) (Figure 1).

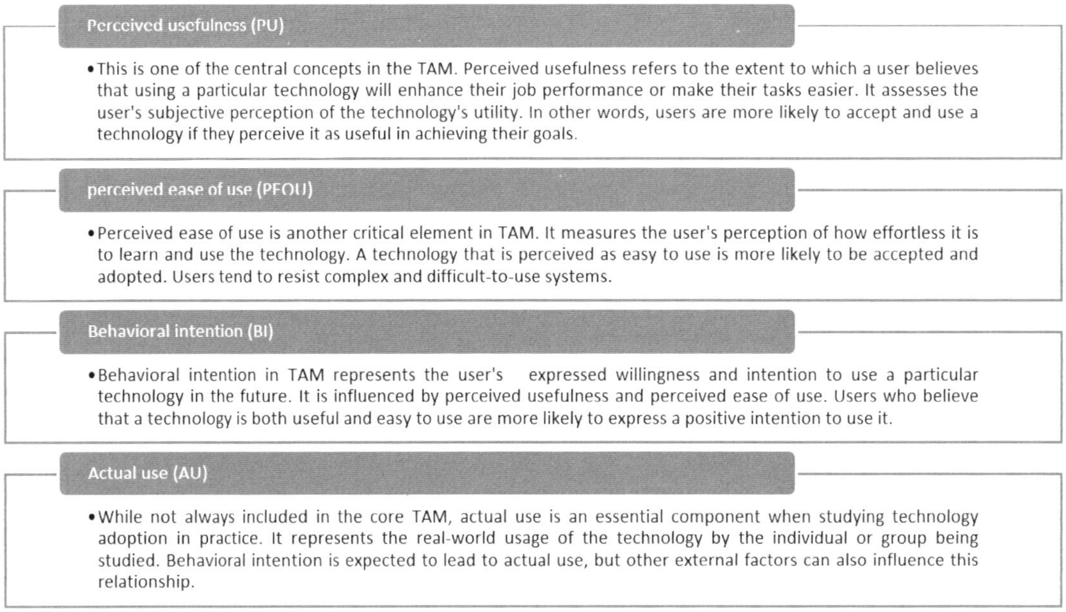

Figure 1. Different stages of TAM method (Abdullah & Ward, 2016; Alfalah, Falah, Alfalah, Qutaishat, & Muhaidat, 2020; Scherer & Teo, 2019)

2. TECHNOLOGY ACCEPTANCE MODELS

In the case of technology acceptance in the field of healthcare, many models have been suggested offering considerable insights into the factors that influence healthcare professionals, patients, and organizations in utilizing healthcare technologies. The Technology Acceptance Model (TAM) is known as the first foundational framework for understanding user acceptance of technology, which was suggested by Fred Davis in 1989. In the case of the healthcare section, this concept is beneficial in investigating the adoption of electronic health record systems, telemedicine platforms, and different medical devices (Zheng, Padman, Krackhardt, Johnson, & Diamond, 2010).

To enhance the TAM capability, many scholars developed TAM to include additional factors such as subjective norm, job relevance, and output quality known as TAM2 or TAM3 providing a better understanding in terms of technology adoption behavior for evaluating the acceptance of advanced healthcare approaches (Kaewsaiha, Chanchalor, & Technologies, 2021; Yazdanpanahi, Shahi, Vossoughi, & Davari Dolat Abadi, 2023). The TAUT which was first suggested by Venkatesh et al. in 2003 (Mohd Sah, Mat Shah, Azmi, & Hassan, 2021), has integrated many models and theories into a unified framework. As a result of the Unified theory of acceptance and use of technology (UTAUT), key determinants of technology acceptance can be identified consisting of performance expectancy, effort expectancy, social influence, and facilitating states (Abbad & Technologies, 2021). The researchers in the field of healthcare utilized UTAUT in cases of adopting electronic health records, mobile health apps, and telehealth services. Recognizing the important factors affecting the acceptance of health information technology, researchers developed a health information technology acceptance (HITAM) model to address healthcare contexts, specifically. Based on HITAM, many factors such as perceived usefulness, perceived ease of use, system quality, information quality, and user satisfaction should be considered. HITAM was applied in studies related to patient portals, health information exchange systems, and clinical decision support systems (Ogundipe, Sim, Emmerton, & Pharmacy, 2022). The IDT by Everett Rogers was determined to be influential in understanding the spread of innovations, including healthcare technologies whereas not exclusively a technology acceptance model (Lampo, 2022). IDT categorizes individuals into innovators, early adopters, early majority, late majority, and laggards based on their readiness to adopt innovations. Healthcare policymakers and organizations have utilized IDT to strategize technology implementation and adoption campaigns. In the subsequent sections of this article, we will delve into the applications, recent advances, challenges, and future directions of these technology acceptance models in the dynamic landscape of healthcare. Understanding these models is fundamental to comprehending the complex interplay between technology and healthcare stakeholders, ultimately shaping the future of healthcare technology adoption and utilization.

3. THE APPLICATION OF TAMS IN HEALTHCARE

Table 1 shows the recent papers on TA applications and their different models in healthcare sections. The main aim of the present paper was to determine the results of studies in the case of model applications and methods in findings related to the use of TAM in different fields. Models are to be included UTAUT and Task-Technology Fit, Robot acceptance model, and so on and methods were considered in the questionnaire survey, structured questionnaire, and raw data for use in different algorithms (Table 1).

Table 1. The recent studies in the field of TAM applications in healthcare

Ref.	Aim	Model Used	Method	Key Findings
(Pai & Huang, 2011)	Evaluating parameters for successful healthcare information system introduction	Information System Success Model (DeLone and McLean and TAM)	Questionnaire survey	Information, service, and system quality affect user intention through perceived usefulness and ease of use.
(Wang, Tao, Yu, & Qu, 2020)	Understand factors influencing consumer acceptance of Healthcare Wearable Devices	Integrated UTAUT and Task-Technology Fit (TTF) models	A self-administered questionnaire, PLS-SEM	Many factors positively affect consumers' intention to use HWDs.
(Kissi, Dai, Dogbe, Banahene, & Ernest, 2020)	Analysis of Physicians' satisfaction with telemedicine services adoption and utilization	Technology Acceptance Model	Structured questionnaire, SEM	Perceived ease of use and usefulness influence physicians' behavioral intentions positively.
(Turja, Aaltonen, Taipale, & Oksanen, 2020)	Propose a model for the intention to use care robots	Robot acceptance model	Data collection	Use intention is predicted by usefulness, enjoyment, social influence, and attitude.
(Ben Arfi, Ben Nasr, Khvatova, & Ben Zaied, 2021)	Examine IoT adoption in eHealthcare from the customer perspective	Extended UTAUT framework	Data collection	Cost is the primary barrier to IoT adoption in eHealthcare.

(Ayaz & Yanartaş, 2020)	Investigate factors affecting the adoption of Electronic Document Management System (EDMS)	UTAUT	Data analysis using R and SEM	Performance expectancy and social influence significantly influence the intention to use EDMS.
(Kuek & Hakkennes, 2020)	Assess digital literacy levels and attitudes toward information systems	-	Survey	The majority reported high digital literacy levels and positive attitudes toward information systems.
(Chen, Lin, & Wu, 2020)	Evaluate organization-driven barriers in implementing a healthcare information system based on big data	Acceptance of wearable technology (ANP) and VlseKriterijumska Optimizacija I Kompromisno Resenje (VIKOR)	ANP and VIKOR analysis	Model to assist in predicting and addressing organizational barriers in implementing a healthcare information system.
(Khan, Saleh, & Quazi, 2021)	Identify factors impacting healthcare professionals' social media usage behaviors	TAM	Self-administered survey	Multiple factors influence perceived social media usefulness, which affects social media usage behavior.
(Nezamdoust, Abdekhoda, & Rahmani, 2022)	Identify factors affecting nurses' use of health-related mobile applications	Combined TAM and diffusion of innovation (DOI) models	Questionnaire survey, data analysis with SPSS	Perceived usefulness and ease of use significantly influence nurses' use of mobile applications.
(Sudaryono, Fadhiil, Syarifah, & Simanjuntak, 2023)	Examine the application of TAM to telemedicine during COVID-19 pandemic	Extended TAM theory	Empirical testing using telemedicine user surveys	Trust is positively associated with the perceived usefulness and ease of use of telemedicine during COVID-19 pandemic in Indonesia.
(Hung & Jen, 2012)	Explore the intention of Executive Master of Business Management students to adopt MHMS	TAM	PLS analysis	"Perceived usefulness" and "attitude" significantly affect the intention to adopt MHMS.
(AlSuwaidi & Moonesar, 2021)	Assess user satisfaction with medical health apps among Dubai Health Authority (DHA) app users	TAM	Quantitative methodology	Statistically significant differences were found based on independent variables.
(Halbig et al., 2022)	Investigate healthcare professionals' needs and concerns regarding the integration of Virtual Reality (VR) applications	Extended TAM	Online survey	Users have a positive attitude toward the VR platform.
(Mouloudj et al., 2023)	Investigate factors influencing customers' adoption of digital health apps in Algeria	Extended TAM	Structured questionnaire survey	Several factors significantly predict customers' intention to use digital health apps.
(Huda & Review, 2023)	Investigate individual acceptance of m-government health services	Integration of TAM and expectation-confirmation (ECM) model	Quantitative analysis	Several factors significantly affect Intention to Use and Satisfaction.
(Farzandipour, Nadi-Ravandi,	Design a new health IT acceptance model based on Iranian users' views	HITAM	Cross-sectional study	Six key factors influencing attitude and use intention were identified.

Gilasi, & Soleimani, 2019)				
(Gharaibeh, Gharaibeh, De Villiers, & Technology, 2020)	Investigate factors influencing the acceptance of mobile health applications among elderly people in Jordan	IDT	Qualitative approach (focus groups)	Factors like relative advantage and observability influence acceptance.
(Lu & Deng, 2022)	Promote successful implementation of an intelligent surveillance system for construction site safety	Intelligent Surveillance System Acceptance Model (ISSTAM)	Questionnaire survey, SEM	Various factors impact use intention, with privacy risk having a negative impact.

Table 1 shows the studies concerned with the use of different TAM approaches in the healthcare sector. As seen, scholars are concerned with a wide range of healthcare-related topics in the case of TAM such as EDMS, healthcare wearable devices, care robots, the use of social media in education, big data-based healthcare information systems, digital literacy levels in healthcare staff, and the adoption of computerized healthcare systems. In addition, the factors influencing user acceptance of technology were investigated by using

TA-based approaches including UTAUT, TTF, ANP, VIKOR, DOI, Extended TAM¸HITAM, Innovation Diffusion Theory, and ISSTAM models. These models help analyze factors such as usability, perceived usefulness, and personal perceptions of technology value. Moreover, researchers have utilized different approaches to provide data such as questionnaire surveys, structured questionnaires, online surveys, self-administered surveys, PLS-SEM, and VIKOR analysis. In addition, different variables including perceived usefulness and attitude showed their place in previous research but it seems that more attention is needed for other study cases. Factors like cost and Perceived ease have been widely investigated.

In (Pai & Huang, 2011) and (Kissi et al., 2020), scholars converged on the adoption of technology in the field of healthcare and utilized TA theories, such as the UTAUT, to investigate the factors influencing user acceptance. They found that the expectancy of performance and social influence significantly impact users' intention to use EDMS. In addition, it was shown that the key barrier in the field of big data-based healthcare is its high costs. In (Wang et al., 2020) and (Turja et al., 2020), researchers concerned the healthcare wearable devices and robots. In (Wang et al., 2020), a hybrid model, consisting of UTAUT and TTF was utilized to understand consumers' acceptance of healthcare wearable devices and determined that factors like performance expectancy, effort expectancy, and social influence positively can affect the behavioral intentions of users. Meanwhile, in (Fielding et al., 2023) the intention to use care robots was concerned, emphasizing factors such as usefulness, enjoyment, social influence, and attitude. It finds that perceived usefulness and social acceptance are among the most important factors in users' perception of care robots. In (Ben Arfi et al., 2021), the digital literacy levels and attitudes of healthcare staff toward information systems were taken into consideration and investigated, especially in the context of implementing electronic health records. the need for targeted education and training for staff with low digital literacy, as this can significantly impact patient care. In (Kuek & Hakkennes, 2020), the adoption of computerized healthcare information systems with a particular focus on the elimination of traditional approaches was assayed. It was determined that factors such as performance expectancy and social influence are known to be vary essential in explaining users' intention to use EDMS in a university setting.

4. ADVANTAGES AND DISADVANTAGES OF TAM APPLICATIONS IN HEALTHCARE

As stated, there are many approaches in cases of TAM-based models successfully applied to various healthcare-related topics, including EDMS, healthcare wearable devices, care robots, social media usage in education, big data-based healthcare information systems, digital literacy levels in healthcare staff, and the adoption of computerized healthcare systems. This wide range of applications demonstrated outstanding results about the adaptability and effectiveness of TAM-based approaches in addressing diverse healthcare challenges. These models also can facilitate an in-depth analysis of related parameters in the acceptance of healthcare technologies. Moreover, users can obtain better apprehension behavior and attitudes by considering variables including usability, perceived usefulness, and personal perceptions. This in-depth analysis can lead to more informed decision-making in healthcare technology implementation and design. As mentioned, in the literature, there are numerous studies, in which TAM models are integrated and developed namely UTAUT, TTF, ANP, VIKOR, DOI, Extended TAM, HITAM, Innovation Diffusion Theory, and ISSTAM allowed researchers to explore complex interactions and dependencies among various factors, leading to a richer apprehension of technology adoption. One limitation of TAM-based models is the lack of generalizability. In this regard, the obtained outcomes from a specific healthcare context cannot be easily transferable to different settings or populations. Healthcare systems and user behaviors can vary across regions and demographics, making it challenging to apply findings significantly. In the process of TAM-based model applications, users' perceptions are commonly simplified into a few key factors, such as perceived usefulness and ease of use. While this simplicity aids in model applicability, it may oversimplify the complex nature of healthcare decision-making. Factors like trust, privacy, and social influence, while important, may not be fully captured by these models.

5. CONCLUSION, FUTURE WORKS AND RECOMMENDATIONS

The integration of technology in different sections of healthcare systems guided a new era of possibilities, shaping patient care, diagnostics, and healthcare systems. It also provides numerous advantages presents new challenges and raises ethical concerns. The future of healthcare technology holds promise in precision medicine, telemedicine, AI, and IoT. Therefore, technology has elevated patient care and efficiency in healthcare, significantly. EHRs enabled quick access to patient data, facilitating informed decisions. Due to enhancing new technologies, patients now have easy access to health information, fostering self-management and proactive health decisions. Noted that the diagnostic capabilities of technology are progressing, remarkably. Medical imaging techniques like MRI and CT scans provide precise diagnoses. AI-based technologies included administrative task automation, robotic surgeries, and predictive analytics for resource allocation in the field of healthcare. Research and development have benefited from technology, accelerating drug discovery and global scientific collaboration. However, its applications are context-specific, limiting generalizability. User perceptions are often simplified into key factors like perceived usefulness and ease of use, potentially oversimplifying healthcare decision-making. Although many studies were conducted in the field of TAM, many problems were introduced in this field that challenge its efficiency. Future research should focus on cross-cultural studies to determine the generalizability of TAM-based findings across different cultural contexts. The influence of cultural factors on TA in healthcare can be investigated to aid in designing culturally sensitive interventions. In addition, longitudinal assaying tracking the adoption and acceptance of healthcare technologies over time can provide insights into the evolving nature of user perceptions. It can be used to identify critical points for intervention and improvement. By advancing technologies including AI, telemedicine, and virtual reality in healthcare, future research should explore how TAM-based models can adapt to assess the acceptance of these emerging technologies. Healthcare organizations should use the insights gained from TAM-based research to tailor interventions that address specific barriers to technology adoption. This may include targeted training programs, user-friendly interface design, or addressing trust concerns. Collaboration between healthcare professionals, technology designers, and researchers is essential. Interdisciplinary teams can leverage TAM-based models to develop user-centered healthcare technologies that align with user needs and expectations. Healthcare organizations should adopt a culture of continuous evaluation and user feedback. Regularly assessing user satisfaction and acceptance of healthcare technologies can lead to ongoing improvements and better outcomes for patients and providers.

REFERENCES

Abbad, M. M. J. E., & Technologies, I. (2021). Using the UTAUT model to understand students' usage of e-learning systems in developing countries. *26*(6), 7205-7224.

Abdullah, F., & Ward, R. (2016). Developing a General Extended Technology Acceptance Model for E-Learning (GETAMEL) by analyzing commonly used external factors. *Computers in Human Behavior, 56*, 238-256.

Ajzen, I. (1980). Understanding attitudes and predicting social behavior. In M. Fishbein (Ed.). Englewood Cliffs, N.J. :Prenticc-Hall.

Alfalah, S., Falah, J., Alfalah, T., Qutaishat, W., & Muhaidat, N. (2020). An Analysis of the Technology Acceptance Model in Understanding The University of Jordan's Students Behavioral Intention To Use m-Learning. *International Journal of Psychosocial Rehabilitation, 24*, 1297-1312.

AlSuwaidi, S., & Moonesar, I. A. (2021). UAE Resident Users' Perceptions of Healthcare Applications from Dubai Health Authority: Preliminary Insights. *Dubai Medical Journal, 4*(1), 10-17. doi:10.1159/000513489 %J Dubai Medical Journal

Ayaz, A., & Yanartaş, M. (2020). An analysis on the unified theory of acceptance and use of technology theory (UTAUT): Acceptance of electronic document management system (EDMS). *Computers in Human Behavior Reports, 2*, 100032.

Ben Arfi, W., Ben Nasr, I., Khvatova, T., & Ben Zaied, Y. (2021). Understanding acceptance of eHealthcare by IoT natives and IoT immigrants: An integrated model of UTAUT, perceived risk, and financial cost. *Technological Forecasting and Social Change, 163*, 120437.

Chen, P.-T., Lin, C.-L., & Wu, W.-N. (2020). Big data management in healthcare: Adoption challenges and implications. *International Journal of Information Management, 53*, 102078.

Davis, F. (1985). A Technology Acceptance Model for Empirically Testing New End-User Information Systems.

Farzandipour, M., Nadi-Ravandi, S., Gilasi, H., & Soleimani, N. (2019). Iranian Health Information Technology Acceptance Model (IHITAM) from Users' Views. *Acta Inform Med, 27*(4), 245-252. doi:10.5455/aim.2019.27.245-252

Felding, S. A., Koh, W. Q., Teupen, S., Budak, K. B., Laporte Uribe, F., & Roes, M. (2023). A scoping review using the Almere model to understand factors facilitating and hindering the acceptance of social robots in nursing homes. *International Journal of Social Robotics, 15*(7), 1115-1153.

Gharaibeh, M. K., Gharaibeh, N. K., De Villiers, M. V. J. I. J. o. A. S., & Technology. (2020). A qualitative method to explain acceptance of mobile health application: Using innovation diffusion theory. *29*(4), 3426-3432.

Gupta, P., & Yadav, S. (2022). *A TAM-based Study on the ICT Usage by the Academicians in Higher Educational Institutions of Delhi NCR.* Paper presented at the Congress on Intelligent Systems: Proceedings of CIS 2021, Volume 2.

Halbig, A., Babu, S. K., Gatter, S., Latoschik, M. E., Brukamp, K., & von Mammen, S. J. F. i. V. R. (2022). Opportunities and challenges of virtual reality in healthcare–a domain experts inquiry. *3*, 14.

Hariyanti, N. K. D., Sanjaya, I. G. N., Sutawinaya, I. P., & Sudhana, I. F. P. (2021). *Conceptual Model for Adoption of Mobile Banking Technology in Savings and Loans Cooperatives.* Paper presented at the International Conference on Applied Science and Technology on Social Science (ICAST-SS 2020).

Huda, M. N. J. P., & Review, G. (2023). Analysis the Critical Factors of M-government Service Acceptance: An Integrating Theoretical Model between TAM and ECM. *7*(2), 109-124.

Hung, M.-C., & Jen, W.-Y. (2012). The Adoption of Mobile Health Management Services: An Empirical Study. *Journal of Medical Systems, 36*(3), 1381-1388. doi:10.1007/s10916-010-9600-2

Kaewsaiha, P., Chanchalor, S. J. E., & Technologies, I. (2021). Factors affecting the usage of learning management systems in higher education. *26*, 2919-2939.

Khan, M. I., Saleh, M. A., & Quazi, A. (2021). Social Media Adoption by Health Professionals: A TAM-Based Study. *8*(1), 6.

Kissi, J., Dai, B., Dogbe, C. S., Banahene, J., & Ernest, O. (2020). Predictive factors of physicians' satisfaction with telemedicine services acceptance. *26*(3), 1866-1880. doi:10.1177/1460458219892162

Kuek, A., & Hakkennes, S. (2020). Healthcare staff digital literacy levels and their attitudes towards information systems. *26*(1), 592-612. doi:10.1177/1460458219839613

Lampo, A. (2022). *How is Technology Accepted? Fundamental Works in User Technology Acceptance from Diffusion of Innovations to UTAUT-2.* Paper presented at the Proceedings of the 8th International Conference on Industrial and Business Engineering.

Lu, Y., & Deng, Y. (2022). What Drives Construction Practitioners’ Acceptance of Intelligent Surveillance Systems? An Extended Technology Acceptance Model. *12*(2), 104.

Marangunić, N., & Granić, A. (2015). Technology acceptance model: a literature review from 1986 to 2013. *Universal Access in the Information Society, 14*(1), 81-95. doi:10.1007/s10209-014-0348-1

Mohd Sah, N. F., Mat Shah, N. S., Azmi, F. S., & Hassan, N. D. J. A. i. B. R. I. J. (2021). A study on the acceptance of e-wallet apps usage amidst mobile phone users in Klang Valley. *7*(3), 65-72.

Mouloudj, K., Bouarar, A. C., Asanza, D. M., Saadaoui, L., Mouloudj, S., Njoku, A. U., . . . Bouarar, A. (2023). Factors Influencing the Adoption of Digital Health Apps: An Extended Technology Acceptance Model (TAM). In *Integrating Digital Health Strategies for Effective Administration* (pp. 116-132): IGI Global.

Nezamdoust, S., Abdekhoda, M., & Rahmani, A. (2022). Determinant factors in adopting mobile health application in healthcare by nurses. *BMC Med Inform Decis Mak, 22*(1), 47.

Ogundipe, A., Sim, T. F., Emmerton, L. J. R. i. S., & Pharmacy, A. (2022). Health information communication technology evaluation frameworks for pharmacist prescribing: A systematic scoping review.

Pai, F.-Y., & Huang, K.-I. (2011). Applying the Technology Acceptance Model to the introduction of healthcare information systems. *Technological Forecasting and Social Change, 78*(4), 650-660.

Purwanto, S., Hartini, S., Premananto, G. C. J. J. o. A., & Finance, S. (2020). Narrative online advertising as external variable in the development of the technology acceptance model of go-pay for millennials. *3*(1), 118-135.

Scherer, R., & Teo, T. (2019). Unpacking teachers' intentions to integrate technology: A meta-analysis. *Educational Research Review, 27*, 90-109.

Sudaryono, N. G. P., Fadhiil, M., Syarifah, S., & Simanjuntak, E. R. J. J. o. W. S. (2023). Application of Technology Acceptance Model (TAM) in Telemedicine Application During Covid-19 Pandemic. *2*(7), 909-921.

Turja, T., Aaltonen, I., Taipale, S., & Oksanen, A. (2020). Robot acceptance model for care (RAM-care): A principled approach to the intention to use care robots. *Information & Management, 57*(5), 103220.

Wang, H., Tao, D., Yu, N., & Qu, X. (2020). Understanding consumer acceptance of healthcare wearable devices: An integrated model of UTAUT and TTF. *International Journal of Medical Informatics, 139*, 104156.

Yazdanpanahi, F., Shahi, M., Vossoughi, M., & Davari Dolat Abadi, N. J. J. o. D. (2023). Investigating the Effective Factors on the Acceptance of Teleorthodontic Technology Based on the Technology Acceptance Model 3 (TAM3).

Zheng, K., Padman, R., Krackhardt, D., Johnson, M. P., & Diamond, H. S. J. J. o. t. A. M. I. A. (2010). Social networks and physician adoption of electronic health records: insights from an empirical study. *17*(3), 328-336.

FOSTERING EMOTIONAL ATTACHMENTS TO CARS: INSIGHTS FROM A FOCUS GROUP STUDY

Mareike Grund[1], Ingo Totzke[1] and Arnd Engeln[2]
[1]*CARIAD SE, Germany*
[2]*Hochschule der Medien, Stuttgart, Germany*

ABSTRACT

The emotional attachment between users and products is shaped by pragmatic and hedonic qualities. Their influence and importance are changing over time and varying across products. While different user groups (owners, lessees, car sharing users) form emotional attachments to cars, the relevance of these product qualities throughout a car's lifecycle (familiarisation, everyday use, malfunctions, farewell) is unknown.
The aim of this study is to provide approaches to strengthen the emotional attachment at each use phase for every user group, considering modern technologies such as digital assistants. Six focus groups, each with five to six participants, who have an emotional attachment to their car, were conducted. Different ideation methods were used.
According to the results, owners focus on ideas that increase identification with their car during the familiarisation phase. Over time, they prefer stimulating approaches, while creating memories is always important to them, especially not losing those memories when they part with the car. Lessees prefer stimulating ideas from the beginning and stimulation remains important throughout the lifecycle, while car sharing users prefer pragmatic and cost-oriented concepts. For all user groups, it is important to personalise the car experience to increase identification. Digital assistants are therefore seen as a potential tool. They can also anticipate user needs and facilitate memory transfer between cars.

KEYWORDS

Emotional Attachment, Focus Groups, Car Use Phases, Ideation, Digital Assistant, Product Qualities

1. BACKGROUND

1.1 Emotional Product Attachment

People can form attachments not only with other people, but also with brands or objects (Page, 2014; Whan et al., 2010). Because of that emotions might play an important role in purchase decisions and brand loyalty. Moreover, users might also experience long-term enjoyment of a product through an emotional attachment (Diefenbach & Hassenzahl, 2017).

Hassenzahl (2005) divided product qualities into two categories: *hedonic* and *pragmatic*. Both qualities influence product evaluation and emotional attachment. Pragmatic qualities, such as usability and utility, are related to the user's immediate goal attainment. In contrast, hedonic qualities focus on the user's subjective feelings when expecting, doing or reflecting interaction with the product. They consist of three dimensions: (1) *stimulation*, which describes the motivational effect of the product through novelty, excitement and curiosity; (2) *evocation*, which measures the product's ability to evoke personal memories and emotions in the user; and (3) *identification*, which refers to the user's tendency to attach individual value to the product and express himself or herself through its use. The more a product can be assigned to the hedonic dimension, the stronger is the emotional attachment (Winder, 2006).

Hassenzahl's (2005) model of hedonic product qualities is partially consistent with Mugge's (2007) findings on emotional product attachment. Mugge (2007) identified four dimensions that contribute to the user's emotional attachment to a product. (1) *Self-expression* describes the user's need to differentiate himself or herself from others through the product and to express his or her own identity. It corresponds in part to Hassenzahl's (2005) concept of identification. (2) *Memories* focus on the product's ability to evoke positive memories and emotions in the user. It parallels Hassenzahl's (2005) dimension of evocation. (3) *Pleasure* describes the immediate pleasure and positive mood that the user feels when interacting with the product. It is not explicitly included in Hassenzahl's (2005) model but can be interpreted as part of stimulation. (4) *Group affiliation* refers to the user's need to feel part of a social group and to experience recognition and acceptance through the product. It has no direct equivalent in Hassenzahl's (2005) model but could be seen as an extension of the concept of identification.

1.2 Factors Influencing Emotional Product Attachment

Considering emotional product attachment an important factor is time. Value perceptions are not static but change over time. Hedonic qualities show more change than pragmatic qualities, which remain more constant (Wilamowitz-Moellendorff et al., 2015). According to Mugge et al. (2005) the dynamic nature of product loyalty can arise through the addition or omission of determinants (e.g., memories associated with the product). The attractiveness may decrease if the product loses novelty (Hassenzahl, 2006) – but may increase as the product becomes better known and more familiar to the user (Hassenzahl, 2006). In addition, the number of memories and the identification with the product increase over time (Karapanos, 2013). Repeated interactions, positive associations and evoked memories lead to lasting positive feelings towards a product (Norman, 2005). Positive memories are particularly important for product loyalty (Mugge et al., 2005). As product-related memories are positively correlated with the degree of product attachment, it can be assumed that product loyalty may also increase over time (Mugget et al., 2005). Kujala et al. (2011) found the strongest changes in product attractiveness at the beginning of the usage. This is in line with the findings of Pettersson (2016), who described the first impression as particularly formative for later product loyalty. However, studies showed that the attractiveness curves over time can vary for different product categories (Wilamowitz-Moellendorff et al., 2015).

Another factor to influence emotions and product attachment are digital products, such as avatars and digital assistants. Studies in human-technology interactions involving a digital assistant showed that users can identify with this non-human object, similar to how they identify with other people (Gelbrich et al., 2021). Duggan (2016) investigated two versions of a digital assistant as a companion in a 30-day fitness programme. The version that used relational strategies such as small talk, expressions of empathy and humour was more respected, liked and perceived as trustworthy by participants than the version that did not use these strategies.

1.3 Application to the Automotive Context

The car is a product with a high emotional value that evokes a wide range of emotions in its users (Sheller, 2004; Steg, 2005). These emotional responses can be attributed to different functions of the car. The car includes instrumental functions by enabling participation in activities and providing comfort through its characteristics such as speed, flexibility and safety. Symbolic functions are fulfilled by the car as a means of self-expression and positioning in the user's social environment. Affective functions are served by associating the car with deeper needs and desires as well as emotions experienced while driving (Steg, 2005). The car therefore serves different functions in our lives: It fulfils pragmatic needs as a means of transportation as well as symbolic functions as a means of self-expression through the choice of the car model or other customisation options. Furthermore, it evokes memories of journeys or special experiences and can have a stimulating effect through new technologies and the driving experience itself (Grund et al., 2024; Steg, 2005).

As Bardhi and Eckhardt (2012) showed, car sharing users (unlike to car owners) do not have an ownership orientation or identification with the car, but instead prioritise the utility value. However, Grund et al. (2024) found emotional attachment to the car also within the group of car sharing users. This attachment is less intense than in the group of owners. In contrast, car sharing users identify with the concept of sharing instead of owning a car. This identification can make them feel more attached to the shared car (Grund et al., 2024). In conclusion, the *duration of use* can have an impact on the emotional attachment (Fraine et al., 2007) for all user groups. Car owners own their cars for several years (instamotion, n.d.), whereas a leasing contract mostly lasts for only two to four years (Leschau & Baumgarten, 2024) and their cars are more often new (Autoscout24, 2023). In the context of car sharing, the use of a car is limited to specific occasions, i.e., it is not permanently available.

Grund et al. (2024) show the attachment curve between users and their cars tending to become more positive over time. But there are differences between user groups. Owners and lessees start their attachment in the positive range, while car sharing users are initially neutral, as they have no experience with the concept and are unsure about their expectations. For owners and lessees, the pleasant anticipation of the new car is predominant, but they also feel some uncertainty at the beginning as they are not familiar with the car at this moment (Grund et al., 2024). The longer the car is used, the greater is the trust in it and the more positive gets the attachment between user and car. For this, factors such as ease of use, identification and attachment are considered as important. In addition, the feeling of safety increases as the user becomes more familiar with the car, its features and functions (Grund et al., 2024.). The attachment to the car can be negatively affected in the short term if defects or malfunctions occur as functionality is impaired and the novelty effect wears off (Grund et al., 2024; Hassenzahl et al., 2015).

Car sharing users are confronted with soiling or damage to the car. In these situations, trust in the car decreases as users feel 'let down'. Once the damage is repaired, the attachment tends to return to pre-damage levels (Grund et al., 2024). The farewell to the car is also difficult for many users and can be associated with negative reactions such as grief - both for the car itself and for the experiences and memories associated with it (Fraine et al., 2007; Grund et al., 2024). This grief is particularly pronounced among owners, but also occurs among lessees and car sharing users. At the same time, the pleasant anticipation of a new car can mitigate negative emotions (Grund et al., 2024).

Four use phases are identified to be important over the lifetime of a car (Grund et al., 2024):

(1) *familiarisation* (received the car a few weeks ago, user has driven the car a few times and has familiarised his- or herself with some of the functions and features of the car),

(2) *everyday use* (use of the car regularly for some time in everyday life, it is no longer new, no problems with the car),

(3) *defects and malfunctions*; for car sharing users: *dirt and dents* (the car gets unpleasant defects or has minor damages that needs to be repaired in a garage; the predecessor left the car dirty) and

(4) *farewell* from the car (decide to hand in the car or total loss; for car sharing users: decide to stop using car sharing or the car is no longer available).

1.4 Research Questions

As previously described, a car is more than just a means of transport for many users who create an emotional attachment (Sheller, 2004; Steg, 2005). This attachment varies over time through different influencing factors. Therefore, the first research question considered different use phases:

(1) Which relevant influencing factors and emotions occur in the different use phases (familiarisation phase, everyday use, defects and malfunctions/ dirt and dents and farewell)?

Furthermore, the aim of this study was to gain ideas on how to support an emotional attachment within different use phases and how an in-car assistant affects the user-car attachment. So, the second research question relates to the support of an emotional attachment:

(2) How can the emotional attachment to the car be strengthened in the different use phases? What role can in-car digital assistants play in positively influencing this attachment?

As already explained different user groups should be considered in the context of cars as each group has specific needs that should be addressed to strengthen the emotional attachment. Therefore, the third research question focussed on user groups:

(3) How do the needs of different user groups (owners, lessees and car sharing users) differ?

2. METHODS

2.1 Research Methodology

Three user groups were focused in the study: (1) owners, (2) lessees and (3) car sharing users. Four use phases were selected as described: (1) familiarisation, (2) everyday use, (3) defects and malfunctions/ dirt and dents and (4) farewell.

As this was an exploratory and hypothesis-generating study, a qualitative descriptive method was used. For data collection and idea generation, six focus groups (two per user group) were conducted with six participants each except from one group with five participants (in line with the recommendations of Krueger and Casey, 2009). This allowed a balance between individual contributions and group cohesion. The first focus group of each user group dealt with use phases (1) familiarisation and (2) everyday use, the second focus group with use phases (3) defects and malfunctions/ dirt and dents and (4) farewell.

Two different ideation methods were used in the focus groups: the *6-3-5 method* and the *random stimulus creativity method*. After the first three focus groups (one focus group per user group), only one of the two methods was continued for each use phase, as the number of generated ideas was sufficient, and it was possible to go more into detail instead. Table 1 shows the use phases discussed from which focus group and the applied ideation techniques.

Table 1. Overview of discussed use phases of the groups and ideation methods that were used

Use phase	Groups (Gr.)	Ideation method
(1) familiarisation	Gr.1 (owner) Gr. 2 (lessees) Gr. 3 (car sharing)	6-3-5 method, Random Stimulus Creativity Technique
(2) everyday use	Gr. 4 (owner) Gr. 5 (lessees) Gr. 6 (car sharing)	6-3-5 method
(3) defects and malfunctions/ dirt and dents	Gr. 1 (owner) Gr. 2 (lessees) Gr. 3 (car sharing)	6-3-5 method, Random Stimulus Creativity Technique
(4) farewell	Gr. 4 (owner) Gr. 5 (lessees) Gr. 6 (car sharing)	Random Stimulus Creativity Technique

The 6-3-5 method was used as a structured brainstorming process in which each participant separately wrote three ideas on a sheet of paper. After five minutes the sheet was passed on to the next participant, who could be inspired by the ideas given of others and developed these existing ideas or added new ideas (Wagner, 2022). After all participants had worked for themselves on all six sheets, there was an evaluation phase in which the ideas were briefly presented, and each participant marked particularly good ideas with sticky dots (Wagner, 2022). This method was used to generate a high number of ideas on how to support the emotional attachment to the car in general during the specific use phases.

The random stimulus technique was used as an ideation method to get people thinking about a topic and to develop creative ideas on what the digital assistant can do to positively influence the attachment with the car. This technique consisted of four steps (Wagner, 2022). In the first step, the topic was written on a flipchart for all participants to see and to ensure that everyone understood it correctly. Then random stimulus words were given (Wagner, 2022). In this study two words were chosen randomly in advance: 'dog' and 'suitcase' for familiarisation and farewell use phases, 'plant' and 'paper' for defects and malfunctions/ dirt and dents. In the third step, these words were analysed by writing down all the characteristics and concepts that the participants associated with the words. Finally, these characteristics and concepts were used as basis to generate creative and innovative ideas for the origin topic (Wagner, 2022).

2.2 Focus Group Procedure

Each focus group session lasted approximately three hours and was conducted by an experienced moderator from an external agency to avoid bias from the authors' expectations. The moderator was briefed by the authors before and was provided with a semi-structured guide. The authors were able to observe the discussion from a separate room where they took notes. Additionally, all groups were recorded on video with tone. All focus groups were conducted in German. The procedure of each session contained four steps:

(1) At the beginning the participants and the moderator introduced themselves and the moderator encouraged the participants to speak freely and to share their views openly.

(2) Then they continued talking about their car situation (e.g., how many cars do they have and since when). To get into the mood for the topic, the participants were asked about their feelings about their car (or,

in the case of car sharing users, in about the car they use regularly). It was discussed how these feelings have changed over time and which events have led to these changes.

(3) Afterwards, the first of the two use phases to be discussed was explained. Groups 1 to 3 dealt with familiarisation, while groups 4 to 6 focused on everyday use. Each focus group firstly discussed the content of the use phase to gain a basic understanding of the main emotional processes before developing ideas for improvement using the 6-3-5 method. In groups 1 to 3 the random stimulus creativity technique was additionally used in a second ideation round for the same use phase.

(4) The same procedure was followed for the second use phase. Groups 1 to 3 discussed defects and malfunctions/ dirt and dents and used both ideation methods, while groups 4 to 6 covered the farewell and ideated using the random stimulus creativity technique with focus on the digital assistant.

Finally, the participants were thanked for their participation.

2.3 Data Analysis

For privacy reasons, each participant was given an anonymous label (e.g., 'TN1-23'). Within the label, the first number represented the user group: '1' assigned to owners, '2' to lessees and '3' to car sharing users. The second number stood for the focus group: '1' is assigned to the first focus group and '2' to the second focus group of each user group. The third number was the participants' number within the group. In this example it was participant three from the second group of owners.

The video recordings of the six focus group sessions were transcribed verbatim. The transcripts were compared with the observers' notes and then analysed using the qualitative data analysis software MAXQDA (VERBI Software, 2018). The data analysis followed the recommendations for qualitative content analysis according to Kuckartz (2016). The data were coded and categorised using the deductive-inductive method. In a first step, the category system was developed deductively based on the semi-structured guide, the dimensions of product qualities according to Hassenzahl (2005) and the results of previous studies (Grund et al., 2024). In a second step, the category system was refined inductively on the basis of relevant text passages: New categories were created and a hierarchical structure of categories was developed. This process was repeated until no further changes in the category system were discernible. A student assistant with experience in qualitative data analysis independently developed a category system. Finally, both category systems were compared. All discrepancies were discussed and a final system was worked out, which was then checked by the second author.

The ideas of the 6-3-5 method were digitised and categorised according to the procedure described above. The number of sticky dots for ideas was also noted. The ideas and statements made in the random stimulus creativity technique were included in the transcripts and analysed with the group discussion.

2.4 Recruiting and Participants

The study was conducted between September 6th and 9th, 2022, in an agency's rooms in Munich. The agency was commissioned to recruit and incentivise the participants. The participants were contacted by phone and selected according to specific criteria given by the authors. These screening criteria were: a certain degree of creativity and technical aptitude as well as belonging to a certain user group: (a) car owning and regularly using a private car (at least twice a week) or (b) leasing and regularly using a car (at least twice a week) or (c) using stationary car sharing with a preference for using a specific model (at least once a month for at least six months). In addition, all participants were required to have an emotional attachment to the car so that they could better empathise with the respective situations emotionally and thus provide more valuable data. For this purpose, quantitative screening questions were used, asking participants to indicate their level of agreement on a four-point Likert scale to various questions such as 'I just love this car' or 'I see the car primarily as a means of transport' (inverted). The screening process and focus groups were conducted in German originally and translated for this publication.

To address ethical concerns, all participants signed a confidentiality agreement. This agreement ensured that they would not disclose any information about the study to the outside world. They were also informed before the study that they would be observed by researchers during the discussion and that the video files would only be used for analysis purposes. The participants' surnames remained unknown to the other participants, the moderator and the observers. All participants participated voluntarily and are allowed to leave the discussion at any time without any disadvantages. No other ethical concerns were recognised.

An equal number of owners, lessees, and car sharing users was required. A total of 36 participants were recruited, one of whom did not participate at short notice due to illness, resulting in a final sample size of $N = 35$ ($n = 19$ men, $n = 16$ women). The age ranged from 22 to 60 years ($M = 41.92$, $SD = 12.09$).

2.5 Quality Criteria

The study used established methods of qualitative data collection and analysis and was guided by the Miles and Huberman (1994) quality criteria to ensure the *credibility* of the findings. There was always more than one experienced researcher involved in the planning, implementation and analysis of this study. An external moderator was chosen to lead the focus groups to avoid a guiding effect. The moderator was also experienced in conducting focus groups and in the application of the ideation methods used. As all participants took part in the discussions voluntarily, it can be assumed that an open and honest basis for discussion was guaranteed. The *dependability* of the study was ensured by a consistent approach to data collection. A guideline ensured that each focus group discussed all relevant issues and a standardised process was guaranteed, without sacrificing individual and situational events and group dynamics. To ensure *confirmability*, all discussions were recorded and logged. In addition, during the analysis, the researchers regularly exchanged information about the procedure and documented each step. Explicit quotes from participants are used to enhance the comprehensibility of the results. *Transferability* is provided by a transparent description of the research design as well as the data collection and analysis.

3. RESULTS

The research questions are answered by presenting the results separately for each use phase and user group. For each user group, the specific emotional characteristics and the ideas generated to increase emotional attachment in the use phases are identified. Table 2 aligns the emerged ideas from the respective use phases of different user groups with Hassenzahl's (2005) dimensions. All quotations are translated from German.

3.1 Familiarisation

Owners reported that they were initially overwhelmed by all the information about the new car. They needed time to familiarise themselves with the car. However, they enjoyed discovering new things and wanted to have their first experiences with the car.

> "You get in the car, and you feel comfortable and you don't want to get out, I emptied the tank on my first trips because I didn't want to get out, I have the sunroof half open, coffee in the car, I drove another lap and another lap, with time driving becomes more and more familiar" (TN1-11).

Experiential activities of all kinds were conducive to strengthen the emotional attachment and to create memories. Photo shoots with the car, visits to drive-in cinemas and joint excursions as well as the conscious enjoyment of driving were suggested. To support their feeling of pride the owners wished to show off their car. Furthermore, they wanted to personalise it to feel more individual. Cleaning and caring for the car were seen as means of maintaining its value and creating an emotional attachment. They wanted the digital assistant to get to know them and help them to personalise the car. "It greets you, recognises where you want to go and automatically sets the navigation system for me" (TN1-24). From a pragmatic point of view, owners wanted to get to know their car and try out new features. Therefore, they mentioned the digital assistant to support them by providing car-specific explanations and feedback on driving behaviour.

Lessees, in particular, reported that the smell of the new car was important to them. A long-lasting scent could strengthen the emotional attachment with the car. Like owners, lessees wanted help with getting to know the car and in personalising it, which they saw as a potential area for digital assistant support. They also valued a unique car pickup and superb service from the dealership (e.g., good accessibility, a personal welcome and an individual approach to fulfil their needs). Lessees also mentioned positive experiences in a more stimulating context, such as new car events or the opportunity to test the car on a racetrack.

Table 2. Ideas mapped to Hassenzahl's dimensions (2005) across use phases and user groups

Use phase	Dimension of mentioned ideas	Owner	Lessees	Car sharing user
(1) familiarisation	evocation	X		
	identification	X	X	
	stimulation		X	
	pragmatic	X	X	X
(2) everyday use	evocation	X		
	identification			X
	stimulation	X	X	
	pragmatic	X	X	X
(3) defects and malfunctions/ dirt and dents	evocation			
	identification			
	stimulation			
	pragmatic	X	X	X
(4) farewell	evocation	X	X	
	identification			
	stimulation	X	X	X
	pragmatic			X

Car sharing users cited various reasons for using car sharing for the first time, with the size of the car being a key selection criterion. They wanted to be able to use the car intuitively and to start driving immediately without having to waste time getting to know the car. In addition, the car should have technology that is easy to use and to understand. It should be well-equipped and provide a high level of comfort. Monetary benefits as free minutes or free test drives were perceived as encouraging. Car sharing users also considered quick availability and cleanliness of the car as important. The digital assistant should act as a friend and companion, recognising the user's individual needs and adjusting the car's settings accordingly. Evocative and stimulating experiences were not considered.

3.2 Everyday Use

In all user groups, the initial 'infatuation' phase had faded into the everyday phase and a certain routine set in. Owners continued to hope for trouble-free use and began to individualise their car. Accordingly, they mentioned that they wanted to personalise their cars in the same way they regularly redecorate their homes. They wished to adapt the car to their lifestyle and escape the 'daily grind'. For example, owners wanted to be able to keep their cars feeling new for a longer time through regular updates or retrofitting of assistance systems, new varnishing or seats with reclining or massage functions. Trips in the car were suggested to strengthen the emotional attachment and to create shared experiences. The car itself should make suggestions for certain destinations or activities. Photos, routes and highlights could be saved as souvenirs. In addition, owners wanted to share their experiences on internet platforms and exchange ideas with other owners of the same model. In addition to these hedonic aspects owners also emphasized pragmatic ideas such as easier tyre changes, regular checks by the car itself and cost optimisation.

Lessees continued to express satisfaction with their car although the initial euphoria had worn off because it still feels as good as new. "The infatuation phase wears off a bit after five to six months, like any relationship, it becomes more familiar, at the beginning it's all "wow cool", then it starts to wear off, but it's still cool" (TN2-22). Compared to owners, cost was a much more important consideration for lessees. They suggested discount promotions (e.g., 'use for twelve months, pay for eleven months') and more flexibility in the duration of lease. Like owners, lessees also wanted changes in appearance and updates and upgrades, although their suggestions were less intense and frequent. Furthermore, Lessees looked for experiences that should increase driving enjoyment and positive emotions. However, they mentioned neither ideas to increase evocation nor identification with the car.

Car sharing users described the everyday routine as boring on the one hand, but also as comfortable and safe on the other, as they already knew how to handle the car. Nevertheless, new and unfamiliar cars could provide variety and highlights. To strengthen the emotional attachment during the everyday phase, car sharing users suggested discount campaigns such as free rides, free minutes or a free car wash for their own car. They also wanted more flexible use of the car, e.g., when travelling abroad. Like owners and lessees, car sharing users wanted the car to provide suggestions for destinations and events as well as the option to share certain routes or experiences via a social media platform. Furthermore, personalisation was important to car sharing users. They wanted the car to recognise them and adapt directly to their needs and preferences. They also suggested welcome rituals, such as flickering lights or honking to greet them.

3.3 Defects and Malfunctions/ Dirt and Dents

Owners reported anger, disappointment and anxiety when defects or malfunctions occurred. There was uncertainty about whether the garage would repair the damage in a way that met their needs and was cost effective. They lacked information about the duration, cost and nature of the damage.

> "I am annoyed, disappointed, I have questions in my head like 'how much will it cost', 'how long will it have to stay in the garage', do you research garages first or is it possible to do it yourself? What tools or spare parts will I need?" (TN1-11)

Quick assistance services, such as showing the nearest garage with user ratings from the car itself, as well as comprehensive information on repairs and damage were considered particularly desirable by owners. Concerns about costs could also be alleviated by reassurance that only necessary repairs will be carried out and that the costs will be covered by, for example, the insurance company or the seller. Discounts offered by garages, such as a free car wash after an appointment or the installation of a free special feature, were seen as attractive. In general, this phase should be made as pleasant as possible by minimising inconvenience and maintaining mobility by providing a replacement car. Calming and distracting the owners would be helpful and could be achieved by various means, such as reminding them of rational reasons ('The main thing is that no one is hurt', 'It's just a car'). The digital assistant could support by providing the desired information, e.g., explaining the damage, organising help and playing relaxing music.

Lessees expressed ambivalent feelings about technical problems. On the one hand, they felt annoyed, but on the other hand, they put the damage into perspective and may already be interested in a new car. One participant commented: "The car is a commodity, I don't mind the garage, maybe I'll start looking for new cars again" (TN2-14), while another participant said:

> "I'm angry because someone drove into my car and I had to pay for it myself, the car should look well maintained as a status symbol, it's expensive, I don't want to drive around in it like a dirty car and if you have dents in it that annoys me." (TN2-16)

Like owners, lessees wanted fast and competent help. They suggested a digital garage via video call or the car itself diagnosing the fault, checking the availability of spare parts in garages, making appointments and explaining the next steps to the user (e.g., in the event of an accident). The digital assistant could also perform these tasks, providing reassurance and safety. Lessees were also concerned about costs and suggested a flat rate for repairs or a combined insurance and lease payment to avoid additional costs. Like owners, they wanted this phase to be as pleasant as possible so they also suggested that a replacement car of at least the same value should be provided. They also wanted coffee and snacks to be available in the garage area or even an all-inclusive, worry-free package.

Car sharing users were concerned that they might be charged for damage to the car. They therefore checked whether any dents or other damage had already been registered before starting their journey. Car sharing users were particularly interested in the pragmatic aspects, such as being reminded to check the car for dirt and damage before use. The digital assistant could provide greater safety by displaying dirt and damage before the journey and making it clear that this is not the user's fault. They also suggested that the car itself should detect defects and collisions and identify the person in charge. If the car was dirty, they reacted with anger and disappointment, but emphasised that this was not the fault of the car but of the previous user or even the fleet provider. Therefore, they supported stricter rules e.g., photos of the car's condition at the end of a journey. Eating and drinking in the car should be restricted and the user should be informed if the previous user had animals with them, especially if the user is allergic to animal hair. Repeated soiling should be penalised. To react quickly in the event of soiling, car sharing users wanted cleaning products in the car, as well as discounts or compensation offers. Additionally, they wanted the digital assistant to give them clear instructions in the event of an accident.

3.4 Farewell from the Car

For owners the farewell from the car and then buying a new one was an emotionally stressful phase. They emphasised the difference between selling a car, which involves some planning and the intention to buy a better car, and an accident, which is unexpected and abrupt. Even if they felt some pleasant anticipation about the new car, albeit with some uncertainty about making the right decision, negative feelings predominated, such as sadness, frustration, anger and the pain of separation. They were saddened by the thought that the memories associated with the car would be lost.

> "Unless you buy exactly the same model again, it might be not so bad, but there are still memories attached to it, but if I say I'm going to get rid of it now and buy the i3, I love it too, but then the question is will I get on with it, is it good enough for me?" (T1-24)

Accordingly, owners wanted the digital assistant to act as the car's 'brain', storing all the memories and settings and transferring them to the new car. This would make it easier to say goodbye, as only the chassis of the car would change, whereas the memories and personal preferences would remain.

> "It's not so hard to say goodbye, it takes everything - including the memories, it knows what my favourite music is, it's got all my memories, it knows my memories, whatever they are, I'm taking it with me, that makes it extremely easy for me, I'm basically taking the head of the whole thing and just leaving the shell there and the shell gets a new look and the old tried and tested gets a new look. (...) The (digital assistant) of the future has remembered things about you, it knows your favourite routes, your favourite restaurant, (...) it has driven with you all your life and it goes with your memories into the next car where more memories will take place." (TN1-21)

Owners also hoped the digital assistant would help to build pleasant anticipation for the new car. For example, it could explain new features, provide regular delivery status updates, and automatically adjust all settings in the new car. However, concerns were also expressed about the feasibility of these features when changing brands.

Lessees also said that a sudden and unforeseen farewell from the car would be much more emotionally stressful than a planned change. They found it sad to say goodbye to a leased car, but not as sad as to a car they owned. The pleasant anticipation of the new car generally outweighed the negative feelings. It was important to lessees that the new car felt like an improvement on the previous model.

> "It used to be worse when I owned a car, you didn't know what was coming next, now the anticipation of the next car is greater than the pain of separation and it makes a difference whether it's a sudden death or whether I can adapt to it." (TN2-22).

Lessees also wanted a digital assistant that could save all settings and memories and transfer them to the new car. One participant commented: "Imagine you could take your assistant from your old car, let's call him Joe, to your new car and he would know all the settings" (TN2-22). However, they were critical of the technical implementation of the data transfer, especially when changing car brands. They also questioned whether they would feel emotional attached to the car itself or to the digital assistant. Nevertheless, they saw great potential for the digital assistant, especially among the younger generation, who have grown up with digital technology and would therefore use it more.

Car sharing users showed a wide range of feelings when thinking about the farewell to a car sharing car. While one said: "It's not mine, you borrow it, it wouldn't be so bad, I'll just take another one" (TN3-23), another one said: "I'll start crying straight away" (TN3-21). This affected the intention to further use car sharing. Some users would use car sharing less frequently after such a farewell, while others would pragmatically continue to use another car. However, car sharing users emphasised the difference of the farewell to their own car. Owning a car is associated with much more emotion, memories and investment. In addition, car sharing users assumed that if a particular model was discontinued, the fleet provider would offer a better replacement model to maintain customer loyalty. They wanted the digital assistant to give them advance warning of an impending car discontinuation, e.g., in the form of "We would like to inform you that the car will be discontinued in three weeks' time" (TN3-23). They would be happy to receive free minutes or kilometres as a parting gift. At the same time, the digital assistant should build pleasant anticipation for the next, better car by advertising it and offering free minutes. The idea of a digital assistant that saves the user's settings and automatically adapts them to the new car was also mentioned. However, unlike owners and lessees, memory storage was not explicitly mentioned.

4. CONCLUSION

4.1 Discussion

The aim of this study was to identify factors that strengthen the emotional attachment between users and cars. By means of focus groups, different user groups: owners, lessees, car sharing users were analysed and looked at important use phases throughout the entire period of use: familiarisation, defects and malfunctions/ dirt and dents, everyday use and farewell. The results of the present study support previous research on hedonic and pragmatic product attributes that influence emotional attachment (Hassenzahl, 2005; Mugge, 2007) and extend existing knowledge to the automotive context. Furthermore, concrete approaches are provided on how to prevent a loss of attractiveness over time. In addition, the inclusion of different user groups allows for a more nuanced view of the results.

It is shown that the relevant product qualities for increasing emotional attachment vary over different use phases. This is in line with the findings of Wilamowitz-Moellendorff et al. (2015), who found a change in the perception of product qualities over time. Hassenzahl (2005) described that the initial stimulation of product novelty diminishes over time, which can lead to boredom, but can also convey a sense of security. This study confirms this observation: In all user groups, pragmatic aspects are relevant at the beginning to familiarise themselves with the car. In addition, suggestions are made to increase identification, with a particular focus on personalising the car. While owners want to create an emotional attachment through evocation (e.g., shared experiences), lessees are more interested in additional stimulation (e.g., special pickup).

After the novelty effect has worn off in everyday use owners also express ideas about how to increase stimulation to maintain the car's novelty. At the same time, they continue to seek shared experiences with the car to strengthen the emotional attachment. This is consistent with the findings of Karapanos (2012) and Mugge et al. (2005), who demonstrated that emotional attachments develop over time through positive interactions and memories. Lessees, on the other hand, continue to favour stimulating and pragmatic aspects, but also attach importance to convenient, flexible use and cost efficiency. This aspect is also considered as important by car sharing users, while evocation and stimulation are less relevant for them. Although Bardhi and Eckhardt (2012) found evidence that car sharing users do not show an ownership orientation or identification with the car, this study indicates that strengthening identification, especially through personalisation, can support the emotional attachment to the car both initially and in everyday use.

In line with the findings of Fraine et al. (2007) and Grund et al. (2024), this study shows that defects and malfunctions or dirt as well as the farewell lead to predominantly negative emotions. This applies to a lesser extent for lessees and car sharing users than for owners (Grund et al., 2024). As the functionality of the car is limited during the occurrence of defects and malfunctions, it is not surprising that pragmatic ideas are mentioned, such as the provision of a replacement car or the fastest and most cost-effective repair possible. Car sharing users also express concern that any damage could be at their expense.

For the farewell all groups highlight the difference between a planned change of car and a sudden accident, with the latter being perceived as significantly more emotionally distressing, which is align with Grund et al. (2024). All groups mention the idea of a digital assistant that can be taken from car to car, storing memories, personal preferences and settings and acting as the 'brain' of the car. In the new car, it can speed up personalisation and identification and ensure that memories of the old car are not lost. In addition, the participants express the wish to stimulate pleasant anticipation of the new car actively in advance.

Modern technologies such as in-car digital assistants offer great potential to strengthen the emotional attachment between users and their cars by facilitating personalisation, anticipating user needs and providing information and support at various use phases. In addition, digital assistants can act as memory storage and make it easier to transfer personal preferences to the new car. They can also build pleasant anticipation for new car features and functions. Although the findings on digital assistants are consistent with those of Duggan (2016), according to whom a digital assistant that focuses on attachment in addition to its functional benefits is more highly valued by users, our findings go further because of the desire for the digital assistant to become the 'brain' of the car. However, it is important to note that there are also limitations to the use of digital assistants in cars: e.g., privacy concerns about the transfer of user data or technical incompatibilities between different car brands may limit the uptake and benefits of this technology.

4.2 Limitations and Future Research

The study is based on a qualitative data approach, which is inherently prone to bias and social desirability. In addition, the study sample is relatively small and consist exclusively of participants who already had an emotional attachment to their car. Although this limitation is necessary so that the participants can better empathise with the respective situations emotionally and thus provide better ideas and more valuable ideas, it limits the generalisability of the results. In addition, the study was carried out in Germany and emotional attachment to the car may vary in different cultures due to different values, car use patterns and social norms. Future research should therefore take greater account of cultural factors to gain a more comprehensive picture of emotional attachment to the car.

This study opens new perspectives by including digital assistants as a means of increasing product loyalty. In this context, an in-depth investigation of the influence and long-term effects of these digital assistants on the emotional attachment between user and products is needed. It is important to clarify whether digital assistants can act as mediators or moderators of emotional product attachments. In addition, the ideas generated in this study should be evaluated to see if they can have an impact on emotional attachment at the different use phases. Nevertheless, this study contributes to the understanding of the emotional attachment between users and their cars. This knowledge can serve as a basis for design, marketing and strategy decisions aimed at increasing user satisfaction, promoting sustainable transport and fostering positive attachments between users and their cars throughout their time of use.

REFERENCES

Autoscout24 (2023). *Auto Leasing in Deutschland: Leasing-Trends 2023 – der große Jahresrückblick* [Car leasing in Germany: Leasing trends 2023 - the big annual review]. https://www.leasingmarkt.de/magazin/leasing/leasing-in-deutschland-2023

Bardhi, F., & Eckhardt, G. M. (2012). Access-based consumption: The case of car sharing. *Journal of Consumer Research, 39*(4), 881–898. https://doi.org/10.1086/666376

Diefenbach, S., & Hassenzahl, M. (2017). *Psychologie in der nutzerzentrierten Produktgestaltung: Mensch-Technik-Interaktion-Erlebnis* [Psychology in user-centred product design: human-technology-interaction experience]. *Die Wirtschaftspsychologie.* Springer.

Duggan, G. B. (2016). Applying psychology to understand relationships with technology: from ELIZA to interactive healthcare. *Behaviour & Information Technology, 35*(7), 536–547. https://doi.org/10.1080/0144929X.2016.1141320

Fraine, G., Smith, S. G., Zinkiewicz, L., Chapman, R., & Sheehan, M. (2007). At home on the road? Can drivers' relationships with their cars be associated with territoriality? *Journal of Environmental Psychology, 27*(3), 204–214. http://dx.doi.org/10.1016/j.jenvp.2007.06.002

Gelbrich, K., Hagel, J., & Orsingher, C. (2021). Emotional support from a digital assistant in technology-mediated services: Effects on customer satisfaction and behavioral persistence. *International Journal of Research in Marketing, 38*(1), 176–193. https://doi.org/10.1016/j.ijresmar.2020.06.004

Grund, M., Totzke, I., & Engeln, A. (2024). *The Emotional Attachment Between Humans and Their Cars: Dimensions, Dynamics, and Implications.* [Manuscript in preparation]

Hassenzahl, M. (2005). The Thing and I: Understanding the Relationship Between User and Product. In J. Karat, J. Vanderdonckt, G. Abowd, G. Calvary, J. Carroll, G. Cockton, M. Czerwinski, S. Feiner, E. Furtado, K. Höök, R. Jacob, R. Jeffries, P. Johnson, K. Nakakoji, P. Palanque, O. Pastor, F. Paternò, C. Pribeanu, M. Salzman, . . . P. C. Wright (Eds.), *Human-Computer Interaction Series. Funology* (Vol. 3, pp. 31–42). Springer Netherlands. https://doi.org/10.1007/1-4020-2967-5_4

Hassenzahl, M. (2006). Interaktive Produkte wahrnehmen, erleben, bewerten und gestalten [Perceive, experience, evaluate and design interactive products]. In M. Eibl, H. Reiterer, P. F. Stephan, & F. Thissen (Eds.), *Knowledge Media Design Grundlagen und Perspektiven einer neuen Gestaltungsdisziplin* (pp. 151–171). Oldenbourg Verlag. https://doi.org/10.1524/9783486593433.147

Hassenzahl, M., Wiklund-Engblom, A., Bengs, A., Hägglund, S., & Diefenbach, S. (2015). Experience-Oriented and Product-Oriented Evaluation: Psychological Need Fulfillment, Positive Affect, and Product Perception. *International Journal of Human-Computer Interaction, 31*(8), 530–544. https://doi.org/10.1080/10447318.2015.1064664

Instamotion (n.d.). *Nutzungsdauer Pkw: Faktoren, die die Lebensdauer Deines Autos beeinflussen* [Car service life: factors that influence the service life of your car]. https://www.instamotion.com/blog/nutzungsdauer-pkw#:~:text=Nutzungsdauer%20Pkw%20im%20Durchschnitt,unter%20normalen%20Bedingungen%20funktionst%C3%BCchtig%20bleibt.

Karapanos, E. (2013). *Modeling Users' Experiences with Interactive Systems. Studies in Computational Intelligence: Vol. 436.* Springer.

Krueger, R. A., & Casey, M. A. (2009). *Focus groups: A practical guide for applied research* (4. ed.). Sage.

Kuckartz, U. (2012). Qualitative Inhaltsanalyse: Methoden, Praxis, Computerunterstützung [Qualitative content analysis: methods, practice, computer support]. Beltz Juventa.

Kujala, S., Roto, V., Väänänen-Vainio-Mattila, K., Karapanos, E., & Sinnelä, A. (2011). UX Curve: A method for evaluating long-term user experience. *Interacting with Computers, 23*(5), 473–483. https://doi.org/10.1016/j.intcom.2011.06.005

Leschau, I., & Baumgarten, A. (2024). *Leasing: So funktioniert die Auto-Miete auf Zeit* [Leasing: How temporary car hire works]. https://www.adac.de/rund-ums-fahrzeug/auto-kaufen-verkaufen/finanzierung-leasing/leasing/

MAXQDA 2018 [Computer software]. (2018). VERBI Software.

Miles, M. B., & Huberman, A. M. (1994). *Qualitative data analysis: An expanded sourcebook.* Sage.

Mugge, R. (2007). *Product attachment* [PhD thesis]. Delft University of Technology.

Mugge, R., Schifferstein, H. N. J., & Schoormans, J. P.L. (2005). A Longitudinal Study of Product Attachment and Its Determinants. In K. M. Ekstrom & H. Brembeck (Eds.), *E - European Advances in Consumer Research Volume 7* (pp. 641–647). Association for Consumer Research.

Norman, D. A. (2005). *Emotional design: Why we love (or hate) everyday things.* Basic Books.

Page, T. (2014). Product attachment and replacement: implications for sustainable design. *International Journal of Sustainable Design, 2*(3), 265–282. http://dx.doi.org/10.1504/IJSDES.2014.065057

Pettersson, I. (2016). *The Temporality of in-vehicle User Experience: Exploring user experiences from past to future* [licentiate thesis]. Chalmers University of Technology, Gothenburg, Sweden.

Sheller, M. (2004). Automotive emotions: Feeling the car. *Theory, Culture & Society, 21*(4-5), 221–242. https://doi.org/10.1177/0263276404046068

Steg, L. (2005). Car use: lust and must. Instrumental, symbolic and affective motives for car use. *Transportation Research Part A: Policy and Practice, 39*(2-3), 147–162. https://doi.org/10.1016/j.tra.2004.07.001

Wagner, K. (2022). Kreativität [creativity]. In: Leyendecker, B., Pötters, P. (Eds.), *Werkzeuge für das Projekt- und Prozessmanagement* (pp.167-194). Springer Gabler. https://doi.org/10.1007/978-3-658-34724-6_7

Whan Park, C., MacInnis, D. J., Priester, J., Eisingerich, A. B., & Iacobucci, D. (2010). Brand attachment and brand attitude strength: Conceptual and empirical differentiation of two critical brand equity drivers. *Journal of Marketing, 74*(6), 1–17. https://doi.org/10.1509/jmkg.74.6.1

Wilamowitz-Moellendorff, M. v., Hassenzahl, M., & Platz, A. (2007). Veränderung in der Wahrnehmung und Bewertung interaktiver Produkte [Change in the perception and evaluation of interactive products]. In T. Gross (Ed.), *Mensch & Computer* (pp. 49–58). Oldenbourg Verlag.

Winder, T. (2006). Emotionen im Marketing [Emotions in marketing]. In G. Schweiger (Ed.), *Werbe- und Markenforschung. Emotionen im Marketing: Verstehen - Messen - Nutzen* (pp. 67–87). Gabler Edition Wissenschaft.

PREDICTING STEM LEARNERS' PERFORMANCE IN SERIOUS GAMES FOR COMPUTATIONAL THINKING USING GAME LEARNING ANALYTICS FRAMEWORK

Fatin Nasuha Abdul Razak[1], Amirrudin Kamsin[1] and Hameedur Rahman[2]
[1]Faculty of Computer Science and Information Technology, Universiti Malaya
50603, Kuala Lumpur, WP Kuala Lumpur, Malaysia
[2]Faculty of Computing and AI, Air University,
Air University, 44000, Islamabad, Pakistan

ABSTRACT

Games, particularly serious games (SGs), have long been embraced in education for their inherent engagement and motivational qualities, especially among younger learners. In the realm of STEM education, SGs have emerged as a technological strategy to enhance student engagement and performance. This paper addresses the growing interest in SG implementation for computational thinking (CT) development within STEM education. Through the introducing of a Game Learning Analytics (GLA) framework, this research explores the predictive potential of technological tools in assessing learners' performance. Focused on the creation of SGs, the GLA framework aims to elucidate the relationship between SG participation and CT skill development. The study proposes a methodological approach for implementing GLA to predict STEM learners' performance in SGs, contributing to the ongoing discourse on leveraging technology to enhance education outcomes.

KEYWORDS

Computational Thinking, Education Games, Serious Games, Game Learning Analytics, Learning Analytics

1. INTRODUCTION

Serious games (SGs) are video games that have an explicit educational objective, such as assisting in the creation of inspiring surroundings, the promotion of important experiences, and the ability to generate systemic concerns (Fernández-Sánchez et al., 2023). SGs are games with non-entertainment aims that are meant to educate, train, and inform (Hauge et al., 2014) and it can be used in education field. Otherwise, SGs are designed to teach, build skills, and induce behavioural change. SGs have demonstrated various benefits when utilised in education to improve student learning. Many teachers still do not consider games to be a powerful tool for improving their teaching (Calvo-Morata et al., 2019). Therefore, SGs have been discovered to offer great educational potential, with the potential to make learning more interesting and enjoyable (Carvalho et al., 2015). SGs are increasingly being employed to boost student engagement and foster the development of relevant cognitive abilities (Yousefi & Mirkhezri, 2019). When engaging students in STEM (Science, Technology, Engineering, and Mathematics) education, SGs can be more effective in teaching and learning. Traditional game-creation environments lack STEM-related support (Yousefi & Mirkhezri, 2019), therefore implementing SGs in the educational field can provide numerous advantages over more traditional learning approaches. Students may be attracted to SGs via engaging and exciting STEM education activities (Ahmad Zaki et al., 2020). SGs concepts are growing rapidly and are recognised as an effective teaching method (Leao et al., 2017). In addition, the use of SGs in STEM education can have a significant impact on both educators and students. Due to the obvious low number of students engaged in STEM education, several technology tools and games have been developed to increase students' motivation and performance. Because SGs are so interactive, they offer users a firsthand simulated experience, which is one of their educational benefits. Interaction data generated by SGs can be used for both formative and summative assessment of learning, and to offer learners with fast feedback, or even to alter game elements on the fly (Freire et al., 2023). Several advantages of using SGs in education, according to the review, include a better learning experience, quick feedback, behaviour change, and the capacity to adapt to most learning situations (Yousefi & Mirkhezri, 2019).

Gamification has been identified as one way for improving engagement in a variety of contexts, including marketing, customer and student engagement, product, and workplace engagement (Dhiraj Upadhyaya & Anchal Garg, 2019). In this situation, SGs can be utilised for purposes other than pure entertainment; they can be used to teach, change an attitude or behaviour, or raise the awareness about a specific topic (Calvo-Morata et al., 2019). Numerous advantages of using games in education are readily apparent in games designed for sheer entertainment. Their approach is fun, engaging, and encourages students to achieve their goals (Cristina Alonso-Fernandez et al., 2017). According to (Celorrio-Aguilera & Freire, 2021), educational games have been shown to be an effective technique for motivating students and improving their learning. They enable high school or college students to understand, connect, and investigate the formulas often found in a STEM curriculum.

However, there are concerns about how to access or predict learners' performance in SGs. Game Learning Analytics (GLA) is one of the keys to help teachers in the application of SGs in the classrooms (Antonio Calvo Morata et al., 2019). After the learning process with the SGs, the outcomes need to be measured by a performance indicator or measuring tool. As a consequence, it was found that, in order to analyse the data in compliance with institutional criteria, an analytical tool is needed to hold practically all of the data. An analytical method for gauging student achievement and predicting interest is learning analytics (LA). A recent field of study called "learning analytics" suggests a connection between learner and educator data. By providing instant feedback on how their students are using SGs in class, this method aims to make SG implementation more informative for teachers (Ángel Serrano-Laguna & Baltasar Fernández-Manjón, 2014). Thus, one of the most important tools for assisting educators in using SGs in the classroom is GLA (Antonio Calvo Morata et al., 2019). On the other hand, practical exercises are used in almost all classrooms to assist students consolidate knowledge and learn new abilities. Students must use their theoretical knowledge to solve specific problems when completing assignments. This helps them to demonstrate their understanding and point out misunderstandings or any issue. This is certainly relevant for scientific subjects, where practise is necessary for learning (Ángel Serrano-Laguna & Baltasar Fernández-Manjón, 2014). When teachers wish to maintain track of their class's progress, they must monitor how learner's complete classroom exercises, among other things (Ángel Serrano-Laguna & Baltasar Fernández-Manjón, 2014). GLA provides for the collection of data from students' engagement with games and the extraction of information that simplifies teachers' tasks. When done in a transparent manner within the gaming environment (i.e., stealth assessment), it can provide evidence-based data on the learners' understanding at any given point in time (Antonio Calvo Morata et al., 2019). In (Hauge et al., 2014) study, there are two modes of SGs analytics which are in-game (real time) analytics, and post-game (off-line) analytics.

In this study, computational thinking (CT) can be applied in SGs by using GLA to predict the performance of STEM learners. The term CT refers to a cognitive skill geared at problem solving using computer science methodologies and concepts (Pires et al., 2019). CT is a method of problem-solving that enables individuals to identify the nature of a difficult situation and identify possible solutions. The solutions can then be displayed in a way that can be comprehended by a computer, a human, or both. They consist of four key techniques to computational thinking: decomposition, pattern recognition, abstraction and algorithms. Figure 1 illustrates the CT techniques.

The main goal of this study is to evaluate the best method for gathering statistical information regarding the impact of playing SGs with GLA frameworks to enhance the development of CT skills and encourage student participation in STEM education. As a result, this study will go over a novel STEM in SGs and GLA framework, as well as serious game elements that can be used in STEM education by using SGs. In a nutshell, recommendations for using it in SGs will be explored. The framework's output will be used as a guideline by developers and educators to create SGs to enhance CT skills to facilitate learning in STEM education based on the features discussed in this research in order to predict learner performance and improve the effectiveness process in STEM education while using SGs. This initiative would aid in the development of students that are digitally savvy, innovative, and exhibit higher order thinking skills.

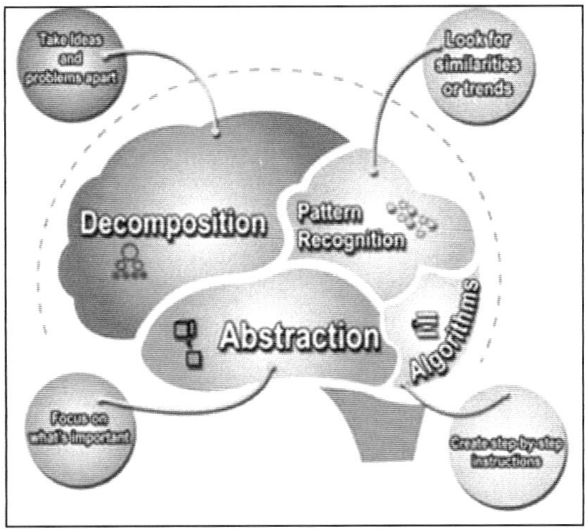

Figure 1. Computational thinking techniques

1.1 Interrelation between GLA and SGs

This study addresses the potential effects of combining LA and SGs for enhancing game quality, measuring and evaluating player behavior, gaming achievement, game development, attaining learning objectives, and user satisfaction (Hauge et al., 2014). GLA can be utilised to pique educators' and learners' interest in exploring SGs because of their engaging and immersive aspects in order to boost learners' motivation and performance in STEM education. SGs and GLA can shed light on how to best optimise the game lifecycle as well as the learning process (Perez-Colado et al., 2021). According to (Ángel Serrano-Laguna & Baltasar Fernández-Manjón, 2014). Through classroom exercises, teachers can use GLA concepts to help them monitor their students on a regular schedule. There are just two conditions we must fulfill: In order for the connected device to relay the resolution process back to the teacher, the students must first complete exercises; and second, this user data needs to pay attention to, analysed, and meaningfully presented to the teacher by a GLA system.

Aside from that, CT skills entail a process that uses computational tools to compute solutions to complicated issues by first reducing them to smaller, more manageable parts, and then abstracting those parts into forms that can be computed. It can define or predict STEM learners' performance. CT seeks to apply the essential abilities and approaches in the design of algorithms to address issues in domains outside than computation, and is built upon the four components of decomposition, pattern recognition, abstraction, and algorithms (Pires et al., 2019). To solve problems with CT, the following procedures are used: to break the problem down into smaller, easier-to-solve parts; to recognise patterns and determine whether there is similarity between two or more problems, allowing the use of the same solution; the identification or abstraction of the essential attributes and the rejection of those that are irrelevant to the problem's resolution; the description of a logical-algorithmic step-by-step procedure that will lead to the problem's solution (Pires et al., 2019). For instance, most of the STEM subjects have a number of problems that are used in real-world situations. So then, in this study, we propose the implementation of SGs for STEM education through the use of CT skills as well as pedagogical approach, as shown in Figure 2. One of the most important aspects to consider when developing a SG is gamification design. A greater understanding of specific game elements may aid designers in making better design decisions (Li et al., 2022) to maximise the benefits of SGs in supporting students' play and learning experiences. In addition, implementing the problem-solving and creative-thinking elements of CT skills into SGs is the most important way to ensure the success of a STEM in SGs application. To sum up, the SGs elements must be involved in the development of the SGs for STEM education.

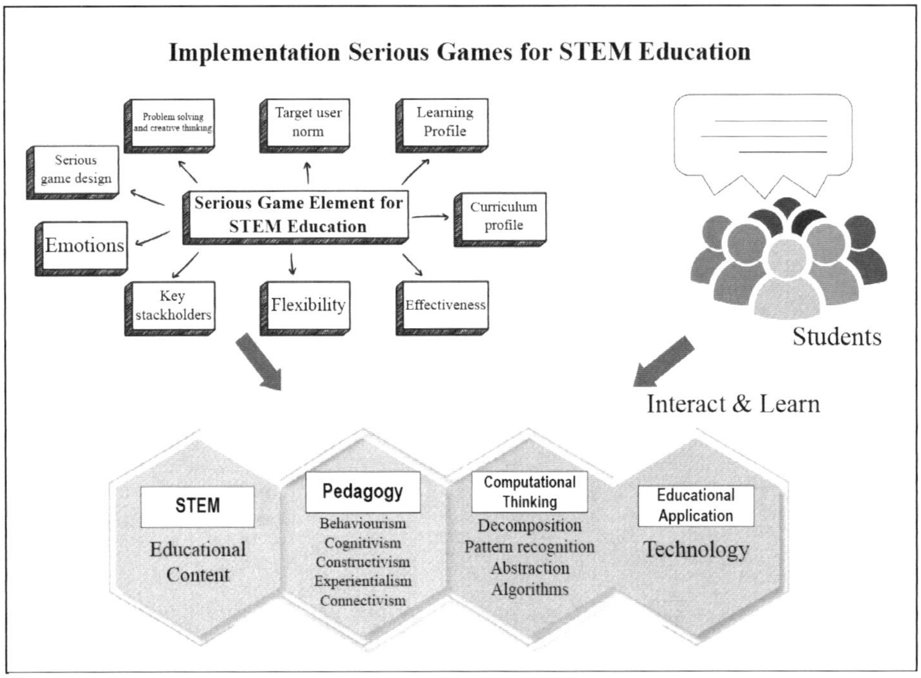

Figure 2. Implementation SGs for STEM education

CT is an essential human skill when compared to other skills such as reading, writing, and performing arithmetic operations since it can be helpful in explaining complicated issues or contexts. Thus, in this study, the solution of problems through CT by using GLA framework can be follow this process as Table 1 below:

Table 1. Computational thinking characteristics and process

Techniques	Process
Decomposition	Breaking down a big problem and take ideas into smaller part.
Pattern recognition	Look for similarities or trends.
Abstraction	Taking the details out of a problem and ignoring irrelevant information which is focus on what's important
Algorithms	Simple rules to follow the solve problem by create step by step instruction

1.2 Game Learning Analytics (GLA) for the Sake of Serious Games (SGs) in STEM Education

How do the above mentioned GLA and SGs interact with one another to predict STEM learner performance? What is the context for such cooperation, and what is the possible outcome? Some of the works reviewed for this article suggest two potential interactions between GLA and SGs, such as: GLA is used for improvement of SGs, and GLA is used to predict STEM learners by using SGs in educational field or curriculum. The combination of LA and SG is known as GLA, which aids in the gathering, processing, and visualisation of data about a learner's interactions with a SGs (Petrov et al., 2019). There needs to be a way to quantitatively and qualitatively assess the educational value of these games (Cristina Alonso-Fernandez et al., 2017). This framework will assist stakeholders in applying analytics to educational gamification data to improve engagement and motivation, thereby improving the teaching and learning process and enhancing student learning (Dhiraj Upadhyaya & Anchal Garg, 2019) in STEM education.

1.3 Serious Games (SGs) for the Sake of Game Learning Analytics (GLA) in STEM Education

How can the GLA benefit from the SGs? How the above mentioned SGs and GLA can interact between each other? SGs can be used to raise the LA's quality in order to respond to this question. GLA is a tool that can be used to streamline the deployment of SGs in educational settings. In addition, GLA also can be used to validate the effectiveness of STEM subjects while using SGs in the education field. In addition, one of the previous studies indicates, because games are highly interactive, when trying to gain insight into or enhance the educational experience for students, LA is ideally suited for recording their interactions with one another (Cristina Alonso-Fernandez et al., 2017). To promote the engagements of GLA and STEM education, which makes it possible in light of the present educational issues, which illustrate students as discouraged and lacking in interest in their studies (Pires et al., 2019). Figure 3 presents how the SGs and GLA can interact between each other by including the SGs elements in design and development of the SGs for STEM education.

1.3.1 Interaction between Serious Games Elements and Game Learning Analytics

The process of GLA application can be into four steps; 1) design new GLA application, 2) improve GLA by adding module, 3) analyze design components, and 4) access the end result.

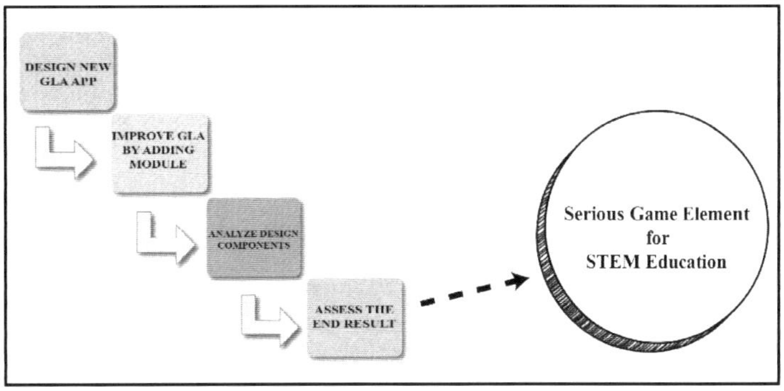

Figure 3. Interaction between SGs elements and GLA

2. METHODS AND BENEFITS

This section explains how to utilise the GLA framework to predict STEM learners' performance in SGs for CT skills, as well as how to construct GLA for learners and the benefits it provides. There are a few ways or strategies for using SGs to execute the LA. These methodologies could assist educators, researchers, and policymakers in collecting huge data sets to analyse the potential of SGs applications in conjunction with LA models.

According to (Petrov et al., 2019), game elements, virtual reality features, and CT skills are all examples of important factors that should be accounted for in the implementation of the GLA framework. Teachers have been complaining about students' lack of motivation and interest as teaching moves online. However, students had negative things to say about dull teaching strategies. By creating innovative and engaging e-learning techniques, such as boosting emotional engagement through games, interactivity, and experience design, research into bettering the teaching and learning process has produced new concepts (Dhiraj Upadhyaya & Anchal Garg, 2019). Using game aspects to increase enjoyment, stimulate people, encourage learning, and solve issues is what is meant by "serious games." An impulse that leads to an action or objective is called motivation, and it's crucial to both learning and gaming. In CT, motivation comes in two forms: extrinsic and intrinsic. When a learner follows through on a proposed course of study out of curiosity and without considering the potential rewards, they are demonstrating intrinsic motivation. In contrast, behaviour resulting from an activity that carries a reward or punishment is known as extrinsic motivation (Pires et al., 2019). To deliver educational content in an engaging and interactive manner within an SGs application and create intrinsic motivation among learners, numerous design strategies can be used, including gamified learning components, real-time feedback, collaborative elements, etc. Gamified learning features include gaming mechanics such as levels, achievements, badges, and leaderboards. This will expose students to an extrinsic motivating experience. The real-time feedback will give learners immediate, constructive feedback on their actions and decisions in the game. Aside from that, incorporating multiplayer or cooperative tasks in which learners can collaborate to solve problems or attain goals might help students improve their problem-solving skills through brainstorming. In a nutshell, learners' engagement in cognitive thinking, practical skills, emotions, and behaviour was lower when they engaged in intrinsic play than when they engaged in extrinsic play.

Thus, in this study, the implementation of SGs and problem solving to predict learner performance through CT skills utilising the GLA framework can be done as follows:

- Decomposition: Determine ways of assessing students' performance in serious games for STEM education.
- Pattern recognition: Look for the technological tools and relevant games that have been introduces to boost students' performance and motivation.
- Abstraction: Identify the issue that has arisen in order to stimulate student interest in STEM education through the use of SGs, such as the pedagogical approach and game elements that can be implemented in the development of SGs.
- Algorithms: Increase student engagement in STEM education through the use of SGs in the classroom. Identify and execute a pedagogical strategy, game elements, and game design in order to create SGs that promote STEM learner engagement through SGs. The implementation of GLA framework is then used as an evaluation tool in the classroom to evaluate and predict the learners' performance.

Figure 4 below illustrates the framework method and the applications of GLA for SGs. Predicting the performance of learners using CT skills requires a real-world experiment involving STEM subjects and SGs. Every piece of information gathered from the game learning process was submitted to the GLA application. Therefore, educators can employ a few functions of the GLA programme, including predicting students' performance or grade level, predicting students' conduct or subject-matter knowledge, making it easier to implement SGs in the classroom, and predicting how well STEM subjects would work in SGs.

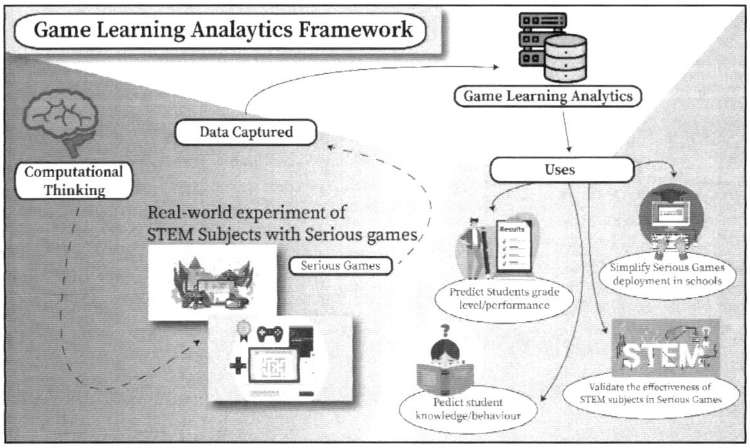

Figure 4. GLA framework

2.1 Implementation of GLA Framework for STEM Education using SGs

Based on the findings of this study, the use of the GLA framework to predict STEM learners in SGs with the deployment of CT skills is visualized in Figure 5.

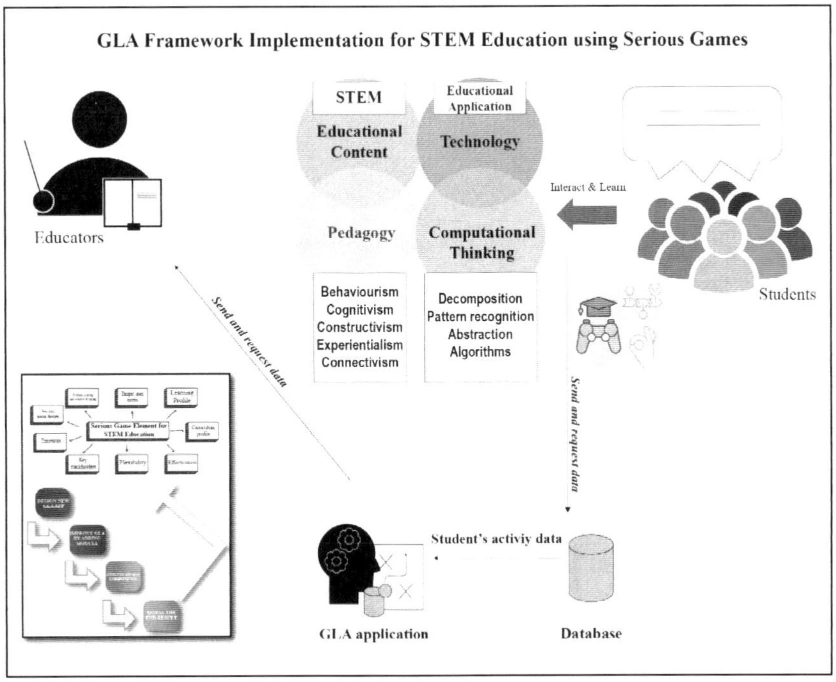

Figure 5. Implementation of GLA framework for STEM education using SGs

The first thing to examine is how a quality design may be performed in order to develop SGs for STEM fields. To get a good game design and to pique the students' interest in learning those subjects, the SGs elements must be included in SGs. The educational application that students can use with the help of technology. Next, students will interact and learn STEM subjects as educational content is integrated in the SGs deployment. In addition, to improve learning with SGs, the pedagogical approach and computational thinking must be implemented in the SGs and GLA implementation process. Using technology, all data from student activity could be transferred to the GLA application. Finally, by sending and requesting data to educators, GLA can be used to assess the end result. Figure 6 illustrates the guidelines for designing GLA applications that support the suggested framework for this study. The implementation of frameworks is divided into two areas: SGs as instructional materials and GLA applications as data analysis tools. This proposed framework can be considered a novel technique in STEM education. According to the previous study, the majority of existing frameworks only focused on conceptual and technical types. There is no relationship with the STEM education field, particularly with specific game elements and pedagogical approaches that can interact and connect with one another.

The SGs and learning analytics model are elaborate below:

- Teachers use SGs as learning resources.
- Teachers assist students by using mobile games to configure SGs as instructional materials.
- Students participate in learning from courses created in SGs, and all data is transformed to the LMS, which has an implementation relationship with the game elements in SGs.
- As students participate in learning, data is created into terms of various logs, grades, etc.
- Various levels and types of analysis is done to measure and predict student engagement, performances, outcomes, and dropout.

- Gamified learning is used in this educational approach to engage and encourage students by incorporating elements of game design and mechanics into the learning environment.
- Through the use of an IT system, adaptive and personalised learning can be accomplished. From the student and domain models to the pedagogical model, feedback is delivered into the learning management system.

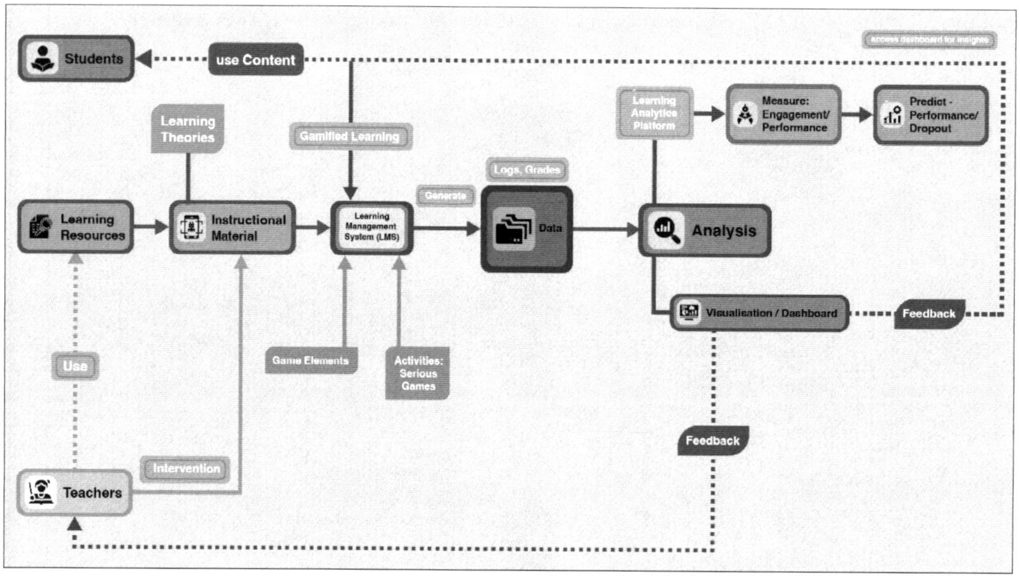

Figure 6. Framework for SGs and GLA

By adopting this design guideline, the stakeholder can use learning analytics to enhance the educational impact of the SGs, ensuring that it is both engaging and effective in achieving its educational objectives.

3. DISCUSSION

This study aimed to provide guidelines for developing a GLA application to forecast STEM learners' performance in SGs based on applied CT skills. We believe that obtaining LA data from SGs is crucial because it sheds light on students' in-game activities and makes it easier for educators to use games in the STEM education context. Through attempts, the LA application may even highlight notable differences between age and gender in terms of interests, abilities, accomplishments, and development (Zapata-Caceres & Martin-Barroso, 2021). SGs can be utilised to increase students' motivation to learn. Students' confidence and experience learning (Kazimoglu, 2020) with CT skills can be enhanced through STEM education and game play, which can then aid in their learning of STEM subjects. When compared to traditional approaches, SGs provides tremendous benefits to educators. SGs should be simple to find, distribute, and integrate in order to maximise its benefits. GLA could be considered as one of the keys to supporting educators in the use of SGs in the classroom.

4. LIMITATION OR CHALLENGES

Educators might not see the clear value in using a game in the classroom even if it meets all the criteria for doing so (Calvo-Morata et al., 2019). Because of their role as educators, they might not be comfortable using the game's technology (Calvo-Morata et al., 2019). Furthermore, the development of real-time procedures for adaptive gaming and personalised support; the appropriate formulation and execution of reliable assessment models and criteria; these are all areas where more research is needed (Hauge et al., 2014).

Another barrier to this research was the lack of a widely accepted conventional method for teaching CT skills to students by having them play SGs in STEM education content (Kazimoglu, 2020). Numerous researchers have supported the idea of teaching CT in schools, but it has yet to gain traction. This has an impact on research study design because it is not always clear what type of intervention can be used in a control group (Kazimoglu, 2020).

Nonetheless, financial issues constantly occur when developing and deploying the GLA application in the educational field. GLA remains an expensive and fragile process (Freire et al., 2023).

5. CONCLUSION

This paper presented a GLA framework strategy for CT skills aimed at SGs in STEM education. This study also seeks to discover and address the usefulness of playing SGs in STEM education. Implementing SGs in STEM education through the use of CT skills must be appropriate and interesting across a variety of courses. This is to keep the game interesting throughout time, it must be updated and upgraded on a regular basis, including the game elements and design which is to maintain track on learner performance on a frequent basis. The discovered CT skills consist of four elements: decomposition, pattern recognition, abstraction, and an algorithm that can be used in this proposed framework. SGs for CT skills can assist students in visualising difficult concepts and provide opportunity for learners to transfer experience into knowledge. Hence, employing GLA allows educators to predict student performance in a variety of categories such as behaviour, knowledge, grade level, and etc. Game designers can incorporate gamification features into the application to improve the learning experience, ensuring that these elements correspond with the learning objectives and foster a sense of fun and engagement. However, since research on CT through the use of GLA is still poorly conducted or possibly ongoing, the number of articles that can be reviewed in this study is limited. This conceptual framework has been developed with reference to previous studies. Thus, studies using actual students as participants are required to validate the suggested framework and determine its upsides and downsides.

ACKNOWLEDGEMENT

This research work has been supported by the Ministry of Higher Education under the Fundamental Research Grant Scheme (FRGS/1/2022/SSI07/UM/02/21), Grant ID Number FP051-2022, in the Game Learning Analytics Framework for Pedagogical Approach of STEM Education using Augmented Reality-based Serious Games. I would like to convey my heartfelt gratitude to my PhD supervisors, Assoc. Prof. Dr. Amirrudin Kamsin and Assoc. Prof. Dr. Hameedur Rahman, for their guidance and assistance during the research process, as well as for providing insightful and kind comments on a previous draft.

REFERENCES

Ahmad Zaki, N. A., Mohamed Zain, N. Z., Noor, N., & Hashim, H. (2020). Developing a Conceptual Model of Learning Analytics in Serious Games for STEM Education. *Jurnal Pendidikan IPA Indonesia*, *9*, 330–339. https://doi.org/10.15294/jpii.v9i3.24466

Ángel Serrano-Laguna, & Baltasar Fernández-Manjón. (2014). Applying learning analytics to simplify serious games deployment in the classroom. *EEE Global Engineering Education Conference (EDUCON), 2014 3-5 April 2014, Military Museum and Cultural Center, Harbiye, Istanbul*.

Antonio Calvo Morata, Cristina Alonso Fernandez, & Manuel Freire. (2019). Game Learning Analytics for Educators. *Proceedings of 2019 IEEE Global Engineering Education Conference (EDUCON) : Date and Venue, 9-11 April, 2019, Dubai, UAE*.

Calvo-Morata, A., Alonso-Fernandez, C., Freire-Moran, M., Martinez-Ortiz, I., & Fernandez-Manjon, B. (2019). Game Learning Analytics, Facilitating the Use of Serious Games in the Class. *Revista Iberoamericana de Tecnologias Del Aprendizaje*, *14*(4), 168–176. https://doi.org/10.1109/RITA.2019.2952296

Carvalho, M. B., Bellotti, F., Berta, R., De Gloria, A., Gazzarata, G., Hu, J., & Kickmeier-Rust, M. (2015). A case study on Service-Oriented Architecture for Serious Games. *Entertainment Computing*, *6*, 1–10. https://doi.org/10.1016/j.entcom.2014.11.001

Celorrio-Aguilera, I., & Freire, M. (2021). Creating serious STEM games by combining a game platform and mathematical software. *Proceedings - IEEE 21st International Conference on Advanced Learning Technologies, ICALT 2021*, 69–71. https://doi.org/10.1109/ICALT52272.2021.00028

Cristina Alonso-Fernandez, Antonio Calvo, Manuel Freire, Ivan Martinez-Ortiz, & Baltasar Fernandez-Manjon. (2017). Systematizing game learning analytics for serious games. *Proceedings of 2017 IEEE Global Engineering Education Conference (EDUCON) : Date and Venue: 25-28 April 2017, Athens, Greece.*

Dhiraj Upadhyaya, & Anchal Garg. (2019). Leveraging on Gamification and Learning Analytics for Improved Student Learning. *2019 International Conference on Computing, Power and Communication Technologies (GUCON) Galgotias University, Greater Noida, UP, India. Sep 27-28, 2019.*

Fernández-Sánchez, M. R., González-Fernández, A., & Acevedo-Borrega, J. (2023). Conceptual Approach to the Pedagogy of Serious Games. *Information (Switzerland)*, *14*(2). https://doi.org/10.3390/info14020132

Freire, M., Calvo-Morata, A., Martinez-Ortiz, I., & Fernandez-Manjon, B. (2023). Bootstrapping serious games to assess learning through analytics. *IEEE Global Engineering Education Conference, EDUCON*, *2023-May*. https://doi.org/10.1109/EDUCON54358.2023.10125177

Hauge, J. B., Berta, R., Fiucci, G., Manjon, B. F., Padron-Napoles, C., Westra, W., & Nadolski, R. (2014). Implications of learning analytics for serious game design. *Proceedings - IEEE 14th International Conference on Advanced Learning Technologies, ICALT 2014*, 230–232. https://doi.org/10.1109/ICALT.2014.73

Kazimoglu, C. (2020). Enhancing confidence in using computational thinking skills via playing a serious game: A case study to increase motivation in learning computer programming. *IEEE Access*. https://doi.org/10.1109/ACCESS.2020.3043278

Leao, C. P., Soares, F., Carvalho, V., Lopes, S., & Gonçalves, I. (2017). A serious game concept to enhance students' learning of statistics. *2017 4th Experiment@International Conference (Exp.at'17)*, 187–190. https://doi.org/10.1109/EXPAT.2017.7984390

Li, J., Van Der Spek, E., Hu, J., & Feijs, L. (2022). Extracting Design Guidelines for Augmented Reality Serious Games for Children. *IEEE Access*, *10*, 66660–66671. https://doi.org/10.1109/ACCESS.2022.3184775

Perez-Colado, V. M., Perez-Colado, I. J., Freire-Moran, M., Martinez-Ortiz, I., & Fernandez-Manjon, B. (2021). A Tool Supported Approach for Teaching Serious Game Learning Analytics. *Proceedings - Frontiers in Education Conference, FIE*, *2021-October*. https://doi.org/10.1109/FIE49875.2021.9637062

Petrov, E. V., Mustafina, J., Alloghani, M., Galiullin, L., & Tan, S. Y. (2019). Learning analytics and serious games: Analysis of interrelation. *Proceedings - International Conference on Developments in ESystems Engineering, DeSE*, *2018-September*, 153–156. https://doi.org/10.1109/DeSE.2018.00037

Pires, F., Lima, F. M., Bernardo, J. R., & Melo, R. (2019). *Gamification and engagement Development of Computational Thinking and the implications in mathematical learning*.

Yousefi, B. H., & Mirkhezri, H. (2019). Toward A Game-based Learning Platform : A Comparative Conceptual Framework for Serious Games. *Proceedings of the 2019 International Serious Games Symposium, ISGS 2019*, 74–80. https://doi.org/10.1109/ISGS49501.2019.9046979

Zapata-Caceres, M., & Martin-Barroso, E. (2021). Applying Game Learning Analytics to a Voluntary Video Game: Intrinsic Motivation, Persistence, and Rewards in Learning to Program at an Early Age. *IEEE Access*, *9*, 123588–123602. https://doi.org/10.1109/ACCESS.2021.3110475

DESIGN GUIDELINES FOR PERSONALITY BASED INTERFACES

Dina A. Zekry, Khaled Nagaty and Gerard T. McKee
The British University in Egypt
El-Sherouk, Cairo, Egypt

ABSTRACT

The research presented in this paper addresses the lack of design guidelines for personalization of interfaces in existing interface design principles, which are general in nature. The research investigates the association between users' dominant personality traits, measured by the Big Five Personality Traits framework, and interface preferences. The research focused on associating five design attributes to the identified dominant traits. The five design attributes are color preferences, information structure, element shape, interface type, and symmetry preferences. Students studying Informatics and Computer Science were invited to participate in the study by taking the Big Five Personality Traits test. Segmentation using K-means did not give distinctive personality clusters. Further analysis using Principal Component Analysis (PCA), however, revealed that openness and conscientiousness accounted for over 50% of the variance in the data. The associations were investigated by designing Learning Management System (LMS) based mobile interfaces with attributes corresponding to these two dominant traits. Using the Chi-squared test, the research identified a significant association between the interfaces designed with the openness and conscientiousness proposed attributes and the users' interface preferences. These findings suggest employing the design attributes as guidelines to facilitate the personalization process for interface designs tailored to openness and conscientiousness personality traits.

KEYWORDS

Interface Design, Personality Traits, Personality-Based Design Guidelines

1. INTRODUCTION

User interface (UI) serves as a gateway that facilitates users' interaction with system functionalities. UI ought to be user centered to cater for the users' needs and offer a satisfying experience. Personalization is an approach rooted in user data that offers insights into user needs and preferences which have been linked to enhance the user engagement and satisfaction. The process of designing interfaces for digital products is guided by general design principles that help lay a foundation for designing interfaces. Creating personalized interfaces is challenging due to the difficulty of choosing design attributes. Also, there are no specific design guidelines that help decide which design attributes should be used in which context. Numerous design attributes contribute to shaping an interface leading to a multitude of possibilities. Therefore, there is a need to have specific guidelines to streamline the design process. The research is conducted in the context of Learning Management System (LMS) for university students.

The research identified two research gaps. First, the lack of specific design guidelines for personalization in interface design. Second, the challenges in translating insights about personality impact into applicable design guidelines. The authors use the Big Five Personality Traits (BFT) framework to identify the users' personality traits and segmented the dataset using K-means and PCA to identify the most dominant user traits. Based on the results, the research associates five design attributes with each of the identified personality traits. Based on the associations, personality-based interfaces are designed for the Learning Management System (LMS). By conducting an experiment and using the Chi-squared test, the research evaluates the association between interfaces that cater to the users' dominant personality trait and the user interface preferences. The research goal is to provide specific design guidelines based on the drawn associations to guide the design of personality-based interfaces.

The paper is organized as follows. Section 2 provides a literature review of interface design and the Big Five Personality Traits framework. Section 3 presents the research methodology including the dataset used, the dataset analysis including K-means and PCA, the design attributes association to the identified personality traits, and the designed interfaces using Figma. Section 4 describes the experiment set up. Section 5 discusses the experiment results. Section 6 provides the conclusion and section 7 discusses future work.

2. LITERATURE REVIEW

This section provides an overview on interface design and the Big Five Personality Traits framework.

2.1 Interface Design

Interface design encapsulates a wide range of design attributes that contribute to the overall design. For instance, layout, color, typography, images, icons, alignment, spacing, element shape and sizes, and many more. Additionally, there are design aspects that should be considered such as consistency, visual hierarchy, navigation, feedback mechanism, interactivity, visual balance, familiarity, and others. Including every design aspect proves challenging due to the vast array of possibilities. Moreover, a single design attribute has diverse applications. For example, a rectangular box can be used as a text box, button, container, and separator.

There are multiple design principles that help guide the design process such as Alan Dix's principles, Gestalt principles, and Nilson's ten usability heuristics. Alan Dix's principles categorizes design principles into three main groups recognizing the multifaceted nature of design attributes (Dix et al., 2004). These principles highlight the importance of flexibility in design. Gestalt principles are rooted in psychology offering valuable insights into organizing visual elements based on users' perception focusing on patterns and their relationships (MacNamara, 2016). Nielsen's Ten Usability Heuristics for interface design act as a general guide advocating for user-centric design and providing a set of criteria to evaluate interactive systems' usability (Nielsen, 1994).

While design principles are significant and have a substantial role in impacting the design process, they have the limitation of being general. The design principles lack specificity regarding which design elements should be employed in various situations to best accommodate user needs. Additionally, the interpretation of the design principles can vary among readers and contexts which leads to diverse implementations. Also, the principles may overlap or express similar concepts further complicating their application in interface design.

Personalization plays a vital role in interface design by profiling users and customizing interfaces to suit their preferences, interests, and unique characteristics (Sili et al., 2016). Personalization acknowledges individual differences rather than treating users as uniform groups. Research has shown that personalized interfaces tailored to users' personalities enhance user performance resulting in improved information flow (Sili et al., 2016; Alves et al., 2020). Personality also influences users' perceptions of design efficiency and users' acceptance and usage behaviors (Sili et al., 2016; Alves et al., 2020). Individuals demonstrate increased user engagement and task completion when encountering interfaces that cater to their personality preferences. Despite the progress in understanding the impact of personality on interface design, challenges persist in translating these insights into guidelines that are applicable and specific to guide the design process.

2.2 The Big Five Personality Traits Framework

The Big Five Personality traits framework (BFT) consists of five traits that are the building blocks of an individual's personality (Goldberg, 1993; McCrae & Costa, 1999). Namely, conscientiousness, agreeableness, openness, extraversion, and neuroticism. Conscientiousness is the tendency to show self-discipline, planning and organization, agreeableness is the tendency to be pro-social and cooperative towards others rather than antagonistic, openness to experience is the degree of intellectual curiosity, creativity, and preference for novelty and variety, extraversion is the positive emotions, activity, sociability, and tendency to seek stimulation in the company of others, and neuroticism is the vulnerability to unpleasant emotions such as anxiety, anger, and depression (Goldberg, 1993; McCrae & Costa, 1999).

Research conducted over the years has associated characteristics to personality traits (Goldberg, 1993; McCrae & Costa, 1999). Conscientiousness individuals are organized, responsible, and dependable. They hold high standards of themselves and strive for achievement. They are known to be detail oriented and able to exert effort towards their goals. Agreeableness individuals are empathetic, cooperative, and prioritize interpersonal relationships. They are known to avoid conflict and their opinions are not hard set. Openness individuals are curios, imaginative, creative, and willing to try new things. They are known to prioritize a global vision and expose themselves to experiences. Extraversion individuals are sociable, energetic, and talkative. They are known to enjoy social settings and being the center of attention.

3. METHODOLOGY

The following section provides details on the gathered dataset, the data analysis using K-means and PCA, the association of design attributes and the identified personality traits, and the designed interfaces.

3.1 ICS-BUE Dataset

The dataset is gathered by the paper author on the campus of the British University in Egypt (BUE). All participants are Informatics and Computer Sciences (ICS) students. The batches chosen for the research are prep year, year one after prep, and year two after prep. All study participants took the Big Five Personality Traits test using Truity website (Truity Psychometrics LLC and Owens). Table 1 shows the total number of participants per batch.

Table 1. Number of participants per batch

Batch	Number of participants
Prep year	30
Year 1 after prep	107
Year 2 after prep	71
Total	208

3.2 Dataset Analysis

The data analysis section discusses the results of implementing K-means and PCA to segment the dataset and identify the dataset dominant trait. The term "trait combination" denotes the arrangement of the five personality traits from the most dominant to the least dominant trait. The term "dominant trait" refers to the highest scoring/ most influential trait in the dataset.

3.2.1 K-means

K-means is a clustering algorithm used to partition data points into K distinct clusters based on their features. Elbow and silhouette methods are used to find the optimum value of K. The elbow and silhouette methods both support K=2 as the optimum value of K. Table 2 shows the cluster density and acronym for K=2 clusters.

Both clusters exhibit openness and agreeableness as their most dominant traits. However, the trait combination varies, where OACEN and OAECN are the acronyms for the produced clusters respectively. The trait combinations indicate that neuroticism is the least dominant trait while extraversion and conscientiousness interchange in the fourth and third positions.

Table 2. K-means results for K=2

Method	Total number of clusters	Cluster density	Acronym
K-means	2	97	OACEN
		100	OAECN

To investigate the variance within the clusters, standard deviation is used to evaluate how much the scores of individuals within a cluster differ from the mean score for each trait within that cluster.

In Cluster 0, individuals demonstrate moderate variability across the Big Five personality traits. Openness, conscientiousness, agreeableness, and extraversion exhibit standard deviations ranging from approximately 10.94 to 14.17 which indicates some diversity within the cluster in these dimensions. However, the variability is not exceedingly high. Neuroticism displays the highest variability with a standard deviation of approximately 14.17 which suggests more difference among individuals within the cluster compared to the other traits.

In Cluster 1, individuals demonstrate moderate variability across the Big Five personality traits but slightly higher variability than the traits in Cluster 0. The standard deviations for openness, conscientiousness, and extraversion range from approximately 11.57 to 13.51, indicating some diversity within the cluster regarding these dimensions. However, the variability is not excessively high. Agreeableness exhibits a slightly lower variability, with a standard deviation of around 10.87, suggesting a relatively consistent level of agreeableness among individuals in the cluster. Neuroticism also shows moderate variability, with a standard deviation of approximately 12.27. Table 3 shows the results of standard deviation for the clusters.

Table 3. Standard deviation results for cluster produced when K=2

Cluster	**Openness**	**Conscientiousness**	**Extraversion**	**Agreeableness**	**Neuroticism**
0	12.142317	10.942910	13.861848	12.318873	14.170391
1	13.414567	11.568934	13.509494	10.869574	12.272788

The research anticipated that clustering using K-means would produce clusters with distinct varying dominant traits. Instead, the clusters produced have similar dominant traits and varying trait combinations. Additionally, within the clusters, the variations are not significantly high which means that the clustering results cannot consider the traits in isolation. The clustering results are beneficial for identifying the trait combination but not the dominant trait. The research aims to identify the most dominant traits to create personality-based designs. Due to the insufficient results from K-means, the research resorted to Principal Component Analysis (PCA) to identify the most dominant trait.

3.2.2 Principal Component Analysis (PCA)

Principal Component Analysis (PCA) is a statistical technique used to reduce the dimensionality of a dataset by transforming the original variables into a new set of uncorrelated variables called principal components which capture the maximum variance in the data. PCA is applied to identify the most influencing traits in the dataset as it has the ability to overcome issues related to variables strongly correlate with each other.

The result of the PCA explained variance ratio is [0.31517963, 0.23423334, 0.17656209, 0.15189813, 0.12212682]. The BFT are represented in the order of openness, conscientiousness, extraversion, agreeableness, and neuroticism which correspond to PC1, PC2, PC3, PC4, PC5 respectively. The first principal component (PC1) explains approximately 31.5% of the total variance in the dataset. The second principal component (PC2) explains around 23.4% of the total variance. The third principal component (PC3) explains about 17.7% of the total variance. The fourth principal component (PC4) explains roughly 15.2% of the total variance. The fifth principal component (PC5) explains around 12.2% of the total variance.

The sum of explained variance ratio of the first two principal components is 55.9% which indicates that openness and conscientiousness collectively account for a significant portion of the dataset's variability. Therefore, these traits have substantial influence over the observed differences in individuals' personalities within the dataset.

To determine the threshold for establishing which traits generated by PCA should be considered as the dominant traits for the ICS-BUE dataset, F-statistic is used. The F-statistic test is able to assess the significance of the differences between the variances explained by different principal components. The p-value associated to the F-statistic represents the probability of observing the results of the statistical test. If the p-value is less than the standard threshold of 0.05, the null hypothesis is rejected, supporting the alternate hypothesis. The null hypothesis proposes no significant difference, while the alternate hypothesis proposes the existence of a significant difference.

The F-statistic is computed to assess the significance of the variance between conscientiousness and extraversion. The F-statistic result is approximately equal to 232 with its associated p-value equal to 1.11×10^{-16}. The p-value is very small and close to 0 which indicates that the observed difference in variances between conscientiousness and extraversion components is highly unlikely to have occurred by chance. This suggests that the conscientiousness and extraversion components captured by PCA are significantly different from each other. Based on the PCA and F-statistic results, a threshold of 20% for PCA influence is established. Only openness and conscientiousness were considered as their influence surpasses this threshold.

3.3 Personality Based Interface Design

The following section details the design associations and the Figma designs.

3.3.1 Design Associations

Based on the data analysis phase, the personality traits to be designed for are openness and conscientiousness. As the research aims to provide detailed personality-based design guidelines, the research focuses on associating five design attributes to the identified personality traits. The five design attributes are color preferences, information structure (breadth-first vs. depth-first), element shape (soft vs. sharp elements), interface type (text-based vs. image-based), and symmetry preferences (asymmetric vs. symmetric). The following are the expected interface design preferences of the identified traits for the five design attributes.

For color preference, openness interface should utilize a diverse and vibrant color palette to appeal to users with a preference for exploration and creativity. Conscientiousness interface should implement a dark color scheme that avoid stimulation, reflecting a preference for structure and order.

In terms of information structure, openness interface should adopt a breadth-first approach, enabling users to quickly scan and explore content globally. This aligns with their desire for a general view of information. Conversely, conscientiousness interface should employ a depth-first approach to arrange information systematically, catering to users who prefer a detailed and structured presentation.

Element shape plays a significant role in interface design. For users with openness traits, softer design elements like rounded shapes and gentle transitions should be integrated to create a welcoming and fluid experience. In contrast, conscientiousness users would prefer sharper elements with clean lines and defined shapes, reflecting their preference for precision and clarity.

Interface type is another aspect where design attributes should vary based on personality traits. Openness users would prefer an image-based approach, stimulating creativity and visual engagement. Meanwhile, conscientiousness users would find a text-based approach more appealing, delivering clear and concise information aligned with their preference for efficiency and accuracy.

Symmetry preference influences interface design aesthetics. Openness interface designs should embrace asymmetry, allowing for creative freedom and unconventional layouts. Conversely, conscientiousness interface designs should prioritize symmetry, presenting balanced and well-organized elements that appeal to users valuing order and structure in design. Table 4 shows a summary of the design attributes association to the identified traits.

Table 4. Five design attributes associated with the identified personality traits

Design attributes	Openness	Conscientiousness
Color preference	Diverse unconventional color palette	Well-balanced color scheme
Information structure	Breadth-first	Depth-first
Element shape	Soft elements	Hard elements
Interface type	Image-based	Text-based
Symmetry preference	Asymmetrical	Symmetrical

3.3.2 Figma Designs

The designed interfaces reflect the intended user flow which are the steps a user takes to accomplish a particular task within a digital product. The intended user flow is for the user to login to be navigated to the LMS dashboard. Then, the user selects a module from semester one to be navigated to the module details screen. The user then selects a week to view the week's content. The user flow is the same for openness and conscientiousness.

Figure 1 shows the interfaces designs that cater for openness trait following the preciously stated design associations. The interfaces are arranged from left to right. The designs prioritize breadth-first structure for easy information scanning where grid views are evident in both the dashboard and module pages. Curved edges and visual elements like images and icons are used throughout the designs. Container sizes and alignments vary with left alignment for text and icons and center alignment for module grid content. The color palette is primarily orange with secondary shades that are vibrant and stimulating while maintaining harmony.

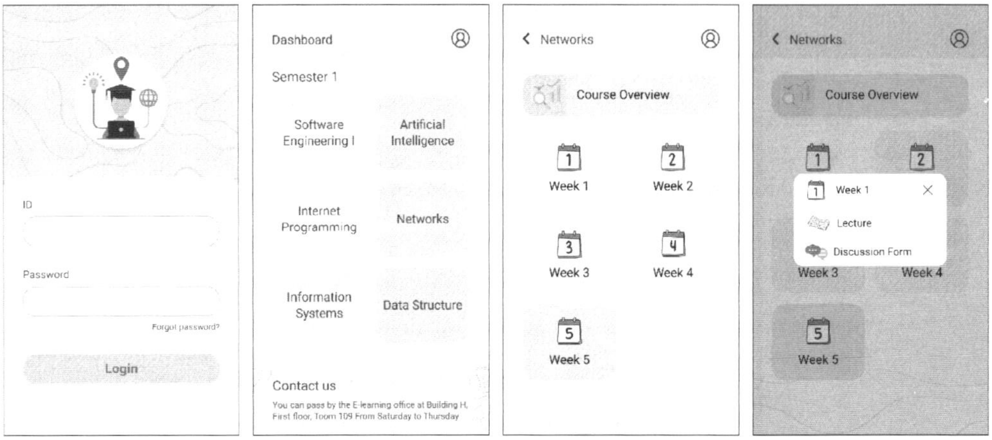

Figure 1. Openness interface designs

Figure 2 shows the interfaces that cater for conscientiousness trait following the previously stated design associations. The interfaces are arranged from left to right. The designs adopt a depth-first structure by presenting essential information first and requiring user interaction to access additional details. Sharp edges are used throughout the interface, with a focus on text to minimize visual stimulation and emphasize detail orientation. Symmetry is maintained with centered text and equal-sized elements. The color palette consists of shades of black to create a dark theme that communicates professionalism and maintains the focus on the interface content.

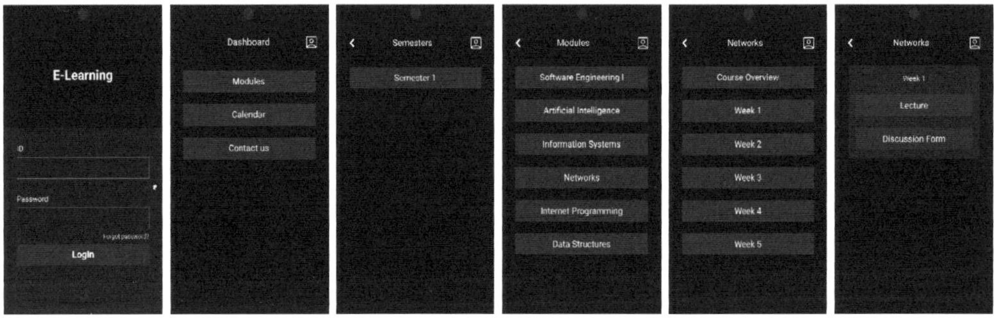

Figure 2. Conscientiousness interface designs

4. EVALUATION OF THE DESIGN ASSOCIATIONS

The following section details the dataset and experiment setup for investigating the association between personality-based interfaces and the users interface preference.

4.1 Subset Dataset

To investigate the validation of the design associations and the users' preferences a subset dataset is extracted from the ICS-BUE dataset. The subset dataset consists of 85 participants, 68 of them have openness as their dominant trait and 17 of them have conscientiousness as their dominant trait.

The clustering results produced the acronym OAECN to represent the trait combination within the ICS-BUE dataset. The cluster shows that openness is the most occurring trait and conscientiousness ranks fourth which indicates its lesser occurrence. Consequently, the subset dataset contains a larger proportion of participants with openness as their dominant trait compared to conscientiousness.

It is anticipated that the 68 participants would prefer the interface tailored to accommodate their personality trait while the same would apply to those with conscientiousness. The openness interface is referred to as "Multi-Colored App" and the conscientiousness interface is referred to as "Dark-Colored App".

4.2 Experiment Setup

The participants were contacted by email. To avoid order bias, two separate emails were sent, each identical except for the link provided to direct the participants to the experiment. The difference between the links is in the sequence order of interfaces presented to the participants. 34 participants who have openness as their dominant trait and 9 participants who have conscientiousness as their dominant trait were directed to the link with the "Multi-colored app", followed by the "Dark colored app". On the contrary, the remaining participants were directed to the link with the opposite order. The experiment is set up using Maze tool which enables participants to interact with Figma prototypes. The test was set up as follows:

The first question asks the participant to enter their student ID which will help correlate if the individual belongs to the openness or conscientiousness segments. The participant is then given a prompt which is "Use the e-learning app to access week 1 lecture for Networks module." After the participant clicks start, he/she interacts with the Figma prototype navigating through the screen to achieve the target goal. The user is presented with one of the interface designs. After the user completes the goal, the user is presented with a similar prompt but interacts with the other interface designs. After the participant completes the target goal, he/she is presented with a question that asks, "Which app did you prefer?" the choices are "Dark colored app" and "Multi-colored app". After the participant selects his/her answer, the participant is navigated to a thank you screen.

5. RESULTS

Chi-squared test is used to assess if there is an association between the dominant personality trait and the preferred interface design. The Chi-squared test is suitable for the evaluation as both the identified dominant traits and the interface preferences are categorical variables which is the type of variables Chi-squared test is designed to analyze. Also, the Chi-squared test assesses whether there is a significant association between variables while assuming independence between them. Moreover, the Chi-squared test is straightforward to implement and interpret facilitating its application. The Chi-squared test hypothesis are as follows: Null Hypothesis (H0): There is no association between dominant traits and interface preferences. Alternative Hypothesis (H1): There is an association between dominant traits and interface preferences.

A total of 85 students received an invitation to take part in the study. The total number of participants in the study reached 72 individuals which is 84% of the targeted participants. Of those participants, 58 have openness as their dominant trait while 14 have conscientiousness as their dominant trait. Of the participants who have openness as their dominant trait, 38 individuals favored the interface tailored to their dominant trait while 20 individuals opted for the alternative interface. From the participants with conscientiousness as their dominant trait, 9 individuals preferred the interface aligned with their dominant trait while 5 individuals favored the other interface. Table 5 shows the number of participants per category.

Table 5. Subset dataset number of participants per category

Category	Number of participants	Total participants
Openness participants who chose openness interface	38	58
Openness participants who chose conscientious interface	20	
Conscientious participants who chose conscientious interface	9	14
Conscientious participants who chose openness interface	5	

The Chi-squared statistic value is 10.4 and its corresponding p-value is 0.005. Accordingly, the results indicate a significant association between the dominant trait and interface preference. The p-value falls below the standard significance threshold of 0.05 indicating enough evidence to reject the null hypothesis. Consequently, it can be concluded that there is a meaningful relationship between dominant traits and interface preferences among the study participants.

This finding is important as it highlights that individuals with certain dominant traits have distinct interface design preferences. Additionally, the findings validate the design associations established by the research where participants preferred the interfaces that cater to their dominant trait. Recognizing these associations enables interface design to better accommodate dominant personality traits and reinforces the research objective of establishing design guidelines for the identified personality traits.

6. CONCLUSION

The research utilized the Big Five Personality traits to identify the target users' personality and implemented segmentation using K-means and PCA to identify the dataset's most dominant trait. Based on the results, openness and conscientiousness were identified to be the most influential traits in the dataset. Consequently, the two traits were associated to five design attributes to personalize interface designs that cater for each of the traits. The design attributes are color preferences, information structure, element shape, interface type, and symmetry preferences. An experiment was conducted with participants who have openness or conscientiousness as their dominant traits. In the experiment the participants interacted with the designed interfaces, then selected their preferred interface design. Chi-squared was used to evaluate the experiment results which showed that there is a significant association between the participants dominant personality traits and interface preference. Accordingly, the design associations tailored to each trait align with the participants' dominant trait preferences and impacted their selection of interface. Consequently, the research proposes using the design associations similarly as guidelines when catering for openness and conscientiousness traits.

7. FUTURE WORK

The authors aim to further investigate the designed personality-based interfaces and their influence on user perception of usability. Additionally, the research intends to collect a broader and more diverse dataset to obtain comprehensive feedback on interface preferences and perceptions of usability.

REFERENCES

Dix, A., Finlay, J., Abowd, G. D., & Beale, R. (2004). *Human-Computer Interaction* (Third Edition). Pearson Education Limited, Edinburgh Gate, Harlow, Essex CM20 2JE, England

MacNamara, W. (2016). Evaluating the Effectiveness of the Gestalt Principles of Perceptual Observation for Virtual Reality User Interface Design. Master's Thesis, Technological University Dublin.

Nielsen, J. (1994). Enhancing the explanatory power of usability heuristics. In The SIGCHI Conference on Human Factors in Computing Systems, 152–158.

Sili, M., Garschall, M., Morandell, M., Hanke, S., & Mayer, C. (2016). Personalization in the User Interaction Design. In: Kurosu, M. (eds) Human-Computer Interaction. Theory, Design, Development and Practice. HCI 2016. Lecture Notes in Computer Science, vol. 9731, Springer, Cham. doi: 10.1007/978-3-319-39510-4_19.

Alves, T., Natálio, J., Henriques-Calado, J., & Gama, S. (2020). Incorporating personality in user interface design: A review. Personality and Individual Differences, 155, 109709. [Online]. Available: https://doi.org/10.1016/j.paid.2019.109709.

Goldberg, L. R. (1993). The structure of phenotypic personality traits. American Psychologist, 48(1), 26–34. doi: 10.1037/0003-066X.48.1.26.

McCrae, R. R., & Costa, P. T., Jr. (1999). A Five-Factor theory of personality. In L. A. Pervin & O. P. John (Eds.), Handbook of personality: Theory and research, 139–153. Guilford Press.

Truity Psychometrics LLC and Owens, M. "The Big Five Personality Test." Truity. [Online]. Available: https://www.truity.com/test/big-five-personality-test.

NATURAL INTERACTION FOR MUSEUM INSTALLATIONS DISPLAYING CULTURAL HERITAGE: A CASE STUDY OF THE RECREATION OF THE TORRE DE LA PARADA

Luis Antonio Hernández-Ibáñez, Viviana Barneche-Naya and Guillermo Franganillo-Parrado
VideaLAB. Universidade da Coruña, Spain

ABSTRACT

Natural interaction can play an outstanding role in the design of museum installations. This paper describes the software architecture and gesture-based interaction scheme utilised in a real application case, the virtual recreation of a 17th-century royal hunting lodge, today lost, that hosted an impressive collection of paintings by European masters such as Rubens and Velazquez. The installation is part of an actual exhibition that puts some of these paintings on display, along with the virtual replica of the building filled with the full collection, hence putting them in context for a better understanding of the painting's history and, at the same time, allowing the visitor to walk through and contemplate the architecture of the historical site. The interaction strategy evolved from a free movement scheme to an assisted one based on users' selection. To achieve such assistance, several active components have been designed and implemented. Virtual paintings, doorways, and spaces intervene to take the visitor from place to place inside the building, so the user is aware of the historical architectural heritage as they control the experience using simple gestures with their body.

KEYWORDS

Natural Interaction, Gesture-Based Interaction, Museum, Digital Architecture, Virtual Archaeology, Cultural Heritage

1. INTRODUCTION

Museums play a crucial role in preserving and disseminating cultural heritage. As technology advances, natural interaction techniques are progressively used to enhance the visitor experience in museum environments. Natural interfaces in virtual museums use methods such as gesture recognition, voice input and eye tracking to create a user experience that reflects natural human behaviour. For example, gesture-based interaction (GBI) allows users to control digital systems through intuitive physical body movements and gestures, offering new ways to engage audiences and bring cultural artefacts to life (Zao et al., 2019; Hernández-Ibáñez et al., 2016; Fanini et al., 2015). By leveraging these intuitive forms of interaction, visitors can navigate virtual spaces and manipulate objects in familiar and effortless ways, shortening the learning curve and promoting a more engaging experience.

These technologies hold enormous potential to transform the museum experience and promote deeper engagement, understanding and learning (Phichai et al, 2021; Manghisi, et al, 2018; Shakroum et al, 2016). While challenges remain, ongoing research and development efforts pave the way for more immersive and accessible museum installations that effectively present cultural heritage to diverse audiences. Additionally, GBI can improve accessibility for users with disabilities and provide an alternative input method that can be more accessible than traditional controllers (Pietroni et al., 2021; Sorce et al., 2018).

When facing the design of a museum installation, it is essential to consider aspects related to diverse user profiles, such as the influence of previous skills in navigating virtual environments. The goal is to find an interface and forms of interaction and navigation in virtual spaces that minimise the attention users need to pay to those tasks. Existing approaches to navigation assistance in virtual environments include automated code generation to incorporate guided tours, as demonstrated in a 3D computer science museum (Chittaro et al., 2004). Alternative approaches leverage computational analysis of the virtual space to predetermine an optimal path for the visitor (Elmqvist et al., 2007). Further research has explored guiding users sequentially through a predetermined series of viewpoints or points of interest (Chittaro et al., 2010), as well as the utilisation of hotspots in the Virtual Regolini Galassi Tomb to facilitate movement between locations within the virtual space (Pietroni et al., 2012).

Integrating natural interfaces with visual cues can create a synergistic effect, improving the usability and satisfaction of virtual museum experiences and making virtual museums accessible to a wider audience. Some studies highlight the potential of natural interfaces and visual cues to improve the user experience and the effectiveness of virtual reconstructions (Verma& Monga, 2023, Pescarin et al, 2013). Effective use of colour coding, lighting effects, and iconography can direct attention, suggest interactions, confirm the success of an action, or clarify navigation paths. It increases the intuition of interaction and supports learning and retention by reinforcing actions through immediate visual responses. By leveraging humans' natural gestures and perceptual processes, these techniques promote a more intuitive, immersive and comprehensive museum experience, allowing visitors to actively engage with the meaning of the cultural heritage on display.

In this paper, the authors describe the use of natural interaction and visual cues in a museum installation designed to contextualise several works of art by Rubens currently on display at the Museo de Bellas Artes in A Coruña, Spain. These paintings were part of an outstanding collection specifically designed to decorate an exceptional, now-lost building, the Torre de la Parada.

The Torre de la Parada (Tower of the Hunting Break) was a hunting lodge in a forest in the surrounding hills of Madrid. It was built in 1547 and renovated in 1635 as part of a major architectural project commissioned by King Philip IV of Spain, a hunting lover. The tower was decorated with works of art by leading painters, including Velázquez and especially Rubens, whose studio produced most of the 173 paintings that adorned the lodge's walls. The building was destroyed by fire in 1714 during the War of the Spanish Succession. Nothing remains of the building today, but many paintings have been saved and are exhibited in museums such as El Prado (Madrid) and the Bellas Artes Museum of A Coruña.

The installation is part of an exhibition organised by the latter, "Torre de la Parada, A Painting Space for Rubens. The virtual exhibition". It recreates a well-founded archaeological hypothesis of the entire form of the building, including the internal distribution of spaces matching to accommodate each painting as described in historical sources (Alpers, 1971). The idea behind the installation is to describe a singular place and let the visitor walk through the rooms to experience the collection as Phillip IV did in the 17th century. The size of the projection screen and the fact that the visitor's body controls the stroll are the keys to immersion in this set. Along the walkthrough, the user can also access information related to the paintings.

Apart from the archaeological and architectural challenge of obtaining a plausible hypothesis about the distribution of the spaces of the lost building, the main technical challenge of this project was to create a natural interaction system that could fulfil the specific and exigent requirements in terms of universal access, ease of use, educational value, robustness, and fun for an installation intended to achieve a double goal: to experience the realistic recreation of the archaeological hypothesis of the building and to provide a context and a medium to describe and provide information about the paintings once hosted there, thus providing a context to better understand them before the contemplation of the real, original artworks.

2. METHODOLOGY

The research on the lost building's shape and the development of the architectural hypothesis carried a considerable effort whose discussion is out of the scope of this paper. Once the building shape was obtained and the inner space distribution was determined, the virtual building was modelled in AutoCAD and ported to Unreal Engine to recreate and apply the historic construction materials and emulate the natural illumination that once lit the former rooms.

The first approach to the virtual navigation of the model consisted of developing a natural interaction scheme to move inside the building that could be used by the visitor to walk through the spaces and approach the paintings for close inspection. The authors had previously researched movement paradigms for body-tracking-based natural interaction applied to architectural walkthroughs (Barneche-Naya & Hernandez-Ibañez 2023; Barneche-Naya & Hernandez-Ibañez 2021). Those schemes proved helpful in applications where the user is minimally trained in using gestures to control the navigation. The first development versions of the installation incorporated one of such locomotion schemes, using a Kinect camera to track the visitor's limbs and applying a step-twist paradigm, as follows: The user starts the experience in a spot marked on the floor. Taking a step forward or backwards from this spot, the camera in the simulation starts moving consequently. Twisting the upper body right or left controls the user's orientation if static or the turn of the movement if moving. This approach soon seemed inadequate for several reasons. Initial test taken showed that:

1. Users needed time to test and familiarise themselves with the movement scheme, taking precious time that, although small in length (less than a minute), is too much for a museum installation.
2. Users tended to hit walls or have difficulties moving backwards when finding obstacles. Although they soon learned how to deal with these situations, the sensation was initially frustrating.
3. When users left the installation, they frequently abandoned the simulation in a location or orientation difficult for the next user to follow (e.g., facing a wall or too close to a painting).

Therefore, after discussing those issues with the museum's representatives, the need for a different approach arose. Users should be able to move along the building to appreciate the virtual reconstruction. However, to avoid the abovementioned drawbacks, the system should control the locomotion from point to point. The simulation should let the visitor choose the destination and then smoothly take the user to the place of interest.

Consequently, a different interaction paradigm was adopted. Now, the user can rotate the view by twisting the upper body. When an object of interest, such as a painting or a passage to another room, falls in the centre of the view, it is highlighted, transmitting the idea of a possible interaction. If the user raises one hand, the system takes them at walking speed, following a spline trajectory calculated on the go. This route keeps the point of interest centred on focus and finishes in a contemplation point associated with the selected painting. Suppose the item highlighted and selected is a door to another room. In that case, the system guides the movement, taking the visitor past the entrance of the corresponding room and placing them in a point with a view direction that permits them to see all elements in the new space to choose from.

2.1 System Components

Several active elements needed to be designed and coded to develop this interfacing scheme. All of them were programmed in Unreal Engine using the Blueprint visual scripting system. The system incorporates both diegetic and head-up-display graphic interface elements.

2.1.1 Smart Paintings

We defined every painting as an interactive actor in the scene, with most of its visual features defined procedurally. Paintings take an active paper in the simulation. They are generated procedurally based on data stored in a database regarding their particular features, which are used as follows:

- Dimensions. Used to procedurally generate and texturise the canvas and frame geometry, location of the contemplation station, location of the wall label, and dimensions of the highlight frame
- Existing/Lost flag. Sketch/Actual painting flag. Sketch dimensions. Sketch images are used when the painting is lost, but its original sketch is preserved so that it can illustrate the presence of the lost painting. When a painting is referred to using its sketch, it is shown with the sketch's original size and stretched to the painting size afterwards.
- Frame. Frames consist of several wooden or golden strips that combine to generate the geometry of every picture frame. Every element is configurable in size, material and moulding types to obtain multiple frame styles.
- Wall label. A descriptive label can be displayed on the wall in a museum-style way. It is used in some cases of non-interactionable paintings.
- Contemplation Station: A visual cue that marks the location of the optimum vantage point to contemplate the painting. The location of this point is derived from the dimensions of the picture and the Field of View of the simulation camera. It can be overridden for exceptional cases.
- User sensor volume. This non-visible volume checks for user presence to activate the display of this painting's info card under user action.
- Highlight frame: A pulsating, shining frame that surrounds the painting when it is selectable.
- The title, author, image, painting technique, collection, description, and other relevant information are displayed in a procedurally generated card written in two languages upon user action. If the user sensor detects the visitor, the user can raise a hand to display the info card. (Figure 1)

Figure 1. Components of a smart painting (up,left) and associated info card displayed upon user action inside the contemplation station (up, right). A visitor using the system (down, left). Components of a smart doorway (down, right)

2.1.2 Smart Doorways

Doorways are highlighted just as paintings do when they occupy the centre of the field of view. Doors and passes contain a highlight frame of a different colour than the pictures and some visual widgets to control their behaviour. Suppose the doorway is highlighted, and the user raises a hand. In that case, the system calculates a spline from the user's position, describing a smooth trajectory to the next room to cross the doorway and enter the adjacent place, releasing the visitor in a vantage point to look at the room, choose a new item and perform an action. The widgets control the destination and view direction at the end of the route. (Figure 1)

2.1.3 Smart Volumes

The user's presence across the building is monitored by non-visible volumes encompassing every room. The volumes act like sensors that react as soon as the user avatar overlaps them, activating the interactivity of related elements, such as paintings and doorways, and redirecting the user input to these elements. Hence, primary actions, such as painting and door selection, only operate on the objects inside the volume. Other secondary actions, some only accessible to museum operators, such as candlelight switching, light temperature selection, activation of special cinematics, etc, are also controlled by those volumes. (Figure 2)

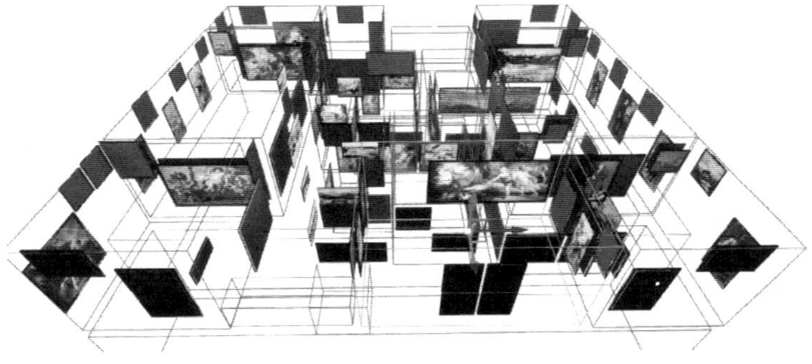

Figure 2. Smart volumes encompass and manage interaction in every room on both floors of the tower

2.1.4 Spline Trajectories System

Every painting has an associated contemplation station that marks the best location to study the artwork, but the route to reach this point can start from any point in the room. Since the system has to take the visitor to the contemplation station following a smooth path, a spline trajectory is calculated starting in the instant location of the user, using the forward vector of the associated avatar as the initial tangent and finishing in the centre of the sensor volume integrated into the contemplation station. The normal vector of the canvas is used as the end tangent of this 2-point spline.

The user's camera view target stays at the centre of the painting as the user advances along the spline, and the speed of the movement is adjusted to obtain a pleasant sensation of approach. (Figure 3). In the case of doorways, the process is similar, but the endpoint and final tangent of the route's spline, used respectively as the vantage destination and final view direction, are defined by the location of the widgets associated with the doorway. (Figure 3).

When the user sends an action on a highlighted element, the system enters automatic mode and takes the visitor to the endpoint of the corresponding spline route. Two semi-transparent, horizontal bars appear at the top and bottom borders of the screen, meaning that the user is being driven along the trajectory automatically, and no input is needed.

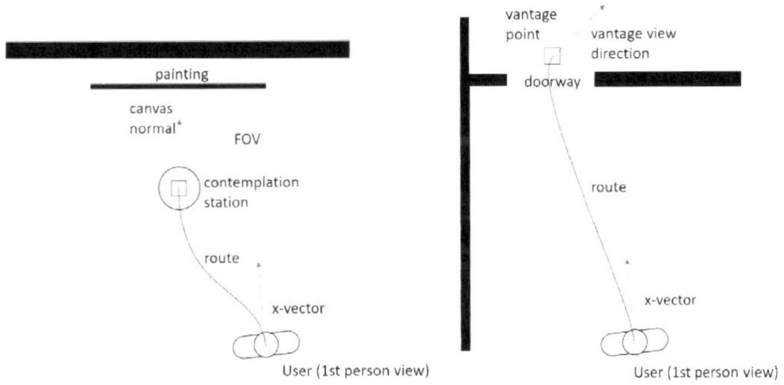

Figure 3. Spline definition for paintings (left) and doorways (right)

2.1.5 Pre-Set Cinematics

Some trajectories and transitions between spaces are too complex to expect the visitor to perform adequately. Examples are going up and down stairs and the trajectory that starts the experience, which begins in a bird's view and ends in front of the main door. The system incorporates some cinematics (preset, non-interactive, real-time rendered animations) that take the user's camera following preset trajectories that are activated by the volumes containing their starting points.

When the system enters cinematic mode, horizontal bars appear on the upper and lower borders of the screen, just as they do in automatic mode.

2.2 Visual Interface

Apart from the diegetic interface elements already described, such as highlight frames for active objects, some visual cues help users along the experience.

The figure shows the visual interface in two different situations. On normal operation (Figure, left), the user can see the room's name in the upper centre of the screen as soon as they enter and several elements at the bottom of the image. On the bottom left, an icon indicates that the user is in place and tracked by the Kinect device. In the bottom centre of the image, a triangle marking the middle of the screen turns yellow or blue when an interactive element reaches this area. This little indicator turned out to be extremely useful in helping users locate the middle of the frame and, consequently, the point where objects become interactable.

On the bottom right, the visitor can check a minimap depicting the layout of the floor on which they are located. A point marks their location, and a triangle displays their current field of view. The map also includes text with the floor number and room name. (Figure 4). In cinematic and automatic modes (Figure 4) some translucid bars appear over the upper and lower edges of the screen. In these modes, user input is disabled as the camera moves.

Figure 4. Visual interface on normal operation (left) and cinematic and automatic modes (right)

2.3 Hardware Interface

Although the system is designed to be configured for different hardware settings, the museum installation is intended to utilise just a Kinect depth camera to control all interactions. This camera is placed on the same wall that hosts the projection, pointing to a spot marked on the floor three meters away. The Kinect checks all users in the room but only considers having a user ready if she or he is placed on the mark and will only react to the gestures of this user. The tracked gestures are:

- Upper body twist: Used to control the camera yaw. The user can turn the camera horizontally or counterclockwise by turning the waist. The Kinect reads the location (coordinates) in the space of the shoulder joints and obtains the angle formed by the line connecting them. The angle between this line and the screen tells the system about the degree of twist. If it surpasses a given threshold, the virtual camera begins to turn with an angular speed proportional to the twist angle. Going back to an idle pose stops the camera turn.
- The depth camera also reads the location of the user's wrists. When one of them is raised, and the height coordinate exceeds that of the wrist, the system considers that an action is invoked and acts consequently.

This is the only set of gestures the user is expected to perform. Other gestures are available to museum personnel; for instance, raising both hands overpassing the head resets and restarts the simulation. A concise representation of the available gestures is presented below the screen. A sign depicting two feet marks the location where the user must be placed. (Figure 5). Aside from this installation configuration, the museum representatives considered having a secondary option for interaction, both as an alternative for people not attracted to using the Kinect system and as a way to incorporate the full capability of the system to explore every corner of the virtual reconstruction. Consequently, we placed a 3D Conexxion Spacemouse on a pedestal nearby. We provided it with the capability of turning the camera by twirling the device clockwise or counterclockwise, sending action orders by pressing it down, and also using it as a joystick to move front, backwards, left, or right. The complete installation can be seen in Figure 5.

Figure 5. Museum installation. Notice the sign below the screen, the spot mark on the floor and the monolith that holds the Spacemouse

After several months of use, the museum personnel reported very little use of the Spacemouse. However, it proved useful for some expert users interested in exploring both the inside and the façade and surroundings of the building.

3. RESULTS

Since the exhibition opened in January 2024, the installation has received visitors daily. Previously, a behaviour evaluation was carried out during the interaction of a group of high school students and museum staff. These observations and feedback provided by those users were important in improving the system, reinforcing some aspects and changing other functions in successive versions of the application.

Both individuals and organised groups use the set every day. In the latter case, the installation is also used as a tool for the museum docents to describe the building and the artworks inside by driving the simulation themselves, which is seen as a spectacular performance by the visitors. The docents also encourage volunteers to try the experience while the rest of the group contemplates the scene and makes comments, fostering a joyful social activity.

Museum managers report that the vast majority of users prefer to control the experience with their bodies and that visitors perceive this as a very easy task. Only a small number of visitors use the Spacemouse, mainly to get an extended experience in contemplation of the building. A video of the experience can be seen at https://videalab.udc.es/Torre_Parada.

4. CONCLUSION

Natural Interaction, and especially Gesture-based Interaction, is an excellent tool for designing and developing museum installations. The vast diversity of museum visitor profiles and the zero-training condition required to use such installations make it necessary for the designers to offer a very limited set of available gestures to control and also a limited set of actions to take. In the case of installations intended to describe three-dimensional environments, such as the virtual recreation of the lost building referred to in this paper, letting the visitor move freely inside the virtual space has several drawbacks that get worse if there is also an intention to describe other objects, such as paintings, during the stroll.

Therefore, the strategy of letting the user choose a destination, then helping them move through the space, and activating the complementary information as described in the paper proved to be an effective way to use an installation of this kind. Museum visitors prefer gesture-based interaction over more traditional hardware and control devices.

A limitation of the study is the study of the visitor experience. In the next version of the application, UX Evaluation is planned. The system will collect, store and use information on user behaviour, such as routes taken, most visited works, and times dedicated to observation. In addition, an on-site questionnaire will be conducted on ease of use, mental and physical fatigue, and overall satisfaction. As a future line of research, we will delve into the patterns of use and gestures and the time visitors use to interact with the installation confidently.

ACKNOWLEDGEMENT

The authors wish to acknowledge the representatives and technicians of Museo de Bellas Artes of A Coruña for their continuous support and Xunta de Galicia for funding this project.

REFERENCES

Alpers, S. (1971). *The Decoration of the Torre de la Parada, Corpus Rubenianum Ludwig Burchard. Appendix II*, pp. 289-364. Phaidon Publisher. London and New York, 1971. ISBN 0714814032.

Barneche-Naya, V. & Hernández-Ibáñez, L. A. (2023). *Assisted navigation for digital architectural walkthroughs in Natural User Interface-based installations*. Universal Access in the Information Society, 1-15.

Barneche-Naya, V. & Hernández-Ibañez, L. A. (2021). *A comparative study on user gestural inputs for navigation in NUI-based 3D virtual environments*. Universal Access in the Information Society, 20, 513-529.

Chittaro, L., Ieronutti, L., & Ranon, R. (2004). Navigating 3D Virtual Environments by Following Embodied Agents: a Proposal and its Informal Evaluation on a Virtual Museum Application. PsychNology J., 2(1), 24-42.

Chittaro, L.; Ieronutti, L.; Ranon, R.; Siotto, E.; Visintini, D. (2010). A high-level tool for curators of 3D virtual visits and its application to a virtual exhibition of renaissance frescoes. In Proceedings of VAST, 2010, pp.11.

Elmqvist, N., Tudoreanu, M. E.; Tsigas, P. (2007). Tour generation for exploration of 3D virtual environments. In Proceedings of the 2007 ACM symposium on Virtual reality software and technology, 2007, pp. 207-210.

Fanini, B., d'Annibale, E., Demetrescu, E., Ferdani, D & Pagano, A. (2015). *Engaging and shared gesture-based interaction for museums the case study of K2R international expo in Rome*. In 2015 Digital Heritage, Vol. 1, pp. 263-270. IEEE.

Hernández-Ibáñez, L. A., Barneche-Naya, V.& Mihura-López, R. (2016). *A comparative study of walkthrough paradigms for virtual environments using kinect based natural interaction*. In 22nd International Conference on Virtual System & Multimedia (VSMM), pp. 1-7. IEEE.

Hernández-Ibáñez, L. A.& Barneche-Naya, V. (2016). *Assisted navigation and natural interaction for virtual archaeological heritage. Implementation of an attractor-based approach using a game engine.* Mediterranean Archaeology & Archaeometry, 16(5).

Manghisi, V. M., Uva, A. E., Fiorentino, M., Gattullo, M., Boccaccio, A., & Monno, G. (2018). *Enhancing user engagement through the user centric design of a mid-air gesture-based interface for the navigation of virtual-tours in cultural heritage expositions.* Journal of cultural heritage, 32, 186-197.

Pescarin, S., Pietroni, E., Rescic, L., Wallergård, M., Omar, K., & Rufa, C. (2013). *NICH: a preliminary theoretical study on Natural Interaction applied to Cultural Heritage contexts*. In 2013 DigitalHeritage, Vol. 1, pp. 355-362. IEEE.

Phichai, P., Williamson, J., & Barr, M. (2021). *Alternative design for an interactive exhibit learning in museums: How does user experience differ across different technologies-VR, tangible, and gesture.* In 2021 7th international conference of the immersive learning research network (iLRN), pp. 1-8. IEEE.

Pietroni, E., Ray, C., Rufa, C., Pletinckx, D.& Van Kampen, I. (2012). Natural interaction in VR environments for Cultural Heritage and its impact inside museums: The Etruscanning project. In 18th International Conference on Virtual Systems and Multimedia (pp. 339-346). IEEE.

Pietroni, E., Pagano, A., Biocca, L., & Frassineti, G. (2021). *Accessibility, natural user interfaces and interactions in museums: the IntARSI project.* Heritage, 4(2), 567-584.

Shakroum, M. A., Wong, K. W., & Fung, C. (2016). *The effectiveness of the gesture-based learning system (GBLS) and its impact on learning experience*. Journal of Information Technology Education: Research, 15, 191-210.

Sorce, S., Gentile, V., Oliveto, D., Barraco, R., Malizia, A., & Gentile, A. (2018). *Exploring usability and accessibility of avatar-based touchless gestural interfaces for autistic people*. In Proceedings of the 7th ACM International Symposium on Pervasive Displays, pp. 1-2.

Verma, D., & Monga, C. (2023). *Exploration of Visual Cues and Guidelines to Increase Visitors' Engagement and Immersion in Virtual Museums*. In International Conference on Research into Design (pp. 535-543). Singapore: Springer Nature Singapore.

Zhao, S. (2019). *Exploring how interactive technology enhances gesture-based expression and engagement: A design study.* Multimodal Technologies and Interaction, 3(1), 13.

AN ANALYSIS OF INTERACTION BEHAVIORS IN PERSONALIZED LEARNING

Emine Cabı[1] and Hacer Türkoğlu[2]
Baskent University, Faculty of Education,
Department of Computer and Instructional Technology Education, Ankara, Turkey
[1]Assoc. Prof. Dr.
[2]Asst. Prof.

ABSTRACT

The purpose of this study is to examine the relationship between students' participation behaviors in online learning analytics (LA) and their academic performance and self-regulated learning (SRL) in learning analytics-based feedback systems. In the study, 73 university students participated. Moodle was used as a learning management system (LMS) to share digital content, communicate with students, and make evaluations. In the flipped learning (FL) environment, LA including different types of activities was made available to students for four weeks. During this process, students were supported with feedback within the framework of instructional design based on learning analytics. Interaction data, achievement test, and SRL Scale were used as data collection tools. The data obtained in the study were examined using K-Means Clustering Analysis and Mann-Whitney U-test. Cluster analysis was performed to classify students with similar behavioral patterns into a homogeneous group. As a result of the analysis, two clusters were obtained: those with high engagement and those with low engagement. Students' interaction behaviors were determined and the relationship between different interaction behaviors and students' academic success and self-regulation skills was examined. As a result, students with high interaction/ engagement spend more time in activities than students with low engagement. Additionally, the academic success and self-regulation score averages (except for help-seeking) of students with high engagement were found to be higher than those with low engagement. When academic achievement and self-regulation skills were compared according to clusters, no statistically significant difference was observed.

KEYWORDS

Interaction Behaviors, Clustering Analysis, Educational Data Science, Learning Management System

1. INTRODUCTION

In online learning environments, studies on students' interaction with learning materials, and analysis and reporting of this interaction data are becoming increasingly common. Learning management systems (LMS) are a widely used tool for hosting learning materials and monitoring student behaviour. Learner interactions within an LMS often depend on how instructors design a module, course, or programme of study. Models of these student interactions, often referred to as learning analytics applications (LAI), can be represented by combining system-level LMS data with course-level design decisions to provide more detailed insights into student behavior (Lancaster et al., 2020). An online learning design in Moodle through learning analytics, providing students with an individualised learning experience (Lluch Molins & Cano Garcia, 2023). Educators can identify student behaviors as they learn online and how these behaviors change over time. In this way, it can reveal the most likely solutions to educational problems and performance improvement (Timmi et al., 2022). Learning analytics can contribute to instructional design with this strength.

Ultimately what makes learning analytics important is its ability to contribute to progress on both immediate and long-standing challenges in learning, not only by improving existing systems but also by considering alternatives for what is and what could be (Wise et al., 2021). The main problems or issues related to education that LA research aims at are (Charitopoulos et al., 2020): recommendation systems to assist students through a study programme or course module; decision-making systems for various stakeholders, be they individuals or organizations; monitoring and reduction of student dropout rates; education system quality assessment covering various aspects of organized education; learning style preferences for individual students; guidance systems; teaching quality assessment

On the other hand, when the related studies are analyzed, the term Educational Data Mining (EDM) is used in this context as well as the term Learning Analytics. Learning Analytics (LA) and Educational Data Mining (EDM) are two distinct and yet closely related research areas that focus on this data aiming to address open education-related questions or issues (Charitopoulos et al., 2020). Cerezo et al. (2024), conducted a study on why these two concepts are used in different or the same sense.

After all, although they both use the same data and share similar goals and interests, EDM and LA are distinct research communities with different origins and focus in their conferences and journals. However, none of the differences are large enough to conclude that LA and EDM follow different paths to improve the teaching-learning process. Therefore, researchers propose to use the term Educational Data Science (EDS) to integrate both LA and EDM with all these related communities. We also used the term both LA and EDM in our study.

1.1 Self-Regulation Skills

Self-regulation is related to the degree to which students actively participate in their learning processes in terms of metacognition, motivation, and behavior (Zimmerman, 1989). Students who are active in their learning processes learn with their efforts. They develop certain strategies to achieve the goals they set and evaluate the effectiveness of these strategies in achieving their goals.

Schunk (2005) defines self-regulation as the process of systematically managing students' feelings, thoughts, and behaviors to achieve their goals. In summary, self-regulated learning is defined as an active and positive process in which students set learning goals, make efforts to control, regulate, and monitor their cognition, motivation, and behavior, and are guided and constrained by their goals and the contextual features of their environment (Pintrich, 2000).

1.2 The Aim of the Study

In online learning design, there are studies investigating the effect of feedback given through learning analytics on students' academic achievement. According to the results of the studies, feedback has a noticeable effect on students' performance (Lim et al., 2023a).

In addition to the contribution of personalised feedback to academic achievement, personalised feedback can be used to improve students' self-regulation skills (Fleur et al., 2023). Self regulation skills could be also affected by the students' interaction with LMS. Cakiroglu et al. (2023) states that content, forum, assignment, assessment are important for environment structuring, task management, and help seeking which cover assessment oriented and content oriented groups.

In recent years, EDM and LA have developed greatly as interrelated research fields and disciplines. Many studies have been carried out in this context (Timmi et al., 2022; Cerezo et al., 2024; Charitopoulos et al., 2020; Akcapinar & Bayazit, 2018). In addition, there are many studies on the effects of online learning students' interactions on their self-regulation skills and academic achievement (Çebi & Güyer, 2020; Lim et al., 2023b). However, there are still gaps or unclear situations in this context.

The sub-problems of the research are as follows;

- How to classify students' participation behaviors in LA supported by LA feedback?
- Is there a significant difference between different behavioral patterns and academic achievement?
- Is there a significant difference between different behavioral patterns and Self-Regulation Skills?

2. METHODOLOGY

2.1 Participants and Context

The study was conducted with 73 teacher candidates (63 female and 10 male) who took the Information Technologies course. First grade of 33 teacher candidates participated in Programs of Primary

School- Classroom Teaching, 13 from the Program of Guidance and Psychological Counseling, 25 from the Elementary Mathematics Education Program, and 2 from the Program of English Language Teaching students.Since all of the students had taken a distance course for a semester before, they were not unfamiliar with the FL environment.

2.1.1 Content and the Procedure

To carry out the training, the necessary learning environments were created for the participants determined by simple random sampling. A total of three hours of training was given in the FL environment, one hour face-to-face and two hours online. This training included teaching the MS Excel calculation table. Various activities and resources (textual resource document, video, mini test, classroom application) were created within the scope of the study. Students were given videos, course resources, mini-tests, and forum activities via LMS to review at home before coming to class. These activities were placed in the learning management system and made available to students. In the classroom, firstly, a Kahoot mini-quiz was conducted to review the topics examined, the subject was reminded, and then in-class Excel applications were made face-to-face under the guidance of the instructor.

To measure students' interaction with the LMS; Time spent on exercises (mini-test), Number of videos accessed, Number of all activities accessed, and Number of access to source documents statistics were analysed.

Until the next week, the students were sent the learning analyses of the previous week as a report to their emails. This report (Individual Learning Analytics Feedback Report) includes: Feedback based on descriptive statistics and graphs from analysis of individual and class data to facilitate students' understanding and help them compare their online activities with those of their classmates. Textual feedback including sending each student a personalised message to assess their performance in light of their recent report.

2.2 Support with Learning Analytics Feedback / Intervention Strategies

In the study, the instructor monitored and analyzed each student's participation status via Moodle. During the process, an "Individual Learning Analytics Feedback Report" was sent via e-mail at the end of each week. They also directed the class to look at their e-mail messages.

This report includes: Feedback based on descriptive statistics and graphs from analysis of individual and class data to facilitate students' understanding and help them compare their online activities with those of their classmates. Textual feedback including sending each student a personalised message to assess their performance in light of their recent report.

2.3 Data Collection Tools

2.3.1 Achievement Test

At the end of the learning process, the achievement test consisting of 30 multiple-choice questions was administered to 83 students, and item analysis was performed.

As a result of the analysis, a test consisting of 30 items with a difficulty index ranging from 0.34 to 0.98 was obtained. The discrimination index of the items varies between 0.29 and 0.84. Kuder-Richardson Formula 20 (KR-20) was applied for the internal reliability of the test and the reliability coefficient indicating internal reliability was found to be 0.76 and the reliability was acceptable (Kline, 2013).

2.3.2 Online Self-Regulated Learning Questionnaire (OSLQ)

The OSLQ was used to collect data on students' perceptions of SRL in the online learning environment. Lan et al. (2004) first created the OLSQ, which was used by Barnard et al. (2008) and later concentrated on 25 Likert-type items. The survey was adapted by Kilis and Yıldırım (2018) and validated with data from 321 students. In this study, the OSLQ factor structure was tested with confirmatory factor analysis (CFA) by administering it to 130 students. The Chi-square value, which is accepted as the initial fit index, was examined first and found to be significant ($\chi 2$ =448.31, SD = 237, p = 0.00). The X2/SD ratio is 1.89, NFI (Normed Fit Index) = 0.92, NNFI (Non-normed Fit Index) =0.95, CFI (Comparative Fit Index) =0.78, GFI (Goodness-of-fit index)=0.78, AGFI (Adjusted Goodness-of-Fit-Index)=0.72, SRMR (Standardized Root

Mean Square Residual index)=0.07, RMSEA (Root Mean Square Error of Approximation) = 0.05. Based on the fit indices of the various types of values obtained in the study, it was determined that the observed values were mostly within acceptable value ranges (Schermelleh-Enge et al., 2003).

2.4 Data Analysis

First, the data was transferred to an Excel spreadsheet and combined with data on academic performance from course instructors. After that, SPSS was used to export the final student dataset for statistical analysis. The way that students interacted with the LA in the online learning environment was investigated using descriptive statistics. Different algorithms such as Two Step Cluster, Hierarchical Cluster, or K-Means Cluster can be used to create clusters in SPSS. The most popular classic data analysis methods used in LA research are (i) Classification, (ii) Clustering, (iii) Regression, and (iv) Correlation (Charitopoulos et al., 2020).

To categorize students' interactions with LA, a K-Means clustering analysis was carried out. K-means clustering is a technique for cluster analysis that seeks to divide n observations into k clusters, where each observation is assigned to the cluster with the closest mean (Tao, 2020). For k-means, the power to detect clustering was primarily dependent on cluster separation, and much less on sample size (Dalmaijer et al., 2022). Before determining their relationship with academic achievement and self-regulation skills of students in different groups, the variables were checked for normal distribution and homogeneity of variance. Since the variables did not meet the assumptions of normal distribution and homogeneity of variance, Mann-Whitney U tests and non-parametric tests were performed. If the dependent variable is at least on an ordinal scale and the observations are independent of each other, the Mann-Whitney U-test is used (Büyüköztürk, 2021). It tests whether the obtained scores obtained from two unrelated samples differ significantly from each other.

3. RESULTS

The sub-problem of the research is "How to classify students' participation behaviors in LA supported by FLLA feedback?" is the question. Descriptive results obtained regarding students' interaction behaviors with LA are presented in Table 1.

Table 1. Descriptive Statistics on Interaction Behaviors

	Minimum	Maximum	$\bar{x}$	Std. Deviation
Time spent on video	0	19066	3017.42	4188.58
Time spent on exercises (mini-test)	0	1473	704.54	348.50
Number of videos accessed	0	51	9.57	11.74
Number of all activities accessed	0	191	65.03	47.08
Number of access to source documents	0	75	12.75	19.26

When the interaction behaviors of the students were examined, it was determined that they spent more time watching videos ($\bar{X}$=3017.42; SD = 4188.58) compared to mini-tests, and they had more access to the source document ($\bar{X}$=12.75; SD = 19.26) compared to video activities (Table 1).

The students' average access to all activities is 65.03. On the other hand, over the 4 weeks, students spent the least amount of time watching videos in Week 1 ($\bar{X}$= 5.84 minutes) and the most in Week 4 ($\bar{X}$=16.59 minutes).

3.1 Clustering Results

To classify students with similar imaging patterns into a homogeneous group, K-Means cluster analysis was performed on 3 variables; Number of videos accessed, Number of access to source documents, and Number of all activities accessed. Before starting the cluster analysis, the boxplot graphs of the variables to be included in the analysis (time spent in each activity) were examined and it was seen that there were extreme values in all three variables.

However, since all differences of individuals were wanted to be taken into account (those who do not use the system or use it excessively should also be taken into account), these values were requested to be kept in the study. The variables were converted into interaction numbers as 1, 2, and 3 (short, medium, long) respectively, taking into account the rate of 33.33%. As a result of cluster analysis, 73 participants were divided into two clusters. These two clusters consist of 38 (52%) and 35 (48%) participants, respectively.

Table 2. Distribution of Interaction Patterns in Each Cluster

	Cluster 1 (n=38)	**Cluster2 (n=35)**
Number of videos accessed	1.37	2.69
Number of all activities accessed	1.39	2.66
Number of access to source documents	1.61	2.43

Cluster 1 contains those with low interaction, and Cluster 2 contains those with high interaction. As a result, the distribution of 2 different clusters is presented in Table 2.

Mann Whitney U test was conducted to compare students' participation behavior and test scores of the two clusters (Table 3).

Table 3. Participation Behavior with Clusters

	Group	**n**	**Mean Rank**	**Sum of Ranks**	**U**	**p**
Time spent on videos	Cluster 1	38	22.75	864.50	123.50	0.000
	Cluster 2	35	52.47	1836.50		
Time spent on the tests	Cluster 1	38	31.80	1208.50	467.50	0.029
	Cluster 2	35	42.64	1492.50		

When the data of the students in the two clusters were examined. A significant difference was found between the clusters in the variables time spent on video and time spent on the test (Table 3). Accordingly, students with high interaction (Cluster 2) spent more time watching videos ($U=123.50$. $p<0.05$) and taking tests ($U=467.50$. $p<0.05$) than students with low interaction. As a result, the group with higher interaction/participation spends more time in activities.

The sub-problem of the research is the question "Is there a significant difference between different behavioral patterns and academic achievement and self-regulation skills of students supported by FLLA feedback". Mann Whitney U test was conducted to test whether there was a significant difference between the academic achievement and online self-regulation scale subscales between the two clusters (Table 4).

Table 4. Academic Achievement and Self-Regulation Skills with Clusters

	Group	**n**	**Mean Rank**	**Sum of Ranks**	**U**	**p**
Academic performance	Cluster 1	38	33.18	1261.00	520.00	0.11
	Cluster 2	35	**41.14**	1440.00		
Goal Setting	Cluster 1	38	35.37	1344.00	603.00	0.48
	Cluster 2	35	**38.77**	1357.00		
Environment Structuring	Cluster 1	38	36.51	1387.50	646.50	0.83
	Cluster 2	35	**37.53**	1313.50		
Task Strategies	Cluster 1	38	36.12	1372.50	631.50	0.70
	Cluster 2	35	**37.96**	1328.50		
Time Management	Cluster 1	38	33.58	1276.00	535.00	0.14
	Cluster 2	35	**40.71**	1425.00		
Help-Seeking	Cluster 1	38	**39.95**	1518.00	553.00	0.20
	Cluster 2	35	33.80	1183.00		
Self-Evaluation	Cluster 1	38	36.97	1405.00	664.00	0.99
	Cluster 2	35	**37.03**	1296.00		

Academic performance (x̄ =41.14.77), goal setting (x̄ =38.77), environmental organization (x̄ =37.43), study strategies (x̄ =37.96), time management (x̄ =40.71) and self-evaluation (x̄ = 37.03) averages of students with high interaction were found to be higher than those of students with low interaction (Table 4). However. the desire for help (x̄ = 39.95) is higher in the student group with low interaction. Despite this, no statistically significant difference was found between the clusters and academic performance in the subscales of SRL skills.

4. CONCLUSION

When the interaction behaviors of the students were examined, it was determined that they spent more time watching videos compared to mini-tests and they had more access to the source document compared to video activities. According to this finding, more space can be given to video-based materials and source documents in learning environments.

To classify students with similar imaging patterns into a homogeneous group K-Means cluster analysis was performed on the number of videos accessed, number of access to source documents, and number of all activities accessed variables. At the end of the analysis, the participants were divided into 2 different clusters: 1st cluster low interaction, 2nd cluster high interaction. In the study, the participation behaviors of the students and the test scores of the two clusters were compared. As a result, a significant difference was found between the clusters in the variables of time spent on video and time spent on test. Accordingly, students with high interaction allocated more time to watching videos and solving tests than students with low interaction. It can be said that the group with high interaction spends more time on activities. Using quizzes is associated with higher goal-setting and self-evaluation skills of learners (Çakiroğlu et al., 2024). This result is in line with the study of Kizilcec et al. (2017) who revealed that learners with stronger goal-setting and self-evaluation skills were more likely to visit assessment activities and spend more time on assessments. According to a similar study, it was observed that students with surface learners made a statistically significant forward search while watching the video compared to students using the deep learner approach (Akcapinar & Bayazit, 2018).

In the study, it was also tested whether there was a significant difference between the academic achievement and online self-regulation scale subscales between the two clusters. The mean scores of academic achievement, goal setting, environmental organization, study strategies, time management, and self-evaluation of students with high interaction were higher than those of students with low interaction. However, the request for help was higher in the group of students with low interaction. Moreover, no statistically significant difference was found between the clusters and academic performance in the subscales of SRL skills. These results partially support the studies on the effect on academic achievement. Studies have found that students with high interaction also have a high academic achievement (Çebi & Güyer. 2020; Lancaster et al. 2020; Gasevic et al., 2017). Although there was no significant difference in our study. When the cluster averages are taken into account, the achievement averages of students with high interaction are also high. Also, Fan et al. (2021) stated that the learners from high-performance groups showed high-level regulation skills through storıng alignment of the choices of tasks provided in the learning design. The results of this study may also help design effective online courses and advanced LA research. The findings obtained here can be used to identify students with low mobility and develop intervention mechanisms for learners.

REFERENCES

Akcapinar. G.. & Bayazit. A.. (2018). Investigating video viewing behaviors of students with different learning approaches using video analytics. *Turkish Online Journal of Distance Education.* *19*(4). 116-125.https://doi.org/10.17718/tojde.471907

Barnard, L., Paton, V., & Lan, W. (2008). Online self-regulatory learning behaviors as a mediator in the relationship between online course perceptions with achievement. *The International Review of Research in Open and Distributed Learning*, *9*(2).https://doi.org/10.19173/irrodl.v9i2.516

Büyüköztürk, Ş. (2021). *Sosyal bilimler için veri analizi el kitabı* (29th ed.). *Pegem .*

Çakiroğlu, Ü., Kokoç, M. & Atabay, M. (2024) Online learners' self-regulated learning skills regarding LMS interactions: a profiling study. J Comput High Educ 36, 220–241 . https://doi.org/10.1007/s12528-024-09397-2

Çebi. A.. & Güyer. T.. 2020. Students' interaction patterns in different online LA and their relationship with motivation. self-regulated learning strategy and learning performance. *Education and Information Technologies*. *25*(5). 3975-3993. https://doi.org/10.1007/s10639-020-10151-1

Cerezo, R., Lara, J. A., Azevedo, R., & Romero, C.(2024). Reviewing the differences between learning analytics and educational data mining: Towards educational data science. *Computers in Human Behavior*. *154*. 108155.https://doi.org/10.1016/j.chb.2024.108155

Charitopoulos, A., Rangoussi, M., & Koulouriotis, D. (2020). On the use of soft computing methods in educational data mining and learning analytics research: A review of years 2010–2018. *International Journal of Artificial Intelligence in Education*. *30*(3). 371-430.https://doi.org/10.1007/s40593-020-00200-8

Dalmaijer, E.S., Nord, C.L. & Astle, D.E. (2022). Statistical power for cluster analysis. *BMC Bioinformatics 23*, 205. https://doi.org/10.1186/s12859-022-04675-1

Fan, Y., Matcha, W., Uzir, N.A. et al. (2021). Learning Analytics to Reveal Links Between Learning Design and Self-Regulated Learning. *Int J Artif Intell Educ 31*, 980–1021 . https://doi.org/10.1007/s40593-021-00249-z

Fleur, D. S., Marshall, M., Pieters, M., Brouwer, N., Oomens, G., Konstantinidis, A., Winnips, K., Moes, S., van den Bos, W., Bredeweg, B., & van Vliet, E. A. (2023). IguideME: Supporting Self-Regulated Learning and Academic Achievement with Personalized Peer-Comparison Feedback in Higher Education. *Journal of Learning Analytics*, *10*(2), 100-114. https://doi.org/10.18608/jla.2023.7853.

Gasevic, D., Jovanovic, J., Pardo, A., & Dawson, S. (2017). Detecting Learning Strategies with Analytics: Links with Self-reported Measures and Academic Performance. *Journal of Learning Analytics*. *4*(2). 113–128. https://doi.org/10.18608/jla.2017.42.10

Kilis, S., & Yıldırım, Z. (2018). Investigation of community of inquiry framework in regard to self-regulation, metacognition and motivation. *Computers & Education*, *126*, 53-64. https://doi.org/10.1016/j.compedu.2018.06.032

Kline, P. (2013). *Handbook of psychological testing*. Routledge.

Lancaster, A., Moses, S., Clark, M., & Masters, M. C. (2020). The Positive Impact of Deliberate Writing Course Design on Student Learning Experience and Performance. *Journal of Learning Analytics*. *7*(3). 48-63.https://dx.doi.org/10.18608/jla.2020.73.5

Lim L-A, Atif, A., Heggart, K, & Sutton, N. (2023a). In Search of Alignment between Learning Analytics and Learning Design: A Multiple Case Study in a Higher Education Institution. Education Sciences. 13(11):1114. https://doi.org/10.3390/educsci13111114.

Lim. L.. et al.Lim, L., Bannert, M., van der Graaf, J., Singh, S., Fan, Y., Surendrannair, S., ... & Gašević, D. (2023b). Effects of real-time analytics-based personalized scaffolds on students' self-regulated learning. *Computers in Human Behavior*. *139*. 107547. https://doi.org/10.1016/j.chb.2022.107547

Lluch Molins, L., & Cano Garcia, E. (2023). How to Embed SRL in Online Learning Settings? Design Through Learning Analytics and Personalized Learning Design in Moodle. *Journal of New Approaches in Educational Research, 12*(1), 120-138. doi:https://doi.org/10.7821/naer.2023.1.1127

Pintrich. P. R.. (2000). The role of goal orientation in self-regulated learning. In *Handbook of self-regulation* (pp. 451-502). Academic Press.

Schermelleh-Engel, K., Moosbrugger, H., & Muller, H. (2003). Evaluating the fit of structurale quation models: tests of significance and descriptive goodness-of-fit measures. *Methods of Psychological Research-Online*, *8*(2), 23-74. Accessed from http://www.mpr-online.de/.

Schunk. D. H.. (2005). Self-regulated learning: the educational legacy of Paul r. Pintrich. *Educational Psychologist. 40 (2)*. 85– 94.https://doi.org/10.1207/s15326985ep4002_3

Tao, J., Zheng, C., Lu, Z., Liang, J. C., & Tsai, C. C. (2020). Cluster analysis on Chinese university students' conceptions of English language learning and their online self-regulation. *Australasian Journal of Educational Technology, 36*(2), 105-119.https://doi.org/10.14742/ajet.4844

Timmi, M., Laaouina, L., Jeghal, A., El Garouani, S., & Yahyaouy, A.. (2022, May). Learning analytics: a review of the literature. In *2022 International Conference on Intelligent Systems and Computer Vision (ISCV)* (pp. 1-4). IEEE.

Wise, A. F., Knight, S., & Ochoa, X. (2021). What makes learning analytics research matter.*Journal of Learning Analytics*. *8*(3). 1-9.https://doi.org/10.18608/jla.2021.7647

Zheng, L., Kinshuk, Fan, Y. (2023). The impacts of the comprehensive learning analytics approach on learning performance in online collaborative learning. *Educ Inf Technol 28*, 16863–16886 https://doi.org/10.1007/s10639-023-11886-3.

Zimmerman. B. J..(1989). A social cognitive view of self-regulated academic learning. *Journal of educational psychology*. *81(3)*. 329-339.https://doi.org/10.1037/0022-0663.81.3.329

FROM A PARTICIPATORY CITY TO A COLLABORATIVE CITY: VIDEO GAMES AS AN EMERGENT TOOL FOR COLLABORATIVE DESIGN

Khalil Morad El Ghilali[1], Iman Meriem Benkirane[2], Vassilis Bourdakis[3] and Giorgos Papakonstantinou[3]
[1]*University of Thessaly (UTH), Greece, Euromed University of Fes, Morocco*
[2]*Euromed University of Fes, Morocco*
[3]*University of Thessaly (UTH), Greece*

ABSTRACT

Involving citizens in city's design process requires resilient communication tools. The limits of communication in architecture are reflected by the complexity of the means used and the technical skills. The architect communicates through technical documents and 3D design software which often requires technical training. The ideas are experienced through the plan, the section, or the drawing. Architectural renderings are designed for construction professionals and are not easily understood by common citizens. Construction professionals remain in a bubble of technical jargon that keeps being incomprehensible by a population unfamiliar with the field of architecture(Friedrich von Borries, Steffen P. Walz, 2007) . On the other hand, video games already propose city planning alternatives. It is intended as an exchange platform on which we can experiment and develop possible futures(Wragg, 2020, p. 67).
There are already existing video games that allow players to actively participate in the design and creation of content, such as "Minecraft" or "Roblox". These games offer a great creative alternative that can be used to explore architecture-related topics. These creative tools are simple and accessible. They make it possible to quickly develop 3D spaces. Ideas are quickly highlighted and understood by non-specialists through a gamified language. They become the support for creating a gaming environment and a participatory and collaborative experience(Wragg, 2020, p. 201).
Through active participation in the game, players learn from their decisions (and the decisions of others) and assess their consequences. Virtual worlds are therefore a space of freedom, where people have the tools to express their creativity without the need of a particular skill. It offers a democratic and accessible experience that can be afforded by anyone.
This paper discusses and explores the potential of video games as tools for participatory and collaborative design as a response to complex issues such as climate change, emergencies and disasters. After presenting and analyzing video games that influenced our perceptions of the built environment. We will provide an extended view of the merging boundaries of the real and digital territories and focus on how values such as sustainability and climate change engagement alternate as parts of the digital sphere and, at the same time, are being pulled apart from their original space and scattered through the public sphere. Finally, we will explore how video games can enhance user engagement and promote inclusivity and social consensus in the urban design process. Shifting the methodology from a merely participatory to a more collaborative approach.
First, we provide a theoretical framework that discusses the concepts of participatory and collaborative cities, video games as tools for design, user engagement, emergency management, sustainability, and consensus. Second, through a comparative analysis, we review a corpus of examples through the lens of these concepts. Third, we present and discuss the results of our analysis, followed by a discussion on the implications of our findings for design and urban planning.

KEYWORDS

Collaborative Design, Climate Change, Emergency, Education Alternatives, Urban Planning, Video Games

1. INTRODUCTION

As cities continue to grow and evolve, there is a need to design spaces that are functional, attractive, and sustainable. The traditional top-down approach to design often overlooks the needs and desires of users, leading to spaces that are underutilized, avoided, or marginalized. To address this issue, a more collaborative and participatory approach of designing spaces is gaining momentum.

However, there are challenges in implementing these participatory approaches. One challenge is the limited engagement and participation of the public, due to the tools used which can lead to a lack of diversity in ideas and perspectives, mainly due to the detachment one can feel toward space. Another challenge is the time and resources required to enhance participatory design processes (de Andrade et al., 2020, p. 1).

With the emergence of wireless networks and digital technologies that have already captured every aspect of everyday life, our behavior towards the built environment has changed, and the space we inhabit is now filled with multiple layers of information that, due to technological advances, we can receive, process, and reproduce to the point of rearranging its form. Video games present a new scenario around the concept of parallel universes, where the user has the chance to shape reality (Friedrich von Borries, Steffen P. Walz, 2007, p. 355). This approach involves engaging users in the design process, allowing for a more user-centered and inclusive design. The architectural connection between a space and a given programmatic function breaks down, and every user can determine its new function and thus the experience they wish to receive.

Games have already shown an important role in the development of civilization. It is a source of joy and amusement but also a smart way to face problems, to occupy one's mind or to escape from everyday life (Bishop et al., 2022).

"From the point of view of form, Games can therefore be defined in short as a free action, felt as fictitious and situated outside of everyday life, capable, nevertheless, of totally absorbing the player; an action devoid of any material interest and usefulness; which takes place in a time and in a space expressly circumscribed, is carried out in order according to given rules and arouses in the life relations of groups willingly surrounding themselves with mystery or accentuating by disguise their strangeness towards the usual world" (Bishop et al., 2022).

From elements of reality, fictions are developed as proposals for a future. Video games become the communication interface to speculate on future developments of our cities (Pearson, 2020a, pp. 114-143.) … They offer a diverse set of mechanics that allows the participants to design and explore generative systems that rely on resource management and ecological inter dependence. Games like Minecraft, Dwarf Fortress, Prison Architect or Factorio, offer excellent case studies to sensitize the population to the quality of the environment. Video games become a design tool at the service of citizens, offering them the opportunity to express themselves, freely, through a playful 3D projection tool (Bob Martens, Gabriel Wurzer, Thomas Grasl, Wolfgang E.Lorenz, 2015).

We are entering an age where exponential design strategies will be necessary to address global problems. No singular architectural initiative will be able to perform or impact the urban environment in a meaningful way unless, models of mass reach and mass customization involving citizens with architects in the design of the city, like video games, will try to redefine what 21st century urbanism is.

2. THEORITICAL FRAMEWORK

The concept of participation involves more than just a collection of practices; it encompasses the notion that one can actively engage with others in decision-making processes that impact the development of social connections, communities, knowledge systems, organizations, politics, and culture. The potential for communication that can lead to social change is also tied to this promise and belief, as well as to media technologies (such as internet forums, blogs, wikis, podcasts, and smartphones) that appear to facilitate increased participation. However, while these possibilities reflect a desire for increased participation, they can also be viewed as mere rhetoric, empty habits, or missed opportunities. This tension between the promises and limitations of participation, including aspirations and disappointments, illusions, and recoveries, is a key focus of recent social, cultural, and political assessments of participation in the context of new media (Barney et al., 2016, p. 8).

We comprehend participatory culture not only as a newly emerging phenomenon but also as a continuously expanding one, largely due to the "spreadability" of new media, which assumes that valuable information will circulate through all available channels (Jenkins Henry et al., 2013). This extensive nature of participation calls for a shift in terminology to disentangle the tensions, contradictions, and potentialities of new media participation in the design process.

This expansion has become so extensive that it represents an essential characteristic of contemporaneity. A standard that has come to gauge the excellence of our social environments and engagements is now synonymous with virtues, such as equality, justice, fairness, community, or freedom (Barney et al., 2016, p. 10).

However, this contemporary participation is akin to a pharmakon, a term drawn from Stiegler's philosophy of technology, that helps to express a fundamental ambivalence built into modern technologies: technology can have either positive or negative effects, depending on how it is used. This implies that it functions as both a cure and a poison, a solution and a challenge, a promise of emancipation, and a form of subjection (Stiegler, 1998).

In Confronting the Challenges of Participatory Culture, Jenkins et al. characterized communication technologies as an element within the complex ecology of participation. Rather than dealing with each technology in isolation, we would do better to take an ecological approach, thinking about the interrelationship among different communication technologies, the cultural communities that grow up around them, and the activities they support. This raises the question of what constitutes significant participation.

2.1 The Participatory Condition: a Pharmakon?

Despite the apparent abundance of opportunities for individuals to engage in activities that align with traditional notions of political action, such as sharing information, voicing opinions, deliberating with others, expressing preferences, making decisions, observing events, and coordinating collective efforts, it remains uncertain whether the level of participation achieved through these activities truly enhances the quality, intensity, or effectiveness of political engagement or promotes a more democratic distribution of power and resources, compared to the time when participation is not yet a routine aspect of social life. In most practice, the exploration of emerging media (from novel forms of performance to innovative investigations of sound, music, movement, voice, and light, and the aesthetic exploration of kinetic and cybernetic techniques, painting, photography, cinema, video games, and the Internet) plays a significant role in the renewal of participatory aesthetics (Darin Barney, Gabriella Coleman, Christine Ross, Jonathan Sterne, 2016, p. 17).

In the current conjuncture, the emancipatory potential of the participatory experience remains entangled with the political trappings of participation: With an action-oriented toward social practice, there is always the risk of moving "from the action of fiction" in the creative process "to the fiction of action" in the world (Fisher, 2011, p. 20).

Throughout each era of media, there has been longstanding conversation about the possibilities, problems, and peculiarities of participation. Alongside its conceptual interaction, dialogue and engagement – participation have played a major role in how media are perceived, evaluated, and criticized. The emergence of technical media to use Friedrich Kittler's term for electrical and mechanical devices in the late 19th century introduced a new range of controversies surrounding participation, particularly around the potential for media to cause distraction and disengagement (Darin Barney, Gabriella Coleman, Christine Ross, Jonathan Sterne, 2016, p. 20).

Of course, distraction does not always have a negative valence. Most famously, Walter Benjamin wrote that the condition of cinema would lead the working classes to apprehend themselves in their totality, echoing Georg Lukacs's theory of reification, where class consciousness and the collective action that would spring from it was only possible after capitalism objectified social relations, rendering them sensible. The situationists' practices of detournement (the deviation of a previous media work, whose meaning is antagonistic to the original) were also built on Lukacs' account of consciousness and action explicitly in Guy Debord's Society of the Spectacle and implicitly in their attempts to turn urban distraction and alienation against itself (Barney et al., 2016, p. 21; Debord, n.d.).

Historical preconditions, including those outlined above, prepare us for the hail of the contemporary participatory condition. It promotes and shapes itself around the promise of participation as well as the anxieties, power struggles, ambivalences, and failures that accompany such a promise.

The following questions must then be raised: In what ways and to what extent have digital media and, specifically video games become a structuring feature of the contemporary participatory condition and to what extent it can be applied to climate urgency resilience and urban design? This is the main questions this article attempts to address.

2.2 Towards a Collaborative City

The answers to these questions are articulated within the confines of fields, such as political science, ecology, sociology, communication studies, anthropology, law, philosophy, urbanism, and design. However, given the commonalities in some of their discussions and discoveries, their findings transcend their respective disciplines. An interdisciplinary assessment of the participatory condition is essential insofar as participatory culture has expanded across all societal fields. This article also shares a primordial concern: the need to be critical of the participatory condition.

The common conclusion is that, although certain attributes of digital media facilitate participation, these attributes alone do not encompass the possibilities, promises, or deceptions of participatory practices. Rather, digital media creates other environments that are ripe for the unfolding of participatory conditions. As anthropologist Tim Ingold has argued in his study of materiality, the properties of materials "cannot be identified as fixed, essential attributes of things, but are rather processual and relational." Participants in new media environments (engineers, policymakers, investors, branders, employers, users, workers, thinkers, hackers, activists, players, dreamers, propagandists, educators, artists, etc.) shape the media as they are shaped by them. Through case studies, this article aims to analyze what, why, how, and when participation can take place within video games(Ingold, 2007, p. 14).

What is ostensibly distinct today is how new media allows humans to bypass institutions and hierarchies, while encouraging direct connections and participation. However, social ties consolidated by new media cooperation are extremely varied, ranging from weak to strong, manifest to latent, and enduring to ephemeral. The idea of participatory cities emphasizes the importance of involving citizens in sustainable urban design and planning (Delaney, 2020).

As Henri Lefebvre would say "the creative capacity of space is always that of a community or collective, a group, a fraction of an active class, an 'agent' or 'actor.' Even if the command and demand fall into different groups, attribution cannot be made to an individual or an entity, but to a social reality capable of investing itself in a space: producing it, with the means and resources at its disposal (productive forces, techniques, and knowledge, means of work, etc.)." (Lefebvre, 2011)

It might well be that participatory practices have generated a condition not only because of their expansion throughout societal fields but also because participation today hails individuals and the public as subjects in the social order of consensus. This order represents the waning of the political as an activity of the possible. In line with what Erik Swyngedouw has said about sustainability, participation, whether taken as a concept or as a practice is now so bereft of political content and elevated as a moral value that it is impossible to disagree with its formulation, goals, and promises of a better life (Bjelland, 2009).

However, the concept of a collaborative city suggests that the creation of spaces can be a collective effort among different stakeholders (Bishop, n.d.). This approach recognizes the potential of collaboration in generating innovative and sustainable solutions to urban challenges.

3. CITIES AND VIDEO GAMES: AN ALTERNATIVE OR A FORCED MARRIAGE?

One strategy that has emerged for addressing these complex challenges in the recent years is the use of video games, which has become increasingly popular among planners and designers seeking to create more resilient and sustainable cities, in a collaborative and participatory way (Wu and Lee, 2015).

Urban design gaming involves the use of computer simulations to model and test different urban design scenarios, allowing planners and designers to evaluate the potential impacts of various development strategies and identify the most effective solutions.

However, urban planners work very little with video game creators and vice versa (with some exception like SIM CITY or CITIES XL). Still, a few initiatives demonstrate the benefits of collaboration between these professions, particularly by relying on these two paradigms. Several companies in the construction sector have shown interest in the issue of appropriation of City Builders. Although BIM is a complex reality to implement due to the organization of the professional sector, several experiments have taken place. The offer is also driven by the software creators themselves who see it as a diversification lever (Yildiz and Yildiz, 2011).

Their motto is simple: "If we want to develop a 3D modelling tool that will allow us to represent a neighborhood under construction and enable its users to immerse themselves in the future neighborhood, then it's like developing a video game" ("Cycle de formation : introduction à la ville de demain — pop-up urbain, cabinet de conseil en prospective urbaine," n.d.).

This is precisely what ENODO, an actor in immersive 3D technology, offers with their software CryEngine, which aims to be more intuitive than BIM tools for businesses. One of ENODO'S projects, the playful application 'PHOSPHORECITY', was developed for EIFFAGE, a French civil engineering construction company, offering the ability to read the city through different grids of interpretation in a Sim City-like approach.

However, the limitation of this approach is that it functions as a simulation of predetermined scenarios and actions. As such, it does not offer players the ability to be creative or to deviate from the rules in order to propose truly original visions (Pearson, 2020b) .

In a way, the solutions provided by players are contained within the basic algorithm. This is why they are primarily demonstration and persuasion tools, where the expression of the self is dictated a purpose orientated design. However, this is an important paradigm identified at the heart of Smart City projects that exploit the idea of managing flows through real control rooms (Gerber and Götz, 2020).

Therefore, it is a strong ideological unconscious that needs to be deconstructed in the future of such projects. Some games have tried to overcome this limitation by operating on the border between board games and video games, as in the Dutch initiative REZONE. In this project, the aim is to simulate choices and teach public authorities the consequences of their actions as decision-makers (e.g. an isolated building loses value and deteriorates).(Wragg, 2020)In the United States, THE PARTICIPATORY CHINATOWN PROJECT aimed to involve residents of this Boston neighborhoods in the redesign of its conception by playing various concrete roles within the city (e.g. finding a job) (Poplin, 2011). This approach offers a more liberating and innovative environment that engage citizens in urban decision-making.

In these "Sim-City like" approaches, there is a significant gap between the game simulation, which is oriented towards storytelling and its effect on the player, and real urban behaviour. According to Stéphane Natkin, for gameplay reasons, the game will allow the player a freedom of design that does not exist in a real city. Nevertheless, there are attempts to build game engine technologies that can address these different simulation needs. For example, research projects such as LA TERRA DYNAMICA led by Thales group a global leader in new technologies or the behavioral engine SpirOps (Stephane Natkin, 2006) that uses gaming technologies to simulate and create artificial behaviors to achieve more sustainable and intelligent scenarios in urban design.

To try to support these approaches and make them more creative, we can integrate the analysis of player journeys by identifying certain moments that are more likely to offer creativity. Indeed, player attitudes not only vary from person to person, but also within the game's life cycle. Thus, Richard Bartle (2003) distinguishes eight types of players based on their attitude within the video game, as well as two types of trajectories for the transformation of the video game player.(Sicart, 2013, p. 107)

Interestingly, the final stage of this process is either a player motivated by their socialization practices or by hacking practices, which means transforming the city in which they play. Therefore, guiding naive users towards transformative and socially involved practices is part of the ludic process itself. Video games can thus involve citizens and change their perspectives and practices towards their own city.

An example of this is the recent fire at Notre Dame Cathedral in Paris: Hundreds of players and fans of the game expressed their attachment to the building on social media and through the game Assassin's Creed Unity, happy to have means to continue having a concrete experience with the building. To the point where some developers and fans of the game speculated that the game had one of the most faithful models to date and could serve as a reference for reconstruction. Ubisoft stated in a statement that the studio did not plan to engage in such an initiative(Pearson, 2020a, p. 5).

Other notable initiatives include: "THE BLOCKHOLM PROJECT", Sweden, 2013. Using Minecraft technology, the goal is to allow external players to propose new buildings, some of which have been submitted to the choice of urban planning teams. On a more local scale, several municipalities have seized the tool to engage citizens in a collaborative approach to digitizing the city (like Rennes craft, Liege Mine Craft, Metaverse City Saint Etienne), to create social emulation around a project and the city(Delaney, 2022).

The "BLOCK BY BLOCK PROJECT" resulted from a partnership between the UN-Habitat (a UN agency that aims to promote human-scale urban development) and Mojang (a Swedish video game development studio). It aims to rethink the urban organization of disadvantaged neighborhoods. The program proposes to recreate a model of the neighborhoods in Minecraft and use it to enable residents to make the modifications they want or use it as a model close enough to reality to demonstrate the value of an installation. Among the emblematic projects, a disadvantaged neighborhoods in Haiti inhabited mainly by illiterate fishermen: installation of streetlights, public toilets, and trees, or even the creation of a soccer field were proposed to the architects involved in the project, who could propose an applicable version(Delaney, 2022).

More radically, video game cities can be an opportunity to experiment with strong hypotheses:

- Explore extreme environments, like games such as PREY or BIOSHOCK (especially the first version of the game and its CITY OF RAPTURE) that created self-sufficient "buildings" by exploring extreme environments (space city, underwater city, etc.).
- Test construction methods using waste, as allowed by the game FALLOUT 4, where players share online the most improbable settlements based on what the game allows. The game also promotes a DIY ideology related to climate issues, but at the risk, as Nicolas Jaujou explains, of excusing the mistakes of current decision-makers by inviting players to play with a "worst-case scenario."
- Inhabit infrastructure: an idea very present in the work of science fiction author Gibson, well represented for example in METRO EXODUS where urban railway bridges have become inhabited colonies.

These diversions of use are called UGC (User Generated Content) and are more or less well integrated by game designers in the form of modules that reproduce exceptional practices or in the form of modules that allow for original tasks that some game users have already started to design. However, as Nicolas Jaujou regrets, this approach finds little echo among most SimCity-type game designers who tend to prioritize the expression of key messages rather than emphasizing the creativity of player communities.

Platforms such as Minecraft or Roblox are much more conducive to player creativity in this regard. By using video games, designers can engage citizens in a more immersive and interactive manner, allowing for more creative and innovative solutions to be generated (Wragg, 2020).

There is therefore an interesting opportunity here to reverse this paradigm to benefit from a tremendous potential for creativity that, to date, remains poorly equipped and exploited. However, the use of urban design gaming is not without its challenges. One major obstacle is the complexity and interdisciplinary nature of urban climatology, which has historically prevented the application of climate knowledge in urban development processes and practices. To address this issue, a framework was developed to provide key information to planners, architects, and engineers working on sustainable designs. The framework aims to link localized climate conditions with energy demand for cooling in urban areas as well as reduce their carbon footprint.

In addition to applying climate knowledge in urban design gaming models through frameworks such as those stated above, other considerations must also be taken into account when designing resilient and sustainable cities that respond effectively to changing climatic conditions or disasters. The complexity of cities and their interactions with surrounding natural environments makes it difficult to simulate every possible scenario within a game.

Another concern about urban design gaming is its reliance on solitary problem-solving by individual players or teams in isolation from other stakeholders who should also have input in decision-making processes related to designing sustainable cities. While games are helpful at raising awareness through education systems, when applied in real-world policy settings, they leave out critical perspectives like public values or community-level concerns necessary for collective action, which style forms building ownership versus renter rights, hence leading potentially towards less participatory approaches. This raises the question of what can video games offer that other media cannot.

3.1 Integrating climate issues in video games, simulating them and playing them out

Cities can be regarded as the quintessential example of complexity. One of the key features of cities is that they are never what they seem to be. For the same kind of patterns can emerge from very different processes. These systems are therefore irreducible, and it is not possible to model or approximate such a system unless the entire system, including its components and their interactions, is simulated. (Johnson, n.d.)

For many researchers, video games provide a great way to answer questions that are extremely difficult to answer in real life. For researchers from the Integrated History and Future of People on Earth (IHOPE), the key issue is the modelling of complex and dynamic systems.

They note that some simulation video games meet these two criteria due to the number of players present, the existence of a system with its rules, and the many interactions allowed. Based on this principle, (Kelly and Nardi, 2014) explain that these games offer opportunities for exercising create participation through Modeling complex social interactions.

Compared to other types of imaginaries present in films or novels, video games allow players to actually interact with the offered environment as well as with other players. When watching a horror movie, the political and social ecosystem is given, and the viewer experiences it. This is not the case in games. As an example, an update for the Minecraft game entitled Global Warming allows players to integrate the consequences of everyone's actions in the game. By introducing carbon dioxide, players realize that their actions can have positive or negative consequences. The introduction of a form of carbon tax then allows players to understand how competition can exist between them while preserving a common future.

In addition to the gameplay dimensions presented earlier, some authors emphasize the critical role of game aesthetics in immersing players "casually" in alternative post-oil futures.

This approach is related to a critique by Abraham (Abraham, 2018) when he explains that games focused on climate considerations are inherently uninteresting given the near impossibility of reconciling growth and sustainability. For the author, this desire to "persuade" the player using game tools can only hold if the game is enjoyable to play.

Rather than attempting to immerse the player in climate issues by having them manipulate elements of the environment, it would be better to directly show them that a better future can exist. The key issue of video games then becomes, not to try to persuade the player, but through what he calls "submission to aesthetics," to present preferable futures. This should enable, according to him, the establishment of "an informal engagement", as it does not directly attack beliefs or practices that may conflict with climate issues.

Here, user creativity appears as a key element because it shows that it is possible to redirect these universes for the benefit of a more virtuous relationship with ecology. Several avenues for redirecting usage are noteworthy.

Firstly, games are a powerful communication tool, either by demonstrating the relevance of a positive imaginary, contributing to spreading the message that virtuous futures are possible or by using the player's audience to disseminate positive messages.

Secondly, games offer an interesting space for creativity to be exploited, particularly in the context of open worlds and sandbox formats. The creativity of the mods mentioned above illustrates players' ability to take on a problem and redirect it. If games offered more interesting challenges, it could be a lever for collective intelligence in problem-solving. This approach is still largely unexplored.

Finally, games are a territory where developers write the rules. It is therefore interesting to work on this point to strengthen some of the currently positive aspects of games, such as setting clear elements that can help players evolve within a framework that is beneficial to enrich collective creativity in the field of urban environmental preservation.

4. CONCLUSION

The case examples analyzed in this study offers a unique approach to urban design and climate engagement.

The analysis of these case examples reveals several key findings regarding the use of video games as a tool for climate engaged urban design. First, collaboration and participation are essential components of successful urban design. Video games like Minecraft and Roblox provide platforms for collaboration and participation that can help to ensure that public spaces are designed with the needs and desires of the community in mind. Second, implementing sustainability and climate change considerations in urban collaborative design are becoming increasingly important but lacks a clear representative way. However games like Eco offer opportunities for players to explore and experiment with sustainable practices and to consider the impact of their actions on the environment. Finally, user engagement and inclusivity are crucial for the success of this new approach. Video games can help to engage a wide range of users, including those who may not typically participate in the design process, and to promote inclusivity through offering a liberating plateform.

While this study provides insights into the potential of video games as a tool for urban design, there is still much to be explored in this area. Future research could investigate the effectiveness of different types of video games technologies for public space design, the impact of video game design on user engagement and inclusivity, and the potential of video games to promote sustainable practices in public space design. Additionally, further research could explore how video games can be integrated into the broader urban planning process, and how they can be used in combination with other tools and approaches to create more livable and sustainable cities.

REFERENCES

Abraham, B. (2018). Video Game Visions of Climate Futures: ARMA 3 and Implications for Games and Persuasion. Games Cult. 13, 71–91. https://doi.org/10.1177/1555412015603844

Barney, D., Coleman, G., Ross, C., Sterne, J., Tembeck, T. (2016). The participatory condition in the digital age, The Participatory Condition in the Digital Age. London. https://doi.org/10.1162/leon_r_01509

Bishop, C., n.d. Artificial hells : participatory art and the politics of spectatorship.

Bishop, C., De Sacher, P., Paul, K., Aghoro, N., Filippaki, I., Kempshall, C., Maccallum-stewart, E., Mccall, J., Pöhlmann, S., Kiefer, B., Borries, F. Von, Walz, S.P., Böttger, M., Kunzelman, C., Yoon, C., Jeux, L.E.S., Hollllles, E.T.L.E.S., Knöll, R., Mezini, M., Gerber, A., Götz, U., Marty, N., Heidegger, M., Lefebvre, H., Lynch, K., Nitsche, M., Wragg, M., Jenkins Henry, Ford Sam, Green Joshua, Bogost, I. (2022). LES JEUX ET LES HOMMES, Revue. New York and London. https://doi.org/10.1145/1640089.1640128

Bjelland, M. (2009). The Sustainability Development Paradox: Urban Political Economy in the United States and Europe – Edited by Rob Krueger and David Gibbs. Econ. Geogr. 85, 113–114. https://doi.org/10.1111/j.1944-8287.2008.01012.x

Bob Martens, Gabriel Wurzer, Thomas Grasl, Wolfgang E.Lorenz, R.S. (2015). REAL TIME-EXTENDING THE REACH OF COMPUTATION 1. https://doi.org/10.18356/28e9151b-en

Cycle de formation : introduction à la ville de demain — pop-up urbain, cabinet de conseil en prospective urbaine [WWW Document], n.d. URL https://www.pop-up-urbain.com/cycle-de-formation-introduction-a-la-ville-de-demain/ (accessed 1.29.24).

Dansey, N. (2013). A Grounded Theory of emergent benefit in pervasive game experiences.

Darin Barney, Gabriella Coleman, Christine Ross, Jonathan Sterne, T.T. (2016). The participatory condition in the difital age.

de Andrade, B., Poplin, A., de Sena, Í.S. (2020). Minecraft as a tool for engaging children in urban planning: A Case study in Tirol Town, Brazil. ISPRS Int. J. Geo-Information 9. https://doi.org/10.3390/ijgi9030170

Debord, G., n.d. la societe du spectacle 1–76.

Delaney, J. (2022). Minecraft and Playful Public Participation in Urban Design. Urban Plan. 7, 330–342. https://doi.org/10.17645/up.v7i2.5229

Delaney, J. (2020). Democracy, video games and urban design: Minecraft as a public par ticipation tool. Architecton. Game Spaces Spat. Log. Virtual Its Mean. Real 277–292.

Fisher, T. (2011). Radical democratic theatre. Perform. Res. 16, 15–26. https://doi.org/10.1080/13528165.2011.606046

Friedrich von Borries, Steffen P. Walz, M.B. (2007). SPACE TIME PLAY COMPUTER GAMES, ARCHITECTURE AND URBANISM: THE NEXT LEVEL, Birkhäuser Basel _ Boston _ Berlin.

Gerber, A., Götz, U. (2020). Architectonics of Game Spaces: The Spatial Logic of the Virtual and Its Meaning for the Real, Architectonics of Game Spaces: The Spatial Logic of the Virtual and Its Meaning for the Real. https://doi.org/10.14361/9783839448021

Ingold, T. (2007). Materials against materiality. Archaeol. Dialogues 14, 1–16. https://doi.org/10.1017/S1380203807002127

Jenkins, H., Ford, S., Green, J. (2013). SPREADABLE MEDIA. New York and London.

Johnson, S., n.d. Emergence: The Connected Lives of Ants, Brains, Cities, and Software Emergence.

Kelly, S., Nardi, B. (2014). Playing with sustainability: Using video games to simulate futures of scarcity. First Monday. https://doi.org/10.5210/fm.v19i5.5259

Kokonis, M. (2014). Intermediality between Games and Fiction: The "Ludology vs. Narratology" Debate in Computer Game Studies: A Response to Gonzalo Frasca. Acta Univ. Sapientiae, Film Media Stud. 9, 171–188. https://doi.org/10.1515/ausfm-2015-0009

Lefebvre, H. (2011). La production de l 'espace (Intro). Revue 93–121.

DOWNFALL SEED SPREAD. A STACK-BASED ALGORITHM FOR THE AUTONOMOUS GENERATION OF 2D MAPS IN VIDEOGAMES

Lenin Acosta-Guevara[1], Félix Fernández-Peña[1,2], Pilar Urrutia-Urrutia[1] and Diana Coello-Fiallos[3]
[1]Universidad Técnica de Ambato
Av. De los Chasquis, Ambato, Ecuador
[2]Universidad Espíritu Santo
Km. 2,5 vía a Samborondón, Ecuador
[3]Escuela Superior Politécnica de Chimborazo
Panamericana Sur km 1 ½. Riobamba, Ecuador

ABSTRACT

The autonomous generation of 2D maps is commonly achieved by using algorithms that produce useful noise interpreted as a height map. By normalizing height maps as matrices of correlated values, it is easy to generate a 2D map. Each value in the matrix is used to choose an asset from an asset library. The problem is thus defined as the need of an algorithm for creating those matrices of correlated values. Ideally, generated matrices must be different each time while maintaining a common specific geometry among them. Procedural algorithms found in the literature can be particularly useful but also complex and time consuming. In contrast to the use of graphs and other complex data structures, we have proposed to use a stack to achieve desired characteristics in automatically generated matrices of correlated values. In this paper, we present the results of the evaluation of this proposal. Specifically, we show how changing hyper-parameters in our approach, we are up to controlling the resulting geometry of 2D maps. The results show that it was possible to successfully generate fractal geometry resembling the box fractal, tree-like geometry in the style of L-System, and caves like those obtained with cellular automata. The obtained results were compared with the findings of other authors. In all cases, results were similar, but the computational complexity of our solution was always lower. Finally, our approach has been successfully used in the generation of three 2D maps deployed in the Godot Engine.

KEYWORDS

2D Map Generation, Procedural Algorithms, Matrix of Correlated Values, Stack Data Structure

1. INTRODUCTION

Procedural Content Generation (PCG) is a well-established concept, dating back to the 1980 game Rogue, recognized as a pioneering example (Toy et al., 1980). PCG involves a range of techniques for dynamic and autonomous content creation, reshaping the landscape of video game development (Dahrén, 2021). These techniques evolve in tandem with video games, incorporating a diverse array of methods and algorithms with varying levels of computational complexity. They are employed to generate a variety of elements in video games, including terrain, music, textures, characters, dialogues, and more (Melotti & Moraes, 2019).

The entertainment industry leverages procedural generation to craft more diverse and creative content to meet demand (Viana & Santos, 2021). Due to its size and resources, this industry often invests a significant portion of its resources in the research and development of proprietary procedural algorithms (Amato, 2017) (Hollstrand, 2020). On the other hand, independent developers or small teams face the challenge of generating more content with limited resources. This compels them to explore new alternatives that are quick and straightforward to incorporate into their workflow (Hollstrand, 2020).

Algorithm design is conditioned by the requirements of the specific video game, resulting in a variety of proposals with different approaches (Dahrén, 2021). Procedural generation techniques often focus on predictable and controllable outcomes, as seen in some studies (Abraham & Stephenson, 2023). These alternatives are based on artificial intelligence algorithms. However, the computational complexity of these algorithms is high and, consequently, computationally expensive (Hollstrand, 2020). Other researchers have focused on innovative, less complex solutions, for procedural generation (Lipinski et al., 2019) (Johnson et al., 2010) (Macedo & Chaimowicz, 2017) (Putra et al., 2023) (Linden et al., 2014). Some solutions involve the use of graphs (Lipinski et al., 2019), computational models like cellular automata (Johnson et al., 2010), and fractals (Putra et al., 2023), to generate the corresponding structure of the respective video game map.

Fractal geometry, renowned for its intricate and visually appealing forms, is studied and applied to address various issues in different fields. Its application spans from the artistic realm (Alghar et al., 2023), through electronics (Li et al., 2024), cybersecurity (Ayubi et al., 2020) (Chang et al., 2023), to procedural generation in video games (Putra et al., 2023) (Linden et al., 2014). Creating fractals involves using iterative functions and elementary rules, significantly reducing algorithmic complexity compared to other alternatives found in the literature (Macedo & Chaimowicz, 2017).

This research focuses on developing an algorithm based on a stack data structure for storing data. By adjusting hyperparameters, this algorithm can produce different geometric configurations, including fractal geometry. These arrangements can be highly useful in 2D map generation, offering a variety of landscapes and topographic features to enhance the user experience. This paper is structured as follows. Section 2 briefly explores related research with different approaches to this topic. Section 3 introduces the proposed approach. Section 4 presents the results of the experiments that were carried out. Finally, we come to conclusions in section 5.

2. RELATED WORKS

The procedural generation of maps for video games is the subject of numerous research efforts, each addressing a specific aspect and proposing diverse and innovative solutions. Zakaria et al.'s (2023) introduce a novel approach to training map generators without an initial dataset. They employ a learning method adaptable to multiple sizes, and denser feedback at smaller sizes eliminates the need for an initial dataset. Moreno et al. (2022) presents a solution based on a hybrid algorithm for procedural generation, combining reinforcement learning and stochastic content generation methods.

The use of genetic algorithms can be an alternative for generating controlled content. Brown et al.'s (2018) focus on implementing these algorithms for creating playable levels for the game "Hotline Miami 2". Meanwhile, Melotti and Moraes (2019) used genetic algorithms for dungeon generation. They modified the fitness function by incorporating diversity as a metric to achieve superior efficiency with similar results. However, their generation process faces challenges inherent to the complexity of genetic algorithms, particularly in terms of performance.

Johnson, Yannakakis and Togelius (2010) proposed the use of cellular automata for efficient real time dungeon generation. This proposal was validated in the creation of games with infinite caves, generating playable maps based on tunnels. However, the output of cellular automata is a binary matrix, which requires additional processing for coherent item placement within tunnels. Other approaches focus on the use of data structures. Pereira et al. (2021) utilized a tree to generate maps requiring environmental information control, essential for mission-based games. On the other hand, Lipinski et al. (2019) focused on the use of graphs for 2D map generation. They proposed three algorithms centered on calculating a minimum spanning tree and edge insertion. Their approach avoids the need for costly matrix operations. However, their approach requires an additional transformation of resulting data to get the actual geometric representation of assets in a 2D map.

Solutions found in literature strive not to be overly complex. Nevertheless, it is important to notice some relevant gaps in their solutions. Lipinski et al. (2019) highlights the need to generate a base graph and process it to connect and correct undesirable irregularities to achieve the expected result. Johnson et al. (2010) require at least four iterations to attain the desired outcome. On the other hand, the approach of Putra et al. (2023) involves recursive functions, which increase the computational costs of the solution. In summary, other works in literature use complex data structures. Using simpler data structures in an algorithm relying on fewer iterations could significantly decrease the computational cost of the 2D map generation.

3. MATERIALS AND METHODS

This research is focused on the definition of an algorithm for distributing correlated values in a 2D space from a seed value. We experimentally evaluated the capabilities of this algorithm. Further, we compared the results with the alternatives we have found in the literature. Following, we analyze the main characteristics of the algorithm, before documenting the results of the experiments that were carried out.

3.1 The Algorithm

The algorithm we propose is named Downfall Seed Spread Algorithm (DSSA). Its formal definition is shown in figure 1. DSSA is structured in three main facets. Firstly, *the value correlation*, which is conducted to generate new values from existing ones. This process ensures that each value maintains a specific relationship with other values, allowing their classification. Secondly, *neighborhood and local rules* which impact the overall dynamics of the rendering process. They imply the selection of values to be managed during the rendering process. Finally, *storage management* determines the way in which data is stored, yielding various geometric shapes in the resulting outcome.

Algorithm 1 Main

$$\alpha = \begin{pmatrix} 0 & 0 & \dots & 0 \\ 0 & 0 & \dots & 0 \\ \vdots & \vdots & \ddots & \vdots \\ 0 & 0 & \dots & 0 \end{pmatrix}_{m \times n}$$

$\delta \leftarrow [\epsilon, i, j]$
$stack \leftarrow []$
$stack.append(\delta)$
while $stack$ has elements **do**
  $\delta \leftarrow stack.pop()$
  $\delta_\epsilon \leftarrow Correlation(\delta_\epsilon)$
  if $\delta_\epsilon \geq \kappa$ **then**
    if $0 < \delta_i < m - 1$ **then**
      if $0 < \delta_j < n - 1$ **then**
        $\nu \leftarrow Neighborhood(\delta)$
        $LocalRules(\nu)$
        $Storage(\nu)$
      end if
    end if
  end if
end while

Figure 1. Formal definition of the main procedure of DSSA

The range of values incorporated into α is intrinsically related to the process to which ϵ is tied. The function established for calculating new values from ϵ is crucial as it determines the multiplicity and spatial deployment of each value. If the function produces values that are intricately correlated, categorizing the resulting values in α can also pose more challenges. In other words, with more complex relationships between the generated values comes a more intricate task of organizing and understanding those values.

3.2 Value Correlation

Based on it, an arithmetic progression function was defined as: *SimpleCorrelation(ϵ)* : $\epsilon \leftarrow \epsilon - C$, where C is a threshold value for the classification of values in α into assets. When replacing generated values with assets in a video game, the value to be used for transitioning from one range to another one would be $C \times d$, where d is the covered range distance.

On the other hand, a stochastic correlation function was also defined. By using *StochasticCorrelation()*, the entropy of the final result is higher. This function determines the distance between the value of ϵ and its initial value. If the calculated distance has a value that is less than the threshold θ, then ϵ is reset to its initial value. Otherwise, the arithmetic progression function determines its value.

3.3 Neighborhood and Local Rules

The neighborhood refers to the contiguous spaces in α with respect to a position (i, j). Using the Von Neumann neighborhood (Chen et al., 2005), the immediate neighbors are positioned up, down, left, and right. The neighborhood ν of a given value δ is calculated based on Chen et al. considerations.

Local rules were defined to determine which values, of the neighbors in ϵ, are included in α, and which values of the neighbors in ν will be subsequently added to the stack. Two main rules were established. The first rule states that a neighbor is added to the stack if its value in ϵ is equal to zero. The alternative rule determines that, if the absolute value of the normalized difference between the values specified in function local() is greater than the threshold λ, then, the neighbor will be added to the stack (see figure 2).

$\epsilon \leftarrow neighbor_\epsilon$
$i \leftarrow neighbor_i$
$j \leftarrow neighbor_j$
$value \leftarrow \alpha_{i=i;j=j}$
if $value == 0$ **then**
  $\alpha_{i=i;j=j} \leftarrow \epsilon$
else
  $sum \leftarrow \epsilon + value$
  $\epsilon \leftarrow \epsilon / sum$
  $value \leftarrow value/sum$
  $diff \leftarrow |\epsilon - value|$
  if $diff \geq \lambda$ **then**
    $\alpha_{i=i;j=j} \leftarrow \epsilon \times (1 - diff)$
  else
    $\nu.delete(neighbor)$
  end if
end if

Figure 2. Definition of local rules in DSSA

As the difference is normalized, λ takes values between *0* and *1*. A value closer to *1* implies that a larger difference is required for the neighbor to be added to the stack, and the value in α is updated based on how significant the difference is.

3.4 Storage Management

The defined storage order functions take ν as a parameter. Then, they separate its values under the assumption that they are in the order A, B, C, D. If ν is passed with its elements in a different order, the result may differ from the expected outcome even if the storage order is appropriate. Two initial storage orders were defined: 1) $A \xrightarrow{then} B \xrightarrow{then} C \xrightarrow{then} D$ and 2) $C \xrightarrow{then} B \xrightarrow{then} D \xrightarrow{then} A$. By rotating the order, three additional storage orders were defined, resulting in four base storage orders.

The selection of one of the eight resulting orders proves useful in constructing diverse configurations while maintaining low algorithmic complexity. It is possible to define additional sorting criteria by combining the basic ones. The result is a nested storage order criterion. We have experimentally evaluated the following storage orders: 4 sequential basic storage orders, 2 sequential basic clockwise storage orders, and 1 sequential of sequentials storage order. Those storage orders were formalized as: SBA ← BC, BA, BD, BB; SBB ← BB, BC, BA, BD; SBC ← BD, BB, BC, BA; SBD ← BA, BD, BB, BC; SBAc ← BAc, BCc, BBc, BDc; SBBc ← BAc, BBc, BCc, BDc; SSA ← SBC, SBA, SBD, SBB. Two other orders were also considered. First, the stochastic order, arrange neighbors within ν in a random order. Lastly, the deterministic order, arrange neighbors within ν as BA, BB, BC, or BD depending on the divisibility of the value in ϵ of the neighbor in the first position of ν. All these criteria were experimentally proved, and they all generated stable configurations. With BA as a chosen criterion, the corresponding procedure for data storage was defined as function storage(), shown in figure 3.

$$
\begin{aligned}
&A, B, C, D \leftarrow \nu \\
&BA \rightarrow C, B, D, A \\
&\nu \leftarrow BA \\
&stack.push(\nu)
\end{aligned}
$$

Figure 3. Definition of the procedure to store data in DSSA

4. ANALYSIS OF THE RESULTS

There is a diversity of 2D maps that can be generated just by adjusting the value of the hyper-parameters. Here, five different setups are included for showing the results of the experimental validation that was carried out. Values of customized hyper-parameters are depicted in table 1. All these setups used $\kappa = 1$, $\epsilon = 100$ and $\lambda = 1$.

Table 1. Experiments setup configuration

N.	Operator	C	m,n	i	j	Storage
1	Substraction	1	100	m-2	m-2	BA
2	Substraction	0.2	200	m/2	m/2	SBBc
3	Substraction	1.6	100	m/2	m/2	SBAc
4	Substraction	0.6	100	20	n-10	SSA
5	Substraction	0.85	100	m/2	m/2	Stochastic

By using setup 1, a tree-like generation was achieved. The result is comparable to a tree-like generation using the L-system proposed by Juhari and Alghar (2021), as depicted in figure 4 (a). Setup 3 was used for creating shapes similar to a box fractal – see figure 4 (b). The result corresponds to a box fractal generated with Wolfram Alpha in five iterations. On the other hand, setup 4 allowed to reproduce the results of Lipinski, as shown in figure 4 (c). Contrary to the outcome when using setup 3, the output includes the geometric intersection of incident edges, particularly rectangular edges.

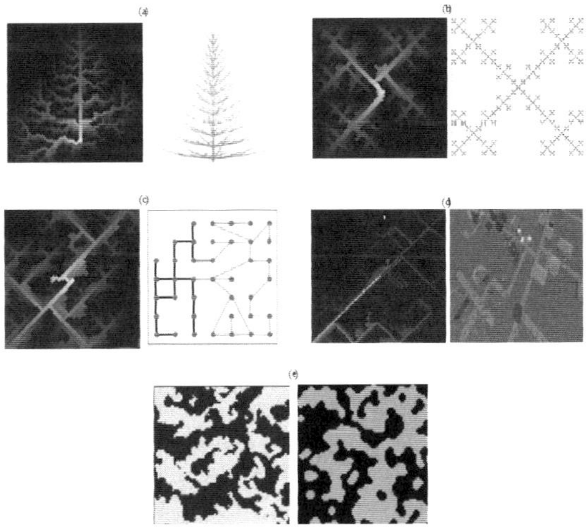

Figure 4. Five experiment results. Our results are presented on the left and the corresponding result from the literature, for each case, is presented on the right

Lipinski uses a graph to manage the connections among edges. He manages the expansion of the abstract model based on a tree data structure. The outcome with our approach not only bears similarities but also offers advantages which are twofold. Firstly, the performance is significantly better when using simpler data structures. Secondly, our matrix allows a direct interpretation into the actual geometry to deploy. For Lipinski, a final transformation is required in order to obtain a polygonal model.

Setup 2 allows to create a corridor geometry, which is the key for linking various spaces or rooms together, following the idea of Dahlskog et al. (2015). This is a fundamental aspect in a number of games, including *Ultima*, *The Battle for Wesnoth*, *Shadowrun: Dragonfall*, *Endless Legend*, and *Minecraft*. Figure 4 (d) shows the result of running this algorithm with setup 2, in comparison to corridors, as they are built up in *Minecraft*. While these results do not exhibit exact similarity to those in the literature, it is noticeable that the distinctive pattern of each case is present. To make sure of cave-type generations, the stochastic order was employed. This result is of the kind obtained by Macedo et al. (2017) and Johnson et al. (2010). They both proposed to use cellular automats which is a far more expensive alternative even when obtaining similar results, as shown in figure 4 (e).

Figure 5 (a) shows the interpretation of the correlation matrix by allocating a color to each cell, in correspondence to the actual value that it contains. This result was obtained using setup 5 from table 1. By modifying λ, it is feasible to obtain a result with varying degrees of noise. Figure 5 (b) demonstrates, for cave-type generations, the result with $\lambda = 0.62$ whilst figure 5 (c) shows the result obtained with $\lambda = 0.98$.

Figure 5. Variations in the configuration. (a) Noise generation with setup 5. (b) Noise generation with $\lambda = 0.62$. (c) Noise generation with $\lambda = 0.98$.

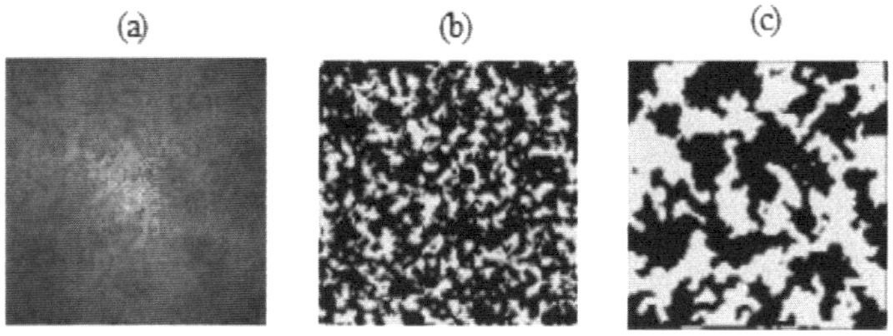

Figure 5. Variations in the configuration. (a) Noise generation with setup 5. (b) Noise generation with $\lambda = 0.62$. (c) Noise generation with $\lambda = 0.98$

Two different hardware configurations were used for demonstrating the applicability of the proposed algorithm in building 2D maps. The first one was a laptop with a CPU Intel i7-8750H, GPU Intel UHD Graphics 630 and 2959 MiB of RAM. The second one was a desktop with a CPU Intel i7- 12700, GPU Intel AlderLake-S GT1 and 15671 MiB of RAM. In both cases, the operating system was Pop!OS 22.04 LTS of 64bits with Godot Engine 4.2 and OpenGL 4.6. Time that it took for rendering the maps was between 150mS and 190mS for the laptop and between 10 and 30 mS for the desktop.

The first two maps in figure 6 (a) and figure 6 (b), respectively, include grass blocks, chests, pillars, stone slabs, and a fountain. Each element has a defined range that controls its location and the probability of spawning within that range. Chests are placed at the end of the path, as rewards, grass blocks are positioned so as not to interfere with the player's route, stone slabs define the area where the player can move, pillars represent items that can appear as player explores, and the fountain represents player's re-spawn point.

The third map, in figure 6 (c), was built using the stochastic order. Ranges are defined and replaced with assets, as needed. In this map, rock and diamond blocks are placed within the range designated as the area where the player cannot move. Dirt slabs are the space where the player can move, and cherries are reward items. Diamonds do not appear on the path but on the rocks, and cherries do not appear on the rocks but on the path where the player has the possibility to find them.

By directly substituting the values of the matrix with assets, we can derive a straightforward top-down 2D game, delineating specific scopes for each set of assets. Nevertheless, the matrix can also be utilized for crafting maps utilized in games such as SMITE, particularly in game modes like joust or assault. To accomplish this, we establish two distinct scopes, partitioning the matrix into two exclusive sections: one dedicated to the pathway where each team will traverse and engage in combat, and the remaining segment, where the developer has the liberty to position the remaining items within the context of the game mode. In this scenario, the matrix values will be replaced not by assets (tiles commonly used in 2D video games) but by pivots of the 3D objects.

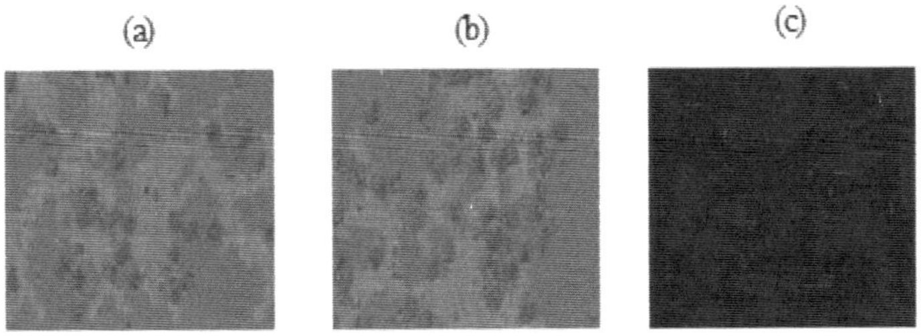

Figure 6. Generated 2D Maps. (a) Noise generation with setup 5. (b) Noise generation with $\lambda = 0.62$. (c) Noise generation with $\lambda = 0.98$

5. CONCLUSIONS

The proposed algorithm was successfully used in the generation of three different types of maps. This result includes tree-like maps, corridor geometry using SBA storage criteria, and cave maps using stochastic correlation function. In all cases, the existing alternatives found in the literature are computationally more complex and significantly more expensive. The successful render of three 2D maps for videogames was achieved through the implementation of algorithm 1 in the Godot Engine.

In summary, the main contribution of this work is threefold. Firstly, the algorithm complexity has been reduced by splitting the generation procedure into 1) correlation, 2) neighborhood and local rules, and 3) storage management. Secondly, the flexibility of the generation process was increased by using thirteen hyper-parameters which customize the output type. Thirdly, the simplicity achieved using a stack instead of more complex data structures used in previous research.

ACKNOWLEDGEMENT

We acknowledge that the *Dirección de Investigación y Desarrollo* (DIDE), from the *Universidad Técnica de Ambato*, has funded this research.

REFERENCES

Abraham, F., & Stephenson, M. a. (2023). Utilizing generative adversarial networks for stable structure generation in angry birds. *Proceedings of the AAAI Conference on Artificial Intelligence and Interactive Digital Entertainment*, (pp. 2-12). https://doi.org/10.1609/aiide.v19i1.27496

Alghar, M. Z., Walidah, N. Z., & Marhayati, M. (2023). Ethnomathematics: The exploration of fractal geometry in Tian Ti Pagoda using the Lindenmayer system. *Alifmatika: Jurnal Pendidikan dan Pembelajaran Matematika*, 5(1) 57-69. 10.35316/alifmatika.2023.v5i1.57-69

Amato, A. (2017). Procedural content generation in the game industry. *Game Dynamics: Best Practices in Procedural and Dynamic Game Content Generation*, 15-25. 10.1007/978-3-319-53088-8_2

Ayubi, P., Setayeshi, S., & Rahmani, A. M. a. (2020). Deterministic chaos game: a new fractal based pseudo-random number generator and its cryptographic application. *Journal of Information Security and Applications*. https://doi.org/10.1016/j.jisa.2020.102472

Brown, J. A., Lutfullin, B., Oreshin, P., & Pyatkin, I. (2018). Levels for hotline miami 2: Wrong number using procedural content generations. *Computers*, 22. https://doi.org/10.3390/computers7020022

Chang, H., Wang, E., & Liu, J. a. (2023). Research on Image Encryption Based on Fractional Seed Chaos Generator and Fractal Theory. *Fractal and Fractional*. https://doi.org/10.3390/fractalfract7030221

Chen, R.-J., & Lai, J.-L. a. (2005). Data encryption using non-uniform 2-D von neumann cellular automata. *2005 9th International Workshop on Cellular Neural Networks and Their Applications*, (pp. 77-80). 10.1109/CNNA.2005.1543165

Dahlskog, S., Björk, S., & Togelius, J. (2015). Patterns, Dungeons and Generators. Presented at the Foundations of Digital Games Conference, FDG, Pacific Grove, U.S.A. (2015). Retrieved from https://urn.kb.se/resolve?urn=urn:nbn:se:mau:diva-16749

Dahrén, M. (2021). The Usage of PCG Techniques Within Different Game Genres (Dissertation). Retrieved from https://urn.kb.se/resolve?urn=urn:nbn:se:mau:diva-46422

Hollstrand, P. (2020). Supporting Pre-Production in Game Development : Process Mapping and Principles for a Procedural Prototyping Tool (Dissertation). Retrieved from https://urn.kb.se/resolve?urn=urn:nbn:se:kth:diva-273926

Johnson, L., Yannakakis, G. N., & Togelius, J. a. (2010). Cellular automata for real-time generation of infinite cave levels. *PCGames@FDG*. 10.1145/1814256.1814266

Li, R., Wang, Z., Wu, Z., Ni, J., He, L., Xiong, M., Kong, M., & Zhang, J. a. (2024). Enhanced cooling performance of stacked chips by structural modification for fractal micro-protrusions. *Applied Thermal Engineering*. https://doi.org/10.1016/j.applthermaleng.2023.121416

Linden, R. V., Lopes, R., & Bidarra, R. (2014). Procedural Generation of Dungeons. *IEEE Transactions on Computational Intelligence and AI in Games*. 10.1109/TCIAIG.2013.2290371

Lipinski, B., Seibt, S., Roth, J., & Abe, D. a. (2019). Level graph-incremental procedural generation of indoor levels using minimum spanning trees. *2019 IEEE Conference on Games (CoG)*, (pp. 1-7). 10.1109/CIG.2019.8847956

Macedo, Y. P., & Chaimowicz, L. (2017). Improving procedural 2D map Generation based on multi-layered cellular automata and Hilbert curves. *2017 16th Brazilian Symposium on Computer Games and Digital Entertainment (SBGames)*, (pp. 116-125). 10.1109/SBGames.2017.00021

Melotti, A. S., & Moraes, C. D. d. (2019). Evolving Roguelike Dungeons With Deluged Novelty Search Local Competition. *IEEE Transactions on Games*. 10.1109/TG.2018.2859424

Moreno-Armendariz, M. A., Calvo, H., Torres-Leon, J. A., & Duchanoy, C. A. (2022). IORand: A Procedural Videogame Level Generator Based on a Hybrid PCG Algorithm. *Applied Sciences*, 3792. https://doi.org/10.3390/app12083792

Putra, P. A., Tarigan, J. T., & Zamzami, E. M. (2023). Procedural 2D Dungeon Generation Using Binary Space Partition Algorithm And L-Systems. *2023 International Conference on Computer, Control, Informatics and its Applications (IC3INA)*, (pp. 365-369). 10.1109/IC3INA60834.2023.10285811

Toy, M., Wichman, G., Arnold, K., & Lane, J. (1980). Rogue. *Comput. Sci. Res. Group UC Berkeley*.

Viana, B. M. F., & Santos, S. R. d. (2021). Procedural Dungeon Generation: A Survey. *Journal on Interactive Systems*. https://doi.org/10.5753/jis.2021.999

Zakaria, Y., Fayek, M., & Hadhoud, M. (2023). Start small: Training controllable game level generators without training data by learning at multiple sizes. *Alexandria Engineering Journal*, 479-494. https://doi.org/10.1016/j.aej.2023.04.019

REHASHING STORYTELLING IN THE MOBILE GAME: 'WALKING DEAD MATCH 3 TALES' CASE

JaeJun Lee and Soyoun Eom
Department of Game Design, School of Arts, Sungkyunkwan University
Seoul, Korea

ABSTRACT

In game development, leveraging well-known intellectual properties (IPs) for rapid development and effective marketing is widely practiced. However, this necessitates deriving a producing strategy that ensures both effective game design and synergy with the chosen IP. Particularly, devising a strategy to incorporate the storyline of the original IP into the game involves determining how it can seamlessly integrate with interactions and storytelling in gameplay, assessing the compatibility of the game content structure and gameplay environment with storytelling, and aligning with the core fun elements pursued by game designers. This paper discusses the decision-making process involved in rehashing the story of "The Walking Dead" to create a new game of puzzle and RPG hybrid genre, considering the aforementioned three aspects. It argues that the process of story rehashing serves as a strategic choice for applying the IP to mobile gaming.

KEYWORDS

Mobile Game, Storytelling, Ludology, Narratology, Puzzle

1. INTRODUCTION

The mobile game is one of the mainstream platforms in the gaming market, alongside PC and consoles. Most mobile games are offered for free, generating revenue through purchases of new stories, maps, or other gameplay-altering features (Sužnjević et al., 2022), or by displaying advertisements. Due to the vast number of free games available, there are limited opportunities for a game to be discovered in the app market and players who download a game often either never launch it or abandon it after just a few days. Therefore, game developers seek to minimize risks by producing games with minimal resources and as quickly as possible. Additionally, game publishers strive to increase marketing efficiency. The strategy of creating enhanced versions of games based on widely recognized IPs with proven game design is employed to mitigate such risks.

The development team in the case study has decided to create a game that combines elements of Match3 puzzles with RPG mechanics, utilizing the "Walking Dead Comics" as its thematic basis. Each stage of the game consists of Match3 puzzles. The game operates on a mechanism where successfully matching puzzle blocks enables the player to attack foes, and upon clearing a stage, the storyline unfolds.

To use "The Walking Dead" in a game, it is necessary to discuss the game design with the comic book publisher, Skybound. The two companies quickly agreed on mechanics, including how the puzzle would work and the mechanic of management of shelters in the game. Following this, the development team designed a storytelling strategy. To incorporate the universe of "The Walking Dead" into a mobile game, the game developer designed the environment, building, and character art styles. Finally, the developer designed the story content and its narrative structure. During this process, a storytelling strategy suitable for the game design was discussed. This paper is a retrospective on the process of deriving the storytelling strategy for "Walking Dead: Match3 Tales."

2. GAME PLATFORM AND FEATURES

In the winter of 2019, the design process for "Walking Dead: Match3 Tales" began. The companies behind the development, Novacore, and Com2US, are specialized in mobile game development and publishing. Consequently, "Walking Dead: Match3 Tales" was designed as a game for mobile platforms. There were disagreements between the IP holder, Skybound, and the developers regarding the use of the original story from the Walking Dead comics. Therefore, the developers analyzed the game platform and its features to summarize the characteristics of games designed for mobile platforms.

The developer analyzed the characteristics of game platforms based on the level of portability and the level of connectivity. The graph's Y-axis represents the level of portability, while the X-axis indicates the level of connectivity. This arrangement naturally associates the level of portability with the level of immersion. Lower portability corresponds to higher immersion, whereas higher portability typically leads to lower immersion. Similarly, a lower level of connectivity tends to result in game content that is focused on strong storylines and game mechanics derived from interactions with the game system. On the other hand, games with a higher level of connectivity are designed around mechanics that arise from interactions among users, as well as competition and collaboration emerging from the user community.

Offline PC or console games, which are enjoyed without internet connection, tend to offer high immersion, and engage players with solo-oriented game content. Notable examples of such games include The Last of Us (Naughty Dog, 2013). Platforms that offer moderate portability and networking capabilities include handheld gaming devices such as the Nintendo DS, Nintendo Switch, and PlayStation VITA. Games like Pokémon (Game Freak, 1996) and Welcome Park (Sony Interactive Entertainment, 2011) are examples of this category.

Games with no portability but moderate connectivity, often referred to as 'network games,' include those that offer both storytelling content and user interaction. A representative example is the Starcraft series (Blizzard, 1998). For online PC games, League of Legends (Riot Games, 2009) serves as an example, designed primarily for user interaction rather than narrative-driven gameplay.

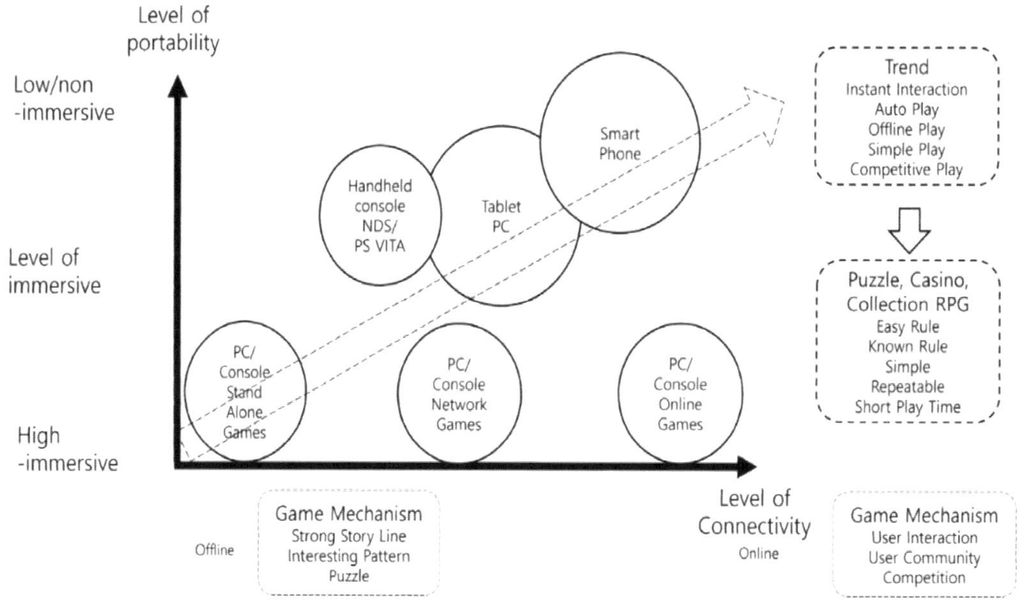

Figure 1. Game Platforms and Features

In Figure 1, moving along the upward diagonal indicates decreasing immersion and increasing connectivity. An example of a gaming platform with these attributes is a tablet and smartphone, and games for this platform are characterized by instant interaction, autoplay, offline play, simple & easy mechanics, and competitive play. These games are designed to be played on the move, which means that gameplay can be interrupted at any time, whether from losing connectivity or from interactions with other users online that can alter the play of the game. Furthermore, calls or various push notifications can disrupt gameplay. For this reason, mobile games are designed with easy-known rules and offer relatively simple and repeatable game mechanics for short play times compared to other platforms.

3. STORYTELLING FOR GAMES

In comparison to other media, the study of video game storytelling is not straightforward when considering interactivity and ludic activities (Tekinbas & Zimmerman, 2003). Unlike films and comics, video games include an element of interaction, and sometimes the objectives of gameplay take precedence over those of storytelling.

Scholars who study games with a narrative focus argue that simulations and games are closely related to narrative, and that even the experience of playing a game without a story is a narrative for the player. Video games have rules for players to follow and scenarios designed by game designers, and players play the game within the confines of the game designer's design. Therefore, even if the play is centered around ludic activities, it is still following a given scenario. Games that prioritize storytelling include The Elder Scrolls V: Skyrim (Bethesda Softworks LLC, 2011), Dragon Age: Inquisition (EA, 2014), Mass Effect 3 (Bioware, 2012), Assassins Creed: Unity (Ubisoft, 2014), and Batman: Arkham Origins (WB Games Montreal, 2013) (Eakins, 2017).

On the other hand, a radical Ludologist believes that everything but pure game mechanics is secondary to the essentials of game aesthetics (Klevjer, 2022). Games centered on gameplay include various puzzle games like Bejeweled (PopCap Games, 2000), Tetris (Alexey, 1985), and various board and card games, as well as player-versus-player focused games like Overwatch (Blizzard, 2016) and League of Legends (Riot Games, 2009).

This debate between narratologists and ludologists is long-standing, and recent efforts have been made to harmonize gameplay and narrative (Kokonis, M. 2014). Even gameplay-centric games like "Overwatch" and "League of Legends" incorporate story elements that focus on individual characters, and our case study game, while designed around game mechanics, has also invested heavily in narrative presentation.

4. STORYTELLING FOR THE WALKING DEAD:MATCH3 TALES

"Walking Dead: Match3 Tales" does not feature storytelling elements directly linked to user interaction. Instead, the game reveals the story after players clear a stage, and then players use the rewards they've earned to construct shelters. The user's attention is divided among the key gameplay elements: battle, shelter construction, and storytelling.

The storytelling in "Walking Dead: Match3 Tales" is conducted through animated comic-style sequences, paneled character dialogues, and text displayed over various backgrounds (Figure 2, Figure 3, and Figure 4). To enhance the immersive experience for players, voice recordings of the characters were made, and expressive facial animations are provided. However, players do not have the option to influence the story by making choices or selecting dialogues. The story progresses linearly. Players must clear stages if they wish to continue viewing the story.

Figure 2. Comic-style sequences

Figure 3. Paneled character dialogues

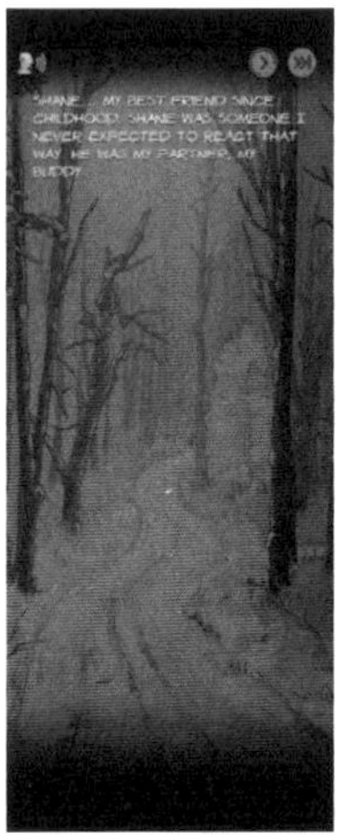

Figure 4. Text displayed over background

"The Walking Dead" has been developed into various forms of transmedia, including The Walking Dead Series (AMC Studio, 2010), The Walking Dead: A Telltale Games Series (Telltale Games, 2012) and OVERKILL's The Walking Dead (Overkill Software, 2018). Each of these adaptations features independent storylines based on the "The Walking Dead" universe. Also, The Walking Dead: Survival Instinct (Terminal Reality, 2013), published by Activision, acts as a prequel to the TV series. Although most transmedia adaptations have their own independent stories, the director of this game decided to rehash an existing storyline for the following reasons.

4.1 Author driven Storytelling

The main difference in storytelling between passive and interactive media is the exposure of key information to advance the story (Damraska, 2022). This perspective can similarly be applied to the distinction between author-driven and user-driven storytelling. In author-driven storytelling, withholding some key information allows the author to move the game in a predetermined direction, but in user-driven storytelling, missing key information prevents the user from making important decisions. It's hard to convey all the key information in a mobile game, and as a result, it's hard to design user-driven storytelling. To fill this information gap, cutscenes, a one-way storytelling method, are used to provide key information to the player (Eskelinen, 2001) A key difference between passive and interactive media is the presentation of important information to tell the story.

Narratives are models of how individuals behave (Cooren, 2000; Czarniawska, 1997), how they construct reality (Weick,1995), and how they think and learn (Bruner, 1960; Schank, 1990). It organizes everything that entered in the brain, gives them meaning, and creates it (McManus & Feinstein, 2006). Therefore, narrative is the form, wherein we organize our experiences and memories (Bruner, 1960). In short, narrative helps individuals construct knowledge through a process of recursivity (Robichaud et al., 2004). The interaction and engagement of games are key to reinforcing this recursivity and are an important element in organizing experience and memory (Jones,1989;1990).

The gameplay for "Walking Dead: Match3 Tales" was already set before the storytelling strategy was developed. The developer did not try to change anything because the developer thought it was the right way to tell a story for mobile. The game has a single story, and it is linear. Players can experience story as a reward for clearing stages. There's no story interaction, and the core mechanics of the game are all about puzzle play. The development team questioned whether they could tell a new story in this way, and wanted to create a balance between gameplay and narrative. Gameplay and story battle for the player's attention (Eakins, 2017). Interaction can distract users and negatively impact their understanding of the story (Ryan, 2011). Additionally, the storytelling method chosen for this game, similar to cutscenes that are not related to user control, fails to meaningfully integrate story and gameplay (Gallagher, 2015). To effectively combine gameplay and story, key dialogues or plot points should be incorporated into gameplay controlled by the user, fostering harmony and enabling players to engage with the game interaction while simultaneously understanding the story (Eakins, 2017). This approach doesn't tell a new story because it can be skipped or unfocused by users.

4.2 Short Length of Session

In comparison to home theaters, viewers who watch films in movie theaters experience a more intense emotional response and tend to have a more favorable opinion of the films (Fröber & Thomaschke, 2021). The immersive environment of movie theaters, isolated from external distractions, enhances the viewing experience. A similar logic can be applied to the storytelling in games, which requires a focused environment and time for players to fully comprehend the narrative. However, mobile games, due to their high portability and connectivity, naturally make it difficult for players to concentrate on content. As a result, mobile games often feature mechanisms that are straightforward and increasingly sophisticated, and they tend to have shorter length of session (Korea Creative Content Agency, 2024). The average session length for mobile games is 30.33 minutes (Adjust, 2023), with casual and puzzle games typically having shorter session lengths than the average (Table1).

The developers expected that each session would last between 10 to 15 minutes considering the game design, during which players would engage in puzzle play and shelter-building activities. It was predicted that about 5 minutes of each session would be dedicated to viewing the story. Additionally, it was anticipated that players would initiate the next session after an interval of 3 to 4 hours. Delivering new story content in 5-minute intervals separated by 3 to 4 hours poses a challenge for effectively conveying and ensuring comprehension of the new narrative elements.

Table 1. Mobile Games length of by genre 2022 (Adjust, 2024)

Genre	Length of session
Puzzle	**30 minutes**
Card	**27 minutes**
Casino	**26 minutes**
Casual	**22 minutes**
Learning	**27 minutes**
RPG	**41 minutes**
Strategy	**33 minutes**
Quiz	**14 minutes**

4.3 Ludic Experience First

The director of the “Walking Dead: Match3 Tales” prioritized the ludic experience over the narrative experience, employing a strategy of "ludic experience first, narrative experience second." By the agreement with the development team, an unnamed reference game combined puzzle and town-building elements. Referenced games provide a narrative at the beginning of the game, with paneled characters appearing from the left and right sides of the screen and having a conversation. Other than the opening, no contents provide a meaningful narrative.

The core mechanic of the game is to clear stages by attacking enemies and triggering the character's skills through match3 puzzles. Players progressed by clearing stages, collecting resources to nurture and combine characters, and forming a battle squad to achieve victory in combat. The end content of the game involved asynchronous online battles against stage-based systems or other players' battle squads. As the game progressed, it evolved from one-on-one duels to team battles.

Based on these references, "Walking Dead: Match3 Tales" was designed to enhance competition among players. Upon entering the game, players were immediately shown a list of other users who had attacked their shelter, with a "Revenge" button available for immediate retaliation. Successful revenge would mostly reclaim stolen resources, and even if revenge failed, the game continuously provided opportunities for revenge to increase the chances of winning battles. Some stages following a predetermined story were designed to set opponents based on other players' battle squad information retrieved from the game server, allowing for natural player-versus-player encounters.

Consequently, players focused on efficiently destroying other players' squads to plunder resources, regardless of the narrative. Players concentrated on acquiring characters and maximizing the battle squad's combat effectiveness through match-3 puzzle gameplay, irrespective of the narrative aspect.

5. ADDITIONAL CHARACTERS

Even though strictly adhering to the original comics, "Walking Dead: Match3 Tales" introduced additional characters, Morris and Tuny (Figure 5 and Figure 6), who do not interfere with the main story plot. In line with Ludic's experience first strategy, this was necessary for the rules of gameplay rather than to showcase a new story and make the game more interesting.

The game features puzzle blocks with five attributes, and the characters are designed to all have one of the five attributes. When aligning puzzle blocks to attack an enemy, the presence of a character in the battle squad with the same attribute as the aligned block increases the damage done to the enemy. The five types of character attributes were necessary at the beginning of the game for the game's combat balance. However, the original story didn't have a character with the "Brutal" attribute at the beginning. To maintain balance in the game's battle play, Morris was created with the "Brutal" attribute. Additionally, the game system includes a shop that needs a character who manages it, but there was no suitable original character who has a shop manager related background story, leading to the creation of Tuny for this role. While these characters do not impact the main plot, they each have their own stories.

Figure 5. Morris

Figure 6. Tuny

When using the Walking Dead IP for a game in this way, the development team would typically create a story and create new characters. In this case, the story and characters are co-owned by the game developer and the original publisher, Skybound. This is one of the strategies for expanding the Walking Dead universe, which is no longer being expanded upon in the finished comics. "The Walking Dead IP" As Kirkman has stated, "The Walking Dead" universe continues to expand through contributions from external writers (Ruditis, 2011).

6. CONCLUSION

This study discusses cases where famous IP stories are applied to games with mobile platform characteristics and author-driven storytelling structures, along with their implications. When opportunities arise to use well-known IPs, the typical strategy involves creating a story with independent entry points based on a Transmedia strategy. However, crafting a new story based on the characteristics of the game platform and the desired content features of the game requires careful consideration. If the targeted game design prioritizes the ludic experience and the storytelling does not integrate with the player's core interactions, conveying the story becomes challenging. In such cases, newly crafted stories are even more challenging to convey, and if game content such as quests are designed with poorly understood or disconnected stories, player immersion becomes difficult.

"Walking Dead: Match3 Tales" adopts well-known stories as they are, even if fragmented and intermittently told, enabling players to understand the storyline. In gameplay-centric designs, players tend to skip the story. However, using a familiar story allows players to fill in skipped timelines with what they already know. In environments where conveying new stories is challenging, adopting a strategy that leverages the influence of IPs based on user nostalgia with an original storyline approach is possible.

ACKNOWLEDGEMENT

Following are results of a study on the "Leaders in INdustry-university Cooperation 3.0" Project, supported by the Ministry of Education and National Research Foundation of Korea

REFERENCES

Tekinbas, K. S, & Zimmerman, E. (2003). *Rules of Play*. MIT Press, Boston.

Czariawska, B. (1997). *Narrating the organization: Dramas of institutional identity*. University of Chicago Press, Chicago

Weick, K. E. (1995). *Sensemaking in organizations*. Sage publications Thousand Oaks, California, Thousand Oaks, CA: Sage.

Bruner, J. (1960). *The Process of Education*. Harvard University Press, Boston.

Schank, R. C. (1990). *Tell Me a Story*. Northwestern University Press, Evanston

Ruditis, P. (2011). *Walking Dead Chronicles: The Official Companion Book*. NY: Abrams, New York

Sužnjević, M., Miklec, M., & Poštić, S. (2022). Case Study of Player Behaviour in a Mobile Free-to-play Interactive Story Telling Game. *IEEE transactions on games*. Vol. 15, No. 3, pp. 450-459.

Eakins, M. J. (2017). Beyond Panels Interactive Storytelling: Developing a Framework for Highly Emotive Narrative Experiences on Mobile Devices. *University of Central Florida*.

Kokonis, M. (2014). Intermediality between games and fiction: The "ludology vs. narratology" debate in computer game studies: A response to Gonzalo Frasca. *Acta Universitatis Sapientiae, Film and Media Studies*, No.09, pp. 171-188.

Damraksa, A. (2022). Thinking About What Can Still Happen: Character Death, The Walking Dead, and Transmediality's Effect on Creator Autonomy. Diss. *Harvard University*.

Eskelinen, M. (2001). Towards computer game studies. *Digital creativity*, Vol. 12, No. 3, pp. 175-183.

Cooren, F. (2000). The organizing property of communication. *The Organizing Property of Communication*, pp.1-288. Vol. 20, No. 2, pp. 142-151.

Robichaud, D., Giroux, H., & Taylor, J. R. (2004). The Metaconversation: The Recursive Property of Language as a Key to Organizing. *Academy of Management Review*, Vol. 29, No. 4, pp. 617-634.

Jones, K. (1989). Running, or stumbling through, simulation. *Simulation/Game for Learning*, Vol. 19, No. 4, pp. 160-167.

Jones, K. (1990). General activity for management education - a deliberate ambivalent. *Simulation/Game for Learning*, Vol. 20, No.2, pp. 142-151.

Gallagher, R. (2013). Pressing Concerns: Comedy, Interactivity and Buttonless Videogame Interfaces. *Online: < http://static. londonconsortium. com/issue09/Gallagher. pdf>. Data dostępu,* Vol 17.

Fröber, K., & Thomaschke, R. (2021). In the dark cube: Movie theater context enhances the valuation and aesthetic experience of watching films. *Psychology of Aesthetics, Creativity, and the Arts*, Vol. 15, No. 3, pp. 528-544.

Korea Creative Content Agency. (2023). Global Game Industry Trend, *Korea Creative Content Agency,* Vol. 2023 Jan + Feb.

Adjust. (2024). Mobile App Trend 2023. *Adjust.*

Klevjer, R. (2002). In Defense of Cutscenes. *CGDC Conf.* Tampere, Finland, pp. 191-202.

McManus, A. and Feinstein, A. H. (2006). Narratology and ludology: Competing paradigms or complementary theories in simulation." *Developments in Business Simulation and Experiential Learning: Proceedings of the Annual ABSEL conference*. Vol. 33, pp. 363-372.

Ryan, M.-L. (2005). Peeling the onion: Layers of interactivity in digital narrative texts. *Based on a talk presented at the Conference "Interactivity of Digital Texts,"* Münster, Germany.

USING GAMIFICATION FOR TEAMBUILDING, COMMUNICATION AND INNOVATION – RESULTS FROM A LEGO® SERIOUS PLAY® WORKSHOP

Julia Thurner-Irmler and Marietta Menner
STEM_Education Team AMU University Augsburg
Universitätsstraße 1a, 86159 Augsburg, Germany

ABSTRACT

LEGO® Serious Play® constitutes a well-established methodology originally developed within the LEGO® corporation. Among other things, the principle of building with clamping blocks is used to gamify processes in order to promote positive effects – such as the visualization of implicit thoughts. The method finds broad application across various contexts, particularly in strategy and prototype development, as well as team building. A workshop, tailored to the administrative domain, was conducted with a team, and subjected to pre- and post-workshop surveys. The inquiries encompassed attitudes and perspectives towards the team and collaboration. After the workshop, additional questions were posed concerning the participants' perceptions and utilization of the LEGO® Serious Play® methodology. Results indicate a favorable response to the method, notably regarding its efficacy in promoting honest communication and raising awareness of issues within the team. Furthermore, it was perceived that the LEGO® Serious Play® method has the potential to contribute to team members feeling of being more heard and integrated.

KEYWORDS

LEGO® Serious Play®, Gamification, Serious Gaming, Workshop, Teambuilding, Communication

1. INTRODUCTION

In recent years, significant changes have occurred in the work context, primarily driven by new possibilities for collaboration. These include, for example, flexible home office regulations or team meetings that no longer exclusively take place in person but can also be conducted digitally with minimal effort (Bansmann, 2021). Leaders face the challenge of supporting their employees in this process and in developing greater autonomy, while also effectively managing the collaboration among team members (Matzat, 2023). Therefore, team-building measures are more important than ever (Fink & Moeller, 2018). One possible measure is a LEGO® Serious Play® workshop. This represents a gamified method for unleashing creative ideas and unlocking the potential of all individuals within a company or a team (Kristiansen & Rasmussen, 2014).

The term ‘gamification’ was coined by Nick Pelling in 2002, who illustrated examples of integrating game elements into everyday scenarios. This was intended to create higher user-friendliness (Pelling, 2011). A broader definition was established, describing gamification as “the use of game design elements in non-game contexts” (Deterding et al., 2011). This refers to game elements such as levels, leaderboards, or points that can be integrated into the design of measures or media (Betts, 2013). However, gamification is not an object you generate, but it “adds game elements to change a process that already exists to change how that process influences people” (Landers et al., 2018). For example, in the area of team building, playful elements can be incorporated to achieve higher motivation among participants and to connect the intervention with positive emotions, especially since the term ‘team building’ does not always evoke great enthusiasm among employees. Often, it only becomes relevant when collaboration is not going well or when work goals cannot be achieved (Matzat, 2023).

The following paper aims to demonstrate how gamification– using the example of a LEGO® Serious Play® workshop – can be integrated into the development of a team strategy. Firstly, the method itself will be introduced, followed by an explanation of the conducted workshop. Subsequently, the questionnaires filled out by participants before and after the workshop will be presented. This will be followed by the results of these evaluations, along with a discussion and an outlook on further steps related to this topic.

2. WHAT IS LEGO® SERIOUS PLAY®?

The starting point of a LEGO® Serious Play® workshop involves a scenario from which a purposeful question suitable for the method can be derived, along with a group of individuals familiar with the scenario. Based on the question, participants begin to visualize their thoughts using building blocks. Subsequently, each person shares their story and impressions of their created artifact to capture all perspectives of the participants present in the workshop. The intervention concludes with a reflection within the group (Hillmer, 2021; Kristiansen & Rasmussen, 2014). The specific components of a workshop entail the following phases: warm-up, building phase(s), presentation, reflection and interpretation, and next steps. A certain etiquette should be followed, assuming that all responses, none of which are right or wrong, are already present within the system and can only be brought forth by the participants through "expressing themselves and listening to each other" (The LEGO® Group, 2010). When the method is applied in this manner, it also becomes evident that social desirability recedes into the background. Through creative, playful engagement, a fear-free and motivating atmosphere can be created, countering this phenomenon. Thus, even in topics that may trigger fears and reservations among employees (introduction of innovations, digitized work processes, etc.), an environment can be created that motivates and actively engages employees (Kranawetleitner et al., 2022). A LEGO® Serious Play® setting can – ideally – be designed to induce a state of flow among participants. This entails a focus on the task at hand, where space and time are forgotten during its execution, one feels a sense of control, and is intrinsically motivated. The required activity should neither over nor underwhelm (Csikszentmihalyi, 1990). A flow state in a LEGO® Serious Play® workshop can be achieved through a balance between challenge and one's own abilities, clear and understandable rules, or the moderator's feedback (Kristiansen & Rasmussen, 2014). The workshop moderator in general plays a central role in this process. By observing the participants and their behavior, for example, and adjusting questions or prompts accordingly, the facilitator can support participants in entering the flow state (The LEGO® Group, 2010).

LEGO® Serious Play® can be regarded, from these perspectives, as a gamified method where challenges are explored, modeled, reflected upon, discussed, and solved using building blocks under structured guidance. The method has already been conducted in different settings and adapted to target groups and contexts, for example in engineering, education, or medicine. Various case studies mention workshop results such as an increased motivation to participate, a positive influence on the sense of responsibility in a group, the expansion of communication channels, the reduction of hierarchical power structures, the promotion of metaphorical thinking or the increased internalization of multiple aspects through the visual and haptic approach (Bulmer, 2011; Cerezo-Narváez et al., 2019; Dann, 2018; Kurkovsky, 2015; Peabody, 2015). Even though the term 'play' is used in its title, it "is almost the opposite; it is hard fun, and it engages your brain in a playful manner to solve a real problem" (Kristiansen & Rasmussen, 2014). Building with bricks and reflection help in translating views and attitudes into visual, auditory, and tactile forms. By constructing conceptual models with hands, it becomes possible to access implicit knowledge and create entirely new connections (Blair & Rillo, 2016). Additionally, it can be noted that these game elements and thus gamified processes exhibit parallels to team building. 'To build' suggests that active action and participation are desired (Matzat, 2023). This activation or active involvement, in turn, can be positively influenced by game-based settings or gamification elements (Menner & Thurner-Irmler, 2023). The use of gamification approaches in form of a LEGO® Serious Play® workshop aims to visualize team building as well as (product) innovation ideas emerging through active collaboration by creating shared models (Blair & Rillo, 2016).

3. EVALUATION OF A LEGO® SERIOUS PLAY® WORKSHOP

The following section describes a specific practical application in which 17 individuals from an administrative team, who in turn manage various projects within the department in smaller units, were tasked with jointly developing a team vision for the next five years. To achieve this, a LEGO® Serious Play® workshop was conducted. Firstly, the framework and preparations of the workshop will be introduced, followed by the presentation of the workshop's procedure and evaluations conducted during the workshop.

3.1 Preparation of the Workshop

Prior to the workshop, the team leader of a department within a municipal administration approached the facilitators to explore whether a gamified method could optimize the creation of a shared team vision. In the initial discussion, it emerged that a LEGO® Serious Play® workshop could indeed be suitable. The method was presented during a team meeting by a certified workshop leader. Two members of the 17-person team expressed concerns about participating in a LEGO® building process, while the remaining participants could envision this playful approach. In a further conversation with a team member and the team leader, two specific topics were identified: The focus was on developing a shared five-year annual strategy as well as team building.

3.2 Conduction of the Workshop

The entire workshop was facilitated by two moderators who are not affiliated with either the team or the organization to which the team belongs. On the day of the workshop, the 17 participants gathered in the prepared seminar room. After conducting the pre-survey, a brief introduction round followed, during which participants were asked to introduce their assigned workshop partner based on the knowledge they already possessed about them. Subsequently, the phases of the LEGO® Serious Play® workshop began. During the warm-up phase, the aim was to break down any inhibitions regarding the use of building blocks and to develop ideas on how the bricks could be used to visualize one's own concepts. The tasks of the warm-up phases were already aligned with the questions to be addressed in the building phase, and participants were asked to build specific terms from their work environment. The other team members were tasked with guessing the built terms. After this gamified initial activation, the fundamental rules, procedures, and etiquette of a LEGO® Serious Play® workshop were explained. Subsequently, the specific task of the first building phase was presented, motivating participants to recreate their current work environment and activities with various aspects like location, colleagues, work topics, skills, etc. Following the building process, individual team members presented their models, thoughts, and impressions. In this context, current challenges mentioned by each participant were also documented by the facilitators in bullet points, made visible to all. Likewise, photos of the models along with all mentioned thoughts were written down in detail by the second moderator in a separate document. The facilitators ensured that the ideas presented were not commented on by other team members.

After a break, the employees were tasked with engaging in a second building phase centered around a fictional scenario. In this scenario, the department received an award for a successfully completed project, and the employees were asked to visualize the steps necessary for this achievement through the transformation of their initial LEGO® structures. Here, too, several possible points of reference were presented, such as communication processes, digitalization, and skills development. Subsequently, the participants presented their new creations, and the steps contributing to the award were documented visibly by the facilitators for all to see. Thus, in two steps, both the challenges and initial solutions got visualized using LEGO®. The written documentation facilitated the comparison between the initial and desired future situations.

In the final step, particular emphasis was placed on team building and problem solving. Participants were instructed to assemble their structures into a comprehensive concept, a large cohesive model, to identify any necessary (new) connections and cross-functional measures. During this building phase, free discussion was encouraged, allowing team members to weigh the pros and cons of various ideas. These were incorporated into the documentation by the facilitators. To conclude, the entire documentation was reviewed and discussed once again, and the key next steps toward addressing or achieving the workshop topics posed at the outset – team strategy and team building – were considered. The discussions were moderated by the workshop leader, who was able to steer the conversation back to the original topics in the event of various situations, deviations, or distractions. Following an outlook, post-evaluation was conducted, and the workshop was concluded.

3.3 Presentation of the Pre- and Post-Survey

To assess the direct effects of the workshop, both pre- and post-surveys were conducted among the participants. The initial survey was administered immediately before the official team presentation to capture the baseline regarding the attitudes and behaviors of the team members. Following the conclusion of the workshop, a second survey was conducted to identify any changes in the aforementioned areas as well as to assess personal method evaluations. The following sections will present the questionnaires, including their contents and items.

3.3.1 Pre-Survey of the Workshop

As part of the study, demographic data of the participants were collected, including gender (female, male, diverse) and age (age groups 20-29, 30-39, 40-49, 50-59, >60 years). Additionally, participants were asked whether they had prior knowledge about the LEGO® Serious Play® method or had previously participated in a comparable workshop. To capture individual expectations and goals of the participants, two open-ended questions were posed: "What is your workshop goal?" and "What do you hope to achieve from the workshop?".

Subsequently, the baseline assessment regarding team evaluation was conducted. Using a 5-point Likert scale (strongly disagree, disagree, neutral, agree, strongly agree), participants were given the opportunity to express their agreement or disagreement with various statements regarding team dynamics and interaction (detailed items in chapter 4.2). These self-formulated items were based on the benefits and objectives of LEGO® Serious Play® workshops described in literature and guidelines (Bulmer, 2011; Cerezo-Narváez et al., 2019; Kristiansen & Rasmussen, 2014; The LEGO® Group, 2010). To minimize systematic response biases, the order of the items was randomized, and some items varied in their polarity.

3.3.2 Post-Survey of the Workshop

In the post-survey, participants were again asked to respond to the identical items used for team evaluation in the pre-survey. This step aimed to capture any changes in team assessment that may have been brought about by participating in the workshop. Furthermore, an evaluation of the workshop itself was conducted. For this purpose, the 5-point Likert scale was employed. Given that the flow state can be conducive to achieving workshop goals and is also a key factor in games or game elements, the selection and formulation of items drew on various flow dimensions relevant to the method (Bulmer, 2011; Csikszentmihalyi, 1990). This question block was supplemented with additional items addressing the workshop's objectives (detailed items in chapter 4.3). The polarity of the items was also randomized. In the questionnaire, the order of the items was randomized as previously done for the team evaluation. In two open-ended questions, respondents could provide more detailed insights into their experiences and wishes regarding the workshop: "What will you remember most clearly from the workshop?" and "What would you like to see as a result of the workshop?"

Furthermore, participants were asked to evaluate the LEGO® Serious Play® method in general. Again, the 5-point Likert scale was provided (detailed items in chapter 4.4). The formulation here also drew on the goals and benefits of the method documented in literature (Bulmer, 2011; The LEGO® Group, 2010). Finally, participants were asked in which areas or on which topics they could also imagine using this method in the future. Additionally, everyone had the opportunity to provide any further comments to the facilitators.

4. RESULTS FROM THE WORKSHOP SURVEYS

The pre-survey was completed by $n_1 = 17$ individuals. However, due to a private incident, one team member had to leave the workshop early, resulting in the post-survey being conducted with $n_2 = 16$ participants. Below, the results of the two surveys are presented.

4.1 Demographics and Workshop Goals

The workshop was attended by eight female and nine male individuals. The distribution of age among the selected ranges was as follows: 20-29 years: three individuals, 30-39 years: seven individuals, 40-49 years: three individuals, 50-59 years: two individuals, over 60 years: two individuals. Six respondents indicated familiarity with the LEGO® Serious Play® method, but none had previously participated in such a workshop.

In total, eleven respondents explicitly stated team building as their primary workshop goal, often linking it with additional aspects such as enhancing efficiency, optimization, improving communication, exchange and acquaintance, finding one's role in the team, team strengthening, as well as better assessment of team members. One person expressed the desire to develop a motto for the team for the coming year, while another aimed at formulating visions and mid-term strategies. The expectation of engaging with a new method and the playful and creative involvement were highlighted by two people. Furthermore, 14 out of 17 respondents expressed specific expectations for the workshop. Getting to know team members (better) was mentioned four times. Optimization of processes, tasks, or even the connections between various task areas were also mentioned four times. Other expectations related to identifying deficiencies, experiencing fun, and developing team strategies.

4.2 Team Assessment

Personal team assessments were recorded using various items in both the pre- (n_1 = 17) and post-survey (n_2 = 16), where responses ranged from 'strongly disagree' (= 1) to 'strongly agree' (= 5). The following table presents the mean scores of the responses for comparison (Table 1).

Table 1. Comparison of mean scores in pre- and post-surveys for team assessment

Item	Pre	Post
I know exactly what tasks each member of our team has.	3.59	3.69
I know exactly where the weaknesses and strengths of my team members lie.	2.94	3.50
I am not responsible for the success of my team. (negative)	2.53	2.63
I can communicate honestly with my team members.	3.71	4.25
I trust the members of my team.	3.76	4.00
I am not aware of the opportunities and challenges within the team. (negative)	2.18	2.63
We work well together as a team.	3.71	4.19
We can achieve our goals as a team.	3.76	4.00

The responses to the items "I know exactly what tasks each member of our team has" and "I am not responsible for the success of my team" remained constant across both surveys. The absence of one response previously rated as "strongly disagree" suggests that the individual who left the workshop prematurely may have held this perspective. Therefore, the mean score slightly increased in the post-survey for these items.

An increase in agreement was observed in assessing the strengths and weaknesses of team members as well as in honest communication, with a mean score change of over 0.5 points to the positive. Similarly, there was a mean score change of almost 0.5 points in evaluating the teamwork. Trust in team members and the perception of being able to achieve goals together as a team also showed a slight increase in agreement. However, the statement of being unaware of opportunities and challenges within the team was more consented in the post-survey than before.

4.3 Workshop Assessment

In the post-survey, participants (n_2 = 16) were asked to evaluate the workshop and their experience overall on the selected 5-point Likert scale. Among the ten items, six pertained to various dimensions of flow (Table 2).

Table 2. Mean scores from the post-survey evaluating the flow dimensions and method goals

Item	Post
The workshop was enjoyable. (flow dimension: positive effects)	4.44
Building with the building blocks came easily to me. (flow dimension: immersion)	4.13
My hands built almost on their own. (flow dimension: immersion)	3.50
I couldn't concentrate properly on the task. (flow dimension: concentration) (negative)	2.31
I felt well-guided throughout the workshop. (flow dimension: guiding)	4.56
We collaborated well as a group. (flow dimension: social)	4.38
I felt that I could contribute effectively.	4.13
I felt not listened to. (negative)	2.00
I became aware of problems and challenges.	4.06
I was able to express my thoughts effectively.	3.88

The highest level of agreement was obtained for the item regarding the guidance of the workshop (mean score 4.56). A similar result was achieved for the dimension of positive effects, enjoyment, that the participants had fun. Regarding the social dimension, ten participants agreed, and six strongly agreed. The negatively polarized item assessing concentration had a mean score of 2.31. One item evaluating the immersion – feeling like the hands were building on their own – was rated differently by the participants (mean score 3.50), while the second immersion item received a higher level of agreement. Among the four items related to the workshop experience or the goals of the LEGO® Serious Play® method, the item "I felt that I could contribute effectively" had a mean score of 4.13. The statement "I felt not listened to" received the highest disagreement overall, although the item "I was able to express my thoughts effectively" was rated high, but not as positive.

In response to the open question about what participants will remember most from the workshop, twelve individuals provided responses. Twice, "more open communication" was mentioned. Three team members emphasized the importance of networking with other departments, while two highlighted the need for adjustments to various (process) structures and work instructions. One person mentioned that they intend to consider other team members more when carrying out their tasks in the future. Other responses focused on the desire to achieve greater well-being within the team through a new work environment or the need for faster and smoother digitalization. Overall, eleven individuals mentioned something they would like to see as a result of the workshop. Seven individuals expressed hope that the suggestions and ideas generated from the workshop would be addressed and implemented. Three individuals noted a desire for improved communication and interaction both within the team and across departments. One participant wrote "nothing special".

4.4 Method Evaluation

At the conclusion of the post-survey, participants (n_2 = 16) were asked to assess the LEGO® Serious Play® method on a scale ranging from 'strongly disagree' (= 1) to 'strongly agree' (= 5) (Table 3).

Table 3. Mean scores from the post-survey evaluating the workshop method in general

The LEGO® Serious Play® methodology...	Mean score
...created a playful and relaxed environment.	4.25
...helped me gain insight into the perspectives and perceptions of my team members.	4.00
...assisted me in better understanding my own perspectives and perceptions.	3.63
...provided me with the opportunity to communicate my perspectives and perceptions.	3.88
...helped stimulate and foster my imagination.	3.94
...aided in presenting the goals of the team.	3.88
...helped link the goals of the team members.	3.88
...contributed to fostering communication within the team.	4.13
...contributed to fostering understanding within the team.	3.94

The item receiving the highest agreement pertained to the creation of a playful and relaxed environment through the method. Also, the improvement in the communication was rated highly positive. The most notable differences in responses were observed in the item regarding the recognition of one's own perspectives and perceptions: one respondent strongly agreed, nine agreed, three were neutral, one person disagreed, and one strongly disagreed. For four items, no respondents expressed any disagreement: presentation of team goals, linkage of team members' goals, promotion of communication within the team, and promotion of understanding within the team.

Seven participants additionally mentioned other areas where they could envision the use of LEGO® Serious Play®, including team building (three mentions), fostering open exchange, addressing team conflicts, aligning visions, identifying and resolving interfaces, promoting equality (ensuring everyone's voice is heard), and promoting team inclusivity. In the comments section at the end of the questionnaire, six individuals expressed gratitude for the engaging, interactive, and well-moderated day.

5. DISCUSSION AND LIMITATIONS

The introductory session immediately highlighted deficiencies in communication flow within the team. It was noticeable that certain team members lacked knowledge about the assigned tasks of their workshop partners. While the knowledge of specific tasks of other team members did not substantially increase in the post-survey, there was an enhancement in the perception of collaboration and trust in other team members as well as in identifying strengths and weaknesses within the team. Noteworthy is also the heightened score regarding an honest communication. However, the assessment of risk and challenge awareness within the department declined – possibly due to the negative framing of the item. Regarding the flow effect, the item receiving the highest rating was related to 'guidance,' i.e., the leadership and facilitation of the workshop. This is particularly encouraging as the guidance dimension is considered essential for achieving a flow state (Csikszentmihalyi, 1990; Kristiansen & Rasmussen, 2014). Further dimensions such as positive effects (enjoyment and fun) and team collaboration (social) were also positively evaluated, while an item related to immersion was rated more neutrally on average. Altogether, the ratings suggest that participants were likely in a personal flow state in this playful environment.

Surprisingly, some participants indicated that they were unfamiliar with the method, despite its prior introduction. The LEGO® Serious Play® approach, aimed at ensuring that all participants are heard through a pleasant, respectful and playful environment was rated above average positively as well as the visualization of implicit thoughts. Especially the item "I felt not listened to" received the highest disagreement. The method contributed to fostering communication within the team, as evidenced by the high ratings of the corresponding items. Numerous suggestions for improving the work climate and team collaboration emerged from the open feedback provided during the workshop. These insights are particularly relevant for leaders and can contribute to the development of a long-term team strategy.

Negatively to note is the premature termination of the workshop by one individual and the lack of pairing between pre- and post-surveys, limiting the analysis of individual developments and the removal of the pre-evaluation results of the person leaving prematurely. The small sample size and absence of a control group (e.g. using another workshop method) also limit the generalizability of the results. Additionally, the presence of the team leader may have influenced the social desirability of responses, warranting further investigation in future studies. The behavior and leadership of the moderators can also have a major influence on the ratings.

However, during the final construction phase, assembling the individual models revealed that the concept could not have been implemented by a single team member. Such workshops require facilitation by an external and trained individual who maintains emotional distance from the workshop themes. LEGO® Serious Play® workshops are characterized by having a clear and understandable goal, and the challenge in the building process must be constantly adjusted and adequately accompanied. This allows for maximum efficiency in addressing the issues (Kristiansen & Rasmussen, 2014; The LEGO® Group, 2010).

6. CONCLUSION AND OUTLOOK

The workshop achieved progress in terms of enhancing an honest communication within the team. The explicit promotion of identifying strengths and weaknesses played a crucial role in its success. Particularly, the perceived high-quality guidance provided during the workshop facilitated a flow experience for the participants. The application of a gamification method and playful elements using LEGO® bricks in a non-gamified process, proved to be an effective method for promoting team building and awareness in this group. This active and hands-on approach has proven to be a valuable tool for enhancing team dynamics in this case. In conclusion, the workshop successfully improved the awareness for communication processes and understanding within the team, despite methodological and conceptual limitations. The results underscore the need to further refine both the methodological implementation and evaluation approaches in future workshops.

To sustainably assess the workshop's effects, a follow-up survey is planned to take place six months after its implementation. This subsequent survey aims to capture potential changes in team dynamics and working relationships. In addition, further workshops with different teams on comparable topics are planned, as this implementation presented here is the first one evaluated in this format by this moderation team. Through expanded application of the methodology across diverse teams, broader data on attitudes and evaluations of the methodology, as well as its potential positive effects – especially through the flow effect – can be collected. These comparative studies are essential for validating and optimizing the effectiveness of LEGO® Serious Play® and similar gamified approaches in various team dynamic and organizational contexts.

The results suggest that innovative, interactive, and gamified approaches for team building, and organizational development are relevant, not only in industrial, but also in administrative businesses. The strategic implementation of playful methods such as LEGO® Serious Play® offers promising prospects for fostering an effective and cooperative team culture. Through continuous evaluation and adaptation of these approaches, organizations can strengthen their teams and optimize collaboration, ultimately leading to increased overall productivity and employee satisfaction.

REFERENCES

Bansmann, L.-M. (2021). *Führen in der COVID-19-Pandemie.* https://doi.org/10.25968/OPUS-1949

Betts, B. (2013). Game-Based Learning. In R. Hubbard (Ed.), *The Really Useful ELearning Instruction Manual* (pp. 175–194). Jon Wiley & Sons Ltd.

Blair, S., & Rillo, M. (2016). *Serious Work: How to facilitate meetings & workshops using the Lego® Serious Play® Method with conscious incompetence*. ProMeet.

Bulmer, L. (2011). THE USE OF LEGO ® SERIOUS PLAY IN THE ENGINEERING DESIGN CLASSROOM. *Proceedings of the Canadian Engineering Education Association (CEEA)*, 1–6. https://doi.org/10.24908/pceea.v0i0.3699

Cerezo-Narváez, A., Córdoba-Roldán, A., Pastor-Fernández, A., Aguayo-González, F., Otero-Mateo, M., & Ballesteros-Pérez, P. (2019). Training Competences in Industrial Risk Prevention with Lego® Serious Play®: A Case Study. *Safety*, *5*(4, 81), 1–24. https://doi.org/10.3390/safety5040081

Csikszentmihalyi, M. (1990). *Flow: The Psychology of Optimal Experience*. Harper & Row.

Dann, S. (2018). Facilitating Co-Creation Experience in the Classroom with Lego Serious Play. *Australasian Marketing Journal*, *26*(2), 121–131.

Deterding, S., Dixon, D., Khaled, R., & Nacke, L. (2011). From Game Design Elements to Gamefulness: Defining "Gamification". *MindTrek '11: Proceedings of the 15th International Academic MindTrek Conference: Envisioning Future Media Environments*, 9–15. https://doi.org/10.1145/2181037.2181040

Fink, F., & Moeller, M. (2018). *Purpose Driven Organizations* (1. Auflage 2018). *SPH Management 2020, SPH Management 2021, SPH Management 2019.* Schäffer-Poeschel; C.H. Beck eLibrary. https://doi.org/10.34156/9783791040356

Hillmer, D. (2021). *PLAY! Der unverzichtbare LEGO® SERIOUS PLAY® Praxis-Guide für Trainer, Coaches und Moderatoren. Hanser eLibrary.* Hanser. https://doi.org/10.3139/9783446470552

Kranawetleitner, T., Krebs, H., Menner, M., & Pistoll, D. (2022). Spielend "leicht" Daten erheben: Anwendung von Gamification-Ansätzen zur Erhebung von Bedarfen in branchenübergreifenden Digitalisierungsprojekten. In B. Mahrin & S. Krümmel (Eds.), *Digitalisierung beruflicher Lern- und Arbeitsprozesse. Impulse aus der Bauwirtschaft und anderen gewerblich-technischen Sektoren* (pp. 298–311). Universitätsverlag der TU Berlin.

Kristiansen, P., & Rasmussen, R. (2014). *Building a better business using the LEGO® Serious Play® method.* Wiley. https://learning.oreilly.com/library/view/-/9781118931370/?ar

Kurkovsky, S. (2015). Teaching Software Engineering with LEGO Serious Play, 213–218. https://doi.org/10.1145/2729094.2742604

Landers, R. N., Auer, E. M., Collmus, A. B., & Armstrong, M. B. (2018). Gamification Science, Its History and Future: Definitions and a Research Agenda. *Simulation & Gaming*, *49*(3), 315–337. https://doi.org/10.1177/1046878118774385

Matzat, A. (2023). Die Rolle und Bedeutung von Teambuilding bei hybriden Arbeitsmodellen. In J. Bath & K. Winkler (Eds.), *Hybrid Work: Wie Führungskräfte ihre Arbeitsorganisation für die Zukunft transformieren* (pp. 141–150). Haufe. https://doi.org/10.34157/978-3-648-16790-8_8

Menner, M., & Thurner-Irmler, J. (2023). Lead Playfully—Technical Innovations Communicated Through Gaming. In N. Pfeffermann & M. Schaller (Eds.), *New Leadership Communication—Inspire Your Horizon* (pp. 409–424). Springer, Cham. https://doi.org/10.1007/978-3-031-34314-8_29

Peabody, M. A. (2015). Building with purpose: Using LEGO SERIOUS PLAY in play therapy supervision. *International Journal of Play Therapy*, *24*(1), 30–40. https://doi.org/10.1037/a0038607

Pelling, N. (2011). *The (short) prehistory of "gamification"...* https://nanodome.wordpress.com/2011/08/09/the-short-prehistory-of-gamification/

The LEGO® Group. (2010). *Introduction to LEGO® SERIOUS PLAY®.* www.seriousplay.com

EXPLORATORY STUDY ON QUANTIFYING COMPLEXITY IN THE TEMPORAL STRUCTURE OF ELECTROACOUSTIC MUSIC

Jumpei Hayata[1], Shingo Honda[1], Soma Arai[1, 3], Hidefumi Ohmura[2] and Takuro Shibayama[1, 3]
[1]*Tokyo Denki University*
Ishizuka, Hatoyama, Hiki, Saitama 362-0074, Japan
[2]*Tokyo University of Science*
2641 Yamazaki, Noda, Chiba 278-0022, Japan
[3]*Tokyo College of Music*
1-9-1 Kamimeguro, Meguro, Tokyo 153-0051, Japan

ABSTRACT

The music created by this study's authors was electroacoustic, which is more complex than ordinary popular music. Individuals often consider highly complex music as being difficult to understand; however, this study's social activities, in which individuals were encouraged to create their own electroacoustic music, indicated that all participants enjoyed it. This indicated that efforts in this social practice may be changing "difficult things" into "fun things." This process of extending "fun things" is useful for extending the concept of "entertainment" in Game and Entertainment Technology. Therefore, this study aimed to verify that complexity in music increases in the order of "normal (8-beat, etc.) music, experimental popular music, electroacoustic music, and noise music." To test this hypothesis, this study attempted to compare the rhythmic structure of "normal music" and "experimental popular music." The results indicated that the rhythmic structure of the experimental popular music was more complex than that of normal popular music. Furthermore, it is strongly suggested that electroacoustic music, which has no rhythmic structure, has a more complex rhythmic structure. Furthermore, it can be stated that inexperienced individuals enjoyed the creation of "music" that has no clear rhythmic synchronization. This extended these individuals' traditional concept of "entertainment", and can be further extended by deepening this activity in the future.

KEYWORDS

Expansion of Domain of Entertainment, Computer Music, Electroacoustic Music

1. INTRODUCTION

Electroacoustic music is more intricate than typical popular music. Complex musical compositions are often disregarded by individuals as being too challenging to comprehend. However, this study's social gatherings, where participants were actively urged to create their own electroacoustic music, indicated that all participants derived pleasure from electroacoustic music.

1.1 Features of Electroacoustic Music (EAM)

This study, which was conducted in the author's laboratory, involved the creation of Electroacoustic Music (EAM) using computers and the practice of sharing this music with individuals from multiple generations who had no prior experience in creating music. EAM refers to concrete music, which originated in France, and electronic music, which originated in Germany. The EAM created in this laboratory exhibited a higher structural complexity level than popular music. While popular music is generally more accessible, it can be challenging for individuals to comprehend highly complex music; consequently, it is often avoided. EAM is a prime example of such music. However, this study observed that inexperienced participants uniformly enjoyed creating EAM through workshops. These workshops indicated that, although highly complex music can give individuals the impression that it is difficult to understand, it can be enjoyed through the creation of complex music. The authors believe that this estrangement is caused by the "esoteric" nature of EAM's cultural background and the "complexity" of EAM's musical structure. Therefore, by analyzing the reasons why EAM is considered challenging to comprehend and making explicit the intricacy of EAM, this study aimed to demonstrate that creating complex music can lead to enjoying complex music.

1.2 "Esotelism" of EAM in the Inaudible Domain

This segment delved into the "intricate (esoteric)" intricacy fostered by the cultural context of EAM. The 19th and 20th centuries witnessed the expansion of music into entertainment, particularly in the 20th century. Entertainment music, such as pop and rock, has gained widespread appeal and is enjoyed daily. However, the philosophical realm of music evolved more abstractly and experimentally. In the early 20th century, music shifted away from traditional tonal structures and ventured into new territories, including atonal, noise, and electroacoustic music. The New Vienna School of Music, a group of composers active in the early 1900s, played a pivotal role during this evolution. They established the principle of atonal music, which transcended the conventional concept of tonality and considered all notes as equal, as exemplified by Schoenberg's twelve-tone technique. Music lacking a conventional tonal framework enables free artistic expression. Simultaneously, the noise genre emerged through the Futurist movement, an avant-garde art movement that primarily occurred in Italy at the beginning of the 20th century. Futurists embraced themes such as "speed," "motion," and "noise," which were integral to industrial machine civilization and urbanization, and they expressed these themes through various means, including sports, automobiles, airplanes, cities, trains, and machines. In 1913, the Futurist composer Luigi Russolo published his treatise "The Art of Noise," marking the birth of noise music. Among other innovations, the development of public address systems and technology has been closely linked to the emergence of theremins and electronic organ synthesizers. The advent of new technologies led to the creation of new forms of music, including electronic expressions in music production and musical expressions. In the mid-20th century, concrete and electronic music emerged as distinct styles. Concrete music, which was introduced by Pierre Scheffert in 1948 with his composition Etude aux Chemins de Fer, is characterized by the use of recorded everyday sounds that are processed and montaged. Conversely, electronic music was founded by Karlheinz Stockhausen and Herbert Eimert in 1951 and utilizes electronic sounds and sounds produced by mechanical objects, such as synthesizers and other electronic circuits. These two forms represent a shift in the perception of music from mere entertainment to a more philosophical and experimental pursuit. The foundation of contemporary music was laid by Stockhausen and Eimert, who explored compositional techniques through electronic means such as acoustic synthesis. Contemporary music has broadened its scope to encompass unlimited expressive possibilities, and the term "complexities (esoteric)" is used to describe the intricate and esoteric nature of this music.

1.3 "Complexity" of EAM in the Audible Domain

Previous studies on methods for defining music complexity were reviewed, and methods for defining the complexity of the musical structure of EAMs were discussed. This study referred to two previous studies on music complexity.

1.3.1 Complexity of Normal Music

Previous studies proposed three methods for assessing musical complexity: a) root patterns, b) substrings, and c) rhythmic balance, uniformity, and entropy. Shmulevich and Povel (2000) suggested two methods for defining music complexity: a) using root patterns and b) employing substrings. Method (a) was based on the concept that rhythmic patterns are developed at various levels through musical elaboration, with complexity defined as the maximum number of root patterns required to generate rhythmic patterns. Method (b) utilized a method for measuring the complexity of finite sequences proposed by Lempel and Ziv (1976), in which the complexity is increased by one each time a new substring is discovered during the analysis of a sound sequence. Milne and Herff (2020) proposed method (c), which was based on rhythmic balance, uniformity, and entropy, all of which affect the perception of and preference for musical rhythmic complexity. These studies focused on methods for defining musical complexity; however, these studies' definitions of complexity were specific to Western music. To assess the complexity of the EAM music, its frequency characteristics should be explored.

This study believes that the complexity of EAM's structure in the audible domain arises from the fact that EAM is not based on conventional music theory, has more complex frequency characteristics in timbre than conventional music, and possesses higher complexity in its rhythmic structure.

1.3.2 Complexity in EAM

First, this study defined complexity in EAM, due to EAM not being based on traditional music theory. Compared to conventional music, EAM is characterized by complexity owing to compositions that are not based on musical theory. Given that Western music is based on music theories, the complexity of Western music is formed by the complexity of the musical structure within rules. Music theory includes musical elements, such as melodies, chord progressions, and tonality. For example, tonality is present when a melody or chord is composed in association with a tonal center. Thus, the complexity of Western music is formed in musical theory, in which the complexity of musical structures is formed. Conversely, EAM has a complex musical structure that is detached from the rules because there are no rules. This is because EAM is composed independently of conventional music theory and its structure differs from that of Western music theory. EAM involves editing recorded sound materials and montaging them along a timeline. Owing to the creation of EAM not being based on the correctness or incorrectness of Western music theory, but being produced by montage and allowing for greater freedom in composition, makes the structure of EAM music more complex than that of Western music.

1.3.3 Complexity of Frequency Characteristics in Timbre Compared To Conventional Music

The sounds produced in Western music exhibit tonal resonance. This is because Western music uses musical tones, which are sounds played by instruments that have a pitch derived from a certain frequency and are tuned. The melodies and chords of musical tones have tuned sounds because they consist of a scale, which is a set of musical tones with different pitches. Conversely, EAM has a complex sound with many overtones due to EAM using a noisy sound. Unlike musical sounds, noise has no regular frequency oscillation. This noise cannot be identified in terms of sound height owing to the short vibration time of the sound. EAM uses noisy sounds because it utilizes recorded everyday environmental sounds. In this study's social activities, music was composed by montaging sounds recorded from everyday objects. Recorded environmental sounds and sounds emitted from daily necessities were not tuned. Therefore, electroacoustic music composed of noisy sounds is assumed to have a significantly more complex acoustic structure than normal music composed of musical sounds. Thus, the frequency structure of electroacoustic music composed of clamorous sounds is significantly higher than that of tuned musical sounds. Finally, EAM has a more complex rhythmic structure than conventional music; Western music has a rhythmic structure within a defined timeframe. This is because Western music uses a duration or timeframe determined by the musical notes. These notes have defined timelines of notes, rests, beats, and measures. Notes and rests are indicative symbols; the length of a note and the length of a nonnote. A beat is an indication of how many of a particular note is a beat, and how many of those notes are in a block. For example, in the case of 4/4 times, a quarter note is considered one beat, and four of those quarter notes form a single measure. Therefore, there are four beats in a measure and each beat is a quarter note in length. A measure represents a box associated with a beat to separate each beat, making the score easier to read. From these, music is heard within a defined timeframe and note length. Regarding the definition of the rhythmic (horizontal axis) complexity of EAM. Given that EAM uses noisier sounds, but untuned sounds do not have a definite rhythmic structure, the rhythmic structure of EAM can be described as an overlap of montaged tones. The rhythmic structure created by this overlap of sounds includes the rhythmic structure originally possessed by the recorded sounds. Additionally, it includes the rhythmic structure of sounds created as a result of sound editing, such as changing the speed of the recorded sound or playing it backward. This includes the rhythmic structure created by arranging phonemes regularly and that created by arranging phonemes irregularly. This makes EAM more complex than Western music, which has a clear rhythmic structure.

2. PROBLEM DEFINITION

In social practice, at the author's laboratory, several individuals enjoyed the creation of EAM, which they considered difficult. This may indicate that highly complex music is not necessarily "difficult." Therefore, this "enjoyment" may be caused not by "appreciation" of EAM, but by "creation." Therefore, the hypothesis that the "creation" of EAM extends the realm of "enjoyment" for individuals can be considered valid. A foundation to support this hypothesis may be established by clarifying the complexity of EAM. A detailed description of the subject matter of this study follows.

2.1 Regarding the Workshops Organized in the Authors' Laboratory

The workshops targeted a large number of inexperienced students, from elementary school students to adults, both on- and off-campus. The workshops used Audacity, a free digital audio editor. The workshops were conducted as follows:

(1) Listen to electroacoustic music listening materials and conduct a cognitive experiment to evaluate the impressions of the electroacoustic music using the Semantic Differential (SD) method.

(2) The sounds of everyday objects brought about by the participants were recorded and transferred to Audacity.

(3) Using Audacity, the montage of the recorded sound materials was performed.

(4) First, create a one-second EAM.

(5) Subsequently, complete this 1-second EAM as a mono soundtrack of 10 to 20 s using sound contrast and Audacity effects.

(6) To this end, prompt and use words such as a) high–low, b) hard–soft, c) moving–no movement, and light–dull during the montage as appropriate to capture the image of the sound and electronic music to draw contrasts.

(7) In addition, describe the effects provided in Audacity, ensuring that a particular state of contrast (i.e., high-contrast - low-contrast duration) is not followed by a high-contrast-low-contrast duration.

(8) The effects described here include sound inversion, pitch and speed changes, and volume changes.

(9) Complete as a mono-soundtrack of 10 to 20 s.

(10) Collect each participant's data and critique while listening to the sample.

(11) Listen to electroacoustic music listening materials and conduct a cognitive experiment to evaluate the impressions of the electroacoustic music using the SD method.

Through this process, EAM was created using a computer, the recorded acoustic materials were edited from everyday items brought in by the participants, and a montage of these materials was created along a timeline. The workshop focused on abstract sound movements and emphasized the participants' direct experience of the dichotomy of acoustic phenomena. This dichotomy meant considering the "abstract" sounds in the score not as a mere sequence of sounds, but rather as the essence of sound, and to perceive sound "concretely" within its totality. Instructing students to directly experience this dichotomy corresponds to processes (6) and (7) of the workshop. In steps (6) and (7) of the workshop, the sound material was perceived concretely and created using pictorial images of the sound material and antonyms. This workshop confirmed that all participants enjoyed electroacoustic music when asked to create their own electroacoustic music. This suggests that these efforts may be changing "difficult things" into "fun things."

2.2 Previous Studies in the Authors' Laboratory

Similar findings were confirmed in a previous study conducted in the authors' laboratory in Arai in 2023. As indicated in the workshop process, a cognitive experiment was conducted to evaluate the impressions of EAMs using the SD method by listening to the listening materials of EAMs before and after the workshop implementation. This cognitive experiment intended to measure the effectiveness of the workshop's creation of EAM by examining how impressions of EAM changed before and after workshop implementation. Before and after the workshop, the participants were asked to listen to three pieces of electroacoustic music.

2.3 Where the Problem is

The authors aimed to expand the scope of activities for experimental music creation using computers. Therefore, by attempting to analyze the reasons why EAM is considered difficult, and by making the complexity of EAM explicit, this study attempted to show that by creating complex music, complex music can be enjoyed. Based on EAM's frequency structure and the concept of rhythmic complexity in previous studies, this study focused on the temporal structure of EAM and proposed a method to make its complexity explicit. The noise sound used by EAM has a shorter vibration time than musical sounds. Therefore, this study focused on the attack (the time from playing the instrument until the sound reaches its maximum volume) on the sound. Noise has a short oscillation frequency, which means that the sound of noise has a short time to reach its maximum volume, and the starting point of the attack is unclear. However, because the musical notes were tuned, the frequencies were clear and the starting point of the attack was considered well-defined. Given that the structure of the position in which the attack occurs is likely to be complex and in light of previous studies, this study argued that focusing on the attack can be useful to emphasize the complexity of EAM, as it has already been shown that a sense of rhythmic balance and uniformity affects the perception of complexity.

Therefore, this study examined whether it is appropriate to focus on the attack and whether it is appropriate to use the attack to make the complex temporal structure of the EAM explicit for songs created in the workshop.

3. HYPOTHESIS VERIFICATION

This study aimed to verify the hypothesis that complexity in music increases in a specific order: from normal music (e.g., 8-beat music) to experimental popular music, and subsequently, to electroacoustic music (EAM) and noise music. To test this hypothesis, the rhythmic structures of regular and experimental popular music were compared. These two types of music were selected because they are distinct and clearly demonstrate the complexity of EAM in their attack structure.

3.1 Regarding the Two Pieces of Music for Which the Attack is to be Detected

The music selected as the target of attack detection were normal music and experimental popular music.

(A) Japanese popular music, PONPONPON (2011).

(B) Japanese experimental popular music, Birds Must Be Eliminated (2000).

To ensure similar music conditions, songs with 128 beats per minute (BPM) were selected for both songs. BPM refers to the music's speed. Music (A) was defined as "Sample 1" and music (B) as "Sample 2." Sample 1 was a piece of popular music that the authors judged to be composed of musical notes that everyone can relate to. Sample 2 was an experimental popular music piece that the authors judged to have a more complex attack structure than Sample 1. Attack detection was performed for both songs.

3.2 Detecting Attacks in Audio Files Using Max/MSP

Max/MSP was used to detect the attacks. Max/MSP is a graphical integrated development environment (visual programming language) for music and multimedia developed and maintained by Cycling 74, a San Francisco software company. Max/MSP allows users to build their own synthesizer systems, create visual art, and analyze acoustics. Using Max/MSP, this study built a system to detect attacks. Max/MSP uses patches, which are objects that have functions. The functions of the constructed system were as follows:

(1) Specify an existing audio file and load it into Max/MSP.

(2) Create a new audio file at a specified location.

(3) Play an audio file.

(4) Detect attacks in audio files.

(5) Play a sine wave when an attack is detected.

(6) Record a specific sound in an audio file.

Therefore, using these Max/MSP functions, Sample 1 was loaded and the audio was played back to detect attacks. When an attack was detected, a sine wave was heard and the sine wave was recorded in a newly created audio file. This audio file recorded the attack location. Sample 2 was examined similarly.

Subsequently, the attack appearance locations were recorded from the audio files in which the attacks were detected and ProTools was used to record the attack-appearance points. The BPM of ProTools was set to 128, and the attack appearance points were recorded. The ProTools time signature was set for each note (quarter, eighth, sixteenth, and thirty-second note). At each beat, the point at which the attack occurred was recorded. Figures 1 and 2 present screenshots of the attack recorded in ProTools. Figure 1 shows the existing audio file detected, and Figure 2 shows the audio file in which the attack points were recorded.

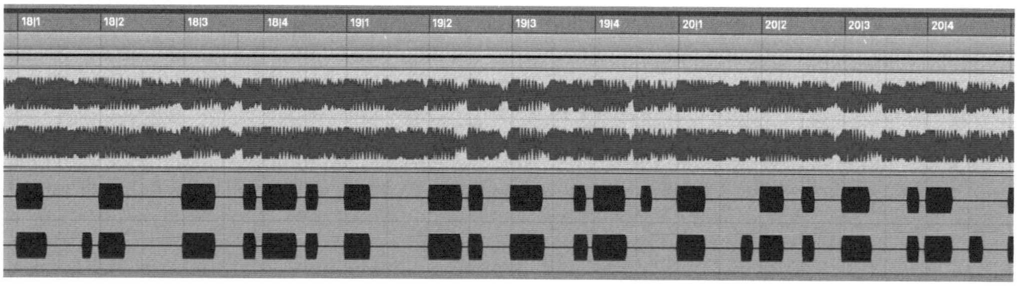

Figure 1. Sample 1 audio file and attack points

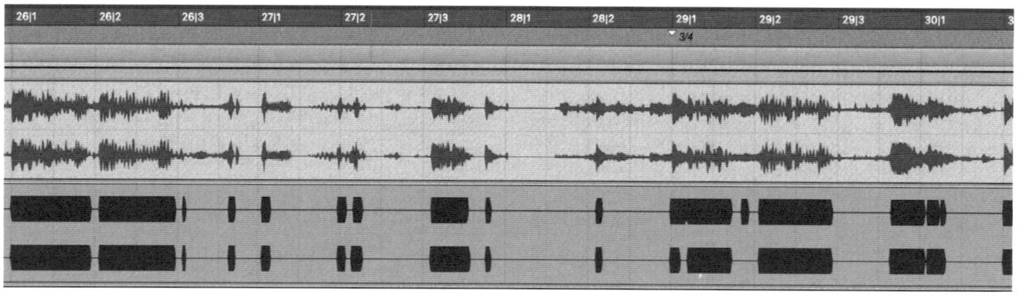

Figure 2. Sample 2 audio file and attack points

4. RESULTS

The attack occurrence and absence rates for each beat were calculated from the attack occurrence locations recorded during hypothesis testing. The attack occurrence rate was calculated using the following formula: total number of beats where an attack occurred / total number of beats × 100. The attack absence rate was calculated using the following formula: total beats - total number of beats where attacks occurred / total number of beats × 100.

Table 1. Attack occurrence rate

			Attack occurrence rate			
Beat	Sample 1	%	Sample 2	%	Total 3/4	Total 4/4
4	36	100	10	27.78	36	36
8	52	72.22	11	15.28	72	72
16	59	40.97	17	11.81	144	144
32	59	20.49	34	11.81	288	288

Table 2. Attack absence rate

			Attack absence rate			
Beat	Sample 1	%	Sample 2	%	Total 3/4	Total 4/4
4	36	0	10	72.22	36	36
8	52	27.78	11	84.72	72	72
16	59	59.03	17	88.19	144	144
32	59	79.51	34	88.19	288	288

4.1 Attack Occurrence and Absence Rates for Quarter Notes

The attack occurrence and absence rates were calculated for both samples by dividing the measures into quarter-note intervals. Regarding Sample 1, the attack occurrence rate was 100% when the measure was divided into quarter-note intervals. As expected, when popular music was divided into quarter-note intervals, the structure of the music indicated that attacks occurred where they were supposed to. This is evident from popular music using musical tones. However, in Sample 2, when the measure was divided into quarter-note intervals, the attack occurrence rate was 27.78% and the attack absence rate was 72.28%. An attack absence rate of nearly 70% indicates that nearly 70% of the attack occurrences were unpredictable. This indicates that the attack structure of experimental popular music was significantly more complex based on the analysis of quarter notes. Additionally, the structure became more complex when the music had an experimental meaning.

4.2 Attack Occurrence and Absence Rates for Eighth Notes

The attack appearance and absence rates were calculated for both samples by dividing the measures into eighth-note intervals. Regarding Sample 1, the attack appearance rate was 72.22% when the measure was divided into eighth-note intervals. When a measure is divided into eighth-note intervals and the attack structure is analyzed, the complexity appears to increase more than when the measure is divided into quarter-note intervals and the attack structure is divided. In contrast, in Sample 2, when the measure was divided into eighth-note intervals, the attack occurrence rate was 15.28%, and the attack absence rate was 84.72%. This indicated that the attack structure of experimental popular music was significantly more complex, even in the eighth note.

5. DISCUSSION

As expected from the validation, the resulting attack structure of the experimental popular music was considerably more complex than that of the popular music. This indicated that an attack was useful for manifesting complexity. Notably, EAM has an even more complex attack structure. Additionally, music seems to increase in complexity when it has experimental meaning. As a consideration, the fact that inexperienced participants enjoyed the creation of "music" that does not have clear rhythmic synchronization may be an extension of their traditional concept of "entertainment," and could be further extended by deepening this activity in the future. To extend this activity, this study explored the significance of creating highly complex music. The significance of creating highly complex music was summarized as a) the significance of creating electroacoustic music using computers and b) the optimal complexity model for music proposed by Berlyne (1971).

5.1 What it Means to Create Electroacoustic Music Using a Computer

This creative method of composing music by creating a montage of recorded sounds is a method of composition unique to computers and fundamentally differs from traditional composition, which is based on musical notes and notated on a score. This allows for repeated trial and error while directly listening to the sound of the creation. Trial and error in this study involved three elements: a) trial and error of the sound itself, b) awareness of the musical structure, and c) creation using Audacity's effects. First, trial and error concerning the sound itself refers to reductive listening based on the dichotomy of acoustic phenomena. This allows one to explore and deepen one's understanding of the nature of sounds. Regarding the awareness of the structure. The use of a computer allows one to instantly identify objects and clearly grasp their front-back relationship, making it easier to understand the before and after relationship. Regarding Audacity's effects. This refers to the compositional techniques and effects enabled through the use of computers. This allows for the exploration of musical expressions and effects that cannot be obtained using conventional methods. Through these creative activities, receptivity may be expanded and new musical approaches and ideas may emerge. Furthermore, the goal of completion is not brought about by music theory norms, or right and wrong, based on musical sounds. Therefore, everyone can experience music creation and the process of discovering and solving music problems.

5.2 Optimal Complexity Model in Music Proposed by Berlyne

Berlyne (1971) proposed an optimal complexity model that shows how the high complexity of music is related to the perception of pleasantness or unpleasantness using the inverse U-function, as shown in Figure 3.

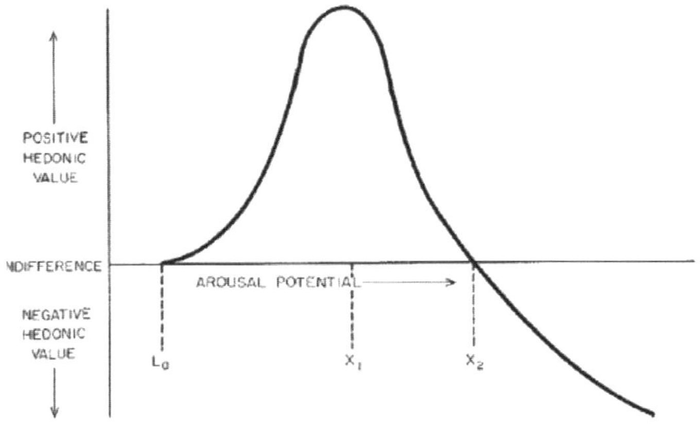

Figure 3. Berlyne's inverted U function

The x-axis of this inverted U hypothesis indicates the level of complexity, whereas the y-axis indicates the value of pleasure. Berlyne (1971) indicated the need for music to have a moderate level of complexity for listeners to derive pleasure. The inverted U hypothesis suggests that this complexity index decreases the value of pleasure when the complexity is too high or too low and decreases to a negative value when the complexity is excessive. This study defined it as popular music that uses musical sounds in its musical composition. Popular music, with its moderate complexity, may fall in the middle of the inverted U hypothesis. Three reasons for this may be applicable: a) moderate complexity can be perceived from its tuned sound; b) moderate complexity can be perceived from its structure, as defined by music theory; and c) it is music that is regularly listened to. First, popular music is composed of musical tones and thus has a tuned sound, from which moderate complexity is perceived. Second, an appropriate degree of complexity is formed by elements such as chord progressions, melodies, and rhythms using musical notes within the rules established by musical theory. Third, regarding regularly listened music, while individuals are accustomed to regularly listening to it, individuals are aware of the lyrics, modulations, and the author's intentions. Based on the above, popular music that uses musical sounds may fall within the middle of the inverse-U hypothesis.

Conversely, EAM may exist in a position in the inverse-U intervals where it is too complex to experience pleasure. Three reasons for this may be applicable: a) it contains significantly high harmonic overtones, making it highly complex; b) it has a structure that is free from musical theory, making it highly complex; and c) it is music that is not used for hearing purposes. First, because EAM is composed of noisier notes, it contains significant overtones, and its resonance gives the impression of a high degree of complexity. Second, EAM is free from musical theory and provides the impression of a high degree of complexity. Conversely, EAM may exist in a position in the inverse-U intervals where it is too complex to experience pleasure. Three reasons for this may be applicable: a) it contains significantly high harmonic overtones, making it highly complex; b) it has a structure that is free from musical theory, making it highly complex; and c) it is music that is not used for hearing purposes. First, because EAM is composed of noisier notes, it contains significant overtones, and its resonance gives the impression of a high degree of complexity. Second, EAM is free from musical theory and provides the impression of a high degree of complexity. Third, music was not used for hearing purposes. What is the significance of creating highly complex music, such as electroacoustic music?

In a previous study, participants' receptivity to electroacoustic music was enhanced through their experience in creating electroacoustic music. This indicates that the inverse U-shaped function shifted to the right through the experience of creating electroacoustic music. The shift to the right may have changed the complexity of the music that was found pleasurable, indicating that electroacoustic music may now be considered pleasurable. This shift is consistent with the process in which listening materials that could not previously be recognized as "music" are recognized as "music" as the participants' sensory domains expand, as presented in Figure 4.

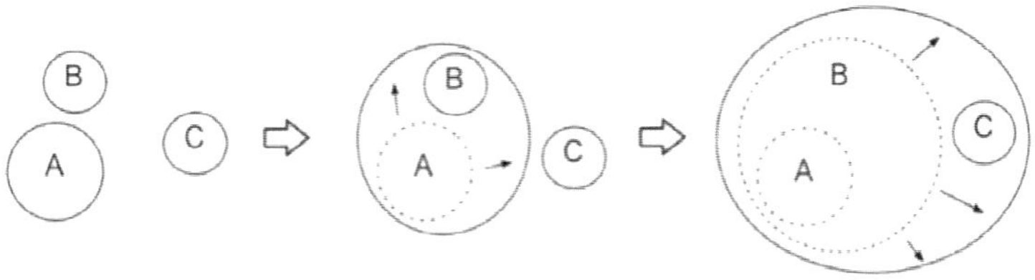

Figure 4. Kansei's process of expansion (Shibayama et al., 2017)

5.3 Everyone is an Artist

This study believes that workshops for creating electroacoustic music can disrupt the composition of music supply and demand. Currently, the relationship between the supply and demand of music is structured as one artist for many listeners. This study believes that workshop activities can make this social structure of "creation (production) - appreciation (reception)" visible and conscious, which has not previously been consciously recognized and can gently dismantle it. This gradual dismantling of the situation in which a small number of "makers" require a large number of "viewers," which is common in most artistic creation, is meant to approximate the "large number of makers" and "large number of viewers" through the perspective of reviewing artistic culture back to its origins, as Huizinga indicated in Homo Ludens (1938), and to increase the clutter in the structure of artistic creation and reception. This also implies increasing unclutteriness in the structure of the creation and reception of art.

6. CONCLUSION

This study focused on the structure of EAM over time and verified a method to make its complexity explicit. From this verification, this study found that focusing on the attack was useful for making the complexity of EAM explicit. In addition, this study discussed the significance of creating electroacoustic music. Future studies should consider strengthening teaching methods. In recent years, there has been a high demand for thinking ability. This study focused on "dimension of thinking," one of the methods of teaching thinking. "Dimension of thinking" is characterized by the fact that the teaching method is attributed to critical and creative thinking.

This study would like to take advantage of this feature to develop instructional methods that allow greater creativity to take place within future workshops.

ACKNOWLEDGEMENT

This work was supported by JSPS KAKENHI (grant #19K00227, #20K12126, and #23K00243), and by Research Institute for Science and Technology of Tokyo Denki University Grant #Q23-02.

REFERENCES

Arai, S., Yaguchi, H., Ohmura, H., Brümmer, L., & Shibayama, T. (2023). Quantifying the extended acceptance of pioneering art music through the creation of electroacoustic music. *Sound and Music Computing Conference (SMC)*, pp. 296–303.

Berlyne, D. E. (1971). *Aesthetics and psychology.* Appleton Century Crofts, New York, USA.

Heizinga, J. (1938). *Homo Ludens: A Study of the Play-Element of Culture*. Routledge & Kegan Paul, London (1949).

Lempel, A., & Ziv, J. (1976). On the complexity of finite sequences. *IEEE Transactions on Information Theory*, IT-22(1), pp. 75–81.

Milne, A. J., & Herff, S. A. (2020). The perceptual relevance of balance, evenness, and entropy in musical rhythms. *Cognition*, *203*, 104233.

Shibayama, T., Ohmura, H., Takahashi, T., & Furukawa, K. (2017). A tentative assumption of the electroacoustic music as an enjoyable music for diverse people. *14th International Conference on Advances in Computer Entertainment Technology (ACE)*, pp. 139–152.

Shibayama, T., Ohmura, H., Yaguchi, H., Hamano, T., & Bümmer, L. (2021). Proposal for the design of the workshop method for the Denshi Onkyo People Project. *Journal of Environmental Art and Design*, pp. 50–55.

Shmulevich, I., & Povel, D. J. (2000). Complexity measures of musical rhythms. In Desain, P., & Windsor, L. (Eds.), *Rhythm perception and production* (pp. 239–244). Swets & Zeitlinger, NL.

Okamoto, S. (1998). A Study on the Creative Thinking in School Music Education: The Effectiveness of Metacognition in Interpreting and Expressing Music. *Japan Society for Educational Methodology*, vol. 24, pp. 105–113.

UNFOLDING EDUCATIONAL GAMES AS SOFTWARE: GAME DESIGNERS' PRACTICES AND PLAYERS' PSYCHOLOGY

Mifrah Ahmad
Design and Creative Technology Vertical, Torrens University, Melbourne, Australia
196 Flinders St, Melbourne, Vic, 3000

ABSTRACT

Game designers consider a player's psychology as one of the most essential components of their designing process. The literature suggests many existing theories, concepts and types of players that can potentially engage with the gameplay created by game designers (GDs). However, not many researchers have explored the idea of game designers' practices and experience on players' psychology in educational games (EGs). For instance, *what matters to their design process? Do they use any published theories? How do they use it? How do they empathize with their players when educational games are considered?* Therefore, this paper discusses 17 game designers' perspectives on how they consider players' psychology in their designing process of EGs and how their experience of designing various games influences their practice. This research is conducted in an Australian context, through a phenomenology approach, where semi-structured interviews were designed and grounded by theory of experience by John Dewey. The audio data collected was thematically analyzed using NVivo and interpreted using the interpretivism paradigm to contextualize the *essence* of GDs' experiences in their practice and unfold their considerations on players' psychology and gameplay experience. As a result, a list of essential theories and concepts that GDs apply in their practice is correlated with GDs' initiation tool(Ahmad, 2023b) to further explore the possibilities of improvising the efficiency of EG designing research in academia, gaming research, and also for new GDs understand the success of conceptualizing players' psychology in designing and developing process.

KEYWORDS

Educational Games, Player's Psychology, Motivation, Cognitive Load Theory, Self-Determination

1. INTRODUCTION

Games have proven to be an effective educational tool as users engage in learning objectives while having fun (Malone, 1980, Malone, 1983, Kultima et al., 2020, Ke, 2016). Many studies have reported positive outcomes of using games in an educational setting (Clark et al., 2016, Ke, 2016), as they provide a more learner-centered environment (Wang et al., 2011), and are effective in subjects such as languages (Razak et al., 2012), mathematics (Barab et al., 2005), and sciences (Shute et al., 2013). Players use their skills in a gameplay activity freely, and consciously experience choices through their play, hence, resulting in *flow* experiences (Gaver, 2002). Researchers have argued that gameplay needs a state of 'flow', where the player experiences deeper absorption and immersion through play (Czikszentmihalyi, 1990).

Undoubtedly, games have become a normalized activity across the educational and entertainment industry where communication, the expression of versatility in ideas and the creation of memorable experiences are concerned (Gee, 2005, Adams, 2014, Perry and De Maria, 2009). For decades, games have been a valuable and efficient learning tool for mental and physical exercises in different contexts such as classrooms or outside (Clark et al., 2016, Connolly et al., 2012). However, Kultima's article argued that games are not entirely extraordinary as what is valuable in games, or good game design, needs more explicit clarification (Kultima et al., 2020). For a player, this means freedom within a virtual environment, which leads a 'relaxed state' of absorbing subject-related material efficiently (Bisson and Luckner, 1996). Due to the adaptive nature of game design, no explicit models are linked to producing the desired end product, as games are a multidisciplinary field of research that positions the players/intended audiences as end-users (Perry and De Maria, 2009, Hagen, 2011, Swartout and van Lent, 2003). Kultima (2018) also argued that game making is not a part of basic education; hence, it has the potential to be misunderstood. It is because game design praxeology sheds light on the experiences that creators go through while making, designing, and developing such games.

The game development and designing process is centered around 'who are the audience or the players of the game'. This is because it influenced the decision-making process of selecting designing core elements with the notion of player experience as a priority (Adams, 2014, Fullerton, 2014, Schell, 2008). Hagen (2011) called this approach designing for player experience. Hagen (2011) posited that Dewey's *art* as experience (Dewey, 1934) is relevant to user experience, and advocated for using *function* (usability of the game) and *experience* (look and feel) in game design (Mills, 2003, Hagen, 2011). Hagen (2011) reported autobiographical responses of a game design team (GD, developer, lead designer, etc.) and suggested the need to encourage GDs to reflect upon their experiences and practices or employ different approaches that could be insightful in gaming industry. However, Hagen acknowledges that the experiences of GDs are subjective, and that interviewing one design/development team does not provide rigorousness in understanding the design experience. In relevance with experience of GDs and players, an *expanded game experience* (EGE) model was proposed to consider a wide range of factors (Kultima and Stenros, 2010). The EGE model provides a detailed description of stages and the game states that GDs can consider when making conflicting design choices, however, it is yet to be applied by GDs in practice. The factors include:

(1) Whether the focus of the game is relevant to a formal structure,
(2) The experience required through play,
(3) The continuum of gameplay experience.

As described above, a conventional software design process is driven by a list of requirements or specifications; however, in most cases, it is driven by the user's experience (Swartout and van Lent, 2003, Perry and De Maria, 2009, Schell, 2008). Here, GDs' position themselves in the players' minds where they anticipate what the latter will experience, and then consider their decision-making by designing the game with compelling experiences, similar to achieving desired play experience (Swartout and van Lent, 2003). Moreover, this is also considered experience-based communication, which seeks to "impart knowledge or skills to users," as it is crucial for the game to influence players' personal beliefs and attitudes (Swartout and van Lent, 2003).

EG's remarkable motivational power includes challenges that excite players, teach, and master achievements; "*It is the act of solving puzzles that makes games fun... with games, learning is the drug*"(Koster, 2013). Several publications have examined the motivational factor that drives the compelling nature of EGs (Fisch, 2005, Mohd et al., 2023), and some suggested that player motivation is associated with the goals and rewarding strategies that are presented within the game (Amory et al., 1999, Nadeem et al., 2023) . While the flow state (addressed earlier), has also been associated with factors that contribute to satisfying players' psychological needs, such as competency, relation to the real world, and autonomy (Deci and Ryan, 2010, Pacheco-Velázquez et al., 2023). Furthermore, factors such as players' learning immersion, its relationship to their achievements, and socialization (within and outside of the game) have been suggested as a motivational boost for players (Pacheco-Velázquez et al., 2023). Considering game design and these factors, the autonomy of a player is activated through different trajectories or progressions of the desired goal (e.g. puzzle games), or it may be perceived as an interactive story through the game play, which allows for an experience as players explore the designed world (Barab et al., 2010, Sotamaa, 2010).

Some researchers argue that effective EG designers must understand learners' capabilities and preferences before including learning content while offering adaptive, engaging and immersive play experiences (Kickmeier-Rust and Albert, 2010, Hamdaoui et al., 2019). Adaptive design is a multi-faceted approach, in which the player's needs and learning through gameplay, weaknesses and preferences to maintain immersive flow are considered part of the design and are considered feedback throughout the design process (Sotamaa, 2007, Ciloglugil and Inceoglu, 2012). The gaps identified by these studies include:

(1) Current lack of dialogue between researchers and practitioners in the gaming field (Tahir and Wang, 2018, Könings et al., 2005, Könings et al., 2014, Wilkerson, 2017).
(2) The need for empirically validated frameworks or ones applied practically in the field by GDs to identify whether they are useful (Tahir and Wang, 2018, Santos and Fraternali, 2015, Ahmad, 2023a)
(3) Only two frameworks: Level-up (Eagle, 2009) and the Experiential gaming model (Kiili, 2005) had empirical evidence to support their credibility based on experiential learning, as reported in Tahir and Wang (2018),

(4) Uncertainty about how theoretical or design principles can be applied within game design practice (Santos and Fraternali, 2015, Wei and Li, 2010).

Therefore, the current research focuses on GDs' perspectives, experiences in their industrial practice as well as their thought-processes that are established in their EG design process where player's psychology is positioned. The practice of designing any genre game and EGs requires parallel discussion, as it is currently niche (Keogh 2021).

2. THEORETICAL AND CONCEPTUAL RELEVANCE OF DATA ANALYSIS AND INTERPREATION

The conceptual and theoretical framework adopted in this paper relates to Dewey's theory of experience (1938) concepts: *growth of experience, purpose, continuity, interaction and situation*. As these concepts are related to the epistemology and ontology of research, constructivism belief is a paradigm that allows for the construction of new knowledge, allowing the subjectivity of individual experiences and embracing their practice experience (Dewey, 1938). The *growth* of experience represents how individuals grow in their careers, experience everyday activities to gain knowledge, learn to achieve their goals, sustain their understanding of the phenomenon, and continue to grow in their experience. The aspects of '*growth*' are driven by one's desire to formulate a '*purpose*' that reverts to the growth of experience with the *intelligence* of one's mind. In this context, the adults whose learning methods combine work and studying, or theoretical and practical exposures are highly familiar and productive in their expertise.

The *purpose* is simple when a desirable quality "*...which identifies freedom with power to frame purposes and to execute or carry into effect purposes so framed. Such freedom is, in turn, identical with self-control; for the formation of purposes and the organization of means them are the work of intelligence*" (Dewey, 1938, p.67). Dewey's description of an actual purpose is that it begins with an impulse. It is always equipped with "end-view" – which is involving "the foresight of the consequences that may result from acting upon that impulse" (1938, p.67). GDs create meaning and constantly reflect through their actions as the games are play-tested, designed, prototyped, iterated, or conceptualized. Hence, deriving an enriched experience shows an individualized aspect of comprehending how GDs differentiate games and EGs, how they distinguish between those above, and their dilemmas in the decision-making process that necessarily require their attention.

The principle of *Continuity* is where each experience taken from the past affects the future experience of the individual. In contrast, *interaction* refers to the situational and GDs' influence on players' or students' experiences. Dewey believes that the elements of *interaction* and the *situation* occur concurrently. Some challenges may be encountered despite the importance of experience, such as "*that all experiences are genuinely or equally educative*" (1938, p.13). Hence, the GDs must first comprehend the nature of human experience, stating that the effect judges the experience's value that this experience has on the individual's present and future, an individual's ability to contribute to society. Therefore, it is directly relevant to how GDs evaluate players' experience while playing the game. In this context, it does not matter whether the player is a gamer or a learner. This is placed directly to the idea of how GDs interact with every individual's needs, to be able to support their cultural and social differences, and to allow them to learn/play equally and freely. Experience, which may be enjoyable, may not contribute to personal growth or experience with no coherence to a situation that does not necessarily result in a cumulative learning foundation for future learning.

The theory of experience has been discussed and applied in many types of fields, and the prominent Kolb's cyclic model (1984) of experiential theory was built on the works of Dewey and has provided its means in the field of education and EGs. As described above, experiential learning is simply defined from the perspective of how learners experience a phenomenon and use that to facilitate learning. It has become an essential for GDs attempting to integrate game-based learning with education (Salen and Zimmerman, 2004, Appelman, 2005, Kolb, 1984): learning involves participation in the real-world, there are intimate relations between experience and education, understandings are derived from and modified through experience, meaningful learning consists of *action* and *reflection*, and *experiential* learning is also based on the belief that people learn best *by doing*.

2.1 Participant Recruitment Criteria, Data Collection Method and Analysis

Based in Australia, the researcher adopted criterion and snowballing recruitment procedures to recruit the GD participants (Table 1). The qualitative semi-structured interviews were designed based on theoretical and conceptual understanding, where unfolding their experiences in designing games and EGs was mapped onto the concepts described in the previous section. Overall, there were 17 GDs who participated through an interview session of approx. 2 hours and 30 minutes (individually) which provided an in-depth reflective experience on participants' game/EG designing practice. This paper interprets one sub-theme of a central theme: EG designing approaches that was identified during coding analysis (Braun and Clarke, 2012). Consequently, the phenomenological approach is adopted to allow the researcher to uncover the *essence* of *lived* experiences described as the qualitative researcher pursues to identify the phenomenon of human experience and then derive a description representing the nature of experience (Kafle, 2011). The *essence* should not be viewed as a vague idea but rather the ability to identify the meaning embodied in the lived experience (Merleau-Ponty and Smith, 1962). Please note that all names are pseudonyms in the analysis.

Table 1. Participant recruitment criteria in this study

Criteria	Participants Details
Location	Within Australia (Victoria, New South Wales, Queensland, South Australia)
Years of Experience	Between 5 years – 15 years
Type of experience	Game designing and Developing (all types of genres; specifically, EG) in Gaming studios and companies
Types of Players' Demographic	All Demographics. Primary school players' demographics are beneficial.
Participants in the study	17

Lastly, it is crucial to mention that experiential learning is also based on the belief that people learn best by doing. Hence, game playing, playtesting and iteration of concepts that GDs go through enables their experiences to grow in the field of game designing.

2.2 Data Analysis and Interpretation Approach

The semi-structured qualitative interviews were audio-recorded, transcribed, and time-stamped. An initial hand-coding approach was adopted before an in-depth thematic analysis using NVivo 10 software was completed. Consequently, the researcher adopted a six-step thematic analysis approach (Braun and Clarke, 2006, Braun and Clarke, 2012) to rigorously achieve commonalities between participants' experience (see Figure 1). The data collection was sufficient once saturation was achieved. This analysis aims to allow GDs' perspectives discuss through reflective experience, their experience designing both types of gaming systems (its *growth* and *continuity*), and the way they analyze the conceptualization of EGs before they are designed (framing the purpose of designing games) and how do they understand their players for EGs. With qualitative approach and phenomenology, the results were interpreted by adapting the interpretivism paradigm, where hermeneutic analysis is adopted to allow the subjectivity of GDs' experience.

Consequently, the results are rigorously discussed to unfold their experience in designing games, their approaches to players' psychology and how they involve their players in the EG designing process, and how they reflect on their practices to describe their designing processes. For data validity and trustworthiness, the authors adopted bracketing where researchers' preconceptions should be used as self-interpreter, as quote presents (Miller and Crabtree, 1992): *"must 'bracket' her/his own preconceptions and enter into the individual's lifeworld and use the self as an experiencing interpreter."* The researcher have bracketed themselves consciously to understand, in terms of the participants' interview that "*the focus [was] on an insider perspective*" (Mouton and Marais, 1988). Other techniques used to establish credibility around multiple-realities adhere to quality interpretive results include: (1) Prolong and persistent engagement with the data, open-discussion (Lincoln and Guba, 1985), and (2) Triangulation where multiple sources of data or multiple theories are used to examine an assertion (Leavy, 2022). The type of triangulation in the current study includes data triangulation, theoretical triangulation, and investigator triangulation.

Lastly, the analysis also correlates and is critically interpreted through researchers' epistemology and ontology position as well as concepts of the theory of experience (Dewey, 1938). Please note that all participants' identifiers are pseudonyms to maintain anonymity.

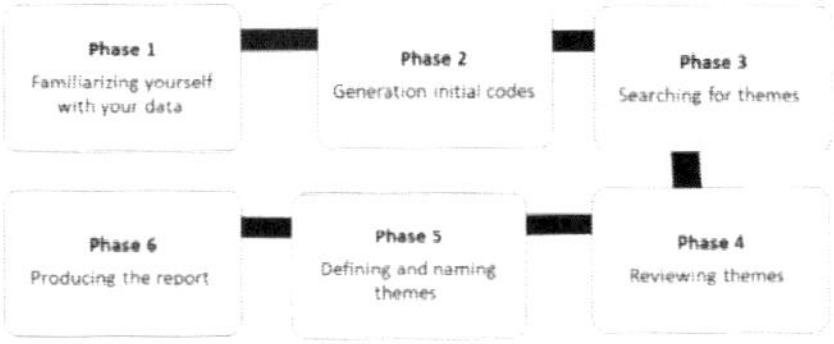

Figure 1. Steps of thematic analysis (adopted from (Braun and Clarke, 2006, Braun and Clarke, 2012)

3. INTERPRETIVE RESULTS AND DISCUSSION

Game designers (GDs) study the players' cognitive and age-specification, as well as intellectual abilities to aid their decision-making processes with the features (Ahmad, 2023b). Here, I prompted the following question: *How do you ensure you have a good understanding of the players you are designing EGs for? For instance, for primary school learners as players?* GDs emphasized the importance of understanding who their audiences are, players and learners as their designing processes require an initial understanding of for whom the game is being designed. As argued by Kiili et al., (2014, p.5), "*when designing EGs, we should consider the constraints of human cognition and design the gameplay according to the target group's skills, characteristics, and prior knowledge*". For instance, Ross asserted:

> *"Well, there is no magic checklist to make your game perfect... it's a combination of arts and science... designing a game mixes various discipline, what it takes to understand game design is an infinite possible way this conversation can go...".*

Firstly, some GDs participants highlighted the use of ***classical conditioning*** during decision-making processes for designing features and mechanics. Briefly, classical conditioning is when an individual's response is tied to a new stimulus within their environment (Kalmpourtzis, 2018). It is closely related with cognitive load theory where a GD considers what the player can keep in their working memory while successfully playing and learning. For instance, Joel described:

> *"...sometimes, I refer to the behaviour nature of the players and if I am considering primary school kids, I need to think of their environment, the classroom... they play with their friends and that changes their response and actions they take in the game too."*

Alternatively, some GDs mentioned the consideration of ***operant conditioning***. Operant conditioning refers to the process where people learn a behavioral response because certain kinds of behavior are rewarded or punished. For instance, Nora added: "*... I know that rewards are crucial, and I use operant conditioning to ensure I have a balance between both encouragement and failure rewards*". This also relates with *situation*, *interaction*, and *continuity* principles; may also integrate the use of *social control* and *freedom* through the game design (Dewey, 1938). It is reasonable to mention that GDs shape the actions or choices that the players are likely to make in their future game plays into consideration.

Most GDs participants advocated the need to have a flow in experiences and considering their game designing decisions based on the interactions and actions that encourage learning processes such as Paige mentioned: "*sense of controlling their [players'] actions and feelings through the design decisions*" , or Cathy added: "*concentration or focused to complete a goal*", and other participants also showed a contemplating thought around identifying sufficient rewards, i.e. Paige mentioned, "*if the design has clarity of representing the content can infiltrate players' mind*". All of these factors are present within the flow theory/flow framework proposed for EGs (Kiili et al., 2014), where the GDs suggest the need to understand their players and ensuring that the flow state is achieved through the designing processes was observed.

With flow state, all GDs mentioned the need to ensure that the ***experiential*** learning occurs, in the form of *optimal*, *memorable*, and *worthwhile* experiences. This relates to *optimal* experience and a complex cognitive condition where coherent motivational and emotional components coexist (Delle Fave, 2009). It relies on GDs' perspectives of positioning and accepting the subjectivity, values, and priorities of individual learners/players and demonstrating the role of designing a game and features constructively. For instance, Paige suggested: "... *achieving a positive balance between in-game challenges and player's skill level that interacts through the 'optimal channel' of activities within the game is tough, but it needs to be done to get them to experience what I design*".

For GDs, players' interaction and progression through the play is when learning occurs as they actively explore and discover the game world to find solutions to a given problem. Anne emphasized: "*experience is so important because as they play, they develop a knowledge representation in their minds and discover an inconsistency, or a change, between their current knowledge and actively experiencing through play*". Participants mentioned ***experiential*** and ***flow*** learning that impacts player's *growth* of experience and making decisions that inform GDs' approach to designing EG. For *worthwhile* experiences, Zack emphasized:

[Zack]: The game needs to be sufficiently challenging, ensuring that players feel something through the play and having a worthwhile experience when they play.

All GD participants advocated their need to understand the cognitive levels of their players, (***cognitive load theory***) their mental structures, and that learners as players have similar yet distinctive levels in which they process information. *Cognitive load* may be affected by the intrinsic nature of the material (intrinsic cognitive load), the manner in which the material is presented (extraneous cognitive load), or by the effort needed to process and take action within the game environment (Sweller et al., 1998). As Nora argued: "*for little kids 4-5 years of age, the design choices and features will be different to players of age 6 to 8! This can't be overlooked!*". It can be observed that cognitive load theory refers to the brain's functional capacity and quantity of information that is represented within the game design for free exploration for players is necessary. For instance, Cathy added:

"... we as adults have different working memory capacities, and we need to be considerate of how children's cognitive load can process the design of the games ... so understanding cognitive load helps in designing and merging all features in the designing to ensure it is not loaded!".

Interestingly, Terry mentioned that the players' psychology is thoroughly explored during his EG designing process as he employs ***self-determination theory*** which he learned through his psychology course: "*... we need psychology knowledge to predict how players might respond to a gameplay experience*". He elaborated on the need for GDs to expand knowledge on a player's psychology and claimed it is deeply relevant to motivation (intrinsic and extrinsic). Terry further explained:

"So, there's an exciting psychological theory called self-determination theory, which has been used to show that video games are incredibly effective at meeting people's psychological needs, more so than any other entertainment medium that humans have devised so far. That's based on meeting competence, autonomy, and relatedness aspects. So, in designing a game, you need to think about those three factors."

The ***self-determination theory*** has the following concepts that are highly crucial to learn about the players: (a) *competence* (feeling effective at one's activities), (b) *autonomy* (having a choice and being able to be yourself), and (c) *relatedness* (feeling connected to others or having a sense of belonging) (Deci and Ryan, 1985). As defined, *extrinsic motivation* is a drive to behave in specific ways based on external sources, and it results in external rewards, whereas *internal motivation* comes from within an individual – the inspirations, values, interest, and personal sense. Furthermore, Gemma also explained its relevance to learning and engaging with playtesting: "*how players behave in the situation, interact with the game, and continuously provide involuntary feedback; all relates with their prior understanding of gameplays, their experiences and personal interests*". It can be assumed that their best source of learning about their players is to observe (playtesting) their players, which influences their iterative processes in designing phases more profoundly and accurately.

The following summarizes the type of theories that GDs mentioned and explained, along with their emphasis on demographic data needed to contextualize their player's learning intellectuals. According to the data analysis, there are six theories/techniques that GDs' participants usually pursue:

(1) ***Classical conditioning*** explained under behaviourism as "conditional stimuli can lead to conditional responses" (Kalmpourtzis, 2018, Pavlov, 1927).
(2) ***Operant conditioning*** expanded on classical conditioning by proposing that the environment impacts our behaviour by either a reinforcement or weaking particular traits, see Kalmpourtzis (2018, p.94) cited Skinner's concept (Skinner, 1948),
(3) ***Flow theory*** as a concept that constructs experiences for players during play (Csikszentmihalyi, 1990),
(4) ***Experiential theory/learning***

(5) ***Cognitive load theory*** to bridge gaps between information structure and human cognitive architecture to efficiently use their working memory during play (Paas et al., 2004),

(6) ***Self-determination theory*** relevant with ***motivational theory*** (Deci and Ryan, 1985), that includes intrinsic and extrinsic factors associated with players' engagement and motivational levels).

Lastly, this is associated with how GDs approach to designing games and EGs, where the current author previously proposed an initiation tool (see Figure 4 in (Ahmad, 2023b), that GDs go-through in their decision-making processes of designing games/EGs and how the GDs' values and reflective practices influence their designing processes in industry. Thus, it also has a reciprocal relationship with their gameplay, their players game play and the experience they intend to design for their players. Therefore, adapting and combining the position of GDs' initiation tool with players' psychology to demonstrate its position in the designing process of EG as GDs' practitioners recommended (see Figure 2).

4. CONCLUSION

GD participants described using the theorists' point of view to link players' psychology as they seem not always to have play-testers available. This demonstrates their *growth* of experience and the *quality* of experience that *contextualised* themselves in the position of players' minds, behaviours, and reactions anticipated by them and revealed those during playtesting. I argue that the iterations for every game design prototype reform its *formation* of unity (the interactivity between game design elements within the game). That means the *formation of purpose* of designing an EG becomes more explicit and more apparent throughout this process. The data revealed that there are six (6) dominant theoretical and/or conceptual published works that are highly adapted by GD participants in the designing process of games and EGs (GDs' initiation tool, see Figure 2). It enables them to empathise and contextualise their sense of understanding around player's skills and motivations to continuously engage with the game/EGs.

The limitation here would be that more GDs could be involved in the interpretive and data collection process. The current context is based in Australia; hence the focus is towards Australian gaming industry. This can further expand and apply in various other contexts to comprehend the similarities and differences. It is essential to understand the current practices to help identify what matters to their practices and how the gaming researchers, communities, and academics can contribute the mentioned works above to expand the use of the aforementioned theories/concepts by participants to help practitioners in the field to achieve more thorough understanding of these concepts.

Further recommendation is to conduct research that can potentially be employed through various genres of games. The current paper discusses video games and educational games (digital); as this paper is a part of a larger project. Another approach is to adopt a participatory design approach, with empathy technique and multiple stakeholders to help identify a sense of collaborative experience and a deeper understanding of the wants and needs of GDs.

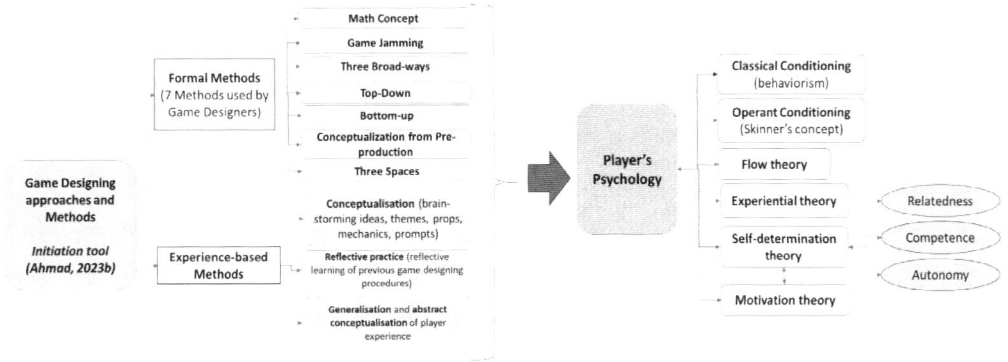

Figure 2. Game Designing Player's Psychology: The *link* between Game Designers' initiation tool and Player's psychology

REFERENCES

Adams, E. (2014). Fundamentals Of Game Design, In: New Riders Publishing.

Ahmad, M. (2023). Discovering Educational Game Design Through 'Conversation Starters': Teachers' And Game Designers' Perspectives. Proceedings Of The 17th European Conference On Games Based Learning., 5-6 October 2023 2023a Enschede, Netherlands., 1-12.

Ahmad, M. (2023b). Towards Standardizing Game Designing Processes: Game Designers' Initiation Tool. *In:* Pietriková, B. S. A. E. (Ed.) *Computer Science For Game Development And Game Development For Computer Science.*: Intechopen.

Amory, A., Naicker, K., Vincent, J. & Adams, C. (1999). The Use Of Computer Games As An Educational Tool: Identification Of Appropriate Game Types And Game Elements. *British Journal Of Educational Technology,* 30, 311-321.

Appelman, R. (2005). Designing Experiential Modes: A Key Focus For Immersive Learning Environments. *Techtrends,* 49, 64-74.

Barab, S., Thomas, M., Dodge, T., Carteaux, R. & Tuzun, H. (2005). Making Learning Fun: Quest Atlantis, A Game Without Guns. *Educational Technology Research And Development,* 53, 86-107.

Barab, S. A., Gresalfi, M. & Ingram-Goble, A. (2010). Transformational Play: Using Games To Position Person, Content, And Context. *Educational Researcher,* 39, 525-536.

Bisson, C. & Luckner, J. (1996). Fun In Learning: The Pedagogical Role Of Fun In Adventure Education. *Journal Of Experiential Education,* 19, 108-112.

Braun, V. & Clarke, V. (2006). Using Thematic Analysis In Psychology. *Qualitative Research In Psychology,* 3, 77-101.

Braun, V. & Clarke, V. (2012). Thematic Analysis.

Ciloglugil, B. & Inceoglu, M. M.(2012). User Modeling For Adaptive E-Learning Systems. International Conference On Computational Science And Its Applications, 2012. Springer, 550-561.

Clark, D. B., Tanner-Smith, E. E. & Killingsworth, S. S. (2016). Digital Games, Design, And Learning: A Systematic Review And Meta-Analysis. *Review Of Educational Research,* 86, 79-122.

Connolly, T. M., Boyle, E. A., Macarthur, E., Hainey, T. & Boyle, J. M. (2012). A Systematic Literature Review Of Empirical Evidence On Computer Games And Serious Games. *Computers & Education,* 59, 661-686.

Czikszentmihalyi, M. (1990). *Flow: The Psychology Of Optimal Experience*, New York: Harper & Row.

Deci, E. L. & Ryan, R. M. (1985). Intrinsic Motivation And Self-Determination In Human Behavior. *Perspectives In Social Psychology.*

Deci, E. L. & Ryan, R. M. (2010). Self-Determination. *The Corsini Encyclopedia Of Psychology*, 1-2.

Delle Fave, A. (2009). Optimal Experience And Meaning: Which Relationship? *Psihologijske Teme,* 18, 285-302.

Dewey, J. (1934). *Art As Experience.,* New York, First Perigee Printing.

Dewey, J. (1938). *Experience And Education: Kappa Delta Pi,* Rochefeller Center, New York, Ny 10020, Touchstone Ny.

Eagle, M. (2009). Level Up: A Frame Work For The Design And Evaluation Of Educational Games. Proceedings Of The 4th International Conference On Foundations Of Digital Games, 2009. 339-341.

Fisch, S. M. (2005). Making Educational Computer Games" Educational". Proceedings Of The 2005 Conference On Interaction Design And Children, 2005. 56-61.

Fullerton, T. (2014). *Game Design Workshop: A Playcentric Approach To Creating Innovative Games*, Crc Press.

Gaver, W. (2002). Designing For Homo Ludens. *I3 Magazine,* 12, 2-6.

Gee, J. P. 2005. Learning By Design: Good Video Games As Learning Machines. *E-Learning And Digital Media,* 2, 5-16.

Hagen, U. (2011). Designing For Player Experience: How Professional Game Developers Communicate Design Visions. *Journal Of Gaming & Virtual Worlds,* 3, 259-275.

Hamdaoui, N., Idrissi, M. K. & Bennani, S. (2019). Educational Games Design: How To Create Adaptive, Engaging, And Fun Learning Experiences. *Handbook Of Research On Immersive Digital Games In Educational Environments.* Igi Global.

Kafle, N. P. (2011). Hermeneutic Phenomenological Research Method Simplified. 181-200.

Kalmpourtzis, G. (2018). *Educational Game Design Fundamentals: A Journey To Creating Intrinsically Motivating Learning Experiences,* New York, Ak Peters/Crc Press.

Ke, F. (2016). Designing And Integrating Purposeful Learning In Game Play: A Systematic Review. *Educational Technology Research And Development,* 64, 219-244.

Kickmeier-Rust, M. D. & Albert, D. (2010). Micro-Adaptivity: Protecting Immersion In Didactically Adaptive Digital Educational Games. *Journal Of Computer Assisted Learning,* 26, 95-105.

Kiili, K. (2005). Digital Game-Based Learning: Towards An Experiential Gaming Model. *The Internet And Higher Education,* 8, 13-24.

Kiili, K., Lainema, T., De Freitas, S. & Arnab, S. (2014). Flow Framework For Analyzing The Quality Of Educational Games. *Entertainment Computing,* 5, 367-377.

Kolb, D. A. (1984). *Experiential Learning: Experience As The Source Of Learning And Development*, Prentice Hall.

Könings, K. D., Brand-Gruwel, S. & Van Merriënboer, J. J. (2005). Towards More Powerful Learning Environments Through Combining The Perspectives Of Designers, Teachers, And Students. *British Journal Of Educational Psychology,* 75, 645-660.

Könings, K. D., Seidel, T. & Van Merriënboer, J. J. (2014). Participatory Design Of Learning Environments: Integrating Perspectives Of Students, Teachers, And Designers. *Instructional Science,* 42, 1-9.

Koster, R. (2013). *Theory Of Fun For Game Design,* United States Of America, O'reilly Media, Inc.

Kultima, A., Lassheikki, C., Park, S. & Kauppinen, T. (2020). Designing Games As Playable Concepts: Five Design Values For Tiny Embedded Educational Games. Proceedings Of The 2020 Digra International Conference: Play Everywhere, Tampere, Finland, 2020.

Kultima, A. & Stenros, J. (2010). Designing Games For Everyone: The Expanded Game Experience Model. Proceedings Of The International Academic Conference On The Future Of Game Design And Technology, 2010. 66-73.

Leavy, P. (2022). *Research Design: Quantitative, Qualitative, Mixed Methods, Arts-Based, And Community-Based Participatory Research Approaches*, Guilford Publications.

Lincoln, Y. S. & Guba, E. G. (1985). Naturalist Inquiry. Beverly Hills, Ca: Sage.

Malone, T. W. (1980). What Makes Things Fun To Learn? Heuristics For Designing Instructional Computer Games. Proceedings Of The 3rd Acm Sigsmall Symposium And The First Sigpc Symposium On Small Systems, 1980. 162-169.

Malone, T. W. (1983). Guidelines For Designing Educational Computer Programs. *Childhood Education,* 59, 241-247.

Merleau-Ponty, M. & Smith, C. (1962). *Phenomenology Of Perception*, Routledge London.

Miller, W. L. & Crabtree, B. F. (1992). Primary Care Research: A Multimethod Typology And Qualitative Road Map.

Mills, T. (2003). Experience Design: It's Not Just For Disneyland Anymore. *Available At Mills' Personal Web Site: Http://Www. Inajar. Org/Other/Experience. Pdf [2010-04-30].*

Mohd, C. K., Nuraini, C. K., Mohamad, S. N. M., Sulaiman, H., Shahbodin, F. & Rahim, N. (2023). A Review Of Gamification Tools To Boost Students' Motivation And Engagement. *Journal Of Theoretical And Applied Information Technology,* 101, 2771-2782.

Mouton, J. & Marais, H. C. (1988). *Basic Concepts In The Methodology Of The Social Sciences*, Hsrc Press.

Nadeem, M., Oroszlanyova, M. & Farag, W. (2023). Effect Of Digital Game-Based Learning On Student Engagement And Motivation. *Computers,* 12, 177.

Paas, F., Renkl, A. & Sweller, J. (2004). Cognitive Load Theory: Instructional Implications Of The Interaction Between Information Structures And Cognitive Architecture. *Instructional Science,* 32, 1-8.

Pacheco-Velázquez, E., Salinas-Navarro, D. E. & Ramírez-Montoya, M. S. (2023). Serious Games And Experiential Learning: Options For Engineering Education. *International Journal Of Serious Games,* 10, 3-21.

Pavlov, I. (1927). Conditioned Reflexes (Gv Anrep. Transl.) Oxford University Press. *London, Uk.*

Perry, D. & De Maria, R. 2009. *Game Design: A Brainstorming Toolbox*, Course Technology, A Part Of Cengage Learning.

Razak, A. A., Connolly, T. & Hainey, T. (2012). Teachers' Views On The Approach Of Digital Games-Based Learning Within The Curriculum For Excellence. *International Journal Of Game-Based Learning (Ijgbl),* 2, 33-51.

Salen, K. & Zimmerman, E. (2004). *Rules Of Play: Game Design Fundamentals*, Mit Press.

Santos, A. D. D. & Fraternali, P. (2015). A Comparison Of Methodological Frameworks For Digital Learning Game Design. International Conference On Games And Learning Alliance, 2015. Springer, 111-120.

Schell, J. (2008). *The Art Of Game Design: A Book Of Lenses.,* Burlington, Usa, Morgan Kaufman

Shute, V. J., Ventura, M. & Kim, Y. J. (2013). Assessment And Learning Of Qualitative Physics In Newton's Playground. *The Journal Of Educational Research,* 106, 423-430.

Skinner, B. F. (1948). 'Superstition'in The Pigeon. *Journal Of Experimental Psychology,* 38, 168.

Sotamaa, O. (2007). Perceptions Of Player In Game Design Literature. Digra Conference, 2007.

Sotamaa, O. (2010). When The Game Is Not Enough: Motivations And Practices Among Computer Game Modding Culture. *Games And Culture,* 5, 239-255.

Swartout, W. & Van Lent, M. (2003). Making A Game Of System Design. *Communications Of The Acm,* 46, 32-39.

Sweller, J., Van Merrienboer, J. J. & Paas, F. G. (1998). Cognitive Architecture And Instructional Design. *Educational Psychology Review,* 10, 251-296.

Tahir, R. & Wang, A. I. (2018). Insights Into Design Of Educational Games: Comparative Analysis Of Design Models. Proceedings Of The Future Technologies Conference, 2018. Springer, 1041-1061.

Wang, Y., Liu, X., Lin, X. & Xiang, G. (2011). An Evaluation Framework For Game-Based Learning. Proceedings Of The 15th Global Chinese Conference On Computers In Education. Hangzhou, China, 2011.

Wei, T. & Li, Y. (2010). Design Of Educational Game: A Literature Review. *Transactions On Edutainment Iv,* 266-276.

Wilkerson, M. H. (2017). Teachers, Students, And After-School Professionals As Designers Of Digital Tools For Learning. *Participatory Design For Learning,* 125-138.

A PLAYFUL APPROACH TO EXTENDED REALITY GAME DEVELOPMENT BY INTEGRATING TANGIBLE AND VIRTUAL INTERFACES

Hengbin Zhang, Xinyi Wu, Xiaoyang Wu and Ruowei Xiao
Southern University of Science and Technology, Shenzhen, Guangdong, China

ABSTRACT

Extended reality game technology transcends the boundaries between reality and virtuality, offering an unprecedented gameplay experience. It not only grants game designers and developers with new creative opportunities, but also challenges for traditional game development paradigm. This exploratory study proposes a playful approach that integrates tangible and virtual user interfaces specifically for XR game development. By utilizing experience prototyping and the Wizard-of-Oz experiment, we were able to simulate the proposed hybrid interfaces and gather preliminary user feedback. We further conducted quantitative and qualitative analyses, as well as adopted a rigorous thematic analysis method. Five design implications with generalizable design knowledge were ultimately synergized, with the aim of guiding our subsequent design iterations and inform future game development research within the domain.

KEYWORDS

Extended Reality, Mixed Reality, Game Development, Tangible Programming Interface

1. INTRODUCTION

Extended reality (XR), as an umbrella term that encompasses Virtual Reality (VR), Augmented reality (AR) and Mixed Reality (MR), refers to spatial, immersive technologies that enable human-beings to observe and interact in a fully or partially synthetic digital environment (Milgram et al., 1995). Specifically, immersive social XR platforms featuring massive multiplayer online video games and open game worlds, are believed not only the literary origin, but also the technical archetype of the hyped term, "Metaverse" (Mystakidis, 2022). Recently, many IT tycoons like Apple, Meta, Microsoft have heavily invested in this sector.

Despite the great potential of XR games, merging physical reality with digital virtuality brings about new challenges for game designers and developers. One of them is that the conventional development paradigm for video games was established with an intensive, if not exclusive, emphasis on the virtual, synthetic contents. Game creators often find themselves busy dealing with all kinds of integration and interoperability issues among heterogeneous physical devices and components, instead of focusing on the design of game mechanism and playful experience per se. Thus, it entails a unified, consistent mechanism to merge, manage and coordinate between diverse physical entities and virtual assets, so as to reduce the technical barriers and development cost. Moreover, many XR games are staged in the application scenarios that require on-site deployment and playtest, e.g. in classrooms, museums, smart factories etc. It indicates the need also for on-the-fly programming and debugging, also known as the "live coding" (Rein et al., 2018).

In this study, we conducted exploratory research to investigate a playful, hybrid approach that combines both virtual and tangible programming interfaces. To be explicit, we first introduced Finite State Machine (FSM), which was also widely adopted in the early game AIs (Sweetser and Wiles, 2002), as a unified model for heterogeneous in-game virtual assets and physical entities, and constructed a compatible experience prototype (Buchenau and Suri, 2000) accordingly. Second, we carried out a Wizard-of-Oz (WoZ) experiment (Dahlbäck, Jönsson and Ahrenberg, 1993) with 25 participants to elicit their feedback regarding the proposed method. The results were analyzed both quantitatively and qualitatively, and synergized into generalizable design implications for guiding our next iteration and possibly future research in this domain.

a) b) c) d) e)

Figure 1. a) Side view and b) top view of a container. Physical widgets for c) state transfer, d) transfer triggers and e) links

In the following sections, we will introduce current state-of-the-art research in Section II. Section III outlines the overall research methodology and Section IV presents the processes and outcomes of both quantitative and qualitative data analysis, and V provides a summary of the limitations and contributions.

2. BACKGROUND

The integration of XR technologies with tangible user interface (TUI) has garnered significant interest in the research community in recent years. For example, BlockXR (De Siqueira, Feijóo-García and Stanley, 2021) explores the fusion of physical block programming with projection-based AR and tangible interactions. This integration enables programming actions and feedback to occur seamlessly, thereby minimizing distractions. GeoGate (Ssin et al., 2019) integrates AR with a ring-shaped TUI to facilitate dataset navigation, enabling users to focus on AR content. Similarly, CodeCubes (Cleto et al., 2020) utilizes physical paper cubes as interfaces for manipulating virtual elements, while Draw2Code (Im and Rogers, 2021) and AR-Maze (Jin et al., 2018) combine AR with physical programming blocks, enabling programming in a tangible form and executing generated code within a virtual environment. These approaches provide users with a cohesive view of the operational space, thereby enhancing user understanding and interaction.

Additionally, existing studies have incorporated other technologies to facilitate cross-reality interoperability. For instance, Zanzibar (Villar et al., 2018) introduces a flexible mat interface for tangible user interaction and gaming experiences. It employs NFC and capacitive footprint detection for object tracking, facilitating portability and diverse cross-reality interaction. Similarly, Tlogic (Deng, Wang and Jin, 2019) and Lighters (Wang et al., 2023) utilize image recognition technology to build tangible programming blocks that assist children in problem-solving. Manipulating, placing, and arranging physical objects in space as input allows users to more easily grasp abstract concepts (Li et al., 2022).

The aforementioned studies imply that there is a growing belief among the research community that the hybrid approach can contribute to enhanced novelty, playability and interactivity. Given extant research are mostly education and/or entertainment oriented, there is a rarity of research specifically targeting XR game development tools and the particular challenges that it's confronting. While general-purpose tools like Zanzibar (Villar et al., 2018) emphasize the interactions on a two-dimensional plane, e.g. a desktop, our research distinguishes itself as it explores the design space of three-dimensional spatial interactions and live coding mobility, rendering a layer of playfulness atop the conventional game development approach.

3. METHODOLOGY

We based our study on an existing open framework for Radio Frequency IDentification (RFID) enhanced XR development (Xiao et al., 2022), as our technical foundation. It consists of three major components:

1) A cardboard VR application that runs on smartphones. We opted to utilize the existing Cardboard VR module because it does not rely on any specialized head-mounted display equipment, instead using a smartphone as the display device. This ensures that it can reach a broader user base at a relatively low cost.

Meanwhile, we chose to sacrifice some display quality to achieve lighter weight and higher portability, making it suitable for outdoor or other frequently mobile application scenarios.

2) A Real Time Kinematic (RTK) positioning module coupled with Google Map 3D for tracing users' realtime locations and mapping the virtual reality to the actual physical environment.

3) A passive RFID-based interactive module that complements and enhances the restricted interactability of the cardboard VR, which is originally equipped with only one magnetic press button. The RFID module enables a variety of physical-virtual user interactions such as detecting users' body movement, teleporting between different virtual locations, or dynamic loading virtual assets, by simply scanning passive RFID tags.

The above RFID-XR development framework has been proved its technical feasibility and potentials as a novel approach towards cross-reality game genres such as pervasive MR games. However, users currently have to modify a database file to associate RFID tags with their intended operations or effects; for more complicated logic control and functions, user will have to modify or rewrite the source code by themselves. It thus results in insufficient usability and a relatively high technical threshold. To bridge the gap, we hence propose an FSM-based hybrid programming interface that further conceals the underlying technical architecture and facilitates user-defined coordination among both virtual and physical in-game objects.

3.1 Experience Prototype Design

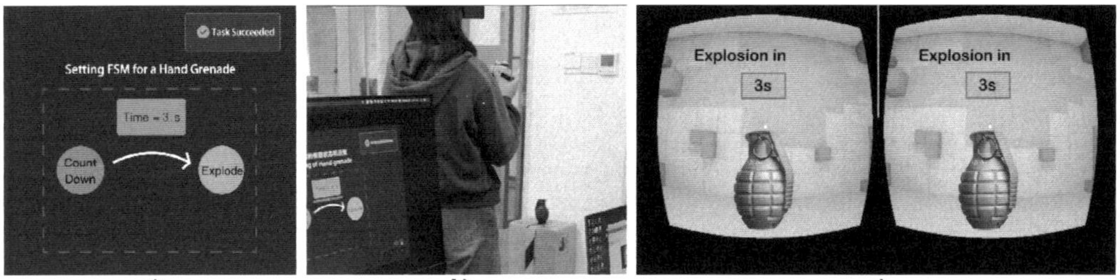

a) b) c)

Figure 2. a) Pseudo-GUI in desktop display. b) A participant used the proposed tool to field debug in front of a physical toy grenade. c) User view in cardboard VR

We designed our programming interface by referring to the previous research by Xiao et al. (Xiao, Wu and Wang, 2019). The authors devised a domain-specific language for composing IoT devices based on FSM model, from which we adopted some basic notions like the "state transfers" and "state transfer mappings", made them into tangible forms, and extended the targets to both virtual and physical game objects. While programming using a domain specific language, it is highly likely for beginners to create syntax or grammar errors, we applied Token+Constraint (Ullmer, Ishii and Jacob, 2005) method to avoid this kind of obvious bugs, by applying physical constraints like the shape of notch and pluggable widgets in our TUI design.

We adopted an experience prototyping method (Buchenau and Suri, 2000), by utilizing low-tech methods and basic materials to simulate possible interactions and user experience at a relative reasonable cost. Our experience prototype includes both pseudo graphical user interface (GUI) as shown in Figure 2 a), and TUI that consists of several types of tangible components. Together they simulated different use scenarios, including both desktop development as well as field debug/playtest which primarily focuses on fine-tuning of some game parameters and settings. The TUI part was designed based on the concept of "physical analogy of the FSM". Some abstract concepts regarding FSM, e.g. "state transfer", "transfer condition/event" etc., all possess their corresponding physical forms, as shown in Figure 1. Additionally, we also decided to take advantages of fun factors from existing toys like the Rubik's cubes and the LEGO bricks. These playful blocks can not only be easily reused to construct non-functional design prototypes, but also naturally signify the affordances and interactions by drawing upon users' previous experience.

As shown in Figure 1, there are four different types of physical components in our experience prototype:

1) **Containers:** The main body of a container is in the form of a Rubik's cube, which is supposed to accommodate an RFID reader in future stage of functional prototype. A Lego-made notch stays always on its top side, and when a physical widget embedded with an RFID tag is plugged in, a game object will be loaded and its corresponding FSM shown in the GUI. Combined with the feedback from the pseudo-GUI, users can rotate upper row of the cube horizontally for selecting between multiple parameters, while the lower row of

the cube for increasing and decreasing the values of the selected parameter. Middle row currently reserved for future use. No vertical rotation is allowed as it affects the position of the top-side notch.

2) **Physical Widgets:** Standard Lego blocks with each representing a pair of state transfer. To specifically note that, the text icons attached to the widgets are only for WoZ experiment purpose. In actual implementation, each physical widget is supposed to be reusable for multiple state transfers.

3) **Transfer Triggers:** A specific type of physical widgets represents the condition or trigger event for a state to transfer to another, e.g. a timer set to three seconds. Also reusable for different conditions and events.

4) **Links:** A specific type of physical widgets for concatenating two or more pairs of state transfer, or two or more FSMs. Additional mapping functions can be attached to a link, e.g. linear, coordinate conversion etc.

3.2 Wizard-of-Oz User Experiment

To gather user feedback about the preliminary design, we conducted a WoZ experiment with 25 participants (16 males, 9 females). In a WoZ experiment, subjects interact with a system that subjects believe to be autonomous, but which is actually being fully or partially operated by a human being (Bella and Hanington, 2012). It was chosen because of our non-functional prototype. Most participants are from fields like design, computer science, and mechanical engineering, ranging from novices to VR/XR experts with over 5 years of experience. The experiment leveraged pseudo-GUIs displayed on both screens and in VR to simulate real-time feedback when the participant performed a task. Each participant was asked to complete three game programming tasks using the proposed prototype within 30 minutes. After completion, the participants filled out a questionnaire and participated in a semi-structured interview. We adhered to the Helsinki Declaration and ethical guidelines from our institution's ethics committee, ensuring informed consent.

During the whole experiment session, the participant was encouraged to apply Think Aloud strategy (Charters, 2003) and required to complete three sequential tasks with a growing complexity. Task I asked the participant to set a grenade from the state "countdown" to the other state "explode", by specifying using a "Timer" type of event trigger. After that, the participant was instructed to don a cardboard VR headset, hold the container, and proceed to a physical location where a toy grenade with embedded RFID tags was placed for field debugging, as shown in Figure 2 b). When participant used the container to scan the RFID tag attached to the grenade, grenade model's appearance, position and parameters will be displayed in cardboard VR view for the participant to further adjust, as shown in Figure 2 c).

Task II asked the participant to switch a door's states between "open" and "locked" using another pair of "true" and " false" states of keys. While the Task III involved the most complicated control logic of establishing a linear mapping between the state transfers of a dice and of a game character, i.e. the state transition of the dice between "idle" and "rolling" will result in randomized dice number, thus triggering the game character's current state to transit from "idle" to "walking" and take the corresponding number of steps.

The participants were asked to respond to the post-experiment questionnaire using a 7-point Likert scale ranging from 1 (strongly disagree) to 7 (strongly agree). We have referred some of our metrics to established assessment indices like Technology Acceptance Model (Davis, 1989) and NASA-TLX (Hart, 2006), while the others were more specific questions related to the proposed hybrid method and FSM model respectively.

4. RESULTS AND ANALYSIS

4.1 Quantitative Analysis Results

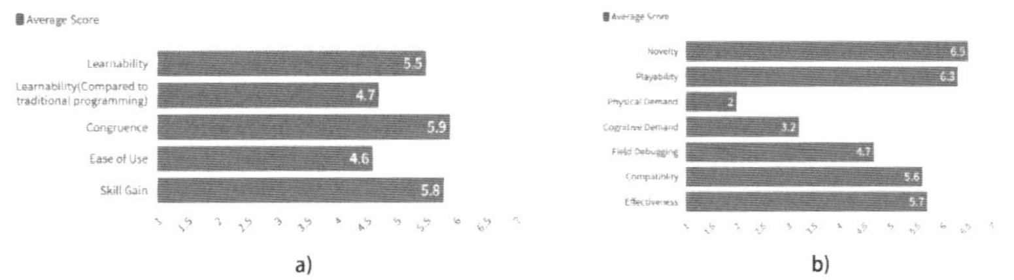

Figure 3. a) User-perceived overall performance of proposed FSM model. b) User-perceived overall performance of the proposed hybrid user interface.

In this subsection, we present the quantitative analysis results, as shown in Figure 3. To specifically note that, the authors claimed NO statistical significance given the limited sample size. While we acknowledge the discrepancies between the experience prototype used at this stage and the final functional prototype, the primary objective of analyzing quantitative data here, was not to provide rigorous statistical verification but to highlight specific aspects that could guide in-depth follow-up inquiries during subsequent interviews.

According to experimental records, the average completion times for Tasks I, II, and III were 172.44s, 183.88s, and 373.38s, respectively. Observations indicate that participants quickly grasped linking two simple state transfers, resulting in similar times for Tasks I and II. However, Task III required significantly more time due to confusion in mapping state transitions between two different FSMs (dice and game character) using two Rubik's cubes.

Our analysis shows that novices in traditional programming perceived the FSM model more intelligible and learnable. Participants generally found FSM usability as neutral and agreed that FSMs effectively describe behaviors of XR game objects, aiding in understanding these objects and their behaviors in the game.

For the hybrid programming interface, the overall data trend indicates that most participants found it novel and playful. The cognitive and physical burdens during use were minimal, with cognitive load slightly higher than physical load. Most participants affirmed the feasibility of using this tool for field debugging, though a minority were uncertain. Additionally, most agreed that the hybrid interface and its spatial interaction were well aligned with the FSM model.

4.2 Qualitative Analysis Results

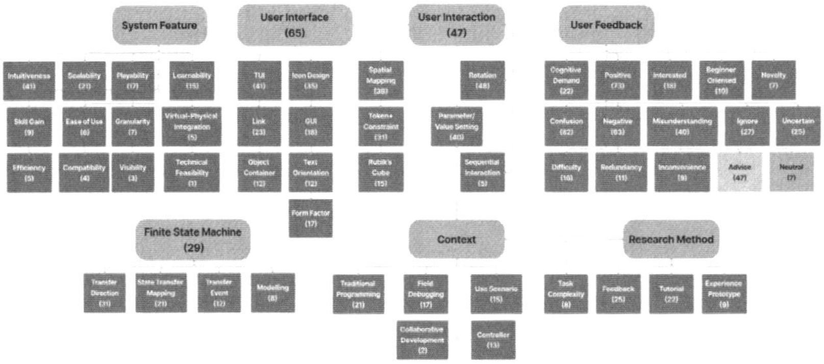

Figure 4. Affinity diagram showing codes and major themes

We conducted a thematic analysis based on the qualitative data gathered from our user interview. The interview audio was transcribed into text and proofread by one of the authors manually before distributed to the whole team. All authors then separately coded the first three interviews and established the initial code set through discussions. After the coding scheme was set up, we went through an independent coding process to ensure inter-rater reliability as possible (Braun and Clarke, 2021). All discrepancies emerged from the results of two independent coders were addressed by group discussion to achieve a final agreement over 99%.

The open coding process resulted in a total of 56 codes, and 7 major themes emerged from the codes via affinity diagramming, as shown in Figure 5. Further, by carefully examining the concurrency between codes, we retained and visualized the strongest thematic connections into a chord diagram, as shown in Figure 4. MAXQDA was used as the coding and matrix analysis tool in this process. The authors discussed and highlighted the recurring and unique patterns across different thematic connections, as well as the quotations related to them. Five design implications were extracted and interpreted from the aforementioned thematic analysis results, as elaborated in the following:

1) **Physicalization:** Participants preferred TUI as it enables physicalization (P5, P9, P11, P22, P24) of coding process based on an abstract model, i.e. the FSM, which facilitates embodied interactions and learning, (P4, P20) and intuitive feedback (P4, P19). But some participants also expressed confusion when they realized that a transfer event also is represented by a physical widget. As the participants put it:

P4: "*Compared with just seeing and memorizing it, the tangible interaction might be more effective... It connects the form of LEGO assembly with the underlying programming logic, which I find quite meaningful and intriguing. Traditional LEGO might construct concrete things, but this forms logical connections.*"

P5: "*Because I used to consider the state transfer a very abstract concept, but you have created something very concrete, a physical object corresponding to an abstract concept. I think it is very interesting.*"

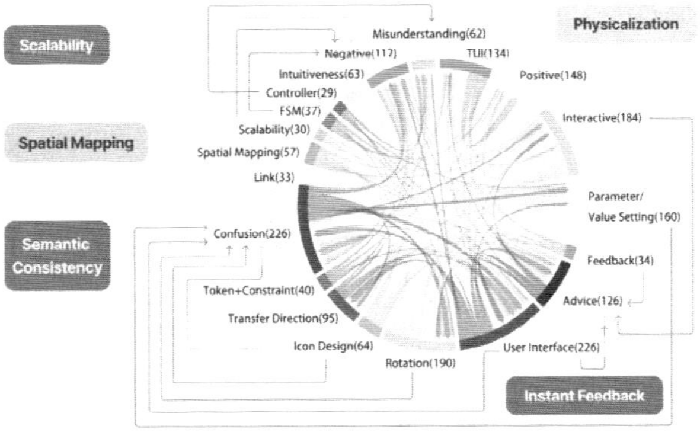

Figure 5. Chord diagram showing strongest thematic connections

P11: "*The most interesting part is tangible programming, a process of exploration and discovery using disorganized materials to create novel interactions, feeling like a game with a strong sense of achievement.*"

P10: "*I don't understand what 'the state transition condition named Timer' in the tutorial means; I didn't realize it actually refers to something physical.*"

2) **Semantic Consistency**. Participants expected a consistency between the design of programming interface, the interaction it provides and its associated meaning (P5, P7, P10, P15, P16, P17, P18, P21). Specifically, the visual elements like icons play an important role and offer supplementary instructions to the users, when the token+constraint is not intuitive enough for them to notice (P2, P3, P22, P24). For instance, multiple participants confused the link used in Task II with the one in Task III. Also, some participants expressed the difficulty they encountered when turning the Rubik's cubes, especially when two cubes were connected by a link piece. As the participants put it:

P13: "*Both actions occur on a horizontal plane, and these two actions somehow overlap. but they're quite different—one involves switching parameters, the other adjusting their values. They could be represented using horizontal and vertical axes respectively to distinguish this different.*"

P16: "*When turning the cube, I felt confused and often turned it the wrong way. Despite the stickers, my instinct was that clockwise should increase the value. Also, when trying to turn the top layer, I ended up turning both cubes, likely due to my personal habit of playing with Rubik's cubes.*"

P17: "*After using one link piece, I mistakenly thought another link piece was the same, leading to several failed attempts. It was challenging, but that's where I found it valuable and positive.*"

3) **Scalability**. As the scale and complexity of the game increase, participants expressed their concerns and uncertainty about both how to utilize FSM for modeling complicated, sequential in-game behaviors (P3, P5, P13), and how users deal with the growing amount of game objects and parameters etc. when scales up (P2, P10, P12, P14). It connects to the user-perceived redundancy, indicating that we should carefully consider the reusability of the physical components when designing and implementing tangible widgets (P19):

P2: "*I'm unsure if the state machine model can handle a vast number of parameters in the future.*"

P3: "*In some XR scenarios, you'll interact with objects whose behaviors can't be easily described by a few parameters, including their reactions to your actions. For example, if I push something, you might install a sensor to measure the force. Then the question becomes how to process and program the related data.*"

P19: "*Make it both fundamental and powerful in functionality, using a limited number of basic widgets to achieve various functions than requiring a specific widget for every single task.*"

4) **Spatial Mapping**. A few participants tend to ignore some spatial attributes, e.g. physical slots, form factors and icon design (P7, P8, P19); On the other hand, tangible programming interface in a three dimensional space entails a stricter, more carefully designed token+constraint strategy (P8, P15, P19, P22).

Considering that XR games set in physical venues often require on-site debugging and live coding, the TUI component thus must be portable and mobile, which excludes most desktop or board-based designs. As a three-dimensional object, a Rubik's Cube can fully utilize its form factor as well as spatial motion attributes such as speed, orientation, tilt angle and axis rotation, possibly captured by inertial measurement units (IMU) and other sensors, to provide a sufficiently rich interaction and operation space as a programming tool:

P7: "*First, I believe the exact spatial relationship isn't that important. For physical widgets like Link, I don't mind if the length matches exactly. A spatial mapping doesn't align well with intuition. As long as it's connected, it can be used. This component doesn't seem very intuitive to me.*"

P8: "*Because I haven't seen exactly how the connection structure works, I just thought that as long as they are connected, it would be used. I possibly didn't consider the deeper logic behind it...*"

P13: "*If you're considering using an axis, maybe the icons attached to the Rubik's cube surface aren't necessary. Once you start turning it, it becomes chaotic. Just indicate which side is facing up. Since the center cubelet in each face doesn't change position, you can use them to anchor the directions.*"

5) **Instant Feedback**. Participants usually expected immediate feedback (P1, P5, P9, P12, P17) or traceable history (P24) to facilitate debugging and learning. This kind of expectation or need also to some extent leads to the participants' misunderstanding that the tool acts as a game object controller (P12, P13, P25). Although most participants mentioned about visual feedback, either in conventional GUI or inside VR, the organization and presentation of feedback information should be carefully designed, because elements like texts, icons, pop-ups, menus etc., which traditional 2D GUIs primarily rely on, may cause extra visual fatigue and difficulties in a 3D development environment. Additionally, for hybrid programming approaches, it is still underexploited to further integrate multimodal feedback such as sound and haptics.

P5: "*I wish you could show me the effects of my programming in VR after I set the grenade to explode.*"

P24: "*There could be a step-by-step recording feature that shows how to backtrack. I tried many times just now and can't remember the steps I took. Having a backtrack record would allow for quicker debugging.*"

5. LIMITATION AND CONTRIBUTION

In summary, the first limitation of this study lies in the research method. The authors are fully aware of the inherent constraints of the non-functional prototype and the WoZ user experiment: It is not feasible to offer identical functionality with that of a functional prototype, e.g. manual operations lead to delayed feedback. Also, when compared with other approaches, the FSM model, which we grounded our entire prototype on, has its own pros and cons: while it is a concise and general model that offers cross-reality interoperability, FSM also falls short of scalability, and the programming structure can become overwhelmingly complicated, e.g. the nesting of multiple FSMs, which the TUI design may fail to capture. Particularly in the context of XR games, it may not be suitable for modeling fine-grained and continuous interactions.

As a result, the proposed programming method seems more suitable for targeting game programming education aimed at beginners with no prior experience, or for the composition and playtest with pre-defined FSM templates, such as user-customized XR games for specific application scenarios like museums. More future work can be done with the refinement of the token+constraint design for the tangible interface and related three-dimensional spatial interaction. In our next iteration, the authors plan to implement a fully functional prototype with sensing and actuating modules, e.g. IMU sensors, vibrators etc., with the aim of incorporating richer spatial motion information and multimodal feedback.

As the contribution of this research, we explored a playful, hybrid approach for XR game development, integrating both virtual and tangible user interface. Grounded on an existing open RFID-XR development framework, we further introduced an FSM-based hybrid programming method atop to achieve cross-reality interoperability and embodied, playful interaction, thus to further lower down the technical threshold and development cost for XR game creators, with or without programming skills. By leveraging experience prototyping and WoZ experiment, we were able to collect preliminary user feedback, signaling very positive potentials regarding the novelty and playfulness of the proposed approach. As a result, five design implications were synergized, respectively, physicalization, semantic consistency, scalability, spatial mapping and instant feedback. We expect the overall research outcome to offer novel and informative insights to guide our forthcoming design refinements and future research endeavors in this domain.

REFERENCES

Bella, M. and Hanington, B., 2012. Universal Universal Methods of Design: 100 Ways to Research Complex Problems, Develop Innovative Ideas, and Design Effective Solutions. MA: Rockport Publishers, p.204.

Buchenau, M. and Suri, J.F., 2000, August. Experience prototyping. In: Proceedings of the 3rd conference on Designing interactive systems: processes, practices, methods, and techniques, pp.424-433.

Braun, V. and Clarke, V., 2021. One size fits all? What counts as quality practice in (reflexive) thematic analysis?. Qualitative Research in Psychology, 18(3), pp.328-352.

Charters, E., 2003. The use of think-aloud methods in qualitative research an introduction to think-aloud methods. Brock Education Journal, 12(2).

Cleto, B., Sylla, C., Ferreira, L. and Moura, J.M., 2020. Codecubes: Coding with augmented reality. In: First international computer programming education conference (ICPEC 2020). Schloss-Dagstuhl-Leibniz-Zentrum für Informatik.

Dahlbäck, N., Jönsson, A. and Ahrenberg, L., 1993, February. Wizard of Oz studies: why and how. In: Proceedings of the 1st international conference on Intelligent user interfaces, pp.193-200.

Davis, F.D., 1989. Perceived usefulness, perceived ease of use, and user acceptance of information technology. MIS Quarterly, pp.319-340.

Deng, X., Wang, D. and Jin, Q., 2019. TLogic: a tangible programming tool to help children solve problems. In: E-Learning and Games: 12th International Conference, Edutainment 2018, Xi'an, China, June 28–30, 2018, Proceedings 12. Springer International Publishing, pp.255-262.

De Siqueira, A.G., Feijóo-García, P.G. and Stanley, S.P., 2021, October. Blockxr: A novel tangible block-based programming platform. In: 2021 IEEE Symposium on Visual Languages and Human-Centric Computing (VL/HCC), pp.1-4. IEEE.

Hart, S.G., 2006, October. NASA-task load index (NASA-TLX); 20 years later. In: Proceedings of the human factors and ergonomics society annual meeting, 50(9), pp.904-908. Sage CA: Los Angeles, CA: Sage publications.

Im, H. and Rogers, C., 2021, June. Draw2code: Low-cost tangible programming for creating ar animations. In: Proceedings of the 20th Annual ACM Interaction Design and Children Conference, pp.427-432.

Jin, Q., Wang, D., Deng, X., Zheng, N. and Chiu, S., 2018, June. AR-Maze: a tangible programming tool for children based on AR technology. In: Proceedings of the 17th ACM Conference on Interaction Design and Children, pp. 611-616.

Li, Y., Kothiyal, A., Weber, T., Rossmy, B., Mayer, S. and Hussmann, H., 2022. Designing Tangible as an Orchestration Tool for Collaborative Activities. Multimodal Technologies and Interaction, 6(5), p.30.

Milgram, P., Takemura, H., Utsumi, A. and Kishino, F., 1995, December. Augmented reality: A class of displays on the reality-virtuality continuum. In: Telemanipulator and telepresence technologies, 2351, pp.282-292. Spie.

Mystakidis, S., 2022. Metaverse. Encyclopedia, 2(1), pp.486-497.

Rein, P., Ramson, S., Lincke, J., Hirschfeld, R. and Pape, T., 2018. Exploratory and live, programming and coding: A literature study comparing perspectives on liveness. arXiv preprint arXiv:1807.08578.

Ssin, S.Y., Walsh, J.A., Smith, R.T., Cunningham, A. and Thomas, B.H., 2019, March. Geogate: Correlating geo-temporal datasets using an augmented reality space-time cube and tangible interactions. In: 2019 IEEE Conference on Virtual Reality and 3D User Interfaces (VR), pp.210-219. IEEE.

Sweetser, P. and Wiles, J., 2002. Current AI in games: A review. Australian Journal of Intelligent Information Processing Systems, 8(1), pp.24-42.

Ullmer, B., Ishii, H. and Jacob, R.J., 2005. Token+ constraint systems for tangible interaction with digital information. ACM Transactions on Computer-Human Interaction (TOCHI), 12(1), pp.81-118.

Villar, N., Cletheroe, D., Saul, G., Holz, C., Regan, T., Salandin, O. et al., 2018, April. Project zanzibar: A portable and flexible tangible interaction platform. In: Proceedings of the 2018 CHI Conference on Human Factors in Computing Systems, pp.1-13.

Wang, X., Xing, Q., Jin, Q. and Wang, D., 2023. "Be a lighting programmer": Supporting children collaborative learning through tangible programming system. International Journal of Human–Computer Interaction, pp.1-19.

Xiao, R., Vianto, A., Shaikh, A., Hamari, J. and Virkki, J., 2022. Exploring the application of rfid for designing augmented virtual reality experience. IEEE Access, 10, pp.96840-96851.

Xiao, R., Wu, Z. and Wang, D., 2019. A Finite-State-Machine model driven service composition architecture for internet of things rapid prototyping. Future Generation Computer Systems, 99, pp.473-488.

A METHOD FOR EMBEDDING BIOMETRIC AND OTHER INFORMATION IN COLOR IMAGES OF FACES

Nazym Kaziyeva[1], Georgy Kukharev[2] and Kalybek Maulenov[3]

[1]*Department of Radio Engineering, Electronics and Telecommunications, L.N. Gumilyov Eurasian National University,Satpayev Str. 2, Nur-Sultan, Republic of Kazakhstan, 010008*

[2]*St. Petersburg Electrotechnical University "LETI", Professor Popov str. 5 litera F, St. Petersburg, Russia, 197022*

[3]*Non-profit Limited Company Akhmet Baitursynuly Kostanay Regional University, Baytursynov Street 47, Kostanai, Republic of Kazakhstan, 110000*

ABSTRACT

The article presents a new fast method for generating a biometric multimedia file consisting of a color image of a face with a color QR code embedded in it, containing biometric data about the face, as well as documentary information about the person to whom this face belongs. Embedding is implemented by simultaneously replacing three LSB slices in the RED, GREEN and BLUE components of a color face image with a color QR code. At the same time, the embedded QR code does not detect the fact of its existence in the multimedia file. To improve the understanding of the idea of the method, the proposed solutions and the algorithm implementing the method, the article presents graphic illustrations with appropriate descriptions and explanations. The solutions proposed in the article have a number of qualitative characteristics presented and discussed in the article. The areas of application of the proposed solutions are marked.

KEYWORDS

Color QR Code, Biometric Multimedia File, Color LSB Layers, Container, Color Images of Faces With Embedded QR Codes

1. INTRODUCTION

As you know, confidentiality of information is a key element in maintaining integrity and protecting against leakage of information that is not intended for general use. First of all, these are personal data of people, state, military and commercial secrets. One of the methods of preserving the confidentiality of information is digital steganography, which provides the possibility of hidden storage of information. There are many methods of hiding data in digital images, including the method of replacing the least significant bits (LSB), which are not noticeable in the filled image to the human eye. However, digital steganography is too complicated in the implementation of its cryptographic part and, therefore, is not always appropriate for a wide and individual application. Especially if the preservation and transfer of confidential information must be carried out within the framework of the required GOST standards. Unlike classical steganography, the work presents approaches that include replacing the contents of LSB layers with a binary QR code containing information embedded in it. In this case, binary QR codes embedded in images are the keepers of hidden information and can be used to protect information in various tasks. Binary QR codes have a significant capacity for recording and storing ASCII information, which provides ample opportunities for storing various data in them. The use of colored QR codes further expands these possibilities.

The aim of our article is to present a new (fast) algorithm for embedding a color QR code into a color image. As an example, the problem of forming a multimedia file based on a color image of a face with a color QR code embedded in it containing biometric data about the face, as well as documentary information about the person to whom this face belongs, is considered. At the same time, a similar algorithm for embedding color QR codes can be applied to any other color images, as well as the information embedded in QR codes may also be different. It is important to note that the use of a color QR code embedded in the face image as a keeper and carrier of all facial information will ensure the protection of this information by restricting open access to it. At the same time, the conditions for the exchange of information according to standards and international channels are maintained without losing any part of it and/or replacing it. These advantages are very important when creating and using biometric databases, as well as when exchanging facial biometric data as confidential information. At the same time, QR codes embedded in a color image do not reveal the fact of their existence in the image. The information embedded in QR codes can be read and decrypted only in accordance with the preparation rule and the encoding method of the original messages that were used to generate QR codes.

Based on the technology of steganography, we recall that it involves the use of an empty container to discreetly conceal classified information in it. After placing the information in the container, it becomes a filled container. In our case, the empty container is the original color image of the face, which becomes a filled container with a QR code embedded in it, which contains biometric and documentary information. In the file form, we previously called this construction as a color BIO QR code. However, if we take into account the platform, the color BIO QR code falls into the class of a multimedia file, as a biometric multimedia file.

2. GENERAL SCHEME OF EMBEDDING BIOMETRIC INFORMATION IN COLOR IMAGES OF FACES

Our solutions relate to facial biometrics and its applications, so we work with images (portraits) of faces that meet all GOST requirements. These portraits have the following geometric characteristics: the image size is at least 320×240 pixels; the face area must be in the vertical axis of the image and must occupy at least 80% of its area; the distance between the centers of the eyes must be at least 60 pixels (here the minimum allowable value for W = 240 pixels).

The general scheme of embedding biometric information (Figure 1) includes several stages. Stages 1-2 show the following processes: obtaining a color image of a face at input "A" and adjusting it in size and placement on the image field, calculating the biometric characteristics of ANTRO and PHENO images of a face; obtaining documentary information about the person to whom this face belongs at input "B". In step 3, the corresponding alphanumeric messages are generated for all data and three QR codes (ANTRO, PHENO and INFO) are generated, each of which represents the unique characteristics of a particular person. Next, a color QR code is generated, which includes generating an empty color image and placing three QR codes (ANTRO, INFO and PHENO) in it, in place of the RED, GREEN and BLUE components. In step 5, the color QR code is embedded in the color image of the face. As a result, the original color image of the face, which was an empty container, becomes a filled container with a color QR code embedded in it, containing facial biometric and documentary information. The results obtained in the first three stages are shown in Figure 2, where two color images of the face are presented, of which the first is the original, the second is corrected according to the requirements of the biometrics standard. The asterisk in the center of the right eye is associated with checking the correct placement of the face area on the field of the corrected image. On the second, lower level, Figure 2 shows three binary QR codes (INFO ANTRO and PHENO) representing the unique characteristics of a particular person. The size of these QR codes is 177×177 pixels. A colored QR code is shown in the upper right corner - the keeper of all facial (biometric and documentary) information. This color QR code also falls under the classification of a multimedia file and can be used independently for the purpose of storing and transmitting biometric and documentary information.

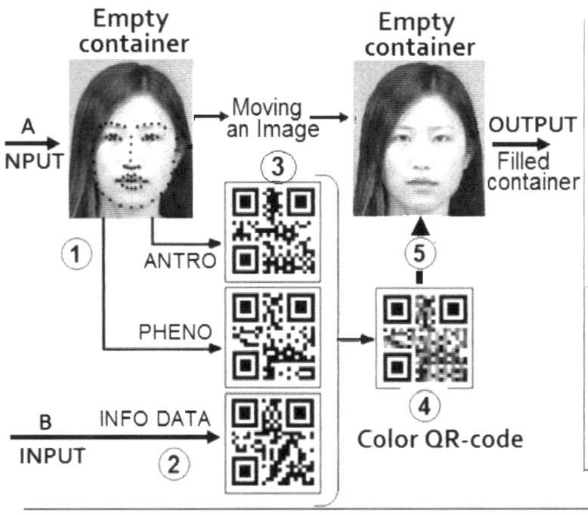

Figure 1. The scheme of embedding biometric information in color images of faces

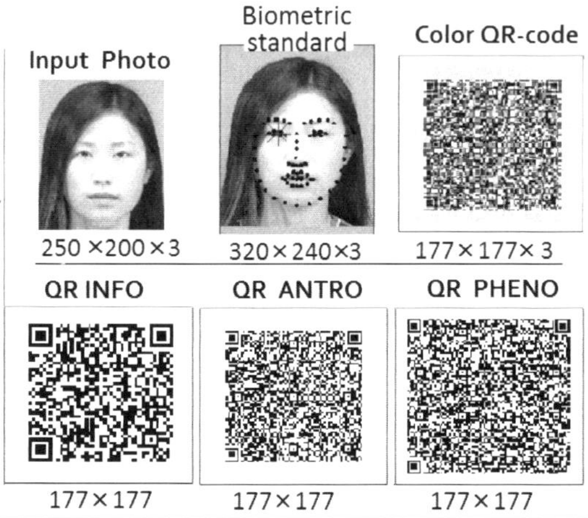

Figure 2. Results obtained in stages 1-3: Faces in biometric standard, binary and color QR-codes

2.1 Description of the Algorithm

At the first step, the system receives a FaceColor face image at input "A", which can be obtained from the camera at the check-in desk at the checkpoint or as a 2D image coming from a biometric database of facial images.

Step #2 intend for preprocessing the face image. Based on the requirements of GOST for Biometrics, image size correction performs to values of 320×240 pixels and correction of the position of the face area on the field of this standard size. This step ensures that the image of the face and its facial biometric characteristics are presented within the boundaries of the accepted standard. This is important for later use in the creation of biometric databases or when exchanging data on request.

In step 3, 68 key points of the face are determined using the algorithm (Kazemi et al., 2014), the procedure of which is publicly available in the OpenCV library. But today more modern tools are available, for example Mediapipe with the BlazeFace model (Lugaresi Camillo et al., 2019), which allows you to determine almost 400 key points on faces, as well as the heights of the face relief at these key points.

At step 4, two sets of facial data are generated: the coordinates of 68 key (anthropometric) points of the face and the brightness features of the face in these coordinates.

In step 5, the values of biometric data are translated into messages (string data type), which are arranged with additional information and boundary signs that support the form adopted for messages intended for QR codes.

At step 6, the messages generated at step 5 are encoded into ASCII characters. In this case, the choice of encoding methods will determine the number of final characters represented in the QR code. In our practical examples, the encoding of the digital values of the coordinates of the key points looks like this:

message = [date, '/FAP' char(NAME),char(pts(:)')];

where:

- FAP - “Facial Anthropometric Point” - additional information defining the name;
- pts - a matrix (size 2×68) of coordinates of key points;
- char(pts) - the procedure for encoding a set of digits into ASCII characters.

A fragment of the encoding of the message data looks like this (the encoded digital data is underlined):

11-Apr-2024TAP Photo:001/#1877: >GUew$> “p^AAADMWbl, 5! ±wwwvkqw~„NUAe] T<’>£oe“irx~.->

The message encoding procedure is standard and depends on the programming language used, which distinguishes it from cryptography.

The message encoding procedure is standard and depends on the programming language used, which distinguishes it from cryptography.

In step 7, two QR codes are generated from the received data: QRANTRO and QRPHENO.

The formation of a "QRINFO" with documentary information is a simpler structure process compared to the previous one, which does not require steps 1-5. It is enough to have only documentary information about the person. This information may include full name, year of birth, citizenship, passport number, date and other information. It is also possible to include a short biography. The volume of documentary information can contain up to 4,296 alphanumeric characters.

Next, you need to convert all the generated binary QR codes into byte format, for example, by writing them to memory in the ".png" format and reading them from memory.

After completing the algorithm for collecting and processing data and generating QR codes, a color QR code is created based on the generated binary QR codes: "QRANTRO", "QRINFO" and "QRPHENO". Mathematically, this process is represented as follows:

- Creating of a three-component zero matrix "QRcolor" according to the size of QR codes:

$$QRcolor = zeros\ (Mqr, Mqr, 3), \quad (1)$$

where Mqr - the number of rows and the number of columns of the zero matrix;

- We replace the three components of the empty Q R color matrix with three QR codes QRANTRO, QRINFO and QRPHENO so that:

$$QRcolor\ (: , : , 1) = QRANTRO;$$
$$QRcolor\ (: , : , 2) = QRINFO; (2)$$
$$QRcolor\ (: , : , 3) = QRPHENO.$$

As a result, we get a color QR code.

When the QRcolor matrix is graphically displayed, we get a color image, and in fact - a color QR code containing three QR codes with biometric and documentary information embedded in them. An example of this color QR code is shown in Figure 2 in the upper right corner.

2.2 Embedding Biometric and Documentary Information in Color Images of Faces

The embedding of biometric and documentary information into a color image of a face (container) is carried out in the block of step 5 of the general scheme, as shown in Figure 1. Two images "meet" here: a size-adjusted color image of a face (FaceColor) and a color QR code pre-generated at the previous stage. A color QR code is immediately embedded in a color image of a face. The embedding operation is implemented by simultaneously replacing three LSB slices in the RED, GREEN and BLUE components of the face image with the components of the same color QR code.

Let a FaceColor matrix of size M×N×3 represent a size-adjusted color image of a face, and a QRcolor matrix of size Mqr × Mqr ×3 represent a color QR code.

Then, mathematically, the embedding method represented as follows:

1. We perform the modulo 2 operations for the FaceColor matrix and obtain an LSBcolor matrix of size M×N×3 representing three LSB slices (red, green and blue) of a colored face image.

In Python it looks like this:

$$LSBcolor = (FaceColor)\ \%\ 2; (3)$$

2. We form a three-component zero matrix NewLSBcolor, which simulates the basis of a new LSB color slice:

$$NewLSBcolor = zeros\ (M, N, 3); (4)$$

3. We replace the highlighted place in NewLSBcolor with a colored QR code:

$$NewLSBcolor\ (1{:}\ Mqr, 1{:}\ Mqr, :) = QRcolor; (5)$$

4. We subtract the LSBcolor matrix from the M×N×3 FACEcolor matrix and add the result obtained with the NewLSBcolor matrix, and save the result in the FACEfull matrix:

$$FACE_{FULL} = (FACEcolor - LSBcolor) + NewLSBcolor, \quad (6)$$

Where $FACE_{FULL}$ - a matrix representing a filled container image that arrives at the output (see Figure 1).

Thus, the $FACE_{FULL}$ image now contains three QR codes embedded in it (in the RED, GREEN and BLUE components) in accordance with the order in which the color QR code was formed. The full view of the color slices for the empty container and the new LSB color slice for the filled container are shown in Figure 3. The embedded color QR code is clearly visible on the second level. The fifth level shows the difference between empty and filled containers. In the table below the figure, the first row shows the numbers of colored slices, the second row shows their weight values. The difference in slices between empty and filled containers is below the rows of the table.

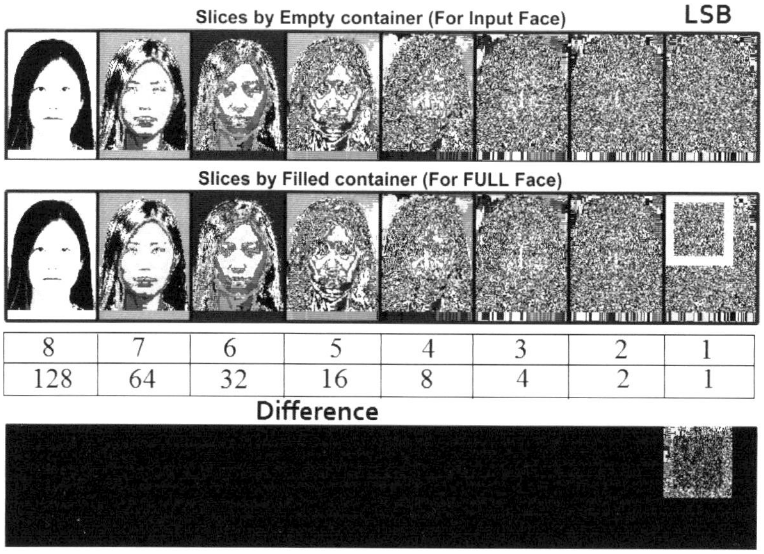

8	7	6	5	4	3	2	1
128	64	32	16	8	4	2	1

Figure 3. Eight colored bit slices of a colored face image for an empty (first line) and filled container (second line). LSB slices are marked with LSB

If we present the bit slices of each of the components ("RED", "GREEN" and "BLUE") separately, then the graphical picture will contain all 24 binary bit slices, as shown in Figure 4.

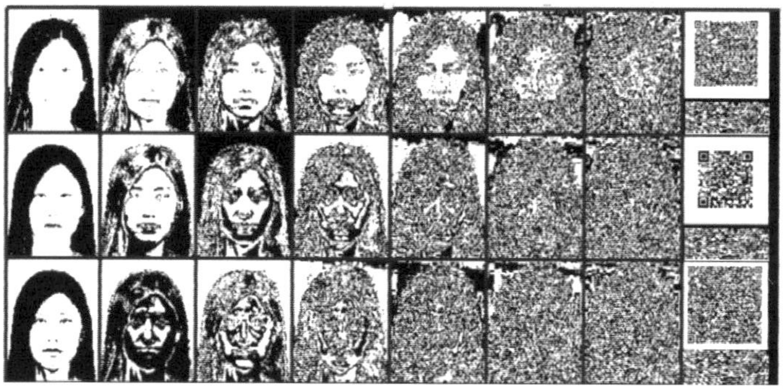

Figure 4. 24 bit slices of a color image of a filled container

At the final stage of the procedure for embedding QR codes in a color image of a face, a compact representation of complete facial information, graphic, biometric and documentary information is finally formed. At the same time, the color image of the face "retains" the basic biometric information with the necessary documentary data, providing versatility of presentation and an increased degree of protection of all information. Also, note that the color QR code can be used independently and can be sent very quickly on demand to transmit the information contained in them. Finally, sometimes there is a need to preserve biometric and/or documentary data about people over long periods of their lives. In this case, the new information is stored in a new QR code, which is embedded in the slices on the left side of the LSB. The result of embedding three-color QR codes is shown in Figure 5.

As an advantage of the above facts, we note that usually in biometric databases, facial images, biometric data and documentary data are stored in different catalogs, which over the course of life leads to their loss and/or difficulties in storing and searching them.

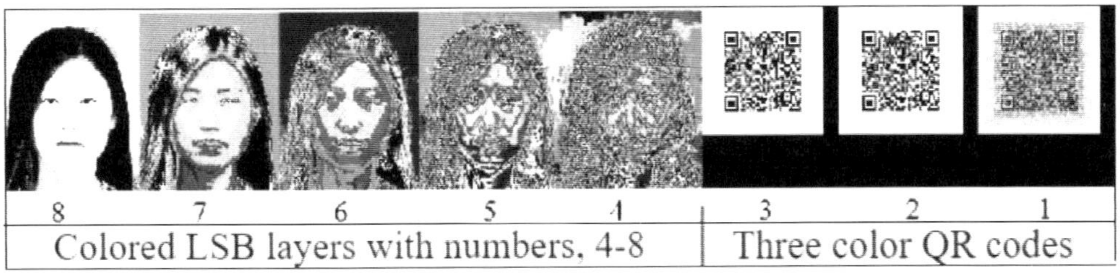

Figure 5. Colored bit slices of a filled container with three embedded color QR codes. The number of all embedded binary QR codes will be nine!

It was previously shown that the difference in slices between an empty and a filled container is visible only in slices containing QR codes. Now let's show that the face image, with QR codes embedded in it, also does not differ from the original image. Figure 6 shows the images of the faces of an empty and filled container from our previous examples. The following is the absolute difference between these color images, as graphic objects or numerical matrices. Obviously, the difference is due only to the difference in the texture of both images in the LSB area (see Figure 3). The fourth place in Figure 6 is occupied by the graphical result of the phase correlation between the images of faces for an empty and filled container. The correlation coefficient was 0.985! This means that the built-in color QR code did not affect the appearance of the image. Note that phase correlation is very sensitive even to the smallest (almost invisible) changes in the texture of images and, therefore, is often used to compare images by texture.

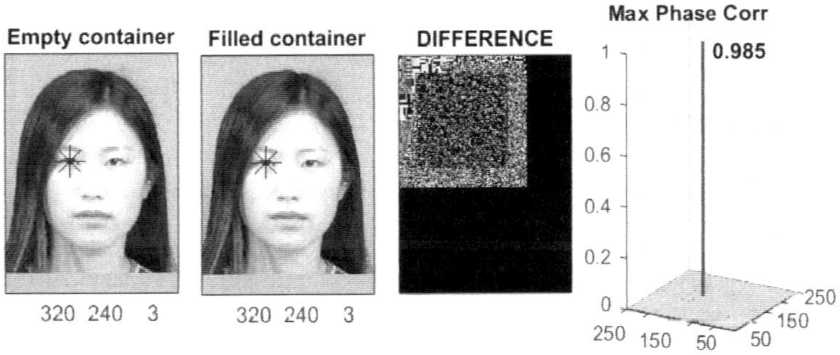

Figure 6. Comparison of textures of images of faces of an empty and filled container. The asterisks in the center of the right eye indicate that these facial images meet the requirements of GOST for facial biometrics

3. CONCLUSION

This article presents a new fast method for generating a biometric multimedia file consisting of a color image of a face with a color QR code embedded in it. At the same time, the color QR code contains biometric data about the person, as well as documentary information about the person to whom this person belongs. It was demonstrated that embedding is implemented by simultaneously replacing three LSB slices in the RED, GREEN and BLUE components of a color image of a face with a color QR code. It is shown that the embedded QR code does not detect the fact of its existence in a multimedia file, which will be interesting for tasks related to the storage and transmission of confidential information. The article presents original graphic illustrations with appropriate descriptions and explanations, which simplified the understanding of the ideas of the method, the proposed solutions and the algorithm implementing the method. In addition, the solutions proposed in the article have a number of qualitative characteristics presented and discussed in the article. Thus, the improvement of graphical data is achieved by the ability to adjust the input color image to the size and requirements of GOST standards for biometrics. Solutions for facial biometrics have increased versatility and high representativeness, which is achieved by their joint representation on a common coordinate grid of key points of the face. Together, all these factors will expand the scope of the proposed multimedia file, not only in biometrics, but also in digital anthropometry, criminology, medical morphological research and other applications. For example, the algorithm for generating biometric multimedia files can be used in systems for automatic registration of people at the border crossing line (e-border) and the creation of biometric and registration databases.

ACKNOWLEDGEMENT

This research was funded by the Science Committee of the Ministry of Education and Science of the Republic of Kazakhstan (grant no. AP19678000).

REFERENCES

Akshara M. Gaikwad, Kavita R. (2015). Embedding QR code in color images using halftoning technique. *International Conference on Innovations in Information, Embedded and Communication Systems (ICIIECS)*, DOI: 10.1109/ICIIECS.2015.7193016.

Mukherjee S., Singh A., & Dutta P., (2019). An adaptive data hiding technique based on QR code. *International Conference on Recent Innovations in Electrical, Electronics & Communication Engineering (ICRIEECE)*, pp. 1-5.

Fernando D.B.S., Parthiban A., Rajesh R., & Vinithra M., (2021). Steganography of Messages Encrypted With QR-Code. *IJSART* - Volume 7 Issue 3, March 2021.

Kukharev G.A. and Kaziyeva, N., (2019). Algorithms of color QR codes formation for biometry tasks. *Scientific and Technical Journal of Information Technologies, Mechanics and Optics*, 19(5), pp. 955–958. doi: 10.17586/2226-1494-2019-19-5-955-958.

ISO/IEC 18004:2015. Information technology — Automatic identification and data capture techniques — QR Code bar code symbology specification. Available at: link.

ISO/IES 19794-5:2011. Information technology. Biometrics. Biometric data interchange formats. Part 5. Face image data. Update date 01.01.2021. Available at: link.

CUHK Face Sketch Database (CUFS). Available at: link (accessed: 03.04.2019).

Kukharev, G.A., Maulenov, K., & Shchegoleva, N.L., (2023). A method for embedding biometric information in a color image of a face and a device for its implementation. PATENTON. URL: https://patenton.ru/patent/RU2771789C1

Kazemi V., & Sullivan J., (2014). One millisecond face alignment with an ensemble of regression trees. *Proc. 27th IEEE Conference on Computer Vision and Pattern Recognition (CVPR)*, 1867–1874. doi: 10.1109/CVPR.2014.241.

Lugaresi C. et al., (2019). MediaPipe: A Framework for Building Perception Pipelines. *ArXiv abs/1906.08172.*

Kukharev G.A. and Kaziyeva, N., (2019). Algorithms of color QR codes formation for biometry tasks. *Scientific and Technical Journal of Information Technologies, Mechanics and Optics*, 19(5), pp. 955–958. doi: 10.17586/2226-1494-2019-19-5-955-958. (in Russian)

Kukharev, G.A., Kaiyeva N. M. & Shchegoleva N.L., (2020). Method of forming color qr-code based on images of faces and device for its implementation. Patent RU 2714741C1. Available at: link.

TEXTILE PATTERN DESIGN GENERATION USING GENERATIVE ADVERSARIAL NETWORKS

Diogo Araújo, Luís Romero and Pedro Miguel Faria
Instituto Politécnico de Viana do Castelo, Portugal

ABSTRACT

In textile design, patterns are traditionally printed on clothing, often comprising repetitive elements. Designers create these patterns, which are then assembled into a complete design. The use of Generative Adversarial Networks (GANs) offers a novel approach, enabling designers to draw inspiration for new ideas by generating textile patterns. Various GAN variants, with advantages in diverse fields, including fashion, have been proposed for this purpose. This paper explores the integration of deep learning, particularly Generative Adversarial Networks, to generate textile designs to provide ideas and facilitate the creative process of the designers. Leveraging Wasserstein GAN and Wasserstein GAN with Gradient Penalty, this study compares their performance in generating pleasant aesthetic results, taking into consideration simples conditionalization of the models. The GAN framework, consisting of a generator and discriminator, refines the image generation process through collaborative learning. A comparison between the models is done visually and by loss stability. This research also addresses the need of dedicated machine learning algorithms for textile design, providing insights into the intersection of technology and creativity in the textile industry.

KEYWORDS

Textile Pattern, Design, Generative AI, GAN, Conditional GAN

1. INTRODUCTION

The textile industry, often regarded as a bastion of creativity and artistry, is undergoing a transformative shift into the realm of knowledge-driven enterprises. While the artistic aspect of textile design remains paramount, the industry increasingly relies on technology, allocating substantial resources to stay at the forefront of innovation. The integration of digital tools, crafted by seasoned professionals and available online, has become a defining feature of this evolution. In this dynamic landscape, machine learning emerges as a powerful catalyst for change, offering an avenue to understand and replicate intricate design patterns. Machine learning, as a discipline, revolves around the identification of patterns within selected data to predict outcomes or generate new material. Recent advancements in technology and processing power have catapulted machine learning into various applications, spanning data classification, statistical analysis, image recognition, and the development of intricate systems. One notable offshoot of machine learning, deep learning, relies on artificial neural networks to unravel complex patterns. This includes specialized neural network architectures such as convolutional neural networks (CNN), generative adversarial networks (GAN) and recurrent neural networks (RNN), each designed to excel in specific applications. Generative Adversarial Networks (GAN) are based on neural networks used for the generation of images (Goodfellow et al., 2014). It mainly consists of two parts, a generator and a discriminator or critic. The generator generates images through latent space and noise as its weights. These generated images are passed onto a discriminator which compares the generated images with the real images and calculates the error/loss value. These loss functions are passed onto the generator and discriminator to fine-tune according to loss function to produce better images and making better predictions.

A method of textile image generation using Wasserstein Generative Adversarial Networks (WGAN) (Weng, 2019) and Wasserstein Generative Adversarial Networks with Gradient Penalty (WGAN-GP) (Gao, 2020) is introduced. According to our knowledge, few algorithms exist that are dedicated to generating proper textile patterns, resulting in the need of testing and evaluation of current models, and fine-tuning them. We have compared the performance of 2 image generative algorithms such as WGANs (Weng, 2019;

Arjovsky et al., 2017a), WGANs-GP (Gao, 2020), and added the concept of conditionality through the embedding of categories/classes. These models were chosen because they represented significant advancements in the field of Generative Adversarial Networks (GANs) and have addressed some of the limitations associated with traditional GANs, such as:

- Stability and Convergence: Where WGAN addresses the issue of training instability and mode collapse that can be observed in traditional GANs. It introduces a more stable training procedure by replacing the Jensen-Shannon divergence with the Wasserstein distance in the objective function.
- Wasserstein Distance: The use of Wasserstein distance allows for a more meaningful and continuous measure of the difference between the generator and real data distributions. This helps in avoiding vanishing or exploding gradients during training.
- Gradient Penalty: While WGAN improves stability, WGAN-GP further refines the training process by incorporating a gradient penalty. The gradient penalty addresses the problem of weight clipping used in WGAN, which can lead to suboptimal convergence. WGAN-GP penalizes the norm of the gradient of the critic (discriminator) with respect to its input, enforcing smoother convergence.
- Mode Collapse Mitigation: WGAN-GP has been observed to be less prone to mode collapse compared to some traditional GAN formulations. Mode collapse occurs when the generator collapses to producing a limited set of similar samples.

This paper is divided into five sections: the present one which introduces the study carried out, followed by a section of related work about some utilities of the GANs, possible activities in the range of image manipulation and some case studies of GANs, in the textile pattern generation; then the implementation section describes a prepared dataset and explains the process of building a GAN model and its conditionalization; the next section refers to the analysis of obtained results, through visual and loss stability assessments; and the last section indicates some conclusions about the study presented here.

2. RELATED WORK

Extensive research has been done in the field of GANs from generating simple images as simple as generation of bird images (Huang, 2018) to more complex subjects as medical studies (Cepa, 2023) and complex designs (Liu, 2020). In the last few years, the evolution of GANs has resulted in different variants and has shown great results in many industries. Models in machine learning can be broadly classified into two categories: generative models and discriminant models. In general, the generated model can perform tasks like reasoning, density estimation, and sampling. The generation model can be separated into unconditional generation and conditional generation based on the various inputs (Yoshimura, 2016). Image synthesis is an important research area within the field of computer vision (Yi, 2023). Its primary function is to transform images between different image domains, including applications such as image super-resolution generation, image coloring, image filling, style transformation, and attribute transformation. (Aittala, 2016) uses CNN to learn the mapping between input images and output images, and (Ren, 2017) decomposed the hidden space of an image into a domain-invariant content space and a domain-specific style space and obtained multimode output. A deep network model based on edge enhancement is proposed for image super-resolution reconstruction, and a deconvolution network is used to achieve the goal of edge enhancement.

Considering textile design, (Yar, 2023) introduces the use of Generative Adversarial Networks (GANs), leveraging the image generation capabilities of GANs, the study curates a dataset of 17,000+ textile design images, categorized by design class. The authors employ a Deep Convolutional GAN (DCGAN) to collectively generate patterns and fine-tune it for specific pattern types, such as cheetah. The paper claims three main contributions: dataset collection and classification, the introduction of GANs in textile design, and the training of a versatile DCGAN for efficient pattern generation. As for the paper (Fayyaz, 2020), the study proposes an innovative approach to automated textile design pattern generation using generative models, claiming that the accuracy of classifying textile design patterns is enhanced by 2% through data cleaning and pseudo labelling. Performance comparisons among Wasserstein Generative Adversarial Networks Gradient Penalty (WGANs GP), Deep Convolutional GANs (DCGANs), and Convolutional Variational Autoencoders (CVAEs) are conducted on a dataset for individual classes, assessed using the inception score.

3. IMPLEMENTATION

It was decided to do an experimental study and some steps were followed. First, it was necessary to acquire and process data related to the problem of generating textile designs, to implement the desired algorithms and build an architecture, in order to be able to train the models.

3.1 Data Acquisition

Before we started the process of textile patterns image generation, we had the need of a data set about textile patterns. We used a dataset made from different sources such as TexGan (Yar, 2023), clothing-pattern-dataset (Alexander et al., 2021) and some hand-picked images from sources such as Freepik and Vecteezy. The dataset consists of 13,000 images, and some of them are exemplified in Figure 1.

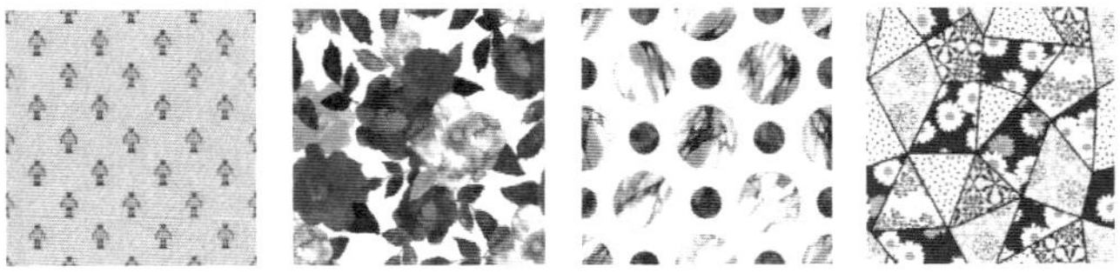

Figure 1. Four pattern examples used from the dataset

The dataset was built using images of several resolutions, and we pre-processed all images before feeding the data models. As the images were loaded, we resized them to 64×64 pixels dimension and established the color channels as 3 (RGB), due to the lack of some computational power, in order to experiment with larger images.

3.2 Models

For this study, the developed structures were based on the proposed algorithms represented in Figure 2, from (Arjovsky et al., 2017b), and represented in Figure 3 from (Gulrajani, 2017). Some considerations were also based on (Soumith and Denton, 2017) GAN-hacks.

Following the Figure 2, for each step the generator takes during the training process, the discriminator will take n steps. As in basic GANs, we take the latent noise sample and the dataset sample to compute the gradient. RMSProp is the optimizer used and it is applied the clipping technique, which clips every weight parameter in the network to be conformed within a certain range. Then the generator is trained, computing the gradient, and using the same optimizer.

Following the Figure 3, for each step the generator takes during the training process, the discriminator will take n steps. Instead of clipping, it is introduced the concept of gradient penalty where it is added the interpolation of the generated sample and the dataset sample, and computed the norm of the gradient, which is desired to be approximately 1 for every interpolation, to satisfy the Lipschitz constraint. In this case the optimizer used is Adam.

Simply put, the biggest differences between the algorithms are the introduction of clipping and gradient penalties that attempt to enforce the Lipschitz condition differently, and the difference between optimizers.

Require: : α, the learning rate. c, the clipping parameter. m, the batch size. n_{critic}, the number of iterations of the critic per generator iteration.
Require: : w_0, initial critic parameters. θ_0, initial generator's parameters.
while θ has not converged **do**
  for $t = 0, ..., n_{\text{critic}}$ **do**
    Sample $\{x^{(i)}\}_{i=1}^{m} \sim \mathbb{P}_r$ a batch from the real data.
    Sample $\{z^{(i)}\}_{i=1}^{m} \sim p(z)$ a batch of prior samples.
    $g_w \leftarrow \nabla_w \left[\frac{1}{m}\sum_{i=1}^{m} f_w(x^{(i)}) - \frac{1}{m}\sum_{i=1}^{m} f_w(g_\theta(z^{(i)}))\right]$
    $w \leftarrow w + \alpha \cdot \text{RMSProp}(w, g_w)$
    $w \leftarrow \text{clip}(w, -c, c)$
  end for
  Sample $\{z^{(i)}\}_{i=1}^{m} \sim p(z)$ a batch of prior samples.
  $g_\theta \leftarrow -\nabla_\theta \frac{1}{m}\sum_{i=1}^{m} f_w(g_\theta(z^{(i)}))$
  $\theta \leftarrow \theta - \alpha \cdot \text{RMSProp}(\theta, g_\theta)$
end while

Figure 2. WGAN proposed algorithm (Arjovsky et al., 2017b)

Require: The gradient penalty coefficient λ, the number of critic iterations per generator iteration n_{critic}, the batch size m, Adam hyperparameters α, β_1, β_2.
Require: initial critic parameters w_0, initial generator parameters θ_0.
while θ has not converged **do**
  for $t = 1, ..., n_{\text{critic}}$ **do**
    for $i = 1, ..., m$ **do**
      Sample real data $\boldsymbol{x} \sim \mathbb{P}_r$, latent variable $\boldsymbol{z} \sim p(\boldsymbol{z})$, a random number $\epsilon \sim U[0, 1]$.
      $\tilde{\boldsymbol{x}} \leftarrow G_\theta(\boldsymbol{z})$
      $\hat{\boldsymbol{x}} \leftarrow \epsilon \boldsymbol{x} + (1 - \epsilon)\tilde{\boldsymbol{x}}$
      $L^{(i)} \leftarrow D_w(\tilde{\boldsymbol{x}}) - D_w(\boldsymbol{x}) + \lambda(\|\nabla_{\hat{\boldsymbol{x}}} D_w(\hat{\boldsymbol{x}})\|_2 - 1)^2$
    end for
    $w \leftarrow \text{Adam}(\nabla_w \frac{1}{m}\sum_{i=1}^{m} L^{(i)}, w, \alpha, \beta_1, \beta_2)$
  end for
  Sample a batch of latent variables $\{\boldsymbol{z}^{(i)}\}_{i=1}^{m} \sim p(\boldsymbol{z})$.
  $\theta \leftarrow \text{Adam}(\nabla_\theta \frac{1}{m}\sum_{i=1}^{m} -D_w(G_\theta(\boldsymbol{z})), \theta, \alpha, \beta_1, \beta_2)$
end while

Figure 3. WGAN-GP proposed algorithm (Gulrajani, 2017)

3.2.1 Generator Architectures

Both models have a similar generator architecture, consisting of 4 deconvolutional blocks (deconvolutional layer, normalization and ReLU activation function) and a final deconvolutional layer. Each deconvolutional layer refers to a certain dimension such as 4x4, 8x8, 16x16, 32x32 and 64x64. The difference between the architectures is the Tanh activation function at the end of the WGAN generator structure, which ensures that the generator output is restricted to the range between -1 and 1. For the WGAN-GP we used no activation function since it was pretended to produce an unconstrained output.

3.2.2 Discriminator Architectures

Both models have the same discriminator architecture, consisting of a convolutional layer and a LeakyReLU activation function, 3 convolutional blocks (convolutional layer, normalization and LeakyReLU activation function) and a final convolutional layer. Each convolutional layer refers to a certain dimension such as 64x64, 32x32, 16x16, 8x8 and 4x4.

3.3 Conditional Models

Following the models i.e., conditional adaptations of the models were developed. For these, we introduced categories/classes, as each image in the dataset belongs to a class such as Floral, Geometric, Cultural, Abstract, etc. Concerning the Generator and Discriminator Architectures, for this case, we kept both models' architectures i.e., but we embed the existing classes of the dataset and add the respective class of each image into the generator and discriminator. This way, both Generator and Discriminator will take into consideration this new characteristic.

3.4 Training Hyperparameters

The computational resources consisted in a laptop with a Quadro RTX 4000 MAX-Q Design, Intel I7-10875H and 32GB RAM. In terms of functional hyperparameters, we defined the necessary ones as follows:

- Learning rate = 5e-5
- Batch size = 64
- Image size = 64
- Color channels = 3
- Noise dimension = 100
- Discriminator characteristics = 64
- Generator characteristics = 64
- Discriminator iterations = 5
- Number of cycles = 200
- Embedding noise dimension = 100

4. RESULTS ANALYSIS

Following, the training parameters i.e., for each epoch, the model weights were stored and can be implemented to transfer learning. The results were evaluated through visual and loss stability assessment.

4.1 Unconditional Models Loss Stability Assessment

Knowing that, in practical terms, optimizers try to minimize loss functions, we can compare the performance of the discriminator and the generator. Therefore, an analysis was carried out on the losses of each model throughout the training process, as observed in Figure 4. The discriminator loss aims to maximize the mean of scores for real samples (encouraging correct classification of real samples) and minimize the mean of scores for synthetic samples (encouraging correct classification of fake samples). The generator loss aims to maximize the mean of discriminator scores assigned to its synthetic samples, thereby encouraging the generator to produce realistic samples that fool the discriminator.

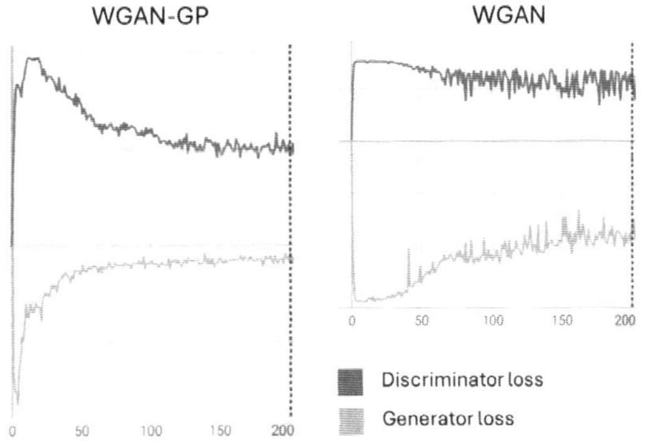

Figure 4. Losses during training of both unconditional models

For the WGAN model, the losses gradually decreased over time, whoever the stabilization seems lacking in comparison with the WGAN-GP model, where the convergence appears to be cleaner and stable. This, however, does not mean that the results obtained are good. Even if we consider that the WGAN-GP model had a better stabilization, the discrepancy between the loss values indicates that the Generator performed poorly compared to the Discriminator. This means that refinement is needed to reduce the discrepancy. Overall, both the Generator and Discriminator did their job and the accuracy calculated (probability of the synthetic image being recognized as real) was on average 35% for the WGAN model, and 10% for the WGAN-GP model.

4.2 Unconditional Models Visual Assessment

Based on the performed training, Figure 5 shows the images generated by the models, after training for 200 epochs. The first set of 32 images were generated by the WGAN model, while the other set were generated by the WGAN-GP model.

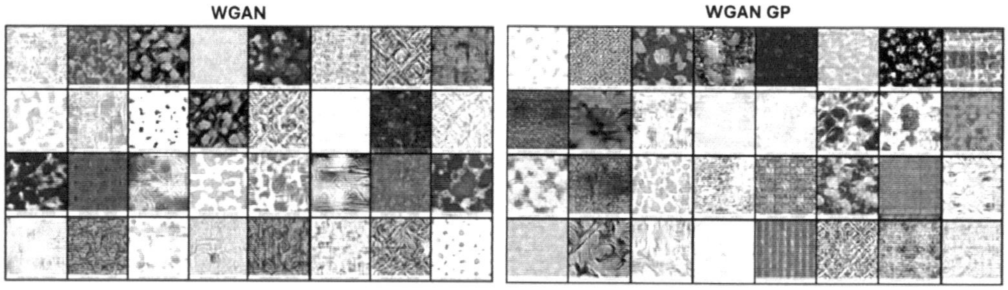

Figure 5. The 32 generated images from each model

From the beginning of this study, we expected that the lack of a higher resolution would make the visual comparison, between the models, more complicated and less viable. As such, some generated examples from both models, appear to resemble some characteristics of textile patterns, even if mostly hard to perceive.

4.3 Conditional Models Loss Stability Assessment

For the Conditional WGAN model, as represented by Figure 6, the losses gradually decreased over time, but the losses oscillations are not desirable. The accuracy calculated as an average of 40%. This indicates that the conditionalization made the accuracy goes up by 5%, but still, the accuracy is considerably low, which shows that there is a lot of room for improvements.

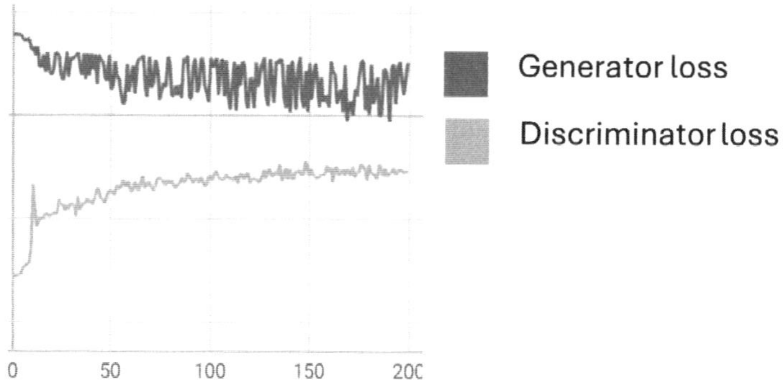

Figure 6. The 32 generated images from each model

For the Conditional WGAN-GP model, represented in Figure 7, the losses presented an unexpected behavior, where the generator loss started to increase, from the 50 epochs forward. Aside from this, the Discriminator loss stabilized and decreased very fast, as expected, based on the Unconditioned WGAN-GP model, which is also not optimal. The accuracy was also calculated, but for this case the output was always 0%.

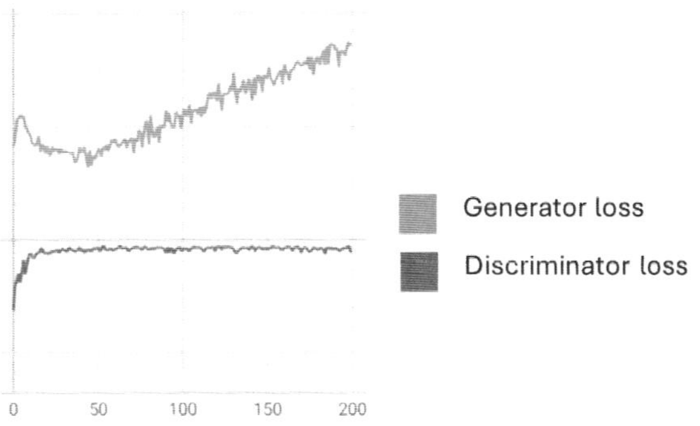

Figure 7. Losses of the Conditional WGAN-GP

4.4 Conditional Models Visual Assessment

Figure 8 shows the generated images by the conditional models. The first set of 16 images were generated by the Conditional WGAN model, while the other set by the Conditional WGAN-GP model. Most of the samples show some characteristics of the class they belong to, even if hard to perceive as it lacks detail.

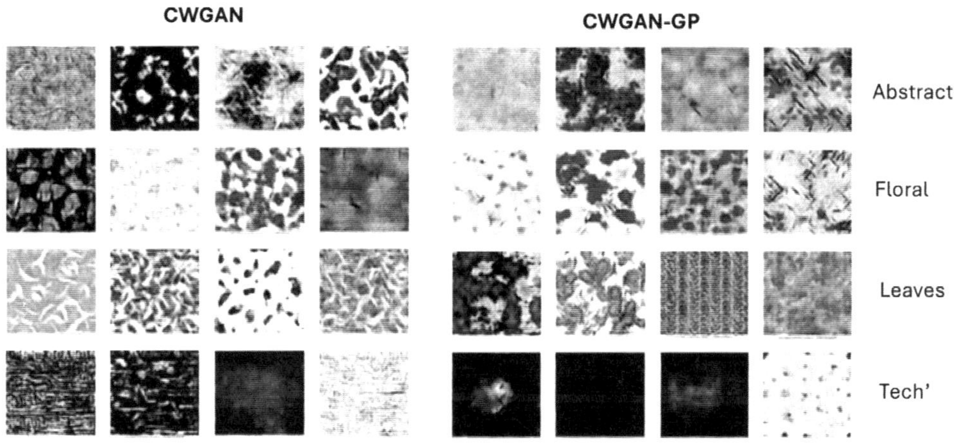

Figure 8. The 4 generated samples per selected class

The first set of samples were easy to pick, since the generator didn't deviate much. As for the second set, the generator had a hard time generating satisfactory samples. This may be because the training of the WGAN-GP model showed some unexpected behavior, as mentioned on the stability assessment.

5. CONCLUSIONS

In this paper, we implemented two models to solve the problem of unique textile pattern generation. As shown through results, both models worked, but there is a lot to take into consideration going forward. Using higher dimensions is quite necessary if we want to do visual assessments, which in this case we could not analyze any type of defined details. Also, for both models, the losses absolute value gradually lowered, which is desired, but the WGAN-GP model needs refining, so the Generator can keep up with the Discriminator. Based on the accuracy calculated, there is a long way to go until we reach desired results. Based on the accuracy results, knowing that the conditionalization of the WGAN model upgraded in average 5%, it showed a positive value. We may change our approach into the problem, taking in consideration various characteristics of the patterns such as composition, key elements, style, and padding, to verify if it can further upgrade the accuracy. Also fine-tuning in general is need for the aim of 90%+ accuracy, for such we will completely change the architecture of the generator and discriminator to fit the needs of the problem. We also intend to seek opinions from professionals within the area of textile design for a better understanding of future results.

ACKNOWLEDGEMENTS

This research was supported by PRR (Plano de Recuperação e Resiliência) under the development of the project entitled "TEXP@CT - Pacto de Inovação para a Digitalização do Têxtil e Vestuário", through the European Union (NextGenerationEU).

REFERENCES

Aittala, M., Aila, T., et al. (2016). Reflectance modeling by neural texture synthesis, ACM Transactions on Graphics, vol. 35, no. 4, pp. 65.1-65.13.

Alexander, J., et al. (2017). Recognizing Clothing Colors and Visual Textures Using a Finger-Mounted Camera. *An Initial Investigation, Proceedings of the 19th International ACM SIGACCESS Conference on Computers and Accessibility - ASSETS '17.*

Arjovsky, M. Chintala, S. et al. (2017b). Wasserstein Generative Adversarial Networks. *Proceedings of the 34th International Conference on Machine Learning*, in Proceedings of Machine Learning Research 70:214-223 Available from https://proceedings.mlr.press/v70/arjovsky17a.html.

Arjovsky, M., Chintala, S. et al. (2017a). Wasserstein GAN. [online] Available: http://arxiv.org/abs/1701.07875.

Cepa, B., Brito, C. et al. (2023). Generative Adversarial Networks in Healthcare: A Case Study on MRI Image Generation. *2023 IEEE 7th Portuguese Meeting on Bioengineering (ENBENG)*, Porto, Portugal, pp. 48-51, doi: 10.1109/ENBENG58165.2023.10175330.

Fayyaz, R. A., Maqbool, M. et al. (2020). Textile Design Generation Using GANs. *2020 IEEE Canadian Conference on Electrical and Computer Engineering (CCECE)*, London, ON, Canada, pp. 1-5, doi: 10.1109/CCECE47787.2020.9255674.

Gao, X., Deng, F., et al. (2020). Data augmentation in fault diagnosis based on the Wasserstein generative adversarial network with gradient penalty. *Neurocomputing*, Volume 396, pp. 487-494, ISSN 0925-2312.

Goodfellow, I. J., Pouget-Abadie, J., et al. (2014). Generative adversarial nets. *Advances in Neural Information Processing Systems*, vol. 3, no. January, pp. 2672-2680.

Gulrajani, I, et al. (2017). Improved Training of Wasserstein GANs, vol. 30, Available from https://proceedings.neurips.cc/paper_files/paper/2017/file/892c3b1c6dccd52936e27cbd0ff683d6-Paper.pdf

Huang, Z. (2018). Bird Generation with DCGAN.

Liu, X., Huang, H. et al. (2020). Intelligent generation algorithm of ceramic decorative pattern. *2020 IEEE 6th Intl Conference on Big Data Security on Cloud (BigDataSecurity), IEEE Intl Conference on High Performance and Smart Computing, (HPSC) and IEEE Intl Conference on Intelligent Data and Security (IDS)*, Baltimore, MD, USA, pp. 122-126, doi: 10.1109/BigDataSecurity-HPSC-IDS49724.2020.00031.

Ren, R., Gu, L., et al. (2017). Super-resolution algorithm based on sparse representation and wavelet preprocessing for remote sensing imagery. Journal of Applied Remote Sensing, vol. 11, no. 2, pp. 14, 2017.

Soumith, M. and Denton, M. (2017). How to Train a GAN? Tips and tricks to make GANs work. GitHub, [online] Available: https://github.com/soumith/ganhacks.

Weng, L. (2019). From GAN to WGAN. DOI: https://doi.org/10.48550/arXiv.1904.08994

Yar, G., Taha, M., et al. (2023). TexGAN: Textile Pattern Generation Using Deep Convolutional Generative Adversarial Network (DCGAN). *2023 IEEE International Conference on Emerging Trends in Engineering, Sciences and Technology (ICES&T)*, Bahawalpur, Pakistan, pp. 1-6, doi: 10.1109/ICEST56843.2023.10138848.

Yi, M. et al. (2023). Research on Artificial Intelligence Art Image Synthesis Algorithm Based on Generation Model. *2nd International Conference on 3D Immersion, Interaction and Multi-sensory Experiences (ICDIIME)*, Madrid, Spain, pp. 102-106, doi: 10.1109/ICDIIME59043.2023.00026.

Yoshimura, M. and Kasahara, S. (2016). Enhanced ray tracing algorithm to generate penumbra by point light. Journal of Environmental Engineering (Transactions of AIJ), no. 724, pp. 81-572, 2016.

BIDIRECTIONAL FEATURE PYRAMID FOR FACE DETECTION IN DENSE CROWD SCENES

Yajuan Wei[1,2], Zhiejie Xu[2], Chuan Dai [2] and Wanju Zhang[1]
[1]*Xi'an University of Posts and Telecommunications, Xi'an, China*
[2]*University of Huddersfield, UK*

ABSTRACT

Face detection algorithms based on deep learning approaches have made significant advancements in the last decade. However, recognising faces in dense crowd scenes remains challenging, particularly in situations with overlapping and obscured small targets. This paper introduces a lightweight model based on YOLOv5s, which replaces the Pyramid Attention Network (PANet) in the original network neck with a bidirectional feature pyramid network (BiFPN) for effective handling of varied feature sizes. The original YOLOv5s framework has a high down sampling ratio that leads to difficulties in learning the features of small objects. The devised model has deployed an additional output head to prioritise small object detection. Based on ablation and benchmarking experiments, the original network's loss function is substituted with the SIoU Loss Function, which not only aggregates regression metrics between predicted and ground truth bounding boxes but also identifies their mismatched orientations, hence enhancing the model's detection accuracy of overlapping targets. Experiments conducted on the COCO128 and WiderFace benchmarks validate the superiority of the proposed model, resulting significant mAP accuracy improvement.

KEYWORDS

Face Detection, YOLOv5s, Bidirectional Feature Pyramid, SIoU, WiderFace

1. INTRODUCTION

Face detection is a critical aspect of face recognition, and the advancement of deep learning-based face detection algorithms has attracted significant attention from researchers. Common large-scale face datasets include CASIA-WebFace (Yi et al., 2014), VGGFace2(Cao et al., 2018), WiderFace(Yang et al., 2016), etc. However, in everyday scenarios like classrooms, subway stations, and crowded squares, multiple faces are often captured within the same video frame. Challenges such as face occlusion and small face sizes significantly escalate the difficulty of face detection, consequently lowering recognition accuracy. Thus, this paper aims to investigate and propose solutions to address this issue.

Currently, there are numerous face detection methods addressing occlusion or overlapping issues. Based on deep learning approaches, they can be broadly categorized into two types: facial feature extraction and facial information restoration.

The principle behind the former method involves enhancing crucial facial features through techniques such as transfer learning, feature fusion, local feature analysis, attention mechanisms, optimization of loss functions, and integration of infrared thermal imaging technology. This approach aims to extract facial identity information from occluded faces, suppressing or eliminating the effects of occlusion. The principle behind the latter method involves considering data augmentation to explore semantic information in facial images through techniques such as facial image restoration, facial feature transfer, and occluded facial information reconstruction. This approach aims to reduce identity differences between occluded and non-occluded faces and mitigate problems caused by self-occlusion and external occlusion, such as missing facial structural information and incomplete facial information. The focus of this paper revolves around facial feature extraction.

Regression-based object detection algorithms have gained widespread attention for their efficiency in feature extraction, surpassing region-based methods that rely on candidate regions. Common regression-based object detection algorithms include SSD(Liu et al., 2016) and various versions of YOLO(Redmon and Farhadi, 2018; Wang et al., 2022). Taking the YOLO series as an example, its network consists of three main components: the Backbone, Neck, and Head. Different choices of Backbone and Neck, varying numbers of outputs in the Head, and different loss functions all have an impact on the detection performance of the object detection network.

This paper introduces a lightweight improved model based on YOLOv5s. In this model, the Pyramid Attention Network (PANet), the original network's neck, is replaced by a bidirectional feature pyramid network (BiFPN) for more effective handling of varied feature sizes. Additionally, to address the high down-sampling ratio in the original YOLOv5s, which poses difficulties for deeper feature maps in learning features of small objects. In the original framework, the output head sizes are 80×80, 40×40, and 20×20. A larger output head size leads to better detection performance for small targets. Therefore, an additional output head with a size of 160×160 is incorporated. This modification increases the number of heads from three to four for a more robust performance on small target Detection. Furthermore, through ablation and comparative study, the network's loss function is substituted with the SIoU Loss Function, which not only aggregates regression metrics between predicted and ground truth boxes but also accounts for their mismatched orientation. This enhancement improves the model's detection accuracy for small and overlapping targets.

The remainder of this paper is structured as follows: Section II provides a brief review of related works on face detection. Section III introduces the proposed face detection framework in detail. Section IV presents the results of the ablation training experiments and analyses the comparisons with state-of-the-art methods. Finally, discussions are presented in Section V to conclude the paper.

2. RELATED WORK

The primary focus of this paper is to utilise convolutional neural networks for face feature extraction, leading to face detection. Consequently, this chapter primarily summarizes several face detection methods based on face feature extraction to address occlusion and overlapping issues, as well as relevant works on face detection implemented through target detection algorithms.

A. Face Detection Based on Facial Feature Extraction

Zhang et al.(Zhang et al., 2022)proposed a generic feature fusion method for end-to-end network feature extraction based on shallow, intermediate, and deep-level features, primarily utilizing each convolutional layer to obtain image features from the perspective of hierarchical characteristics of the network. This method can enhance the recognition accuracy of face recognition under illumination and occlusion conditions. Hariri (Hariri, 2022) firstly locates and removes facial occlusion areas, then utilizes three pre-trained models, VGG-16, AlexNet, and ResNet-50, to obtain deep features of the eyes and forehead, finally applying a multilayer perceptron for classification. Chang et al. (Chang et al., 2021)designed ResSaneNet to integrate CNN with self-attention modules into the same network. Training with occluded and non-occluded datasets can capture global and local information of facial regions for face recognition under occlusion.

B. Face Detection Based Object Detection Method

The cascade CNN(Girshick, 2015) stands out as the initial archetype of deep learning face detectors, employing three sequential convolutional neural networks for face detection. Building upon Faster R-CNN(Ren et al., 2015), it incorporates online hard example mining (OHEM) and multi-scale training techniques to enhance model optimization. Similarly, SSH(Najibi et al., 2017) refines SSD by introducing a multi-branch approach, leveraging various layers within VGG-net to detect faces across multiple scales. This method belongs to regression-based object detection algorithms.

In recent years, regression-based object detection algorithms have been widely praised for their "fast and accurate" characteristics, particularly the YOLO series. Therefore, this paper aims to implement a series of enhancements within the YOLOv5s framework to address face detection tasks in dense crowd environments.

3. FACE DETECTION FRAMEWORK DESIGN

3.1 Overall Detection Flow

The face detection process is extracting video frame images from the video stream, these frames are fed into the detection network for face detection and tracking. Figure 1 illustrates the network architecture of the proposed algorithm. Initially, the CSPDarknet53 backbone extracts facial features. Subsequently, a bidirectional Feature Pyramid Network (BiFPN) module is integrated into the framework's neck to merge features from various scales, which has lower complexity compared to other feature pyramid networks. Furthermore, a new output head is integrated into the framework's head to identify small targets in densely populated scenes. (Figure 2(b) depicts the details of BiFPN block) The detection results for input video frame images are generated using non-maximum suppression (NMS) along with the SIoU loss function. These modifications aim to identify small targets in densely populated scenes and address challenges such as occlusion and overlap between targets. Details are provided later in the next section.

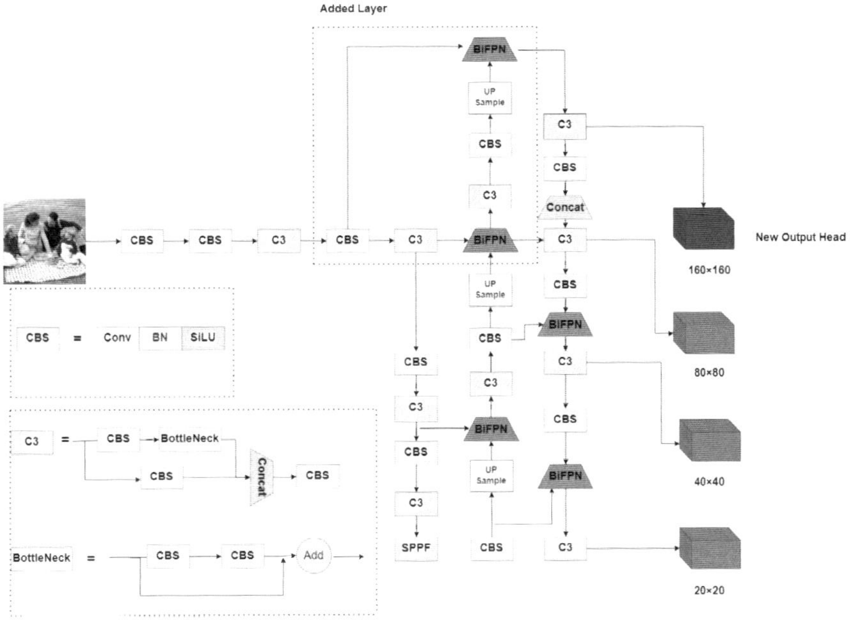

Figure 1. The Overall Face Detection Framework

3.2 Bidirectional Feature Pyramid Network

When the YOLOv5s model detects smaller targets within a crowd, issues of missed detections and false alarms arise. To address this, this study proposes a solution by incorporating the bidirectional feature pyramid network (BiFPN) into YOLOv5s. BiFPN not only effectively mitigates the issue of losing small targets and improves the model's detection accuracy but also simplifies the model's structure and reduces computational complexity.

Building upon PANet, BiFPN refines feature merging by eliminating nodes with minimal impact at different scales. This enhancement has little effect on network performance after the removal of these nodes, simplifying the network structure. To merge features at distinct hierarchical levels, BiFPN increases the frequency of both top-down and bottom-up fusion operations. Additionally, for differential fusion of features with varying importance and improved network efficiency, BiFPN introduces weight fusion. Figure 2 depicts the details of FPN+PANet and BiFPN. The formula for fusion is defined as follows:

$$O = \sum_i \frac{w_i}{\varepsilon + \sum_j w_j} \times I_i \quad (1)$$

Where i and j are the coordinates of the feature information. w_i and w_j are is the learnable, updateable weight of the feature information, constrained by the ReLU activation function to a range of [0,1], with initial values set to 0.5 for all. I_i represents the resolution of the feature map. The parameter ε set to 0.0001.

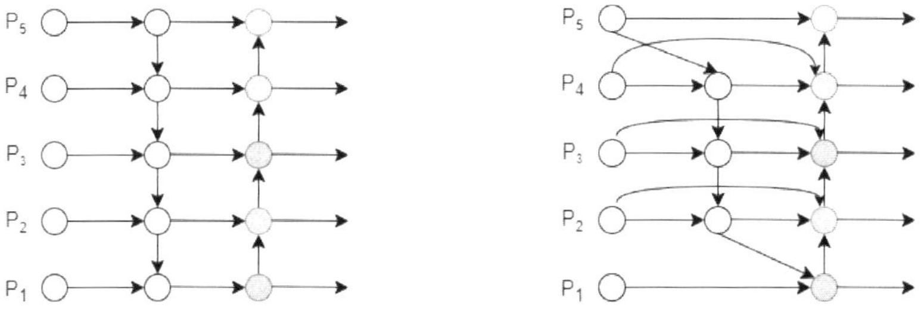

(a) FPN+PANet (b) BiFPN

Figure 2. The Structure of FPN+PANet And BiFPN.

3.3 Loss Function

In the detection of pedestrians in diverse real-world scenarios, there often occurs the phenomenon of target overlap (occlusion). However, for such images, the original YOLOv5 model does not perform optimally in detection. This is partly attributed to the CIoU Loss function used in the original model. CIoU Loss relies solely on regression metrics between aggregated predicted boxes and ground truth boxes. These metrics include factors like distance, overlap area, and aspect ratio, but they overlook the issues of mismatched orientation between predicted and ground truth boxes.

As a consequence, the trained model struggles to effectively detect overlapping targets. To address these challenges, the SIoU Loss not only aggregates regression metrics between predicted and ground truth boxes but also considers their mismatched orientation, thereby enhancing the model's detection accuracy. Hence, this study adopts the SIoU Loss function to replace the CIoU Loss function.

The SIoU loss function consists of four component functions: angle loss, distance loss, shape loss, and IoU loss. The definition of the angle-aware component is as follows.

$$\sigma = \sqrt{(b_{c_x}^{gt} - b_{c_x})^2 + (b_{c_y}^{gt} - b_{c_y})^2} \quad (2)$$

$$c_h = \max\left(b_{c_y}^{gt}, b_{c_y}\right) - \min\left(b_{c_y}^{gt}, b_{c_y}\right) \quad (3)$$

Where, b_{c_x} and b_{c_x} represents the coordinate information of the predicted bounding box; $b_{c_x}^{gt}$ and $b_{c_y}^{gt}$ represents the coordinate information of the ground truth.

The principle of distance loss in SIoU can be defined as follows:

$$\Delta = \sum_{t=x,y}(1 - e^{-rpt}) \quad (4)$$

$$\rho_x = \left(\frac{b_{cx}^{gt} - b_{c_x}}{c_w}\right)^2 \quad (5)$$

$$\rho_y = \left(\frac{b_{c_y}^{gt} - b_{c_y}}{c_h}\right)^2 \tag{6}$$

Where C_w and C_h represents the width and height of the minimum rectangle containing the predicted box and the ground truth box. From the formula, it can be observed that as α increases, the distance loss also increases, leading to an increase in computational complexity.

The formula of shape loss can be defined as follows:

$$\Omega = \sum_{t=w,h}(1 - e^{\omega_t})^{\theta} \tag{7}$$

$$\omega_w = \frac{|w - w^{gt}|}{\max(w, w^{gt})} \tag{8}$$

$$\omega_h = \frac{|h - h^{gt}|}{\max(h, h^{gt})} \tag{9}$$

Where w and h represent the width and height of the rectangle formed by the predicted box and the ground truth box; w^{gt} and h^{gt} represent the width and height of the ground truth box.

IoU loss is computed as the intersection over union. Based on the above, the calculation formula for SIoU can be obtained as follows:

$$L = 1 - IoU + \frac{\Delta + \Omega}{2} \tag{10}$$

4. EXPERIMENT AND RESULTS

4.1 Model Training

In this section, two training datasets - COCO128 and Wider Face - will be utilized to evaluate the proposed face (object) detection algorithm. Thus, the initial evaluation of the proposed methodology is conducted using COCO128, which has a relatively small-scale size. Following this, the effectiveness of our approach on larger datasets is validated through the Wider Face dataset, facilitating comparisons against state-of-the-art (SOTA) methods. Additionally, through ablation experiments conducted under different loss functions and with or without pre-training weight coefficients, the performance of all algorithms based on the YOLOv5s network framework and the proposed algorithm will be compared.

As depicted in Table 1, training will be carried out on the Wider Face dataset. Here, "pretrained" indicates the network framework with pre training weight coefficients obtained from yolov5s.pt, while "CIOU" signifies the loss function used by the original YOLOv5s network. "BiFPN" represents the newly integrated network module in the YOLOv5s network Neck, and "Small Target head" denotes the additional output head. The baseline in this ablation Experiment is YOLOv5s without pretrained weights. Training iterations consist of 10 warm-up training sessions for all YOLOv5s network frameworks to assess their performance, along with 200 training sessions for YOLOV5s+ SIoU and the proposed algorithm.

During the training process, it was observed that the performance improved when using the SIoU and EIoU loss functions compared to the original CIoU loss function. Furthermore, using SIoU resulted in better localization accuracy of the detection boxes compared to EIoU. When training the proposed algorithm (including pre-trained weights) for 200 epochs, it achieved an increase of 2.2% in mAP_0.5, 2.0% in mAP_0.5:0.95, and 1.3% in F1 score compared to the YOLOv5s+SIoU+pretrained framework (including pre-trained weights). Similarly, the proposed algorithm for 200 epochs, it achieved an increase of 30.2% in mAP_0.5, 44.0% in mAP_0.5:0.95, and 20.6% in F1 score compared to the original YOLOv5s framework. Although the addition of modules and output heads in the network increased GFLOPS, the significant improvement in accuracy for densely crowded face targets makes it acceptable. Figure 3 illustrates the trends of relevant loss functions during the training process.

Table 1. Comparative Analysis of Model Training Performance on Wider Face

Model	epoch	GFLOPs	mAP_0.5	mAP_0.5:0.95	F1
Baseline	10	15.9	0.577	0.282	0.63
(pretrained)	10	15.9	0.673	0.350	0.71
EIoU (pretrained)	10	15.9	0.681	0.353	0.71
SIoU (pretrained)	10 200	15.9	0.678 0.735	0.350 0.398	0.71 0.75
+BiFPN (pretrained)	10	16.6	0.661	0.336	0.70
+BiFPN	10	16.6	0.577	0.285	0.63
+BiFPN (pretrained, EIoU)	10	16.6	0.670	0.342	0.70
+BiFPN (pretrained, SIoU)	10	16.6	0.669	0.34	0.70
+BiFPN +Small Target Head (pretrained, EIoU)	10	19.4	0.680	0.347	0.70
Ours	10 200	19.4	0.582 0.750	0.286 0.403	0.62 0.76
Ours (pretrained)	10 200	19.4	0.679 **0.751**	0.344 **0.406**	0.70 **0.76**

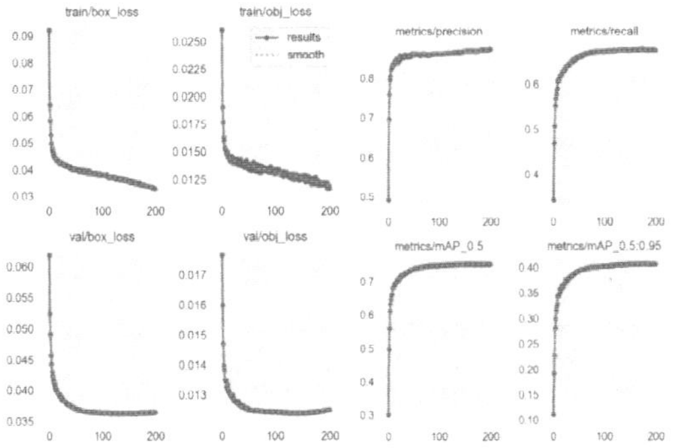

Figure 3. Training Loss Performance After 200 epochs.

4.2 Comparing with SOTA Methods

For this face detection task, five baselines derived from the most advanced deep learning models are employed for comparison. They are YOLOv3s (Redmon & Farhadi, 2018), YOLOv5s, YOLOv7s and the proposed method.

The Yolov3 was first released in 2018. Since then, it has become a well-known method for one-stage object detection, containing the Darknet-53 network structure, anchor frame, FPN, and excellent structures. The YOLOv3s and YOLOv3s-SPP methods are employed to perform detection in this experiment.

YOLOv5 is a lightweight object detection model, which employs a backbone network structure based on Feature Pyramid Networks (FPN). It adopts an anchor-free detection approach, reducing the computational load and parameter count of the model. This approach achieves a fine balance between speed and accuracy.

YOLOv7 is an evolution of YOLOv5, aimed at enhancing the performance and flexibility of its predecessor. Compared to YOLOv5, YOLOv7 has undergone adjustments and improvements in both model architecture and training strategies to enhance detection performance and robustness. It stands out as one of the top-performing detectors known to date, excelling in both speed and accuracy.

Table 2 summarizes the results on Wilder Face. The results are arranged in order of mAP first, followed by GFLOPs, and F1.

Table 2. Performance Comparison on Wilder Face

Method	mAP_0.5	mAP_0.5:0.95	GFLOPs	F1
YOLOv3s	0.777	0.433	154.5	0.78
YOLOv3s-SPP	0.776	0.434	155.4	0/78
YOLOv5s	0.731	0.382	15.9	0.73
YOLOv7s	0.704	0.368	13.2	
Ours	0.750	0.403	**19.4**	0.76

4.3 Visualization

In this section will give a visual expression of the proposed method and original YOLOv5s framework. In Figure 4, visualization results have been presented on Wilder Face. It is found that the proposed algorithm demonstrates superiority in recognizing objects from multiple shooting angles while consuming fewer computational resources. Subsequent efforts will concentrate on enhancing the recognition of facial targets under jittery conditions.

(a) The proposed method (b) Originial YOLOv5s

Figure 4. Wider Face Performance Visualization.

5. CONCLUSION

Face detection in intelligent video surveillance is a fundamental step and aspect of video comprehension. Building upon foundational theories, this paper presents an enhanced YOLOv5 algorithm designed for face recognition under challenging conditions. The key improvement involves integrating a bidirectional Feature Pyramid Network (BiFPN) directly into the YOLOv5 framework's neck. Additionally, an output head is integrated into the framework's head to identify small targets in densely populated scenes. Lastly, the original network's loss function is substituted with Scale-Invariant Intersection over Union (SIoU) to better address challenges such as occlusion and overlap between targets. This integration enables the execution of pre-training tasks on the established COCO128 dataset and the implementation of a targeted facial recognition task on the dedicated Wider Face dataset. Experiments conducted validate the superiority of the proposed model, which resulted in a significant improvement in mAP_0.5 accuracy of over 30.2% (without pretrained weights) and 2.2% (with pretrained weights and SIoU). Future work will focus on improving the YOLO architecture for better handling of complex and ambiguous object shapes, and on generalising the improved algorithms for broader video processing applications. As another future work, the performance of the proposed method can be compared with a capsule network-based classifier since their high performance, particularly in classification of skin diseases, has been shown recently(GOCERI, 2023, 2021).

ACKNOWLEDGEMENT

This research is sponsored by school of Computing and Engineering in University of Huddersfield and Chinese National Undergraduate Training Program for Innovation and Entrepreneurship.

REFERENCES

Cao, Q., Shen, L., Xie, W., Parkhi, O.M., Zisserman, A., (2018). VGGFace2: A Dataset for Recognising Faces across Pose and Age, in: 2018 13th IEEE International Conference on Automatic Face & Gesture Recognition (FG 2018). Presented at the 2018 13th IEEE International Conference on Automatic Face & Gesture Recognition (FG 2018), IEEE, Xi'an, pp. 67–74. https://doi.org/10.1109/FG.2018.00020

Chang, W.-Y., Tsai, M.-Y., Lo, S.-C., (2021). ResSaNet: A Hybrid Backbone of Residual Block and Self-Attention Module for Masked Face Recognition, in: 2021 IEEE/CVF International Conference on Computer Vision Workshops (ICCVW). Presented at the 2021 IEEE/CVF International Conference on Computer Vision Workshops (ICCVW), IEEE, Montreal, BC, Canada, pp. 1468–1476. https://doi.org/10.1109/ICCVW54120.2021.00170.

Goceri, E., (2021). CAPSULE NEURAL NETWORKS IN CLASSIFICATION OF SKIN LESIONS. Presented at the IADIS International Conference Big Data Analytics, Data Mining and Computational Intelligence 2021 (part of MCCSIS 2021), pp. 29–36.

Goceri, E., (2023). Classification of skin cancer using adjustable and fully convolutional capsule layers. Biomedical Signal Processing and Control 85, 104949. https://doi.org/10.1016/j.bspc.2023.104949

Gevorgyan, Z., (2022). SIoU Loss: More Powerful Learning for Bounding Box Regression. https://doi.org/10.48550/arXiv.2205.12740

Girshick, R., (2015). Fast R-CNN. Presented at the Proceedings of the IEEE International Conference on Computer Vision, pp. 1440–1448.

Hariri, W., (2022). Efficient masked face recognition method during the COVID-19 pandemic. SIViP 16, 605–612. https://doi.org/10.1007/s11760-021-02050-w

Najibi, M., Samangouei, P., Chellappa, R., Davis, L.S., (2017). SSH: Single Stage Headless Face Detector, in: 2017 IEEE International Conference on Computer Vision (ICCV). Presented at the 2017 IEEE International Conference on Computer Vision (ICCV), IEEE, Venice, pp. 4885–4894. https://doi.org/10.1109/ICCV.2017.522

Redmon, J., Farhadi, A., (2018). YOLOv3: An Incremental Improvement.

Ren, S., He, K., Girshick, R., Sun, J., (2015). Faster R-CNN: Towards Real-Time Object Detection with Region Proposal Networks, in: Advances in Neural Information Processing Systems. Curran Associates, Inc.

Tan, M., Pang, R., Le, Q.V., (2020). EfficientDet: Scalable and Efficient Object Detection, in: 2020 IEEE/CVF Conference on Computer Vision and Pattern Recognition (CVPR). Presented at the 2020 IEEE/CVF Conference on Computer Vision and Pattern Recognition (CVPR), IEEE, Seattle, WA, USA, pp. 10778–10787. https://doi.org/10.1109/CVPR42600.2020.01079

Wang, C.-Y., Bochkovskiy, A., Liao, H.-Y.M., (2022). YOLOv7: Trainable bag-of-freebies sets new state-of-the-art for real-time object detectors. https://doi.org/10.48550/arXiv.2207.02696

Yang, S., Luo, P., Loy, C.C., Tang, X., (2016). WIDER FACE: A Face Detection Benchmark, in: 2016 IEEE Conference on Computer Vision and Pattern Recognition (CVPR). Presented at the 2016 IEEE Conference on Computer Vision and Pattern Recognition (CVPR), IEEE, Las Vegas, NV, USA, pp. 5525–5533. https://doi.org/10.1109/CVPR.2016.596

Yi, D., Lei, Z., Liao, S., Li, S.Z., (2014). Learning Face Representation from Scratch.

Zhang, J., Yan, X., Cheng, Z., Shen, X., (2022). A face recognition algorithm based on feature fusion. Concurrency and Computation: Practice and Experience 34, e5748. https://doi.org/10.1002/cpe.5748

MESH-POLYPDET: SURFACE MESHES BASED POLYP DETECTION IN VIRTUAL COLONOSCOPY

Ming Ma[1], Chenyang Sun[2] and Na Lei[3]
[1]*Department of Graduate Computer Science and Engineering, Katz School of Science and Health, Yeshiva University, USA*
[2]*School of Software Technology, Dalian University of Technology, China*
[3]*International School of Information Science & Engineering, Dalian University of Technology, China*

ABSTRACT

Colorectal polyps can evolve into colon cancer over time. Early screening or detection of colon polyps using computer-aided detection (CAD) techniques along with removal of the polyps can lower the risk of colon cancer. As an alternative to optimal colonoscopy (OC), virtual colonoscopy (VC) has the advantage of non-invasiveness in the detection of colon polyps. Recent decades have witnessed rapid advancement in VC based polyp detection and false positive (FP) reduction techniques using machine learning or deep learning methods. However, the majority of existing methods are based on the computation using computed tomography (CT) images of patient data, which are in some cases very computationally expensive, particularly in the scenario of necessity of large dataset for model training. In this paper, we propose a novel automatic polyp detection method termed Mesh-PolypDet using the surface meshes of colorectal data. The initial detection of polyp candidates is performed on 3D colon surface meshes, and the subsequent FP reduction is carried out using the visual transformer and conformal mapping. Experiments are conducted to evaluate the performance of the proposed method in comparison with other existing methods.

KEYWORDS

Virtual Colonoscopy, Polyp Detection, False Positive Reduction, Surface Meshes, Conformal Mapping, Visual Transformer

1. INTRODUCTION

Colorectal cancer is the second most common cause of cancer deaths in the United States (Cronin et al. 2022). A colon polyp is a tissue which grows on the wall of the colon. Over time, some polyps can develop into colon cancer, thus early screening or detection of colon polyps along with removal of the polyps can lower the risk of colon cancer (Sharma et al. 2023). In comparison to optical colonoscopy (OC), virtual colonoscopy (VC) is a non-invasive screening technique for detection of colon polyps using computed tomography (CT) scans.

Many computer-aided detection (CAD) techniques have been developed for automatic and efficient detection of colon polyps in VC. These methods mainly leverage various geometric or shape features. Summers et al. utilized the mean curvature, principal curvatures and Gaussian curvature to detect initial polyp candidates (Summers et al. 2001). Zhu et al. proposed a curvature estimation method for polyp detection improvement (Zhu et al. 2011). Li et al. used a wavelet method in the CAD system for polyp detection (Li et al. 2008). In more recent years, various machine learning and deep learning based methods have been proposed for automatic polyp detection. Näppi et al. developed a novel CAD system based on deep convolutional neural network to detect serrated polyps via volumetric shape-based features (Näppi et al. 2017). Zhang et al. proposed a deep learning based method using expert knowledge and multi-scale features for detection of polyps (Zhang et al. 2021). Näppi et al. used photon-counting CT for polyp detection to address the risk of ionizing radiation

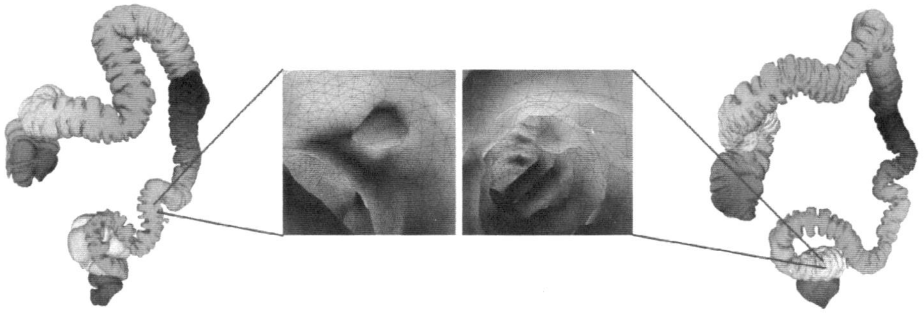

Figure 1. Two colon surfaces with polyps

of CT (Näppi et al. 2023). In addition to these CAD methods on CT images in VC, numerous methods have been presented to automatically detect the polyps in colonoscopy videos acquired in OC. Shin et al. presented a region-based convolutional neural network method for polyp detection in colonoscopy videos via transfer learning (Shin et al. 2018). Lima et al. proposed a two-stage method for polyp detection in colonoscopy images using transformer (Lima et al. 2023). Liu et al. proposed a method based on cross-stage Swin Transformer to extract multi-scale features for polyp detection (Liu et al. 2024).

Existing methods have demonstrated their efficacy and power in polyp detection. However, some issues still lie in the existing methods. The majority of existing methods are based on the computation using CT images of patient data, which are in some cases very computationally expensive, particularly in the scenario of necessity of large dataset for model training. Besides, in spite of promising results achieved by existing deep learning based method using colonoscopy videos acquired in OC, the OC procedure is more invasive than VC. Therefore, we propose a novel polyp detection method in VC based on surface meshes rather than CT images. This not only reduces the computational cost on CT images, but also remains in line with non-invasive screening procedure in VC. Figure 1 illustrates two colon surface meshes with polyps in zoom-in views.

The proposed polyp detection method termed Mesh-PolypDet uses the surface meshes of colorectal data. It consists of initial detection of polyp candidates and false positive (FP) reduction. The initial detection of polyp candidates is performed using shape features and descriptors on 3D colon surface meshes, and the subsequent FP reduction is carried out using the visual transformer based on the 2D images obtained from conformal parameterization of 3D surface meshes.

This work has the following main contributions: (1). A novel polyp detection method termed Mesh-PolypDet based on the surface meshes of colorectal data is proposed; (2). Conformal mapping is introduced into the entire algorithmic framework in conjunction with the visual transformer to improve the polyp detection rate.

2. METHOD

The proposed Mesh-PolypDet method is based on the surface mesh based computation of features and shape descriptors, conformal mapping parameterization, and deep learning based classification using visual transformer. It is comprised of two major components: (1) polyp candidates detection; and (2) FP reduction. An overview of the Mesh-PolypDet is presented in the following subsection, followed by detailed introduction of two major components in the proposed method.

2.1 Overview of Mesh-PolypDet

Figure 2 shows a pipeline of the proposed Mesh-PolypDet method. The method begins with the input of a colon surface, which is a triangulated mesh obtained from original CT image via processing steps including image segmentation and surface reconstruction. Principal curvature ($K1$), mean curvature (MC) and shape index (SI) are computed on the colon surface mesh, respectively. Based on the values of K1, MC and SI on the

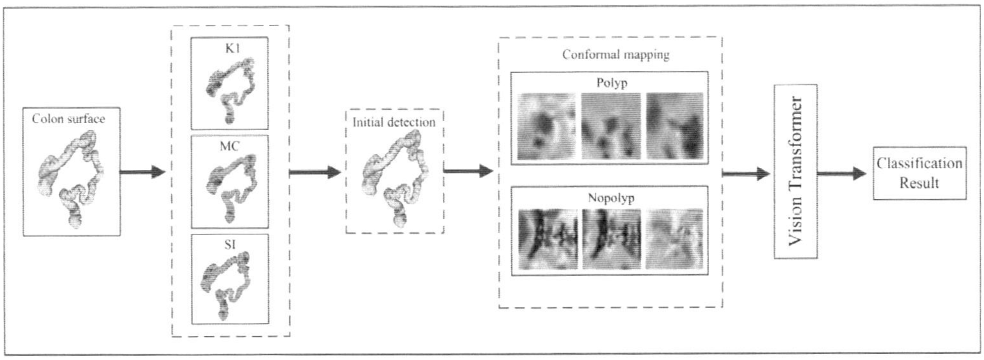

Figure 2. The pipeline of the proposed Mesh-PolypDet method

surface mesh, an initial detection of polyp candidates is performed. To reduce the FP and improve the detection rate, a visual transformer is employed for the purpose of classification. We introduce the conformal mapping to generate the input images for visual transformer. The original 3D colon surface mesh is conformally mapped to 2D domain, and 2D image patches containing either true polyp or FP are generated with color encoded by $K1$, MC and SI values, respectively. These image patches in a specific category ($K1$, MC or SI) are fed into a separate visual transformer for training, leading to three different classification models. The final classification result is obtained using an ensemble strategy to integrate the classification results from three models.

2.2 Polyp Candidates Detection

In the proposed Mesh-PolypDet method, the polyp candidates are detected using automatic algorithm purely on surface meshes of colon data. Figure 3 shows a colon surface in triangulated mesh. Suppose a colon surface mesh is denoted by $M(V, E, F)$ where V, E, and F are the sets of vertices, edges and faces, respectively, and a face $f \in F$ consists of three edges represented by $[v_i, v_j]$, $[v_j, v_k]$, $[v_k, v_i]$ where $v_i, v_j, v_k \in V$. First, the detection algorithm computes $K1$, MC and SI on each vertex $v \in V$. $K1$, MC and SI are calculated according to the following formulas:

$$K1 = H + \sqrt{H^2 - K} \tag{1}$$

where H and K denote the mean curvature and Gaussian curvature, respectively.

$$MC = \frac{1}{2} + (K1 + K2) \tag{2}$$

where $K1$ and $K2$ are the principal curvatures.

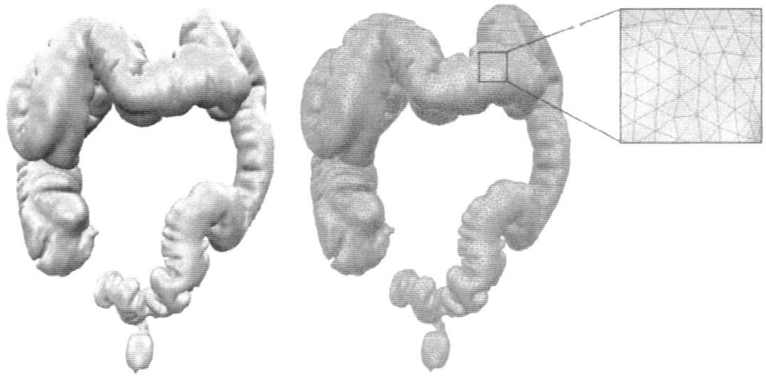

(a) (b)

Figure 3. Colon surface mesh in smooth form (a) and triangular form (b)

$$SI = \frac{1}{2} - \frac{1}{\pi}\arctan\frac{K1+K2}{K1-K2} \tag{3}$$

where $K1$ and $K2$ denote the principal curvatures.

Second, seed vertices are selected according to their $K1$, MC and SI using the threshold. Then, region growing starting from the seed vertex is performed to generate the patch of polyp candidate. Finally, a post-processing step is applied to the initial patches to either merge two close small patches into one patch, or remove the oversized patches which are not considered the polyp candidates. Figure 4 (a)-(c) shows the colon surface mesh with $K1$, MC and SI values encoded in color, on which the polyp candidates detection is performed.

2.3 False Positive Reduction

After the initial polyp candidates detection is completed, a set of detected polyp candidates are generated, which comprises true polyps and FPs. In order to reduce the FPs and improve the detection rate, a deep learning based classification is used for this purpose via visual transformer. To fully utilize the power of visual transformer on 2D images, we employ conformal mapping to transform the 3D colon surface mesh into 2D domain.

2.3.1 Conformal Mapping

Conformal parameterization allows an angle preserving transformation from 3D surface to 2D domain. In this work, the conformal mapping is used to obtain 2D domain images encoding the $K1$, MC and SI values from 3D colon surfaces, which are then fed into the visual transformer for training as input images.

Formally, suppose two Riemannian surfaces are represented by (M_1, g_1) and (M_2, g_2), respectively. A smooth mapping $\varphi: M_1 \rightarrow M_2$ is called conformal mapping, if the pull-back metric $\varphi^* g_2$ induced by the mapping φ and the original metric g_1 differ by a scalar function, i.e.,

$$\varphi^* g_2 = e^{2u} g_1 \tag{4}$$

where $u: M_1 \rightarrow \mathbb{R}$ is a scalar function.

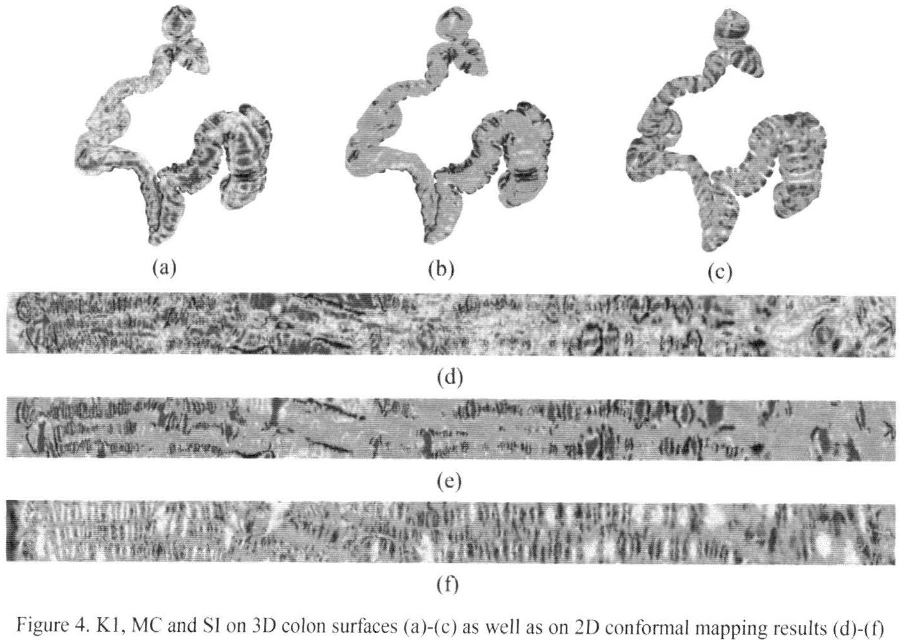

Figure 4. K1, MC and SI on 3D colon surfaces (a)-(c) as well as on 2D conformal mapping results (d)-(f)

Intuitively, conformal mapping preserves angle or local shape. Figure 4 (d)-(f) illustrates the conformal mapping results onto 2D domain from the 3D colon surface as shown in Figure 4 (a)-(c).

2.3.2 Visual Transformer based Classification for FP Reduction

The visual transformer model used in this work is based on Linformer (Wang et al. 2020) with an embedding dimension of 128. It has a depth of 12 layers and 8 heads, and a dimension of 64 for each head. The input sequence length is 49 (7x7 patches) plus one cls-token. The visual transformer model takes input images of size 224x224 pixels, with a patch size of 32x32 pixels and 3 channels. The output consists of 2 classes, one for true polyp class and the other FP. The cross-entropy loss is used as the loss function in this work. Adam optimizer with an initial learning rate 0.00003 is used, and a learning rate scheduler StepLR (Smith et al. 2017) is also applied, where the learning rate was decayed by gamma which was set to 0.7. The visual transformer model was trained using 100 epochs and 64 batch size. Figure 5 shows the architecture of self-attention in the visual transformer.

Three visual transformer models are trained using three separate datasets of patches of 2D images of conformal mapping results from original 3D surface meshes containing true polyps and FPs, including the images which are color encoded by $K1$, MC and SI values, respectively, as shown in Figure 6. Each of such trained visual transformer model is used for classification to reduce the FPs. These three models are denoted as Mesh-PolypDet (K1), Mesh-PolypDet (MC) and Mesh-PolypDet (SI). We also propose an ensemble strategy to integrate the classification results from three visual transformer models to obtain a final classification result. The final model is represented by Mesh-PolypDet (En).

3. EXPERIMENTAL RESULTS

The experiments in this work used 91 colon surface meshes. The dataset contains a total of 101 polyps, all of which have polyp size greater than 5 mm. In the polyp candidates detection stage, all 91 colon surface meshes were used. In the FP reduction stage, the dataset was split into training: validation: testing with a ratio of 60%:20%:20% for training and testing using visual transformer model.

The proposed Mesh-PolypDet method detected 97 polyps, and achieved an average 11.64 FPs/scan in the initial polyp candidates detection stage. In the FP reduction stage, Mesh-PolypDet (K1), Mesh-PolypDet (MC) and Mesh-PolypDet (SI) obtained 3.6 FPs/scan, 4.0 FPs/scan and 3.6 FPs/scan, respectively. The ensemble method Mesh-PolypDet (En) outperformed the above three methods, achieving 2.7 FPs/scan. A comparison with other polyp detection methods is presented in Table 1. As shown in the table, our proposed surface mesh based method is favorably comparable to other CT based methods. Taking into consideration the expensive computation cost in CT based methods, our proposed method has the advantage of less computation cost, particularly in the scenario of necessity of large dataset for model training.

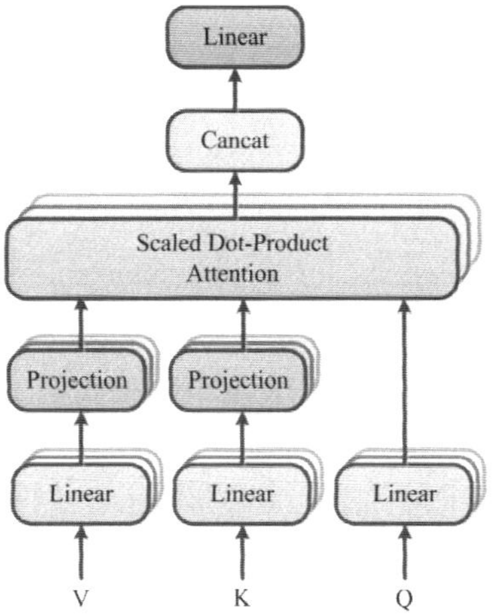

Figure 5. Architecture of self-attention in the visual transformer

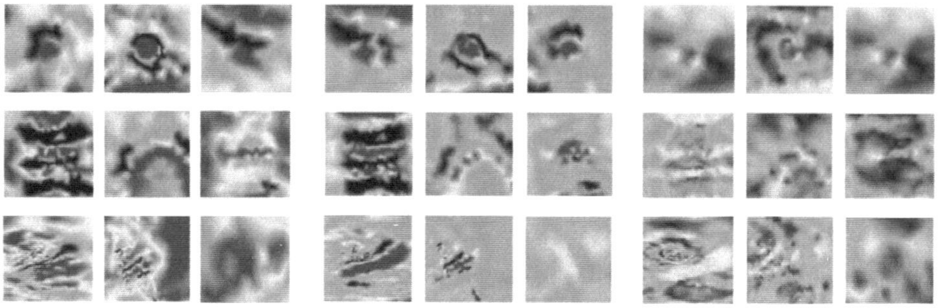

(a) (b) (c)

Figure 6. K1, MC and SI images patches containing the detected polyp candidates as input for classification

Table 1. Comparison with other polyp detection methods

Detection Methods	#Polyps	Polyp Size (mm)	FP Rate
Chen et al.	386	≥5	20.3 FPs/scan
Mang et al.	564	≥6	4.9 FPs/scan
Roth et al.	173	≥6	3.0 FPs/scan
Ren et al.	130	≥5	2.0 FPs/scan
Our Mesh-PolypDet (K1)	**101**	**≥5**	**3.6 FPs/scan**
Our Mesh-PolypDet (MC)	**101**	**≥5**	**4.0 FPs/scan**
Our Mesh-PolypDet (SI)	**101**	**≥5**	**3.6 FPs/scan**
Our Mesh-PolypDet (En)	**101**	**≥5**	**2.7 FPs/scan**

4. CONCLUSION

In this work, a novel automatic polyp detection method termed Mesh-PolypDet was proposed. The Mesh-PolypDet method uses surface meshes of colorectal data for polyp detection instead of CT images, unlike most existing methods. We integrated the conformal mapping into the classification framework to achieve FP reduction via the visual transformer. The proposed method was validated using a dataset of 3D colon surface meshes, and comparative experiments were also conducted to show the competitive performance of the proposed method.

For future work, we plan to improve the transformer architecture in the proposed method, and combine large language model (LLM) with our method to distil patient-specific medical information for enhanced detection efficacy.

ACKNOWLEDGEMENT

We would like to thank all reviewers for their time and efforts in reviewing this manuscript.

REFERENCES

Chen, Y., Ren, Y., Fu, L., Xiong, J., Larsson, R., Xu, X., ... & Zhao, J. (2018, July). A 3D convolutional neural network framework for polyp candidates detection on the limited dataset of CT colonography. In 2018 40th Annual International Conference of the IEEE Engineering in Medicine and Biology Society (EMBC) (pp. 678-681). IEEE.

Cronin, K. A., Scott, S., Firth, A. U., Sung, H., Henley, S. J., Sherman, R. L., ... & Jemal, A. (2022). Annual report to the nation on the status of cancer, part 1: National cancer statistics. Cancer, 128(24), 4251-4284.

Li, J., Van Uitert, R., Yao, J., Petrick, N., Franaszek, M., Huang, A., & Summers, R. M. (2008). Wavelet method for CT colonography computer-aided polyp detection a. Medical physics, 35(8), 3527-3538.

Lima, A. C. D. M., De Paiva, L. F., Bráz, G., De Almeida, J. D. S., Silva, A. C., Coimbra, M. T., & De Paiva, A. C. (2023). A two-stage method for polyp detection in colonoscopy images based on saliency object extraction and transformers. IEEE Access.

Liu, E., He, B., Zhu, D., Chen, Y., & Xu, Z. (2024). Tiny polyp detection from endoscopic video frames using vision transformers. Pattern Analysis and Applications, 27(2), 38.

Mang, T., Bogoni, L., Salganicoff, M., Wolf, M., Raykar, V., Macari, M., ... & Graser, A. (2012). Computer-aided detection of colorectal polyps in CT colonography with and without fecal tagging: a stand-alone evaluation. Investigative radiology, 47(2), 99-108.

Näppi, J. J., Pickhardt, P., Kim, D. H., Hironaka, T., & Yoshida, H. (2017, March). Deep learning of contrast-coated serrated polyps for computer-aided detection in CT colonography. In Medical Imaging 2017: Computer-Aided Diagnosis (Vol. 10134, pp. 114-120). SPIE.

Näppi, J. J., Hironaka, T., Wu, D., Yoshida, S. R., Gupta, R., Tachibana, R., ... & Yoshida, H. (2023, April). Automated detection of colorectal polyps in photon-counting CT colonography. In Medical Imaging 2023: Imaging Informatics for Healthcare, Research, and Applications (Vol. 12469, pp. 187-191). SPIE.

Ren, Y., Chen, Y., Lu, L., & Zhao, J. (2018). Novel 3d radiomic features for computer-aided polyp detection in CT colonography. IEEE Access, 6, 74506-74520.

Roth, H. R., Lu, L., Liu, J., Yao, J., Seff, A., Cherry, K., ... & Summers, R. M. (2015). Improving computer-aided detection using convolutional neural networks and random view aggregation. IEEE transactions on medical imaging, 35(5), 1170-1181.

Sharma, A., Kumar, R., Yadav, G., & Garg, P. (2023). Artificial intelligence in intestinal polyp and colorectal cancer prediction. Cancer Letters, 216238.

Shin, Y., Qadir, H. A., Aabakken, L., Bergsland, J., & Balasingham, I. (2018). Automatic colon polyp detection using region based deep CNN and post learning approaches. IEEE Access, 6, 40950-40962.

Smith, L. N. (2017, March). Cyclical learning rates for training neural networks. In 2017 IEEE winter conference on applications of computer vision (WACV) (pp. 464-472). IEEE.

Summers, R. M., Johnson, C. D., Pusanik, L. M., Malley, J. D., Youssef, A. M., & Reed, J. E. (2001). Automated polyp detection at CT colonography: feasibility assessment in a human population. Radiology, 219(1), 51-59.

Wang, S., Li, B. Z., Khabsa, M., Fang, H., & Ma, H. (2020). Linformer: Self-attention with linear complexity. arXiv preprint arXiv:2006.04768.

Zhang, J., Wang, H., Feng, X., Song, Z., & Neretin, E. (2021, May). Detection of Colorectal Polyps Based on Deep Learning. In Proceedings of the 2021 13th International Conference on Bioinformatics and Biomedical Technology (pp. 190-195).

Zhu, H., Fan, Y., Lu, H., & Liang, Z. (2011). Improved curvature estimation for CAD of colonic polyps in CTC. Academic Radiology, 18(8), 1024-1034.

Short Papers

NONINVASIVE VISUALIZATION OF MUSCLES DURING SWALLOWING USING A MUSCLE DEFORMATION SENSOR

Satoshi Shimabukuro[1,2,4], Ryouta Arashiro[2] and Emi Tamaki[1,3,4]
[1]*Graduate School of Science and Engineering,*
The University of the Ryukyus
1 Senbaru, Nishihara Town, Okinawa, Japan
[2]*Okinawa Rehabilitation Welfare College*
1380-1 Itashiki, Yonabaru Town-, Shimajiri-gun, Okinawa, Japan
[3]*Department of Systems Innovation, School of Engineering,*
The University of Tokyo
7-3-1 Hongo Bunkyo-ku 113-8656 Tokyo, Japan
[4]*H2L Inc.*
3-4-21 Roppongi, Minato-ku, Tokyo, Japan

ABSTRACT

Mealtime is one of the pleasures of daily life and an important factor in ensuring the quality of life. Aging and brain and neurological diseases often complicate eating. In particular, the ability to swallow food directly, such as in dysphagia, has a significant impact on eating. In this study, a new observation method was proposed for the cricopharyngeal muscles, which are important for swallowing. Experiments were conducted on two healthy participants. A muscle deformation sensor was used to observe the cricopharyngeal muscles. The results showed that the contraction and relaxation of the cricopharyngeal muscle during swallowing can be visualized noninvasively and easily using muscle deformation sensors in healthy subjects. Based on this experiment, the possibility of its clinical application in patients with dysphagia is suggested.

KEYWORDS

Swallowing, Noninvasive, Muscle Deformation, Visualization

1. INTRODUCTION

Eating is one of the pleasures of daily life and an important factor in guaranteeing the quality of life. Difficulties with eating include eating and swallowing disorders due to aging and brain and neurological diseases. In particular, many stroke patients experience dysphagia. Rehabilitation speech therapy is necessary for post-stroke feeding and swallowing difficulties. Rehabilitation of feeding and swallowing disorders includes clinical, functional assessment through observation of movement and palpation of neck muscles. In addition, objective tests such as endoscopic swallowing and needle electromyography are often used to confirm efficacy and progress (Ertekin 2002, Wheeler 2006, Celik 2005). The main muscle palpated during clinical functional assessment is the cricopharyngeal muscle (Mu 2002). This muscle is in constant contraction and relaxes during swallowing. It is often anatomically difficult to palpate and requires skill and experience. Objective examination, while superior in terms of understanding the condition, is invasive, patient-intensive, and time-constrained. Therefore, a noninvasive method for visualizing the condition of the cervical muscles during swallowing is desired.

The purpose of this study was to visualize the state of the muscles controlling swallowing function noninvasively using a muscle deformation sensor and to understand the state of swallowing.

The results of this study are used as a stepping stone to estimate the state of swallowing and to develop applications (Figure 1).

2. METHOD AND MATERIAL

2.1 Participants

Two healthy male participants in their 30s were included in the study. The exclusion criteria were as follows: previous neck surgery and fragile skin around the neck. Participants were informed of the nature of the study and their consent was obtained.

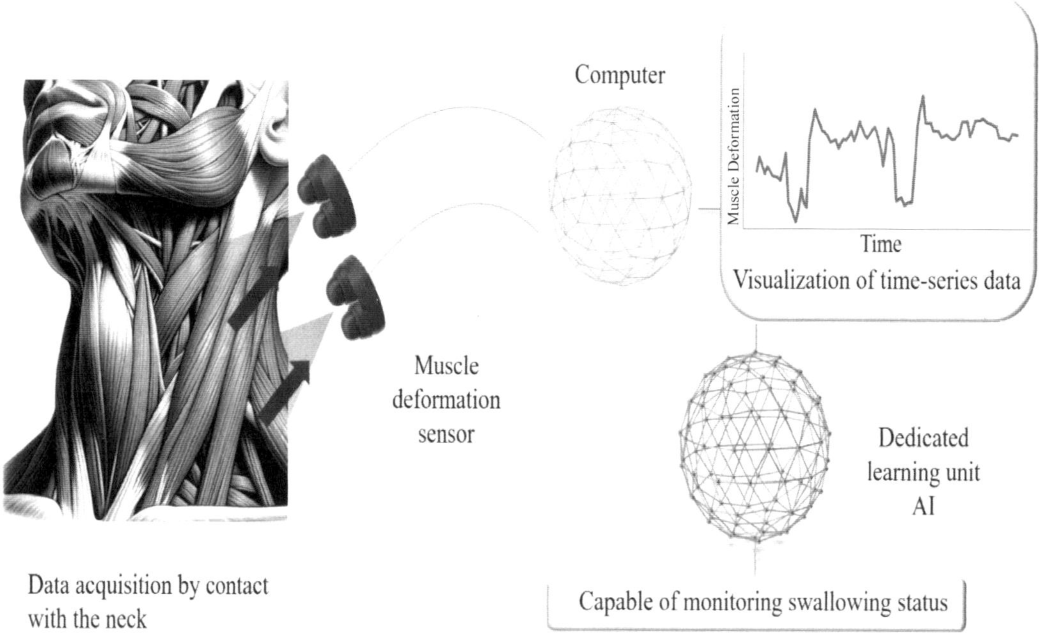

Figure 1. Outline of this study

2.2 Method

For the experiment, a muscle deformation sensor (Tamaki 2019) was used to measure the deformation of the cricopharyngeal muscle. Muscle identification was performed by one speech-language therapist. During the acquisition of muscle deformation, the sensor was placed in contact with the site of the cricopharyngeal pharyngeal muscle (Figure 2c). A portable ultrasound device was used in conjunction with the muscle deformation sensor to confirm swallowing status.

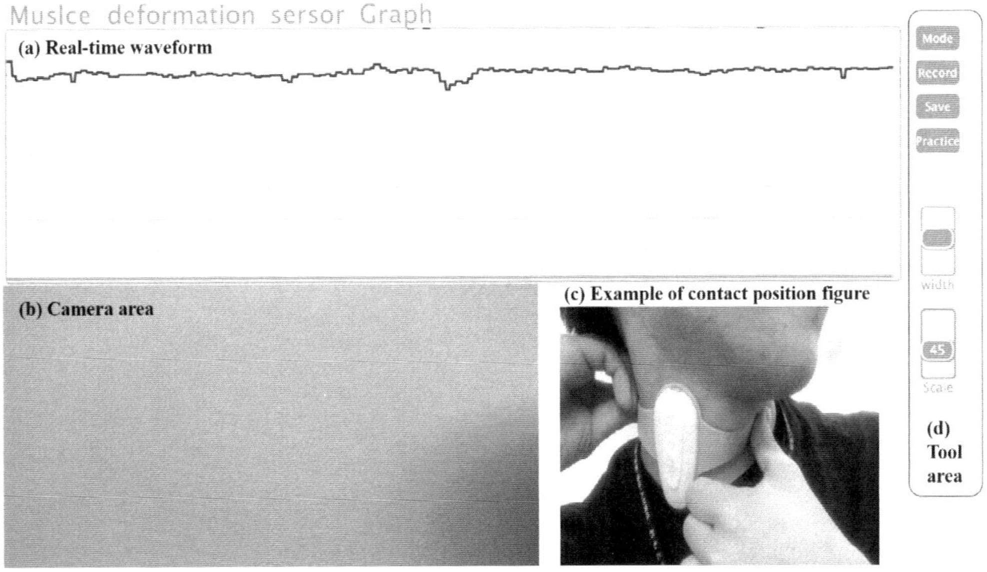

Figure 2. Application Screens
(a) Sensed real-time waveform, (b) Camera area, (c) Sensor contact position, (d) Tool area

2.3 Equipment Used in the Experiment

This study used a muscle deformation sensor array FirstVR (H2L Inc., Tokyo, Japan). FirstVR is a band-type sensor based on near-infrared optical sensing, consisting of infra-light emitting and infra-light receiving. The muscle-deformation sensor array contained 14 optical muscle-deformation sensors. When skeletal muscles are activated, the skeletal muscle deforms by muscle contraction. The reading value in each channel of FirstVR changes when skeletal muscle or skin deforms. The device can be worn by wrapping it around the forearm, similar to a wristwatch, to measure muscle deformation in the forearm and fingers(Shimabukuro 2024, Miyake 2024).

2.4 Data Processing and Visualization with Applications

The reading values were sent to a computer from FirstVR through Bluetooth Low Energy. For the muscle deformation sensor channels, those suitable for the anatomical location of the muscle were selected and visualized in the application. Four sensor channels were selected, and the muscle deformation values for each channel were averaged and extracted. The application was created using processing 4.0. The muscle displacement sensor was connected to the application via Bluetooth, and the muscle status was visualized in real-time (Figure 2).

3. RESULT AND DISCUSSION

In this study, muscle deformation sensors were used to visualize the status of muscles involved in swallowing. It was also possible to observe muscle activity under different swallowing conditions (Figure 3). These were also validated simultaneously with the passage of food and drink by ultrasound device. In the future, this technology could be applied not only during rehabilitation but also in actual eating situations, potentially speeding up recovery. Additionally, it is expected that the technology will be used not only for evaluation but also to provide feedback on muscle activity to patients for therapeutic purposes (Huckabee 2023).

A limitation of this study is that the subject was a two-healthy individual and not a person with dysphagia. In the future, it will be necessary to verify the differences between healthy individuals and those with swallowing disorders.

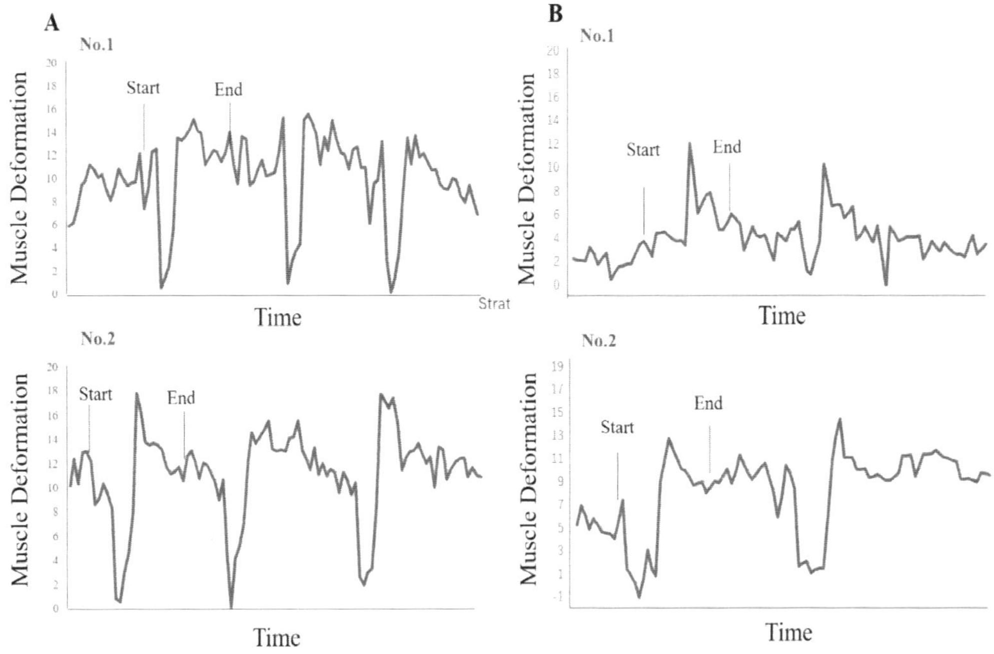

Figure 3. Waveform of muscle deformation during swallowing of food and drink
A: Drink (Water),B: Food (Solid object)
Two participants: No. 1, No. 2

The start is the beginning of swallowing, and the end is the end of swallowing. Swallowing waveforms are three times for liquids and two times for solids.

4. CONCLUSION

This study proposed a new observation method for the cricopharyngeal muscles, which are important for swallowing. The contraction and relaxation of the cricopharyngeal muscle during swallowing could be visualized in a noninvasive and easy manner by using a muscle deformation sensor in a healthy subject. Based on this experiment, the possibility of clinical application to actual patients with dysphagia was suggested.

FUNDING

This work was supported by Council for Science, Technology and Innovation, "Cross-ministerial Strategic Innovation Promotion Program (SIP), Development of foundational technologies and rules for expansion of the virtual economy"(JPJ012495).(funding agency: NEDO)

REFERENCES

Celik, M., Alkan, Z., Ercan, I., Ertasoglu, H., Alkm, C., Erdem, L., ... & Ertekin, C. (2005). Cricopharyngeal muscle electromyography in laryngopharyngeal reflux. The Laryngoscope, 115(1), 138-142.

Ertekin, C., & Aydogdu, I. (2002). Electromyography of human cricopharyngeal muscle of the upper esophageal sphincter. Muscle & Nerve: Official Journal of the American Association of Electrodiagnostic Medicine, 26(6), 729-739.

Huckabee, M. L., Flynn, R., & Mills, M. (2023). Expanding rehabilitation options for dysphagia: skill-based swallowing training. Dysphagia, 38(3), 756-767.

Miyake, T., Minakuchi, T., Sato, S., Okubo, C., Yanagihara, D., & Tamaki, E. (2024). Optical Myography-Based Sensing Methodology of Application of Random Loads to Muscles during Hand-Gripping Training. Sensors, 24(4), 1108.

Mu, L., & Sanders, I. (2002). Muscle fiber-type distribution pattern in the human cricopharyngeus muscle. Dysphagia, 17, 87-96.

Shimabukuro Sr, S., Miyake, T., & Tamaki, E. (2024). Analyzing the Differences in the Degree of Force Application Between Novice and Expert Physiotherapists Using a Muscle Deformation Sensor. Cureus, 16(5).

Tamaki, E., Hosono, S., & Iwasaki, K. (2019, April). Firstvr: A muscle deformation sensors array device to detect finger gestures and noise reduction case. In Proceedings of the 2019 2nd International Conference on Electronics, Communications and Control Engineering (pp. 21-24).Beck, K. and Ralph, J., 1994. Patterns Generates Architectures. Proceedings of European Conference of Object-Oriented Programming. Bologna, Italy, pp. 139-149.

Wheeler, K. M. (2006). Hyoid movement and sEMG activity during normal discrete swallows, Mendelsohn maneuver, effortful swallow and expiratory pressure threshold tasks in healthy adults. University of Florida.

EXPLORING THE BENEFITS OF PHYSICAL FEATURES IN VIRTUAL REALITY ON CUSTOMER EXPERIENCE

Robin Cherix[1], Maud Julmy[2], Marine Capallera[1], Julien Roland[2] and Elena Mugellini[1]
[1]*HumanTech Institute, Haute Ecole d'Ingénierie et d'Architecture,*
Haute Ecole Spécialisée de Suisse Occidentale, Switzerland
[2]*Haute Ecole Arc Ingénierie, Haute Ecole Spécialisée de Suisse Occidentale, Switzerland*

ABSTRACT

Virtual try-out experiences suffer from a lack of physicality. If consumers cannot touch or feel what they see, it is less likely for them to buy it. Here we present work in progress of an immersive luxury watch try-out experience. We added a 3D printed, weighted mock-up to enrich the experience. This mock-up is worn on the wrist, where the virtual watch appears. User tests show that the proposed experience is very well received and sparks interest for such experience.

KEYWORDS

VR, Visuo-Haptic, Watchmaking, User Experience

1. INTRODUCTION

E-shopping and virtual experiences have been a growing opportunity for the business sector over the past decades. With this technology, one can try, compare or customise products before buying. While the experiences become more and more realistic and immersive, they still miss many important aspects of the buying experience: touching, interacting with the product, feeling its weight or its texture for instance. (Ornati, 2019; Racat and Capelli, 2020; Silva et al., 2021). Despite these improvements, the fact that it is not possible to physically touch or feel a product is a massive barrier to the adoption of virtual experiences in specific sectors. Almost 60% of people prefer to buy in a physical shop instead of an online shop because they can feel the product in their hands (KPMG, 2017). This shows that virtual experiences need to include a physical aspect in order to be more convincing.

In this paper, we present a work in progress of a virtual luxury watch try-out experience, including a watch customisation feature and a storytelling about the watch and the brand. For this experience, we used a Submarine 1917 from Tavannes Watch Co[1]. This particular sector presents a business opportunity, as physical stores or events tend to have little stock. This experience includes a 3D printed, weighted watch mock-up to address the lack of physicality. This approach is called "passive haptic", as opposed to active haptic which use vibrations or electricity to elicit haptic sensations.

2. RELATED WORK

Some consumers rely heavily on touch to judge a product, while some don't. (Peck and Childers, 2003) refer to this as "need for touch" (NFT). For people with high-NFT, not being able to touch a product creates a situation of frustration that cannot be attenuated by any alternative, such as textual description. Low-NFT people, on the other hand, can deal with such inconvenience and mitigate their frustration. In the context of luxury watchmaking, our user research leads us to think that consumers of this sector consist mainly of high-NFT people. This highlights the importance of having a haptic component in our experiment.

[1] https://tavannes-watch.swiss/watches/design/submarine-1917/ta-a07-111-stbp02/

In their review, (Petit et al., 2019) insisted on the need for further research regarding multisensory-enabling interfaces. They proposed haptic interfaces for high-NFT people using vibrotactile, body-grounded (attached to the body) tactile or even midair tactile interfaces. Interestingly they didn't mention the passive haptic we adopted for this work.

One sector where touch seems to play a huge role is fashion, similarly to watchmaking. (Ornati, 2019) pointed out the limited development that went into tactile technologies for online retail in fashion. In her paper, she called for more qualitative and quantitative research on the impact of haptics on adopters, as well as qualitative research on managers.

An augmented-reality interactive technology (ARIT) fitting room was created by (Huang and Liao, 2017). They conducted an experiment where users could see their "reflect" (actually a video stream of themselves) with virtual accessories and clothes applied on them. Although close to our work about the virtual try-out experiment, it does not, however, include any haptic component whatsoever.

Closer to our topic, (Morillo et al., 2019) conducted a comparative study in a luxury watch shop. The study proposed to visualize a virtual watch either as a hologram or in augmented reality and customize it. Clients could try the two modalities and choose which they preferred. Although the results did not show any statistical preference, the clients rated the experiment very fun and easy, showing the interest of this population for such digital experiences. As previously explored works, this study did not include any haptics in its experiment. To the best of our knowledge, using passive haptic to enhance a user experience in the context of a virtual luxury try-out has remained unexplored.

3. PILOT STUDY

We conducted user tests to assess the usability and technical quality of our virtual watch try-out system. The tests ran on a laptop equipped with an Nvidia RTX3080 and a Meta Quest 3 through Quest Link. We used Unity 2022 LTS with the HD rendering pipeline. 4 interactions were implemented into the system: thumb-index pinch or full-hand grab to handle the watch, pinch-to-zoom to change its scale, pressing the left palm with the right index to open or close the customisation menu and poke with the index to select a customisation option. These interactions are done using the headset hand-tracking and implemented with the MetaXR SDK. A storytelling about the watch and the brand history is included.

The goal of the user tests was two-fold. First, we wanted to assess the technical quality of our ongoing work. The aspects tested here were the hands self-occlusion resilience, the quality of the interactions with the watch, the customisation menu and the visual quality of the experiment. Second, we wanted to know more about how the users perceived the experience. This includes the storytelling around the model and the brand, as well as the quality of our customisation feature and the importance it plays in the user experience.

5 participants (1 female, 4 males) interested in watchmaking were assigned to 1 of 3 scenarios. During the scenario, the participant could manipulate and customise at will a virtual Submarine 1917 while having a 3D printed mock-up of this model at their wrist. The virtual and mock-up watch match as close as possible, in terms of visuals, weight and wristband material. The scenarios differ around the storytelling. Scenario 1 (S1) had the storytelling outside the virtual environment, while scenario 2 (S2) and 3 (S3) included it as a slideshow with voice-over. In S2, the slideshow starts either when the participant presses the play button, or when they attach the watch at their wrist. In S3, the participant can only start the storytelling by pressing on the play button. 2 users were assigned to S1 and S3, and 1 to S2.

The participant was greeted by a representative of the brand and was invited to choose their preferred wristband material (leather, fabric and rubber). The gestures to interact with the watch and the customisation menu were then shown to the participant (except for participant 1). From there, storytelling was presented to the participant (S1 only), then the participant was invited to put the headset on. Inside the virtual environment, the user was free to play the storytelling (S2 and S3), manipulate the watch, attach it to their wrist and customise it at will. The customisation included the colour of the wristband, crown and dial. While they did so, they were asked to share their feelings about the experiment, in think-aloud. When they felt they could try everything they wanted, the participant was invited to take off the headset and fill in a UX curve and a questionnaire about the experiment. The UX curve addressed: Introduction to the project, storytelling, choice of wristband, putting the headset and the mock-up on and customizing the virtual watch. The questionnaire focused on the quality of the interactions and rendering, as well as open questions about pros and cons of the experiment.

Finally, the participant was handed a real Submarine and was asked to compare it with what they experienced in the virtual environment. Figure 1 shows the different versions of the watch the participant sees and feels during the experience.

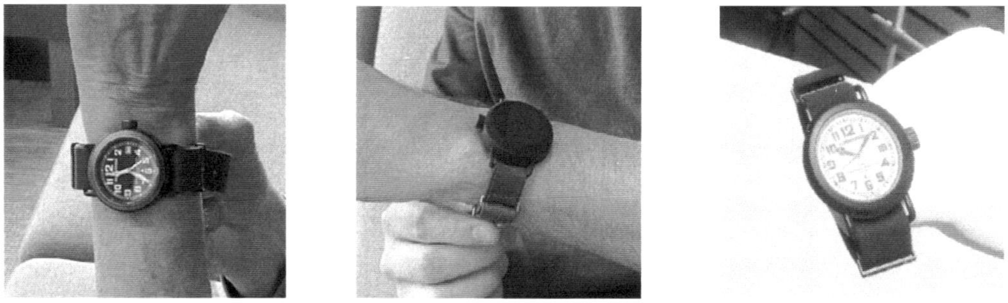

Figure 1. From left to right: The Submarine 1917, the mock-up and the virtual watch

4. EXPERIMENTAL RESULTS

In our experiment, we evaluated various aspects using a 7-point Likert scale. Participants totally agreed (7) that being able to customise the watch is a plus. The storytelling and accompaniment were also highly rated (6.8). Interacting with the virtual storytelling (S2 and S3) was deemed very intuitive (6.6) along with interacting with the customisation interface (6), despite a bug making storytelling and customisation interface visually overlap and some buttons hard to press. Visuals and environment quality rated at 5.8. Watch manipulation got a lower score, but still rated high (5). This score reflects issues some participants encountered when trying to move or rotate the watch. Sometimes the watch would also attach to the wrist unintentionally when scaled up.

These scores highlight the importance of human-to-human interaction in this kind of experience. Storytelling and customisation are key points in a luxury watch try-out. Differences in interaction ease between participant 1 and the others let us think the gestures are good as long as they are introduced before the headset is put on. Overall comments point out that virtual and actual watches felt very similar.

Out of the 4 participants who compared weight between the real watch and the mock-up, 3 were convinced the mock-up was lighter. Our hypothesis is that the watch doesn't have any weight when manipulated mid-air, biasing participants toward a lighter mock-up. This feeling may be increased when the watch is scaled up. The fact that the remaining participant spent considerably more time observing the watch on their wrist and accurately said the mock-up and the actual watch share the same weight backs this hypothesis. Participants imagined several applications where this tool would be a plus: bringing more confidence than buying on a catalogue, presenting prototypes, or helping buyers wait until their watch is ready to ship. Many participants wanted to have more interactions with the watch. For instance, exposing the mechanism, or pulling and turning the crown. The fact that the participants highly rated the experience despite wanting more shows the interest for such experience. While conclusions cannot be drawn definitively from the feedback of five participants, it provides valuable insights for future directions.

5. CONCLUSION AND FUTURE WORK

In this paper, we investigated the effectiveness of visuo-haptic in a luxury watch try-out. Results with 5 participants showed that, despite flaws due to an ongoing work, the proposed experience is convincing.

These results point out a few improvement opportunities: more interactions with the virtual watch, making the customisation interface easier to press and better mid-air manipulation. Participants also suggested applications they could foresee for this experience. The next step is to address these opportunities as well as conducting tests with more users in order to provide stronger results. As of now, the experiment is only available in virtual reality. However, recent devices such as the Meta Quest 3 we used also support mixed reality. This could be an interesting direction for future work, as this would allow people to see themselves wearing the virtual watch, instead of seeing an avatar. This is in line with comments some people made outside the context of the experiment. We plan to investigate the importance of having an accurate weight for the mock-up by comparing well weighted versus badly weighted mock-up evaluations, in terms of user experience. The same investigation could be conducted about mock-up materials. We printed the one we used with filament and thus presented rough details on some spots. Using resin, or even actual materials, for the mock-up would provide a closer experience to the original watch and could lead to improved user experience.

REFERENCES

Huang, T.-L., Liao, S.-L. (2017). Creating e-shopping multisensory flow experience through augmented-reality interactive technology. Internet Res. 27, 449–475. https://doi.org/10.1108/IntR-11-2015-0321

KPMG. (2017). The truth about online consumers.

Morillo, P., Orduña, J. M., Casas, S., Fernández, M. (2019). A comparison study of AR applications versus pseudo-holographic systems as virtual exhibitors for luxury watch retail stores. Multimed. Syst. 25, 307–321. https://doi.org/10.1007/s00530-019-00606-y

Ornati, M. (2019). Touching the Cloth: Haptics in Fashion Digital Communication, in: Kalbaska, N., Sádaba, T., Cominelli, F., Cantoni, L. (Eds.), Fashion Communication in the Digital Age. Springer International Publishing, Cham, pp. 254–258.

Peck, J., Childers, T. L. (2003). To have and to Hold: The Influence of Haptic Information on Product Judgments. J. Mark. 67, 35–48. https://doi.org/10.1509/jmkg.67.2.35.18612

Petit, O., Velasco, C., Spence, C. (2019). Digital Sensory Marketing: Integrating New Technologies Into Multisensory Online Experience. J. Interact. Mark. 45, 42–61. https://doi.org/10.1016/j.intmar.2018.07.004

Racat, M., Capelli, S. (2020). Haptic Sensation and Consumer Behaviour: The Influence of Tactile Stimulation in Physical and Online Environments. Springer International Publishing, Cham.

Silva, S. C., Rocha, T. V., De Cicco, R., Galhanone, R. F., Manzini Ferreira Mattos, L. T. (2021). Need for touch and haptic imagery: An investigation in online fashion shopping. J. Retail. Consum. Serv. 59, 102378. https://doi.org/10.1016/j.jretconser.2020.102378

USER-CENTERED DESIGN OF AN OMNIDIRECTIONAL TREADMILL VIRTUAL REALITY EXERGAME

Daniel Cliburn, Vijay Kumar and Ethan Perez
University of the Pacific
Stockton, California USA

ABSTRACT

Omnidirectional treadmills allow users to walk long distances with 360 degrees of freedom without fear that they will collide with objects in their real-world environment. In this paper, we discuss a user-centered design approach to the development of an omnidirectional treadmill virtual reality exergame. Our findings suggest that exergames for omnidirectional treadmills should emphasize movement objectives that encourage players to travel throughout the virtual environment.

KEYWORDS

Omnidirectional Treadmill Exergame, User-Centered Design

1. INTRODUCTION

Virtual reality (VR) technologies can immerse users in fantastic environments with a feeling of presence not possible through other mediums. Contemporary applications of VR technologies exist for areas such as product design and prototyping, education, medical training, therapy, and entertainment (Hamad and Jia, 2022). VR games have become increasingly accessible to gamers, as the availability of the equipment necessary to play these games expands. A common user task in VR applications is to navigate throughout virtual spaces (Sherman and Craig, 2018). Omnidirectional treadmills allow users to walk in virtual spaces with 360 degrees of freedom, without fear of colliding with objects in the real physical world. However, omnidirectional treadmills are not yet commonplace, and thus the design of enjoyable omnidirectional treadmill games is an area largely unexplored. In this paper, we describe our work in progress to develop a VR exergame for an omnidirectional treadmill through a user-centered design approach.

User-centered design (UCD) actively involves users in the development process, through iterative design and evaluation (Mao et al, 2005). UCD approaches can help to ensure that products are meeting user experience goals. UCD techniques have been used to develop video games for motor-impaired users (Mat Zain et al, 2015), augmented reality games for children (Oppermann et al, 2018), and exergames for seniors (Brox et al, 2017). Through use of UCD techniques, we hope to identify characteristics of omnidirectional treadmill VR exergames that make them both easy and fun for players to play, while also allowing users to meet exercise goals.

2. BACKGROUND

The concept of an omnidirectional treadmill has been around for more than two decades (Darken et al., 1997), and there exists a growing body of research exploring user interaction with them. For example, researchers have compared the use of an omnidirectional treadmill to real walking on the ground (Soni and Lamontagne, 2020; Lewis et al, 2024). Findings suggest that travel speeds tend to be slower when walking on omnidirectional treadmills than on the ground, and that walking on omnidirectional treadmills impacts gait and turning. Other researchers compared use of an omnidirectional treadmill to a uni-directional treadmill (Bashir et al, 2023), finding that subjects reported higher levels of cybersickness, required more effort, and found it more difficult when walking on an omnidirectional treadmill as compared to a uni-directional treadmill. Wehden et al (2021) explored the impacts of a VR headset and an omnidirectional treadmill on the gaming experience. They found that while subjects reported higher levels of game enjoyment when using the VR technologies, subjects also reported higher levels of cybersickness than those who used a standard (non-VR) gaming system. There was no significant difference with respect to game enjoyment between VR gaming with only a VR headset and VR gaming on the omnidirectional treadmill; however, subjects that used the omnidirectional treadmill reported higher levels of perceived exertion. Wehden et al (2021) suggest that this finding may be significant to designers of exergames, games that players play for the purposes of both fun and exercise. Polechoński et al (2023) explored the use of ankle weights to increase physical exertion while playing a game on an omnidirectional treadmill. They report that use of ankle weights significantly increased heart rate, while not significantly affecting game enjoyment.

While previous research suggests that walking on an omnidirectional treadmill is not as natural to users as real walking (Soni and Lamontagne, 2020; Lewis et al, 2024), or walking on a traditional uni-directional treadmill (Bashir et al, 2023), omnidirectional treadmills do have potential to be useful for VR exergames (Wehden et al, 2021; Polechoński et al, 2023). However, little research has explored the characteristics of VR exergames that encourage game players to actually walk (or run) on an omnidirectional treadmill in order to receive a health benefit. The purpose of this project is to design a fun VR exergame that encourages game players to exercise by walking on the Infinadeck omnidirectional treadmill (shown in Figure 1). UCD techniques encourage involving users in software design and evaluation. Our hope is that by involving potential game players in an iterative design and evaluation process, we will develop a game that is usable, fun to play, and provides gamers with a health benefit. The remainder of this paper reports on our first iteration of designing a prototype of our game and evaluating it with potential game players.

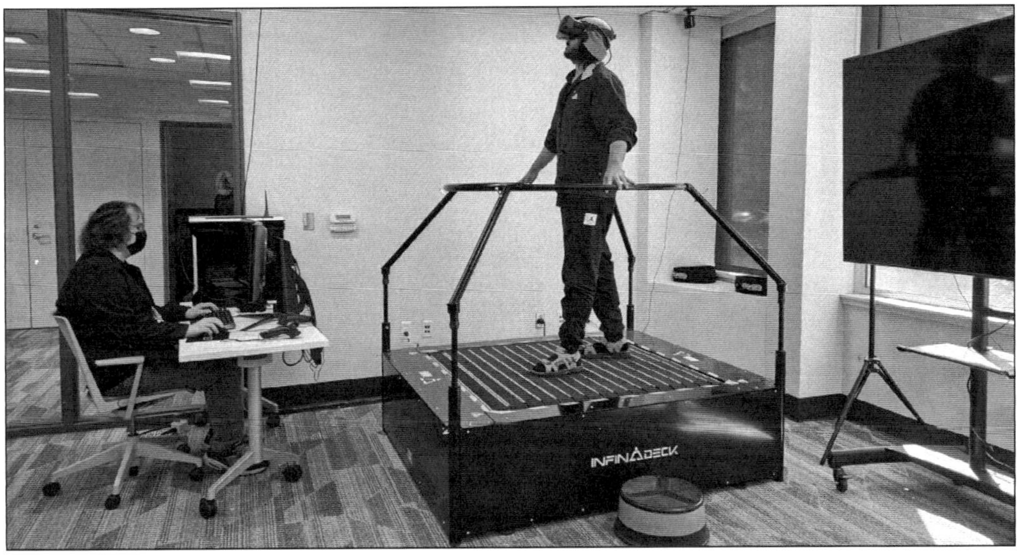

Figure 1. The Infinadeck omnidirectional treadmill

3. VR MECH WARS

In our game, players take on the role of a space marine wearing a mech warrior suit. Since we intend this as an exergame, players walk on the Infinadeck omnidirectional treadmill to move their mech warrior suit. We chose the concept of wearing a mech warrior suit in the game since walking on an omnidirectional treadmill might feel unnatural for users. We thought that having game players believe they are walking in a mech warrior suit while playing the game might add to the realism of the game and increase the sense of presence. To win the game, players must repair damaged terminals while defending their space station from attacking enemy robots. The game was developed using Unreal Engine 5 and the Infinadeck Experience Platform Software Plugin developed by Infinadeck Studios and available on the Unreal Engine Marketplace. As can be seen in Figure 1, users of the Infinadeck typically hold the guardrail while walking on the treadmill. Because of this, we felt it would be impractical for users to hold a controller in their hand while playing the game. Thus, game players fix damaged terminals simply by standing near to them for 14 seconds, and target and shoot missiles at enemy robots simply by staring directly at them for one second. Figure 2 shows a screen shot of the game.

Figure 2. The VR Mech Wars game showing a terminal and enemy robot

4. EVALUATION

Our primary goals with the evaluation of the first game prototype were to determine if the game was usable, what aspects of the game were enjoyable, and what modifications could be made to the game to motivate players to want to play longer. To evaluate the game, subjects were invited to play and provide feedback. Play sessions were designed to last less than 10 minutes, and provide subjects with an exercise experience equivalent to a leisurely walk on a treadmill. Subjects needed to find and repair six damaged terminals in order to complete the game. After playing the game, subjects then wrote their responses to the following items on an anonymous written questionnaire.

1) What was it like for you to experience an omnidirectional treadmill for the first time?
2) Did you find the game to be usable and playable? Please explain your answer.
3) Was there anything you thought you should be able to do that you were not able to do? If so, what?
4) What would have compelled you to keep playing the game longer and for more time?
5) What did you like most about the game?
6) What did you like least about the game?
7) What suggestions do you have to improve the game?

The Institutional Review Board at the authors' university approved this procedure. Twelve subjects played the game and completed at least some portion of the questionnaire. Subject responses to the items on the questionnaire were analyzed to identify general themes. Our findings are as follows.

Subjects described their first experience on the omnidirectional treadmill as "fun", and they found our game to be usable and playable. However, some subjects did comment that it was difficult to keep their "balance" on the treadmill, and they found it challenging to come to a complete stop since the treadmill was always attempting to pull them back to center. Subjects did like that this was a "new experience", "how realistic it was", and being "able to move around the world freely." Interestingly, the least liked aspect of the game was the "aim and shoot" system, as subjects found it "frustrating to have to stare down an enemy" in order to be able to shoot at it. Subjects mentioned wanting "buttons to press," and some wanted to be able to shoot lasers at robots in addition to targeting them with missiles. We designed the targeting system so that game players could keep both hands on the guardrail while playing the game, but apparently this was not intuitive and subjects found it "hard to aim and move at the same time." Perhaps our subjects were used to conventional controls more commonly found when playing first person shooter games. Subjects suggested that we develop a "backstory" to make the game more compelling, add "more objectives," and that we provide a "map" to help them understand "where you have to go." One subject even suggested that the game could require players to find ammunition in order to keep shooting at the robots.

In our next game prototype, we plan to decrease the amount of time that subjects must focus on a robot in order to target it, to the approximate amount of time it would take to press a button on a game controller. We hope that this will make it easier for players to target the robots while continuing to walk on the treadmill, and reduce the amount of time that subjects feel they must come to a complete stop in order to target the robots to destroy them. We also plan to decrease the amount of time that subjects must stand next to terminals in order to repair them. We had thought that subjects would target and destroy robots mostly while standing next to terminals, but in play sessions subjects attempted to target the robots while walking between the terminals. This was difficult to do, and clearly led to frustration for some subjects.

We do consider our findings to be encouraging results, as they suggest that the game was usable, subjects enjoyed moving about the game world, and that future versions of the game should focus on providing players with more movement objectives with more guidance on where to move. These findings also suggest that the game should focus less on tasks that encourage players to stop moving, such as targeting the robots and repairing the terminals. Incorporating these suggestions would likely increase the amount of exercise players perform while playing the game, since players would walk further and stop less in order to complete the game.

5. CONCLUSION

While previous research on the use of omnidirectional treadmills suggests that users find them less natural than real walking, they do support users in walking unrestricted distances in VR applications with 360 degrees of freedom. We report on the design and evaluation of our first prototype of a VR exergame for the Infinadeck omnidirectional treadmill. Findings suggest that subjects found playing our game to be fun, and that as we continue to develop the game we should focus more on movement objectives and less on targeting, since players found it difficult to walk on the treadmill and target enemies at the same time. Future versions of the game could allow players to set workout goals. Players could select their walking speed and the amount of time they want to walk. The game could then generate an environment with objectives spaced at distances requiring players to walk their selected amount of time in order to complete the game. Navigation objectives could also be placed randomly in the environment so that no two gameplay experiences are the same. This would give players more control in how the game is used to help them meet their exercising goals, and provide more variety in the gameplay experience.

One possible limitation to our findings is our sample of subjects. All of our subjects were college and university students, and thus their opinions may not reflect the general population of game players. Future evaluations should include subjects from a more diverse age range. This would help us to determine the viability of the game as an exercising tool for a variety of age groups. Future work could also focus on multiple game playing experiences over a much longer period. This would help to assess the likelihood of players using the game as an exercising tool over an extended period. Nonetheless, we are encouraged by our findings and do believe they support a general conclusion that omnidirectional treadmills have potential as devices that can be used to develop VR exergames.

ACKNOWLEDGEMENT

We would like to thank Veasna Ling, Josh Salyers, and Chris Crawford for their ideas and assistance with the development of VR Mech Wars. We would also like to thank the Department of Computer Science and the William Knox Holt Memorial Library at University of the Pacific for funding this project.

REFERENCES

Bashir, A. et al. (2023). Comparing a Friction-based Uni-directional Treadmill and a Slip-style Omni-directional Treadmill on First-time HMD-VR User Task Performance, Cybersickness, Postural Sway, Posture Angle, Ease of Use, Enjoyment, and Effort. *International Journal of Human-Computer Studies*, Vol. 179, No. C.

Brox, E. et al. (2017). User-Centered Design of Serious Games for Older Adults Following 3 Years of Experience With Exergames for Seniors: A Study Design. *JMIR Serious Games*, Vol. 5, No. 1.

Darken, R. et al. (1997). The Omni-Directional Treadmill: A Locomotion Device for Virtual Worlds. *Proceedings of the 10th Annual Symposium on User Interface Software and Technology*. Banff, Canada, pp. 213-221.

Hamad, A. and Jia, B. (2022). How Virtual Reality Technology Has Changed Our Lives: An Overview of the Current and Potential Applications and Limitations. *International Journal of Environmental Research and Public Health*, Vol. 19, No. 18, p. 11278.

Lewis, M. et al. (2024). Gait Patterns during Overground and Virtual Omnidirectional Treadmill Walking. *Journal of NeuroEngineering and Rehabilitation*, Vol. 21, No. 1, p. 29.

Mao, J. et al. (2005). The State of User-Centered Design Practice. *Communications of the ACM*, Vol. 48, No. 3, pp. 105-109.

Mat Zain, N. et al. (2015). A User-Centered Design: Methodological Tools to Design and Develop Computer Games for Motor-Impaired Users. *Proceedings of the 5th International Conference on Computing and Informatics*. Istanbul, Turkey, p. 130.

Oppermann, L. et al. (2016). Playing on AREEF: Evaluation of an Underwater Augmented Reality Game for Kids. *Proceedings of the 18th International Conference on Human-Computer Interaction with Mobile Devices and Services*. Florence, Italy, pp. 330-340.

Polechoński, J. et al. (2023). Using Ankle Weights as an Effective Way to Increase the Intensity of Physical Activity While Playing Immersive Virtual Reality Games on an Omnidirectional Treadmill. *Applied Sciences*, Vol. 13, No. 20, p. 11536.

Sherman, W. and Craig, A. (2019). *Understanding Virtual Reality: Interface, Application, and Design (Second Edition)*. Morgan Kaufmann, Cambridge, Massachusetts, USA.

Soni, S. and Lamontagne, A. (2020). Characterization of Speed Adaptation While Walking on an Omnidirectional Treadmill. *Journal of NeuroEngineering and Rehabilitation*, Vol. 17, No. 1, p. 153.

Wehden, L. et al. (2021). The Slippery Path to Total Presence: How Omnidirectional Virtual Reality Treadmills Influence the Gaming Experience. *Media and Communication*, Vol. 9, No. 1, pp. 5-16.

REINFORCEMENT LEARNING TO GENERATE LEVELS FOR DESIRED DIFFICULTY

Donghyun Lee and Kyoungsu Oh
Department of Media, Soongsil University, Republic of Korea

ABSTRACT

The field of AI has witnessed considerable advances in recent years, driven by improvements in computing power and the development of various algorithms. A significant proportion of game development time is consumed by level design, which has led to a great deal of research aimed at reducing this time. However, many content generation algorithms depend on training data, making it challenging to efficiently apply them to reduce game development time. This paper presents a novel approach that uses reinforcement learning to train a level generation agent based on difficulty. The method does not require training data, making it particularly useful in scenarios where limited or no training data is available. Our experiments demonstrated the agent's ability to generate levels at high speed.

KEYWORDS

Reinforcement Learning, Procedural Content Generation, Game

1. INTRODUCTION

Reinforcement learning, a subset of machine learning, involves an agent learning to maximize rewards through interactions with its environment. The agent observes the environment's states, selects actions based on these observations, and receives rewards. The primary goal of reinforcement learning is to discover behavior that maximizes rewards. Although commonly applied to gameplay, reinforcement learning also holds the potential for automating game content generation.

This paper proposes the use of reinforcement learning to generate game levels tailored to specific difficulty levels. To assess the efficacy of this approach, experiments were conducted with the Maze game and a simplified version of Candy Crush Saga (King et al., 2012). The agent was trained across various difficulty levels for each game, successfully generating levels that met the desired difficulty.

The design of game levels represents a significant portion of the overall development process, requiring a substantial investment of time and resources. It is of great importance to develop this process efficiently, as this will result in a reduction of both the cost and time spent during game development. One method to achieve this is procedural content generation, in which the game designer sets the rules of the game and employs computer algorithms to automatically generate game content. Supervised learning (Dengyong et al., 2003), which requires training data, is typically generated through manual-level design, and therefore does not result in a reduction of the game development timeline. Genetic algorithms (Sourabh et al., 2020), which do not require training data, are impractical for real-time content generation or bulk production due to the need for repeated evolution cycles for each new content. In contrast, reinforcement learning (Samarth et al., 2020) overcomes these issues by not requiring training data and enabling swift content generation once the agent is trained. The methodology delineated in this paper has the potential to significantly reduce the time and financial resources typically expended during the development of video games.

2. RESEARCH BACKGROUND

The rapid advancement in computer hardware and increasing labor costs have driven the development of various procedural content generation techniques. Adam (Adam et al., 2016) successfully created a design for his Magic the Gathering card by using the denoising sequence-to-sequence method. Tanabe (Tanabe et al., 2021) used LSTMs and sequential encoding to generate levels for Angry Birds. Although there has been significant research on the use of reinforcement learning in gaming (Alex et al., 2019; Niels et al., 2019), its application in content generation remains comparatively unexplored. Khalifa (Ahmed et al., 2020) pioneered this area by employing reinforcement learning to content generation for three games: Binary, Sokoban (Thinking Rabbit, 1982), and The Legend of Zelda (Nintendo, 1986).

3. CONTENT GENERATION

The game development process encompasses four primary phases: planning, development, quality assurance (QA), and release. Development, particularly level design, is the most time- and resource-intensive phase. Procedural content generation methods can reduce these costs because the computer content is generated automatically. Unlike most procedural content generation methods that depend on supervised learning and training data, reinforcement learning does not. Once trained, an agent can rapidly produce content, significantly accelerating game development.

3.1 Environment

The experiments were conducted on two 2D games: a simplified version of Candy Crush Saga, referred to as a Match3 game, and a maze game. The objective was to generate a level that matched the desired difficulty by adjusting the cell type.

3.1.1 Match3

In the Match3 game, there are two types of cells: Empty and Solid. The gameplay mechanics are as follows: the player selects a filled shape within an empty cell and swaps it with an adjacent shape (up, down, left, right). If three or more identical shapes align horizontally or vertically, they are eliminated. Victory is achieved by destroying a specified number of shapes within a limited number of swaps. In contrast to empty cells, which are subject to destruction, solid cells remain intact, ensuring that all empty cells are connected from the top spawn point. The difficulty of the game is gauged by calculating the potential for swaps across all cells within the level and summing these values.

3.1.2 Maze

In the Maze game, there are four types of cells: Empty, Solid, Player, and Goal. The Player can move in four directions (up, down, left, right) and cannot alter its course until it hits a wall or the level boundary. The level must contain exactly one Player and one Goal, with victory being achieved when the Player reaches the Goal. The Player must always have a viable path to the Goal. The difficulty of the game is evaluated based on the path from the player to the goal. This path is identified using a Dijkstra algorithm, which determines the route with the fewest branching paths.

3.2 Training

The PPO (Schulman et al., 2017) algorithm from Stable Baselines was used for training. Figure 1 illustrates the process of training a model.

3.2.1 Model

The model comprises two distinct architectures: the action architecture, comprising eight convolutional neural network (CNN) layers, and the value function architecture, comprising three CNN layers.

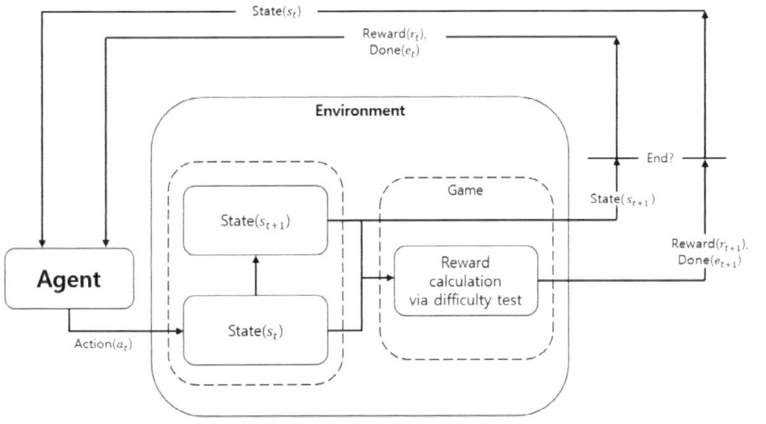

Figure 1. Model training process for content generation

3.2.2 Action and Reward

The level is represented by a two-dimensional integer array, which contains information about different tile types. This array is processed by the agent to produce an action. The agent then processes this action to produce an action defined by a cell type and X and Y coordinates. Once an action is chosen, the level is updated accordingly. A reward is then assigned. If the agent action brings the game state closer to the desired difficulty level, a positive reward is given. Otherwise, a negative reward is assigned. This process is repeated until the agent can consistently generate levels that align with the desired difficulty.

4. EXPERIMENTAL RESULTS

Models were trained on Match3 and Maze games, resulting in the generation of levels of varying sizes and difficulty levels. The agents were found to successfully generate levels that met or exceeded the desired difficulty in more than 70% of cases. All models underwent training for 30,000,000 steps, a value chosen to encompass as many scenarios as possible. However, it is possible to achieve a successfully trained model with fewer steps.

4.1 Level Design

Figures 2 and 3 illustrate the outcome of generating a level that aligns with the desired difficulty of the Match3 and Maze games. The agent was instructed to take a maximum of 1000 actions from a random starting point to achieve this.

5. CONCLUSION

This paper proposes a method for content generation using reinforcement learning. Existing research encounters difficulties with real-time content generation, primarily due to the need for training data, slow generation speeds, or the challenge of producing voluminous content. Conversely, our method does not require training data and facilitates rapid content generation, enabling the production of large volumes of content in real-time. Although the initial training phase may be slower than other methods, once trained the agent can swiftly generate content, significantly reducing time and costs associated with level design, the most time-consuming aspect of the game development process. This approach is expected to make a substantial contribution to streamlining game development.

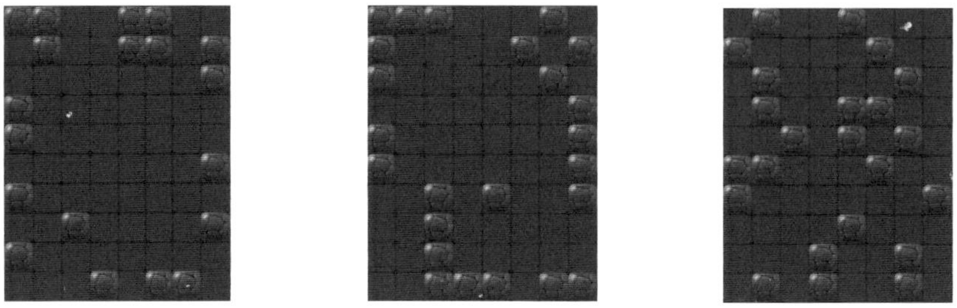

(A) : 500 (B) : 400 (C) : 300

Figure 2. The result of generating levels for a Match3 game by difficulty

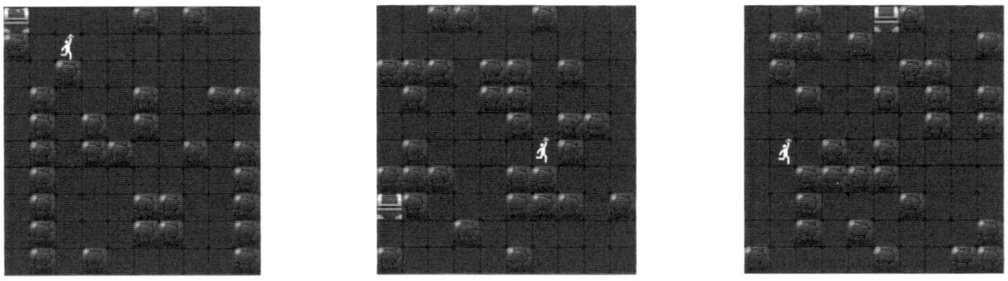

(A) : 5 (B) : 15 (C) : 25

Figure 3. The result of generating levels for a Maze game by difficulty

ACKNOWLEDGEMENT

This work was supported by the Innovative Human Resource Development for Local Intellectualization program through the Institute of Information & Communications Technology Planning & Evaluation (IITP) grant funded by the Korean government (MSIT)(IITP-2024-RS-2022-00156360).

REFERENCES

Dengyong, Z. et al, 2003. *Learning with Local and Global Consistency*. Part of Advances in Neural Information Processing Systems 16

Sourabh K. et al, 2020. *A review on genetic algorithm: past, present, and future.* Multimed Tools Appl 80, 8091–8126 (2021).

Samarth S. et al, 2020. *D2RL: Deep Dense Architectures in Reinforcement Learning*. NeurIPS 2020 Deep RL Workshop

Adam S. et al, 2016 *Mystical Tutor: A Magic: The Gathering Design Assistant via Denoising Sequence-to-Sequence Learning*. Proceedings of the AAAI Conference on Artificial Intelligence and Interactive Digital Entertainment, 12(1), 86-92.

Tanabe T. et al. 2021 *Level Generation for Angry Birds with Sequential VAE and Latent Variable Evolution*. The Genetic and Evolutionary Computation Conference 2021

Alex C. et al, 2019. *Magic: The Gathering is Turing Complete*. Artificial Intelligence (cs.AI); Computational Complexity (cs.CC); Logic in Computer Science (cs.LO)

Niels J. et al, 2019. *Deep Learning for Video Game Playing*. arXiv:1708.07902 [cs.AI]

Ahmed K. et al. *2020. PCGRL: Procedural Content Generation via Reinforcement Learning*. 7 pages, 7 figures, 1 table, published at AIIDE2020.

Schulman J. et al. 2017. *Proximal policy optimization algorithms*. arXiv preprint arXiv:1707.06347.

SERIOUS GAME FOR ADHD DIAGNOSIS

Georgios Liapis[1], Kejsi Rrasa[2], Michael Roditis[1], Kostas Klimantakis[1] and Ioannis Vlahavas[1]
[1]*Aristotle University of Thessaloniki, Greece*
[2]*University of Padova, Italy*

ABSTRACT

Using serious games to assist diagnosis in the medical and psychological fields is an emerging and innovative approach. Attention-deficit/hyperactivity disorder (ADHD), a common neurodevelopmental disorder, lacks fully defined diagnostic methods due to challenges in identifying its specific causative factors. This study introduces a serious game called "MindEscape ADHD", a 3D escape room-type game designed to trigger specific behaviors through tailor-made puzzles and events. The game also provides a theoretical and innovative assisting diagnostic tool for ADHD for adults that eliminates the need for specialized equipment other than a computer. Instead, it will leverage machine learning (ML) techniques, utilizing data collected from gameplay sessions of the serious game designed explicitly for this purpose. The advantages of this approach include reduced subjectivity in decision-making, cost-effectiveness, and enhanced accessibility compared to conventional procedures.

KEYWORDS

Serious Games, ADHD Diagnosis, Machine Learning

1. INTRODUCTION

According to the Diagnostic and Statistical Manual of Mental Disorders (5th ed.; DSM-5; American Psychiatric Association [APA], 2013), attention-deficit/hyperactivity disorder (ADHD) is a neurodevelopmental condition characterized by symptoms of inattention and/or hyperactivity-impulsivity that start in childhood and interfere with functioning or development. These symptoms continue throughout adulthood, posing special difficulties in daily life, professional goals, and interpersonal relationships. During adolescence and adulthood, hyperactivity takes the form of excessive restlessness or inattention or wearing people out with their activity, while impulsivity and poor planning continue to persist (APA, 2013).

In order to address the many effects of ADHD on people's lives all over the world, it is important to raise public awareness of the problems that adult ADHD presents and to underline the need for support and intervention activities while being able to diagnose it correctly. Health specialists typically utilize multi-parametric diagnostic procedures based on systematic reporting, such as self-report measures and questionnaires. Even though these reports are critical for diagnosing ADHD, they are prone to subjectivity when evaluating perceived behavior, which stems from the fact that systematic reports are primarily based on qualitative features, such as the adult's (or child's) responses to the expert's questions.

In this paper, we seek to reach out to the adult ADHD community by proposing a solution that uses a serious game combined with Machine Learning algorithms to distinguish between cases classified with and without ADHD. Our methodology is more cost-effective and accessible than standard approaches for monitoring behavior, while also reducing subjectivity by generating more accurate and reliable data. To attain this aim, we developed MindEscape ADHD, a serious 3D escape room-style game to capture the data of the player, employing triggers camouflaged in the game mechanics.

Every element of the game is designed to trigger a specific symptom of ADHD based not only on the diagnostic criteria included in the DSM-5, which is the main handbook used by healthcare professionals worldwide as a guide for the diagnosis of mental disorders but also incorporating elements from neuropsychological assessment tests.

Contributions of the proposed approach:

- The use of serious games in mental disorder diagnosis
- Puzzles and metrics to generate gameplay data for diagnosis with AI techniques

2. RELATED WORK

Neuropsychological assessment is widely considered to be valuable in complementing clinical observations and self-report measures in the diagnosis of ADHD (Planton et al., 2019). When comparing different neuropsychological evaluation techniques for ADHD, some tests only address one sensory modality. Since vigilance in individuals with ADHD has been demonstrated to be variable, continuous performance tests (CPT; Conners, 1995) are the most commonly utilized test type for neuropsychological evaluation when measuring vigilance (Gentile and Atiq, 2006). However, there is also evidence that adults with ADHD have difficulties in perceptual-motor speed, working memory, verbal learning, and response inhibition (Gentile and Atiq, 2006). In addition, these tests are often administered in an evaluation context without external distractions that may affect attentional performance, lacking ecological validity (Iriarte et al., 2016; Parsons, Duffield & Asbee, 2019).

Recent technological advancements have introduced gamified assessment tools as promising options for the neuropsychological evaluation of ADHD. An early attempt to employ Machine Learning techniques for ADHD diagnosis was the "Groundskeeper" serious game, developed for the Sifteo Cubes interactive gaming system (Faraone et al., 2016). Results showed that "Groundskeeper" could significantly distinguish ADHD patients from patients with other psychiatric disorders, highlighting the potential of integrating digital data into assessment tools for ADHD. Other examples of serious games include "FocusLocus" (Kanellos et al., 2018), designed to diagnose ADHD; however, these games rely on additional sensory devices, virtual, augmented, and mixed reality technology, and do not use machine learning approaches, while other works rely on special equipment. "ADHD360" is another example of a serious game that can be played without specialized equipment (Kouloumpris et al., 2024; Pandria, 2022). This innovative game uses Machine Learning techniques to gather data and differentiate between children with and without ADHD through a runner-style game and a range of entertaining mini-games.

Our own implementation of "MindEscape-ADHD" builds on the central idea of the ADHD360, which is a helpful platform, but it doesn't have enough data to support Machine Learning models with thorough validation. We aim to address this limitation, particularly in its applicability to adult ADHD diagnosis, by innovating to fill these knowledge gaps and leveraging ADHD360's findings. Lastly, to the best of our knowledge, no other research has focused on using a digital escape room for ADHD assessment, and we aspire to introduce this novel approach.

There has also been research (Liapis et al., 2022), about an escape room that can theoretically measure specific gameplay data and metrics regarding a player's personality using specific puzzles and events. In contrast, our work implements game mechanics in a similar environment and events to make an ADHD diagnosis. The use of an immersive serious game environment generates quality data by simulating real-life scenarios and so is able to be an alternative to traditional questionnaires for ADHD diagnosis

3. METHDOLOGY

The methodology discussed in this section applies to the game and how data is created. We present an explanation of the gameplay mechanics.

3.1 Game Mechanics

For our implementation, we decided to use an escape room type of game, because not only could we engage and immerse the player in an entertaining, popular, and modern game environment, but also because the linearity of the gameplay allowed us to create the necessary data for the final assessment. Our game features five puzzles with custom-made game mechanics set in a restaurant theme, as seen in Figure 1, where the player must prepare an order to complete it. This theme simulates a real-life scenario, allowing players to immerse themselves fully. Additionally, it creates opportunities for distractions while solving linear tasks in a fast-paced, multitasking environment. Throughout gameplay, the player's actions are continuously recorded and stored as data points, contributing valuable features to our dataset. The game mechanics and the puzzles were designed by experts participating in this project, guided by the DSM-5 manual, and are specifically connected to various ADHD behaviors. Screenshots of the puzzles and their sequence can be seen in Figure 1 (1–5).

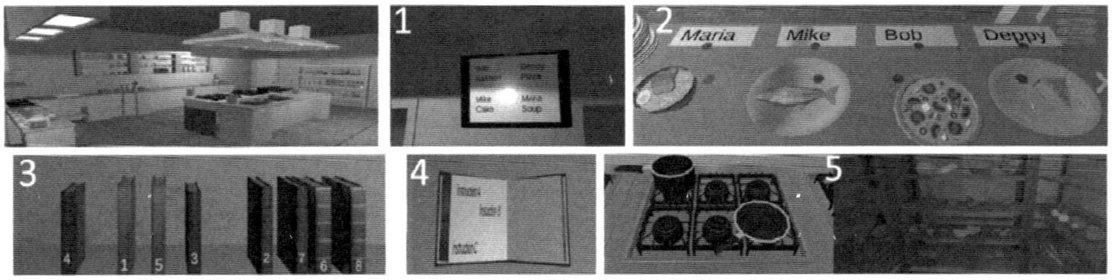

Figure 1. The room and the puzzles

The sequence of puzzles in our game is as follows:

1. Use the monitor to organize orders and their corresponding tables.
2. Identify the order that matches the first order presented.
3. Collect recipe books and organize them sequentially.
4. Rearrange scattered words within a book to form a coherent recipe
5. Prepare the dish by memorizing the recipe and simultaneously gathering ingredients from the pantry.

Additionally, diversions, such as new orders and timers are introduced to observe and collect data on how players handle distractions and multitask.

3.2 Protocol

During the game's testing phase, we use a specific protocol to collect our data. Using the special login information provided to the participants upon registration, players will access the "MindEscape-ADHD" game. All collected data will be anonymized, ensuring that it is impossible to trace individual participants from the dataset. The maximum duration of each participant's gameplay session would be twenty minutes. Upon completion, participants will be asked to answer a short questionnaire regarding the game they played, to ensure user experience. They may also be asked for details about the conditions of their game, to help us determine their level of attentiveness and adherence to the experimental protocol. A possible problem regarding this method is finding a sufficient number of adults who are diagnosed with and without ADHD so that we can evaluate our system.

3.3 Metrics

In this study, we measure multiple data, that rely on both the DSM-5 criteria and on other CPTs in order to develop a tool to assist clinicians in diagnosing ADHD (Fernández-Quirós et al., 2023). First of all, we measure the player's omission errors, which is not responding to the target stimuli, and the commission errors, which are incorrect responses to non-target stimuli, the Hit Reaction Time (HTR) assesses the average response speed for all non-preservative responses; and finally, its standard deviation (HTR SD) that showcases the consistency of response speed throughout the game. Based on these metrics, we evaluate impulsivity, depending on the HRT and the rates of the commission error, while we measure inattentiveness based on the omission and commission errors, the HRT, and the HRT SD. Finally, we assess the sustained attention by measuring the HRT and omission and commission in the later parts of the game.

We must note that the raw data generated during a gaming session is a temporal sequence of in-game events that may be used to reconstruct the full playthrough. For example, such occurrences may correlate to how the player walked, how many mistakes he made, or how he solved the puzzles, like if he recalled the right sequence of objects. These data are stored and can be used to train Machine Learning algorithms. Since we do not yet have labeled data from adults being diagnosed with or without ADHD, we have focused on the initial stages of the data science process for our Supervised Machine Learning models. We have conducted a preliminary design of the structure of data that will be used in the algorithms, and after acquiring labeled data and training our models, we will be able to use them to discriminate between new undiagnosed patients.

Lastly, we can utilize unsupervised learning algorithms to cluster different gameplay styles without prior knowledge of a potential diagnosis. This approach allows us to assess whether distinct play styles emerge sufficiently differentiated to be labeled with very few clinical data.

4. CONCLUSION

In this paper, we introduced "MindEscape-ADHD", an innovative assessment tool that combines a serious game with Machine Learning algorithms to differentiate between adults with and without ADHD. Our approach provides a cost-effective, accessible, and immersive alternative to traditional behavioral monitoring methods. By leveraging the engaging nature of serious games, we minimize subjectivity and enhance ecological validity, due to improved data quality. MindEscape ADHD is a 3D escape room game designed to capture and analyze player behavior through data generated during gameplay. The game's puzzles are strategically designed to trigger specific ADHD symptoms, based on the DSM-5 diagnostic criteria and enhanced with elements from neuropsychological assessment tests.

Although the game has not yet been tested with participants, this approach has the potential to significantly enhance the accuracy and ecological validity of ADHD assessment in adults, while also making the assessment process more engaging. In future studies, we plan to expand our implementation to include more complex puzzles to collect additional data. Moreover, by gathering data from both ADHD and non-ADHD players, we aim to develop more advanced Machine Learning models capable of accurately distinguishing between adults with and without ADHD.

REFERENCES

American Psychiatric Association, DSM-5 Task Force. (2013). Diagnostic and statistical manual of mental disorders: DSM-5™ (5th ed.). American Psychiatric Publishing, Inc.. https://doi.org/10.1176/appi.books.9780890425596

Conners, C. K. (1995). Conners continuous performance test computer program. Toronto, Ontario: Multi-Health Systems.

Faraone, S. V., Newcorn, J. H., Antshel, K. M., Adler, L., Roots, K., & Heller, M. (2016). The Groundskeeper Gaming Platform as a Diagnostic Tool for Attention-Deficit/Hyperactivity Disorder: Sensitivity, Specificity, and Relation to Other Measures. Journal of child and adolescent psychopharmacology, 26(8), 672–685. https://doi.org/10.1089/cap.2015.0174

Fernández-Quirós, J., Lacasa-Cazcarra, M., Alegre-Martín, J., Sanmartín-Sentañes, R., Almirall, M., Launois-Obregón, P., Castro-Marrero, J., Rodríguez-Urrutia, A., Navarro-Sanchis, J. A., & Ramos-Quiroga, J. A. (2023). The Conners Continuous Performance Test CPT3™: Is it a reliable marker to predict neurocognitive dysfunction in Myalgic encephalomyelitis/chronic fatigue syndrome? Frontiers in psychology, 14, 1127193. https://doi.org/10.3389/fpsyg.2023.1127193

Gentile, J. P., Atiq, R., & Gillig, P. M. (2006). Adult ADHD: Diagnosis, Differential Diagnosis, and Medication Management. Psychiatry (Edgmont (Pa. : Township)), 3(8), 25–30.

Iriarte, Y., Diaz-Orueta, U., Cueto, E., Irazustabarrena, P., Banterla, F., & Climent, G. (2016). AULA-Advanced Virtual Reality Tool for the Assessment of Attention: Normative Study in Spain. Journal of attention disorders, 20(6), 542–568. https://doi.org/10.1177/1087054712465335

Kouloumpris, E., Lazaridis, A., Fachantidis, A., & Vlahavas, I. (2024). Diagnosing Attention Deficit Hyperactivity Disorder Using Machine Learning Methods on Serious Game-generated Data. International Journal on Artificial Intelligence Tools, 33(01), 2350059. https://doi.org/10.1142/S0218213023500598

Pandria, N., Petronikolou, V., Lazaridis, A., Karapiperis, C., Kouloumpris, E., Spachos, D., Fachantidis, A., Vasiliou, D., Vlahavas, I., & Bamidis, P. (2022). Information System for Symptom Diagnosis and Improvement of Attention Deficit Hyperactivity Disorder: Protocol for a Nonrandomized Controlled Pilot Study. JMIR research protocols, 11(9), e40189. https://doi.org/10.2196/40189

G. Liapis, K. Zacharia, K. Rrasa, A. Liapi and I. Vlahavas, Modelling core personality trait behaviours in a gamified escape room environment, European Conference on Games Based Learning (Sep 2022) p. 723–731.

Parsons, T. D., Duffield, T., & Asbee, J. (2019). A Comparison of Virtual Reality Classroom Continuous Performance Tests to Traditional Continuous Performance Tests in Delineating ADHD: a Meta-Analysis. Neuropsychology review, 29(3), 338–356. https://doi.org/10.1007/s11065-019-09407-6

Planton, M., Lemesle, B., Cousineau, M., Carlier, J., Milongo-Rigal, E., Carle-Toulemonde, G., Salles, J., & Pariente, J. (2021). The role of neuropsychological assessment in adults with attention deficit/hyperactivity disorders. Revue neurologique, 177(4), 341–348. https://doi.org/10.1016/j.neurol.2021.01.006

T. Kanellos, A. Doulgerakis, E. Georgiou, M. Bessa, S. C. Thomopoulos, A. Vatakis, A. Behan, J. Arambarri and J. Navarra, Focuslocus: Adhd management gaming system ´ for educational achievement and social inclusion, in Smart Biomedical and Physiological Sensor Technology XV 10662, International Society for Optics and Photonics2018, p. 106620E

A DEFORMABLE 3D ZEBRAFISH MODEL FOR BRIGHT-FIELD MICROSCOPY IMAGE SIMULATION

Richárd Jámbor and Attila Tanács
Dept. of Image Processing and Computer Graphics, Institute of Informatics, University of Szeged
Árpád tér 2., Szeged, H-6720, Hungary

ABSTRACT

Due to their rapid reproduction, development, and similar genetic structure to humans, zebrafish are popular animals in various biological research. Their small size and body transparency make them convenient to examine under a bright-field light microscope. However, these provide 2-dimensional projected images, which makes 3D measurements difficult. Usual approaches try to reconstruct 3D structures from series of projected images, that is not always an option. In our paper we propose an approach to model the images acquisition process including the 3D parametric deformable model of the zebrafish and the light conditions in the microscopy environment. Our goal is to simulate images that look similar to the real ones using only a few parameters.

KEYWORDS

Zebrafish, Microscopy, 3D Graphics, 3D Modeling, Simulation, Blender, Three.js

1. INTRODUCTION

The zebrafish genome is about 70% identical to that of humans, and when it comes to genes involved in the development of human-related diseases, the rate is even higher [Goldsmith-2012]. This striking similarity means that zebrafish can easily model human processes in human genetics research. This clearly shows that zebrafish are useful models for understanding human health.

Researchers benefit greatly from the fact that zebrafish embryos are readily available and develop quickly. They collect female zebrafish eggs and are able to monitor their development from the very first moment. The eggs can be easily stored, making large quantities available for research. The transparent bodies of zebrafish offer an additional advantage over mammals such as mice. This allows researchers to follow every moment of the development process inside and out, as the whole body remains transparent. This allows deep insights into the development of embryos and the detailed study of the formation of individual organs and tissues. In addition, zebrafish grow quickly and are easy to test from generation to generation. This means that long-term research can be easily carried out with them and genetic changes can be observed over the long term. If an individual has mutated and then reproduces, it is possible to monitor whether and how these changes appear in the next generation.

Zebrafish embryos can also be used to study the effects of ionizing radiation in human cancer treatment [McAleer-2005, Szabó-2016]. As discussed in [Katona-2019], irradiation-induced DNA damage causes observable morphological changes in the zebrafish embryos, such as in spinal curvature, shortening of body length, yolk sac or pericardial edema, abnormality of the eyes or abnormal development of the head. The severity of these abnormalities are dose-dependent.

The main tissues and organs start to develop within the first 24 hours of embryo development. This allows researchers to follow the whole developmental process of the animal and understand every step of the genetic changes. In the light of these advantages, it is clear that research with zebrafish embryos is of great importance for the understanding of human health and the development of medicine. Because of small size and transparency of their bodies, they are usually examined under a bright-field microscope. The light from the lamp at the bottom passes through the zebrafish, which is captured by the camera at the other end. A typical acquisition setting and an acquired image is shown in Figure 1.

To measure distances and the size of certain organs, researchers often use these 2D projected images, such as in [Katona-2019]. However, due to the spatial rotation of the zebrafish, these projected 2D images are not always suitable for such measurements. Guo et. al. [Guo-2017] proposed a two-phase 3D reconstruction approach based on axial-view imaging computing surfaces of a confidence map that yields precise 3D shape representation and measurements. Their approach requires a more sophisticated microscopic setup called VAST BioImager including a capillary that holds the zebrafish and rotates around to take images from different orientations.

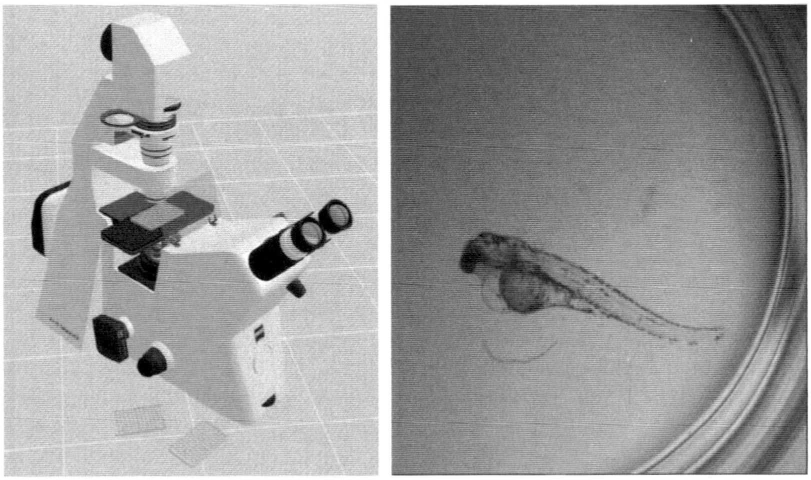

Figure 1. Left: Graphical model of a typical simple bright-field light microscope setting.
Right: A cropped region of a typical bright-field microscopy image acquisition

Our proposed method approaches the problem from another direction. Our goal is to model the image acquisition process including the 3D body of the zebrafish and the light conditions to be able to produce simulated images similar to real ones. We created a deformable 3D zebrafish model in Blender software. The lighting effects are computed using the WebGL based Three.js library.

2. SIMULATION FRAMEWORK

The creation of the simulation framework consists of two main steps. First we need to construct the geometric models, namely the deformable 3D zebrafish model and the spherical well model in which the fish will be placed. Then we need an interactive application that allows the user to set parameters to control the 3D shape and the lighting conditions producing the result image.

2.1 Deformable Zebrafish Surface Modeling

Using reference images, photographs and anatomical atlases, the body of the zebrafish is constructed using the Blender modeling software freely available at https://blender.org/. We divided the body into six main parts: mouth, eyes, back, belly, heart, internal organs (Figure 2).

In each case, modelling started with a simple geometric shape similar in shape to the desired target, and then using simple modelling tools such as scaling, stretching and contracting to create a rough and rudimentary model that is already broadly similar to the one we expected. Once this basic model was ready, we could move on to the detailed development of it using more complex modifiers. Examples include the use of beveling, cutting indentations and holes in the model surface with the Boolean modifier, mirroring to halve the time of certain modelling processes, and the subdivision surfaces modifier. This makes it easy to create complex shapes, in addition to sculpting, which can be thought of as similar to real-life sculpting and provides a means of applying really fine details to the model.

The material property system in Blender is based on PBR ("physically based rendering"), which combines multiple layers into a single easy-to-use node, giving a more accurate representation of how light is refracted and scattered by a surface in the environment, resulting in a more realistic image. The base layer is generated based on user-specified parameters and is a mixture of diffuse, metallic, subsurface scattering and transmission properties. On top of this, there can then be specular layers, sheen layers and clearcoat layers.

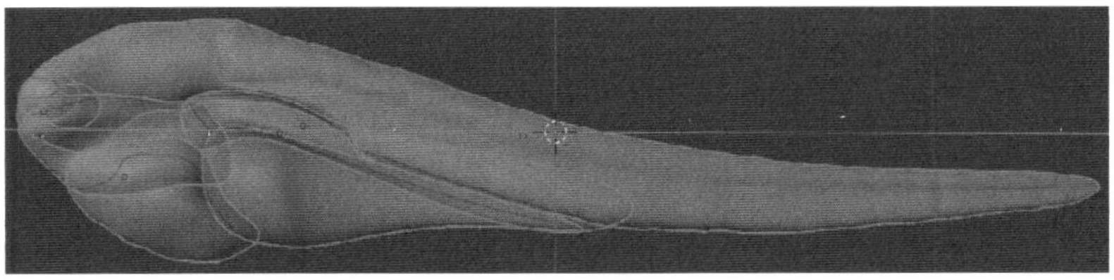

Figure 2. Subdivision of the zebrafish body model into six separate parts. The contours of the body parts are show in orange color overlay in the side view of the model

When examining a zebrafish embryo under the microscope, it is illuminated from below by a bright light, so the different body parts and internal organs are clearly visible. To imitate this, we had to provide the embryo model with material properties that can transmit some of the light but not all of it, thus creating a transparent but still opaque material for the body. To do this, we chose the "Alpha Blend" option instead of the "Alpha Hashed" option in the blend mode parameter of the blend mode used for the transparent materials, which when used in conjunction with the transmission attribute, results in a blend of the base color and the transparency effect. In this case, by adjusting the transparency of the material along the sliders of the alpha and transmission parameters between zero and one, we experimentally found the result that most closely matched the real image.

Textures give a more natural look to the surface model. The 3D surface models were transformed to 2D texture space using "UV Unwrapping", then we used the "Texture Painting" tool to finish painting of surface elements (Figure 3).

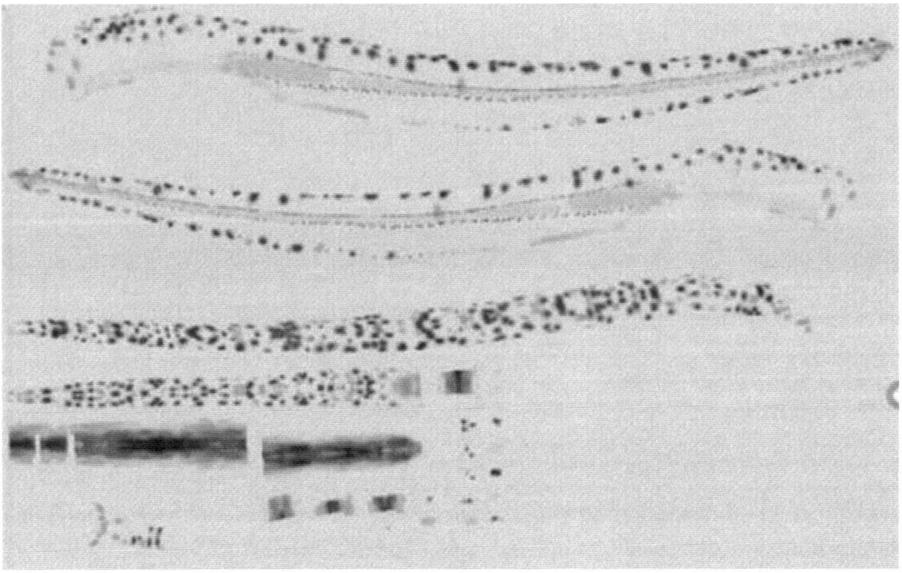

Figure 3. Texture images used to give the surface model a more natural look

To achieve deformability, an armature consisting of hierarchy of bones was added. The main body was divided into four connecting parts, while the pericardium was added directly to the head part (Figure 4). To connect the surface model with the armature, "Armature Deform" with option "With Automatic Weights" option was used. These parts can be rotated and scaled later in the interactive application.

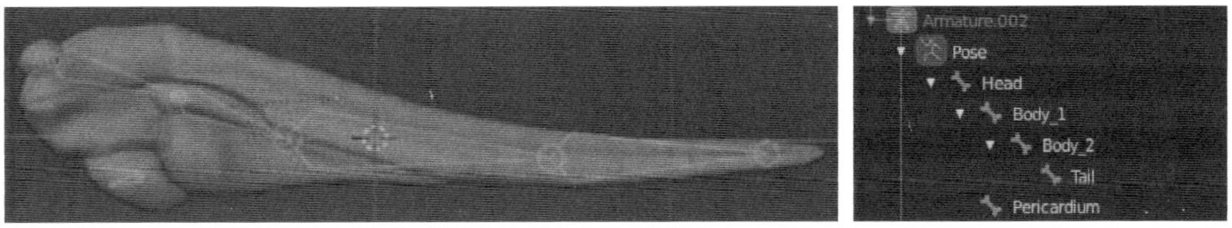

Figure 4. Armature hierarchy of the surface model

2.2 Cylindrical Well Model

Zebrafish embryos are placed in a template containing cylindrical holes, also called wells. As the light from the light source under the template has to pass through this plastic layer, it also affects the illumination of the zebrafish. Figure 5 shows a simple geometric well model. Transparency parameters can be set to reach the desired lighting effect. The height of the well model is arbitrary, it is the interaction with the light that plays a role.

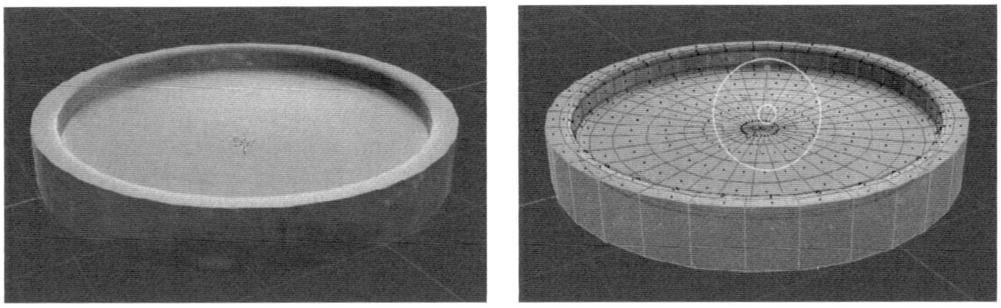

Figure 5. Geometric model of a spherical well. Realistic rendering (left) and Blender model edit view (right)

2.3 Interactive Control Application

An interactive application was implemented in JavaScript using the Three.js 3D graphics library available at https://threejs.org/. The deformable zebrafish model was exported to glTF format from Blender which can be read and rendered directly in Three.js.

Three light sources were defined. One white ambient light to make parts of the model that are not illuminated by direct light sources visible. Two spotlights were placed: one below the ring containing the zebrafish model, and one above at camera location. The light from above was needed to illuminate the camera side of the models with a weak direct light, so that details could be better seen. The light source from the bottom had a much higher brightness value and here we adjusted the angle of the light opening to make it look as similar as possible to the real images.

Interactive sliders are available to change the following parameters of the simulation: rotation of the zebrafish around its main axis and around the center if the microscopy image; scaling and rotation of the armature model parts around the Z-axis; translation of the zebrafish along two camera axes; translation of the light source below the models. These parameters allow modeling of pericardial edema, shrinkage or enlargement of body parts and changes in spinal curvature.

Two simulated images are shown in Figure 6.

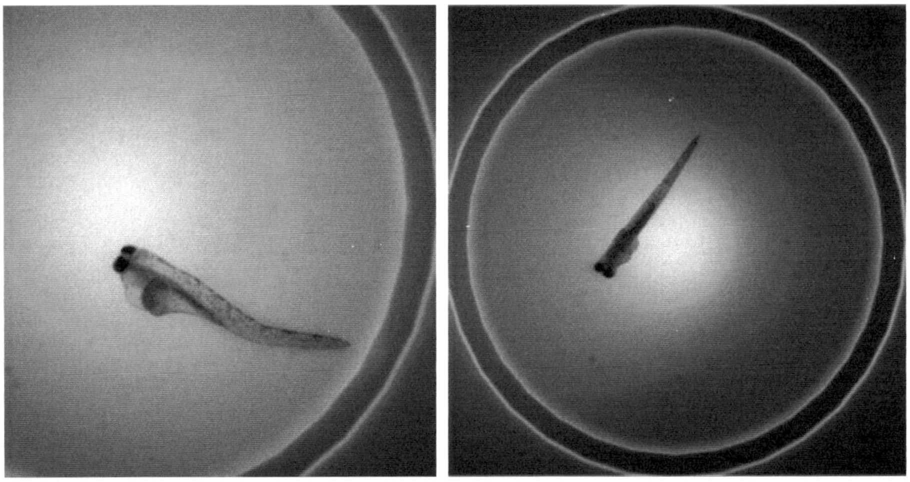

Figure 6. Two simulated images using different deformable parameters

3. CONCLUSION AND FUTURE DIRECTIONS

We constructed a 3D deformable zebrafish model and implemented an interactive application to generate simulated images that look similar to real ones. In the future this application could be extended to e.g., automatically match the 3D model to a real image by finding parameters using an optimization method. In this case, real 3D measurements could be performed using the fitted model. Another possible application is to use the simulation to produce real-like images to augment trainings of deep learning neural networks.

ACKNOWLEDGEMENT

This work was supported by project no TKP2021-NVA-09. Project no TKP2021-NVA-09 has been implemented with the support provided by the Ministry of Culture and Innovation of Hungary from the National Research, Development and Innovation Fund, financed under the TKP2021-NVA funding scheme.

REFERENCES

Goldsmith, J. R. and Jobin, C., 2012. Think Small: Zebrafish as a Model System of Human Pathology. *Journal of Biomedicine and Biotechnology*, Article ID 817341, 12 pages. DOI: 10.1155/2012/817341.

Guo, Y. et al., 2017. A Two-Phase 3-D Reconstruction Approach for Light Microscopy Axial-View Imaging. IEEE Journal of Selected Topics in Signal Processing, Volume 11(7), pp. 1034–1046. DOI: 10.1109/JSTSP.2017.2731742.

Katona, M. et al., 2019. Automatic Segmentation and Quantitative Analysis of Irradiated Zebrafish Embryos. Proceedings of Computational Modeling of Objects Presented in Images; Fundamentals, Methods, and Applications. Lecture Notes in Computer Science volume 10986, pp. 95–107. Cracow, Poland. Springer, Cham. DOI: 10.1007/978-3-030-20805-9_9.

McAleer, M.F., et al., 2005. Novel use of zebrafish as a vertebrate model to screen radiation protectors and sensitizers. International Journal of Radiation Oncology, Biology, Physics 61(1), 10-3. DOI: 10.1016/j.ijrobp.2004.09.046.

Szabó, E.R., et al., 2016. l-Alpha Glycerylphosphorylcholine as a Potential Radioprotective Agent in Zebrafish Embryo Model. Zebrafish 13(6), 481-488. DOI: 10.1089/zeb.2016.1269.

A RECEPTIVE ENHANCED BASED MULTI-SCALE FEATURE FUSION NETWORK

Guojun Mao[1] and Xinchao Zhang[2]
[1]*Fujian Provincial Key Lab of Big Data Mining and Applications, Fujian University of Technology Fuzhou 350118, China*
[2]*School of Computer Science and Mathematics, Fujian University of Technology Fuzhou 350118, China*

ABSTRACT

Camouflaged Object Detection (COD) aims to identify target objects with high similarity to the surrounding environment in complex scenes, and has high application value in military, medical and other fields. This paper proposes a Receptive enhanced based Multi-scale feature fusion network, termed as RMNet. Firstly, it uses the popular pyramid visual network PVTv2 for feature extraction. By overlaying the target area amplification module OAA and deep interaction guidance module DIDM on it, the position ability for camouflaged objects in complex scenes is improved; Secondly, design an enhanced receptive field module REM to enhance the edge perception ability of camouflaged objects; Finally, the feature fusion module MCFM are designed through cross scale hierarchical connections between adjacent levels, effectively improving the accuracy of camouflage object detection. The presented model is evaluated on three highly challenging benchmark datasets, including CAMO, CHAMELEON and COD10K. The evaluation results show that compared with the current popular methods, our method demonstrates superior performance.

KEYWORDS

Camouflaged Object Detection (COD), Multi-Scale Feature Fusion, Receptive Enhancement, Pyramid Visual Network, Deep Interaction Guidance

1. INTRODUCTION

Camouflaged Object Detection (COD) focuses on identifying target objects camouflaged in the natural environment, which can rely on colors, shapes,or textures to hide themselves through the surrounding environment. COD technology has important applications in many fields such as military reconnaissance (Fan D P, et al, 2022), medical image analysis (Chen L, et al, 2017), and criminal investigation (Yang X, et al, 2023) However, due to the low discrimination between the camouflaged object and the background, COD tasks are more challenging compared to ordinary computer vision.

In 2020, Fan et al introduced the concept of COD and constructed the large-scale COD dataset COD10K (Fan D P, et al, 2020), which includes 10000 images and various scenes of 78 object categories. They also proposed the COD model called SINet. In fact, many various COD methods have been proposed, forming relatively independent research branches (Wei J, et al, 2020; Ma M, et al, 2021; Pan Yet, et al, 2021).

This paper proposes a novel RMNet for the COD tasks that combines multi-scale context-awareness with mechanisms simulating the human visual system. The framework adopts a progressive enhancement strategy to improve the overall performance of CODs including object localization, texture feature enhancement, and multi-scale feature fusion.

2. MODEL DESIGN

Figure 1 shows the architecture of the camouflaged object detection network in this paper. For an image to be detected, the pretrained PVTv2 is first used as the backbone network for feature extraction (Wang W, et al, 2022), and then the recognition of camouflaged targets is completed through two relatively independent stages: "target localization" and "target segmentation".

In the "target localization" stage, the extracted multi-scale features are processed sequentially through OAA, DIDM and ASPP modules to gradually determine the coarse bitmap of the target object. In the "target segmentation" stage, the model achieves high-precision segmentation of target object boundaries by designing an enhanced receptive field module REM and a multi-scale collaborative fusion module MCFM.

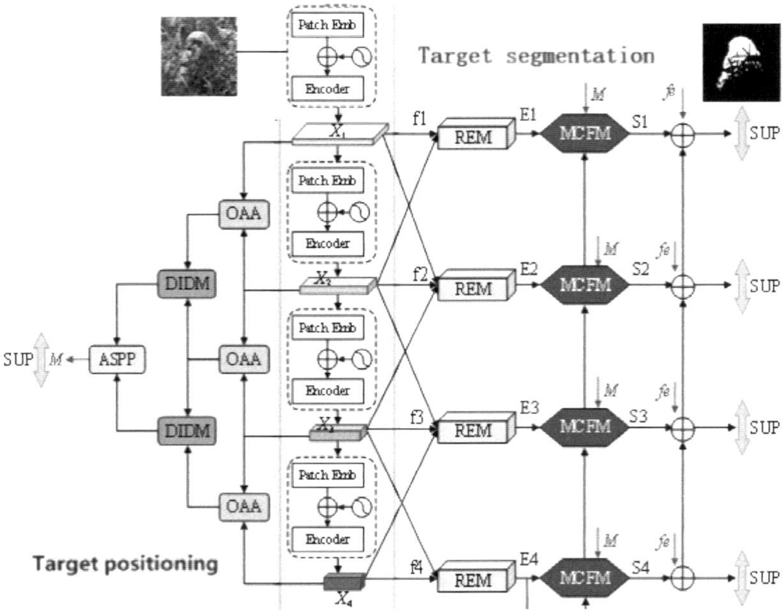

Figure 1. Overall structure of RMNet network

As shown in Figure 1, the stage of target positioning mainly involves gradually summarizing the features X_1~X_4 at four scales through OAA, DIDM and ASPP modules, ultimately forming a coarse localization map M.

The OAA module directly borrowed the design from the reference (Chen L, et al, 2017) and achieved preliminary fusion of multi-scale features using a full cross approach: $\{X_1, X_2, X_3, X_4\} \rightarrow \{b_1, b_2, b_3\}$. The main work of this paper is to design a deep interaction guidance module called DIDM, and the output of DIDM is ultimately generated into the target coarse location image through the hollow pyramid pooling ASPP module.

The calculations corresponding to the DIDM module is as follows:

$$\begin{cases} f_4^{cc} = BC_{(7,7)}(b3 \otimes down(b2)) \\ f_3^{cc} = BC_{(7,7)}(b2 \otimes up(b3)) \end{cases} \quad (1)$$

$$F^{'} = BC_{(3,3)}(f_3^{cc} \oplus f_4^{cc}) \quad (2)$$

In the stage of target segmentation, the enhanced receptive field module REM and the multi-scale collaborative fusion module MCFM are designed. The former is to enhance the multi-scale contextual information capture ability extracted by PVTv2, while the latter mainly utilizes cross scale fusion technology to achieve high-precision boundary segmentation.

The calculation process of the REM module is: first, the expand convolution and asymmetric convolution are used, and then obtain the final output through two 3x3 convolution layers. The specific expression is as follows:

$$E_k = (((Concat\{C_{dil}(f_k), C_{asy}(f_k)\})_{(3,3)} \otimes f_k)_{(3,3)}) \quad (3)$$

The MCFM module integrates the outputs of the REM module with the coarse location map M obtained during the target position stage to ensure effective segmentation of the boundaries of camouflaged objects.

The main calculation of MCFM is completed through two 3x3 convolutions. Assuming that the k-th layer is currently being processed, MCFM will first integrate the outputs of the next level in MCFM module (denoted as S_{k+1}) and the features obtained by the current layer's REM module (denoted as E_k), then depth fusion with the coarse bitmap is achieved through two hyperparameters γ and β. The specific calculation is as follows:

$$S_k = CB(Concat\{CB(S_{K+1}), CB(E_k)\}) \otimes \gamma(M) \oplus \beta(M) \quad (4)$$

3. EXPERIMENTS

To verify the effectiveness of the method proposed in this paper, we conducted comparative experiments on the main detection indicators in three datasets: CAMO (Skurowski P, et al, 2018), CHAMELEON (Perazzi F, et al, 2012), and COD10K (Fan D P et al,2020). Table 1 shows the corresponding experimental results. Comparative algorithms include currently popular computer vision detection ones such as UEDG (Yang F, et al, 2021), FSPNet (Zhou T, et al, 2022), SINet-v2 (Fan D-P, et al, 2022), BGNet (Sun Y, et al, 2022) and OAFormer (Yang X, et al, 2023).

Table 1. Comparison with the popular object detection algorithms

Model	Data	CAMO				CHAMELEON				COD10K			
	Year	$S_\alpha \uparrow$	$E_\phi \uparrow$	$F_\beta^\omega \uparrow$	$MAE \downarrow$	$S_\alpha \uparrow$	$E_\phi \uparrow$	$F_\beta^\omega \uparrow$	$MAE \downarrow$	$S_\alpha \uparrow$	$E_\phi \uparrow$	$F_\beta^\omega \uparrow$	$MAE \downarrow$
OAFor mer	2023	0.866	0.924	0.826	0.048	0.903	**0.960**	0.858	0.022	0.859	0.927	0.773	0.024
UEDG	2023	0.863	0.922	0.816	0.048	0.911	0.958	0.866	0.023	0.858	0.924	0.766	0.025
FEDER	2023	0.804	0.867	0.737	0.071	0.886	0.946	0.834	0.029	0.822	0.899	0.715	0.031
SINet-v2	2022	0.820	0.882	0.742	0.070	0.888	0.941	0.816	0.029	0.815	0.887	0.679	0.036
BGNet	2022	0.813	0.8698	0.748	0.073	0.901	0.943	0.850	0.026	0.830	0.900	0.721	0.032
SINet	2021	0.745	0.804	0.644	0.091	0.872	0.936	0.805	0.034	0.776	0.864	0.631	0.042
UGTR	2021	0.784	0.822	0.683	0.086	0.887	0.909	0.793	0.031	0.817	0.851	0.665	0.035
Ours		**0.869**	**0.926**	**0.830**	**0.047**	**0.913**	0.958	**0.876**	**0.021**	**0.865 5**	**0.929 1**	**0.781**	**0.023**

From Table 1, it can be seen that on the CAMO dataset, compared to BGNet and SINet, there is a significant improvement, and compared with OAFormer, UEDG, FSPNet, and SINet-v2, there were also certain degree of performance improvements of about 0.3%, 0.6%, and 4.9% on S_α. In large-scale COD10K datasets with more complex scenarios, compared with OAFormer, the MAEs have decreased respectively 0.1% and 0.2%. In the challenging CHAMELEON dataset, on the $E_\varnothing$ indicator, except for slightly lower than OAFormer, there is varying degrees of improvement compared to other models.

4. CONCLUSION

This paper proposes a hierarchical feature enhancement aggregation based camouflage object detection network, which gradually restores complete camouflage objects through a feature enhancement mechanism from coarse to fine. The proposed deep interaction guidance, enhanced receptive field and multi-scale fusion methods improved object recognition accuracy and enhance segmentation capabilities of camouflaged objects from different levels. Extensive evaluation was conducted on three highly challenging test datasets, and the latest similar models were compared, fully demonstrating the effectiveness and superiority of our method.

REFERENCES

Chen L., Papandreou G., Schroff F., et al. (2017). Rethinking atrous convolution for semantic image segmentation. *Proceedings of CVPR 2017*, DOI:10.48550/arXiv.1706.05587.

Fan D. P., Ji G. P., Sun G., et al. (2020). Camouflaged object detection. *Proceedings of the IEEE/CVF Conference on Computer Vision and Pattern Recognition*, pp. 2777-2787.

Fan D. P., Ji G. P., Cheng M. M., et al. (2022). Concealed object detection. *In IEEE Transactions on Pattern Analysis and Machine Intelligence,* Vol.44, NO.10, pp. 6024-6042.

Ma M., Xia C., Li J. (2021). Pyramidal feature shrinking for salient object detection. *Proceedings of the AAAI Conference on Artificial Intelligence,* pp. 2311-2318.

Pan Y., Chen Y., Fu Q., et al. (2021). Study on the camouflaged target detection method based on 3D convexity. *In Modern Applied Science, Canadian Center of Science and Education*, Vol. 5, No. 4, pp 152-159.

Perazzi F., Krähenbühl P., Pritch Y., et al. (2012). Saliency filters: contrast based filtering for salient region detection. *Proceedings of CVPR 2012*, pp. 733-740.

Wang W., Xie E., Li X., et al. (2022). PVT v2: Improved baselines with pyramid vision transformer. *In Computational Visual Media*, Vol. 8, No. 3, pp. 415-424.

Wei J., Wang S, Huang Q. (2020). F^3Net: fusion, feedback and focus for salient object detection. *Proceedings of the 2020 AAAI Conference on Artificial Intelligence*, pp. 12321-12328.

Sun Y., Wang S., Chen C., et al. (2022). Boundary-guided camouflaged object detection. *Proceedings of 2022 International Joint Conference on Artificial Intelligence (IJCAI),* https://doi.org/10.48550/arXiv.2207.00794.

Skurowski P., Abdulameer H, Blaszczyk J, et al. (2018). Animal camouflage analysis: chameleon database. *In Unpublished manuscript*, Vol. 2, No.6, pp. 7-12.

Yang F., Zhai Q., Li X., et al. (2021). Uncertainty-guided transformer reasoning for camouflaged object detection. *Proceedings of 2021 International Conference on Computer Vision*, pp. 4146-4155.

Yang X., Zhu H., Mao G. (2023). OAFormer: Occlusion aware transformer for camouflaged object detection. *Proceedings of 2023 IEEE International Conference on Multimedia and Expo (ICME)*, pp. 1421-1426.

Zhou T., Zhou Y., Gong C., et al. (2022). Feature aggregation and propagation network for camouflaged object detection. *In IEEE Transactions on Image Processing*, Vol.31, pp. 7036-7047.

WORK IN PROGRESS: PRINTED CIRCUIT BOARD DEFECT DETECTION WITH PHOTOMETRIC STEREO AND NEURAL INVERSE RENDERING METHOD

Angelika Hable[1,2] and Dieter P. Gruber[1]
[1]*Polymer Competence Center Leoben GmbH*
Sauraugasse 1, Leoben 8700, Austria
[2]*Chair of Materials Science and Testing of Polymers, Montanuniversität Leoben,*
Otto Glöckel-Straße 2/II, Leoben 8700, Austria

ABSTRACT

Defect detection of production components is an important part of industrial manufacturing. In this work in progress paper, we investigate the potential of a Neural Inverse Rendering framework for the use as a defect detection method. This framework combines Uncalibrated Photometric Stereo and Neural Inverse Rendering. Defects on the gold areas of printed circuit boards, which were acquired using a photometric stereo setup, are used for the investigation. The investigated defects have a height characteristic. It was shown that the defects are clearly visible in the depth map and normal map after applying the framework. The quality of the depth map was sophisticated enough to segment the defects from the depth map using a simple thresholding method. However, there are still some problems with the reproducibility of the results and the runtime, so that further research is necessary.

KEYWORDS

Neural Inverse Rendering, Uncalibrated Photometric Stereo, Defect Detection, Printed Circuit Boards

1. INTRODUCTION

During the production of components, it is essential to test the components for defects. This allows defective components to be rejected before they move on to the next process step. Nowadays, automated inspection systems are frequently used for optical inspection. These systems take images of the component surface and evaluate the images using image processing or machine learning methods. For the defects to be detected by the algorithms, they must be visible in the camera image with sufficient contrast. This is a particular challenge with high-gloss surfaces, as defects only become visible when the light source is in a certain position. Photometric Stereo (PS) can be used to make these defects visible (Saiz et al., 2022).

In PS, at least three images of the component are taken under different lighting directions. By knowing the light directions and the images, a normal map can be calculated using least-squares in the simplest case of Lambertian surfaces. A setting where the light vectors are unknown is called Uncalibrated Photometric Stereo (UPS). The normal map represents a color coding of the surface normal of the specimen to be tested. Therefore, defects with a height characteristic become visible (Hable et al., 2023). With the assumption of examining Lambertian surfaces, defects on aluminum alloy castings (Liu et al., 2023), iron pipes (Wang et al., 2023), metal parts (Saiz et al., 2022) and gold areas of printed circuit boards (PCBs) (Hable et al., 2023) were visualized with Photometric Stereo. For defect detection, Hable et al. (2023) used a Convolutional Neural Network (CNN). Normal map and a mean image were used as input, as all defect types are visible in these images. For the detection of defects on aluminum alloy castings, Liu et al. (2023) computed a mean curvature image from the normal map and applied an edge detector to segment the defect from the background. A curvature image, a texture image and a gradient magnitude image were combined into one image by Saiz et al. (2022) and served as input for a segmentation CNN. This network finally detects the defects on steel components.

Perfect Lambertian surfaces do not exist. For solving the PS problem on non-Lambertian surfaces, Jian et al. (2024) uses a photometric near-field stereo approach. Another approach by Cao et al. (2022) uses a CNN to determine the normal map. Images and lightmap were used as input, thereby. For the prediction of the normal map, the CNN was trained purely on synthetic data. Another approach to solving this problem is the Neural Inverse Rendering (NIR) method, with photometric stereo (Li et al., 2023; Li and Li, 2022a; Li and Li, 2022b; Yang et al., 2024). This method uses neural networks to reconstruct the input images. The network is optimized by minimizing the difference between the reconstructed images and the original images. UPS and NIR was combined in a framework by Li et al. (2023) and called it DANI-Net.

In the given work in progress study:

- DANI-Net (Li et al., 2023) is applied to image data of PCBs acquired using a photometric setup.
- This method is being investigated for its usability for the detection of defects on gold areas of PCBs. This includes the investigation of the visibility in the defects in the depth map and normal map as well as considerations on the required inspection time.

The investigated defect types have a height characteristic and in case the defects are visible in the depth map, a segmentation method can be used for defect detection like thresholding. In contrast to supervised learning methods, this offers the advantage that no defect images need to be collected for the training process. This is a huge advantage since it is very difficult to fully cover all defect types in all their different forms in the training data. Additionally, no extensive labeling of defective data, as in supervised settings, is needed.

2. METHODOLOGY

In neural inverse rendering with respect to photometric stereo methods, CNNs (Taniai and Maehara, 2018; Kaya et al., 2021) and multi-layer perceptron (MLP) networks (Li et al., 2023; Li and Li, 2022a; Li and Li, 2022b; Yang et al., 2024) are used. The input is either the image acquisition (Taniai and Maehara, 2018; Kaya et al., 2021) or the pixel position of the examined object in the image (Li et al., 2023; Li and Li, 2022a; Li and Li, 2022b; Yang et al., 2024). The prediction results of the NIR methods are the variables of the rendering equation (Li et al., 2023). The variables of the rendering equation are: light direction, light intensity, normal map, the bidirectional reflectance distribution function (BRDF) and shadow parameter. The rendering equation is used to reconstruct the original image. Based on the difference between the reconstructed image and the original image, the loss is calculated and the learning parameters are adjusted.

In the following, we will take a closer look at the NIR methods which use MLPs and how they predict the parameter of the rendering equation. The framework of these methods is made up of two or three MLPs. The positionally encoded pixel positions of the image objects serve as input for these networks (Li et al., 2023).

Normal map. This parameter is predicted directly from an MLP or calculated via the depth map. Li et al. (2023) use the surface normal fitting method to calculate the normal map from the depth map. The depth map is predicted by an MLP.

BRDF. This parameter is divided into a diffuse and a specular component. The diffuse component is predicted directly by an MLP. The specular part is calculated from the sum of weighted basis functions (Li and Li, 2022a). In the case of Dani-NET, an Anisotropic Spherical Gaussian basis is used (Li et al., 2023). The weights are predicted by an MLP.

Light direction and light intensity. These parameters of the rendering equation are predicted in a UPS problem by a separate pre-trained CNN (Li and Li, 2022b). The image acquisition serves as input. If no UPS problem occurs, these parameters are predefined.

Shadow parameter. Shadows caused by the object itself are considered with the shadow parameter. This parameter is calculated using the depth map and light direction (Yang et al., 2024).

With the parameters of the rendering equation, the reconstructed input image is calculated. The rendering loss is the absolute mean difference between the original and reconstructed images (Li and Li, 2022b). To improve the reconstruction results, additional loss functions are added to stabilize the optimization process (Yang et al., 2024). Additional loss functions are smoothness loss (Li and Li, 2022a), silhouette loss (Li et al., 2023), geometric loss (Li and Li, 2022a) and differential shadow handling loss (Li et al., 2023). The loss function of the framework (framework loss) is composed of the weighted sum of the rendering loss and the additional loss functions (Li and Li, 2022a). The weights of the MLPs and the learning parameters are updated with this loss. The framework is trained over several stages (Li et al., 2023). At each stage, the composition of the loss function of the framework changes with regard to the occurrence of the additional loss functions. The rendering loss is retained throughout the entire training process.

In this work in progress study we use the DANI-NET (Li et al., 2023) framework. The image reconstruction process of DANI-NET consists of three steps:

1) Initialization of light direction and intensity using a pretrained CNN.
2) Prediction of depth map, diffuse and specular components as well as calculation of the normal map via the surface normal fitting method.
3) Reconstruction of the observed images via rendering equation (for details see (Li et al., 2023)), calculation of the loss function and updating of the learning parameters.

The original parameter settings of the DANI-Net framework and the parameter settings we used for this study can be found in Table 1. Furthermore, the composition of the loss function of the framework in the different training stages with which the framework was trained is given.

Table 1. Shows the original parameters of the DANI-Net framework (Li et al., 2023) and the parameters used for our study. Furthermore, the composition of the framework loss during the training process is provided. In addition, the weights that show how strongly the additional loss functions are contributing to the framework loss are shown. The training process is divided into three stages. Stage 1 ranges from 0 to 500 epochs, stage 2 from 500 to 1000 epochs and stage 3 from 1000-2000 epochs

Parameter / function name	Original parameter settings of DANI-NET	Our parameter settings
Trained epochs	2000	2000
Learning Rate	0.001	0.001
Optimizer	Adam	Adam
Learning rate decay	Cosine annealing function	Cosine annealing function
Input of MLPs	Positional encoded pixel positions of the mask of the object	Positional encoded pixel position of the entire image
Rendering equation: shadow parameter	Applied	Not applied (investigated PCBs have a flat geometry)
rendering loss	L1 loss	L1 loss
smoothness loss at normal map	Applied in epoch 0 to 1500; weight: 0.005	Applied in stage 1 and 2 weight: 0.01
smoothness loss at depth map	Applied in stage 1; weight: 0.01	Applied in stage 1; weight: 0.01
Smoothness loss at diffuse reflectance	Applied in stage 1; weight: 0.01	Applied in stage 1 and 2; weight: 0.01
Smoothness loss at specular reflectance	Applied in stage 1; weight: 0.01	Applied in stage 1 and 2; weight: 0.01
Silhouette loss	Applied in stage 1,2 and 3; weight: 0.01	Not applied
Differential shadow handling loss	Applied in stage 1,2 and 3; weight: 0.01	Not applied (investigated PCBs have a flat geometry)

PCB image data. Image data of the PCBs was obtained using the inspection setup (see Figure 1). A detailed description of the inspection setup can be found in (Hable et al., 2022; Hable et al., 2023) The inspection demonstrator captures four images of a PCB under four different lighting directions. The color images are 3050x3050 px in size and have a resolution of 5.5 µm/px.

a) b)

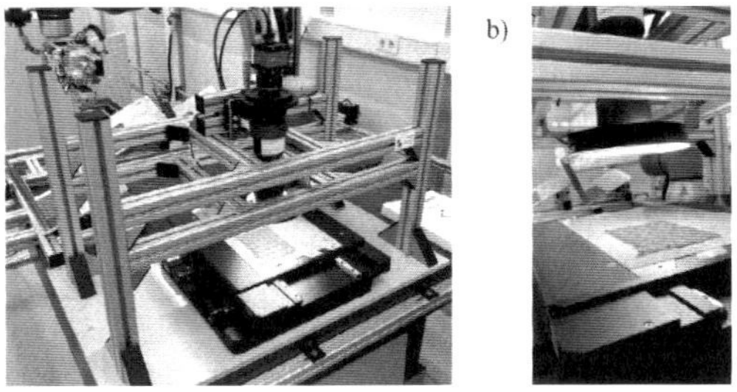

Figure 1. Shows the inspection setup: a) The inspection setup consists of a high-resolution color area scan camera (resolution 5.5µm/px), a telecentric lens, a segmented ring light and an XY-stage. The XY-stage moves the PCB in the PCB array under a camera. b) Close-up of the segmented ring light and a PCB array. The segmented ring light illuminates the PCB one after the other under 4 different lighting directions.

For this study, the defect elevations and dents on the gold areas of PCBs were cut from the images at a size of 150x150 px. The defect image data is resized to 100x100 px and then used as input for DANI-Net. The analyzed image data can be found in Figure 2. The defect images in Figure 2a were originally 150x114 px before being resized to 100x100 px.

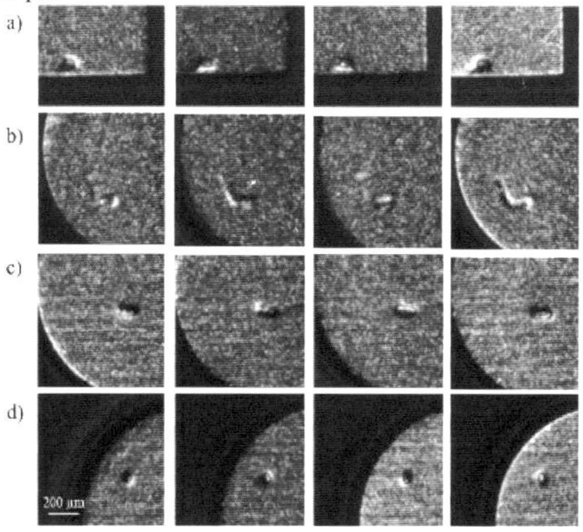

Figure 2. Shows images of the examined defects. Each defect was acquired under 4 different illumination directions. a) and b) show dents, and c) and d) show elevations in the gold areas

3. RESULTS AND DISCUSSION

When applying PCB image data to DANI-Net, we used the parameter settings from Table 1. Training time per image was slightly more than 2 minutes. The results (see Figure 3) show that some of the defects are clearly visible in the normal map and in the depth map. The quality of the depth map was that good, that a simple thresholding procedure was sufficient to segment the defects from the background.

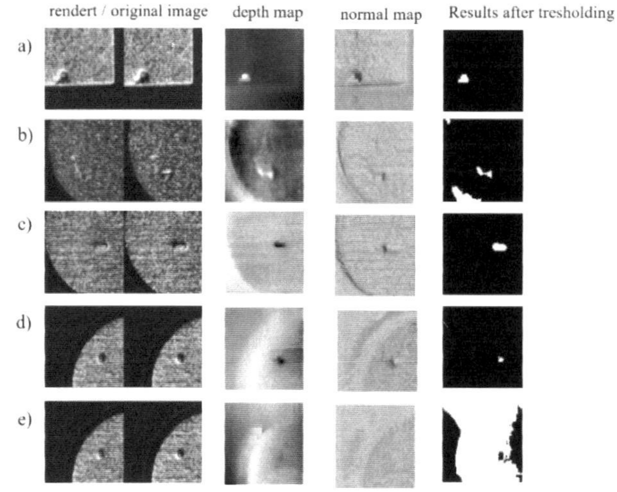

Figure 3. Shows the results achieved with DANI-Net. The defect a)-d) can be seen in depth map and normal map and the thresholded depth map image. e) shows the results of a second run with the defect image data from d)

Elevation defects are shown dark in the depth map because they are closer to the camera. Dents are shown in light color. The process is not always stable in terms of defect visibility (see Figure 3e). When, the same image data was examined sequentially, different results were obtained. In the first observation the defect is visible in the depth map and normal map and in the second observation it is not visible. This is due to the fact that the learning parameters are slightly different optimized in each run. For a defect detection model, the outcome between two runs must be more consistent. This may be achieved by optimizing the CNN used for initializing light directions and light intensities. This CNN was trained on a synthetic image dataset rendered with a point light source. By generating a synthetic dataset that represents the illumination distribution of the PCB image data, a CNN can be trained to predicts more accurate light directions and light intensities. This is assumed to lead to more stable defect detection results.

In this method, defect detection is performed via depth map and normal map during the training process of the neural networks. Therefore, several epochs must be trained in order to obtain a defect detection result. This is a disadvantageous in terms of the runtime compared to supervised detection methods using CNNs. The reduction of the number of training epochs and a delimitation of the examination area, in which only the gold areas of the PCB are examined, can decrease the running time.

4. CONCLUSION

DANI-Net combines a neural inverse rendering method with uncalibrated photometric stereo. This allows normal maps and depth maps of non-Lambertian surfaces to be predicted.

The aim of this work is to visualize defects with a height characteristic in a depth map and in a normal map. In the course of the investigation, we examined several image data with this method. The defects could be successfully segmented from the depth map. The quality of the depth map was sufficient enough to detect the defects with a simple thresholding method. However, the defect detection is not robust enough for practical use. When examining the same image in two different runs, the defect was clearly recognizable in the depth map and normal map in the first run, but in the second run the defect could not be detected.

The reliability of the defect detection may be increased by optimizing the initialization CNN, which estimates the light directions and light intensities. Furthermore, additional research is needed to make investigated defect detection method more stable and to reduce the runtime so that it can be used for defect detection in industry.

ACKNOWLEDGEMENT

The research work was performed at the Polymer Competence Center Leoben GmbH (PCCL, Austria) within the framework of the COMET-program of the Federal Ministry for Climate Action, Environment, Energy, Mobility, Innovation and Technology and the Federal Ministry of Science, Research and Economy with contributions by academic and commercial partners. The PCCL is funded by the Austrian Government and the State Governments of Styria, Lower Austria and Upper Austria.

REFERENCES

Cao, Y. et al. (2022). Photometric-Stereo-Based Defect Detection System for Metal Parts. *In Sensors,* Vol. 22, No. 21, pp. 8374. DOI: 10.3390/s22218374.

Hable, A. et al. (2022). Detection of Printed Circuit Board Defects on ENIG and ENIPIG Surface Finishes with Convolutional Neural Networks and Evaluation of Training Parameters. *Journal of Microelectronics and Electronic Packaging,* Vol.19, No.4, pp. 123–30. DOI: 10.4071/001c.57717.

Hable, A. et al. (2023). Detection of Printed Circuit Board Defects with Photometric Stereo and Convolutional Neural Networks. *Proceedings of International Conference in Central Europe on Computer Graphics, Visualization and Computer Vision (WSCG)*. Plzen, Czech Republic, pp. 300–305. DOI: 10.24132/CSRN.3301.92.

Jian, Z. et al. (2024). Task-Specific Near-Field Photometric Stereo for Measuring Metal Surface Texture. *In IEEE Transactions on Industrial Informatics*, Vol. 20, No. 4, pp. 6019–6029. DOI: 10.1109/tii.2023.3342478.

Li, J. and Li. H. (2022). Neural Reflectance for Shape Recovery with Shadow Handling. *IEEE/CVF Conference on Computer Vision and Pattern Recognition (CVPR).* New Orleans, USA, pp. 16200-16209.

Li, J. and Li, H. (2022), Self-calibrating Photometric Stereo by Neural Inverse Rendering. *Proceedings of European Conference on Computer Vision*. Tel Aviv, Israel, pp. 166–183.

Li, Z. et al. (2023). DANI-Net: Uncalibrated Photometric Stereo by Differentiable Shadow Handling, Anisotropic Reflectance Modeling, and Neural Inverse Rendering. *Proceedings of the IEEE/CVF Conference on Computer Vision and Pattern Recognition*. Vancouver, Canada, pp. 8381-8391.

Liu, H. et al. (2023). A Novel Image Registration-Based Dynamic Photometric Stereo Method for Online Defect Detection in Aluminum Alloy Castings. *In Digital Signal Processing*, Vol. 141, No. 104165, pp. 104165. DOI: 10.1016/j.dsp.2023.104165

Saiz, F.A. et al, (2022). Photometric Stereo-Based Defect Detection System for Steel Components Manufacturing Using a Deep Segmentation Network. *In Sensors,* Vol. 22, No. 3, pp. 882. DOI: 10.3390/s22030882.

Taniai, T. and Maehara, T., (2018). Neural Inverse Rendering for General Reflectance Photometric Stereo, *Proceedings of International Conference on Machine Learning*. Ha Noi, Vietnam, pp. 4857–4866.

Wang, S. et al, (2023). Online micro defects detection for ductile cast iron pipes based on twin light photometric stereo. *In Case Studies in Construction Materials,* Vol. 19, No. e02561, pp. e02561. DOI: 10.1016/j.cscm.2023.e02561.

Yang, Y. et al, (2024). Non-Lambertian photometric stereo via neural inverse rendering and interreflection model. *In Optics and Lasers in Engineering,* Vol. 178, No. 108138, pp. 108138. DOI: 10.1016/j.optlaseng.2024.108138.

VIDEO-BASED PIANO PERFORMANCE EVALUATION VIA DYNAMIC TIME WARPING (DTW)

Vincentius Marcell and Chuan-Kai Yang
National Taiwan University of Science and Technology
No. 43, Sec. 4, keelung Rd., Taipei, Taiwan

ABSTRACT

This paper introduces a novel approach for assessing piano performance through video analysis using Dynamic Time Warping (DTW). Traditional methods of evaluating piano playing often rely on auditory cues or sheet music, neglecting the visual aspects of technique and expression. Our proposed methodology leverages computer vision techniques to analyze pianists' performances captured in video format. The key innovation lies in the application of DTW, a powerful algorithm for measuring temporal variations between sequences, to align and compare the extracted motion features from piano performances.

KEYWORDS

MediaPipe, Pose Estimation, Dynamic Time Warping(DTW), Piano Evaluation, Computer Vision, FFT

1. INTRODUCTION

Piano evaluations traditionally focused on listening or analyzing recordings, missing the visual aspects of a performance that contribute to expression. This research proposes a new video analysis approach to complement traditional methods. By utilizing a special algorithm (DTW), the system can analyze both audio and video data, capturing the nuances of a pianist's technique and expression. This method, tested on a diverse dataset, can reveal subtle variations that enhance performance. This technology has applications in music education, automated feedback systems, and creating more immersive musical experiences. Overall, this research aims to redefine how we evaluate and appreciate piano performances by incorporating both visual and auditory information.

2. RELATED WORKS

People have been interested in developing computer programs to objectively assess piano playing (Modi, D., 2022). Researchers are exploring various methodologies, including analyzing both the pianist's movements and the sounds they produce (Lee, J. et al, 2019; Dmitry, O. G., 2006).

One promising approach utilizes an algorithm called Dynamic Time Warping (DTW) (Ibrahim, A. et al, 2015). Similar to how scientists compare similar shapes or analyze dance movements based on rhythm, DTW compares how well the pianist's timing aligns with the music (Osawa, R. et al, 2020). Another method involves analyzing the sound waves using FFT (Fast Fourier Transform) to understand the specific notes being played (Modi, D., 2022).

By combining these methods, researchers can create programs that assess various aspects of piano playing, similar to how judges score singing competitions in terms of pitch, volume, and rhythm (Tsai, W. H. et al, 2012). Additionally, recent advancements allow computer programs to analyze both audio and video simultaneously, mimicking a human judge's evaluation by considering both the sound and the pianist's movements (Liu, L. et al, 2021).

These interdisciplinary efforts, combining audio analysis with computer vision techniques, are leading to more robust and accurate piano performance evaluation systems (Parmar, P. et al, 2021). Ultimately, these programs can provide valuable insights into musicians' skills and facilitate their continuous improvement (Zhao, X. et al, 2023; Wang, A. et al, 2021).

3. APPROACH

Our Objective is to detect the Hand landmark after that detect the Audio using the Fast Fourier Transform, and lastly, score the evaluation using the distance of DTW between the Teacher Video and Student Video. The resulting distance of DTW will be used in an equation so it will range between 0 and 100. From the result, we can conclude the difference between Teacher and Student Videos.

3.1 Hand Landmark Detection

Hand landmark detection involves using computer vision to locate and monitor particular points on a hand within an image or video. These points, usually about 21 in total and located at the knuckles and the base of the palm, create a skeletal outline of the hand's position. By examining the position and motion of these points, various applications can interpret hand gestures, follow sign language interactions, or interact with virtual objects in augmented reality environments.

This Study will be using the help of MediaPipe Framework. MediaPipe is a framework for building pipelines to perform inference over arbitrary sensory data. With MediaPipe, a perception pipeline can be built as a graph of modular components, including model inference, media processing algorithms data transformations, etc(Lugaresi, C. et al, 2019). Released in 2019, it has gained popularity for its simplicity, flexibility, and efficiency in handling a wide range of multimedia processing tasks.

This framework will be used in This research, to simplify the process for hand detection. Hand detection is one of the major subjects to be used in this research since evaluating hand posture means we need to make sure the computer understands what a hand looks like.

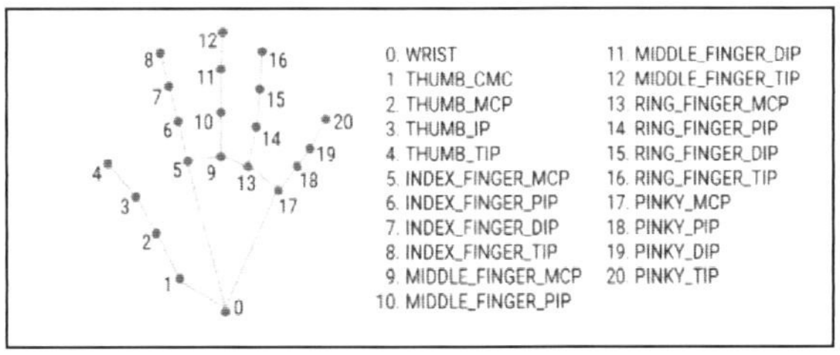

Figure 1. MediaPipe Hand Landmarks list and location of right Hand

The figure above shows how the architecture of MediaPipe understands the shape of a Hand. MediaPipe has 21 places of Hand to differentiate starting from the wrist and each finger.

3.2 Note Detection via Audio Processing

In the realm of digital music analysis, audio processing for note detection addresses the challenge of recognizing musical tones from a recorded audio clip. This task relies on understanding the connection between pitch and frequency, where higher pitches correspond to higher frequencies of sound waves. Through scrutinizing the frequency spectrum of the audio signal, algorithms can identify the prominent frequencies, thereby potentially uncovering the specific musical notes being produced.

This part will use the Fast Fourier Transform (FFT) algorithm. FFT is an algorithm that efficiently computes the Discrete Fourier Transform (DFT) of a sequence, enabling the transformation of time-domain signals into their frequency-domain representations and vice versa. Unlike the straightforward DFT computation with a time complexity of $O(N^2)$, the FFT reduces this complexity to $O(\log_N N)$by employing a divide-and-conquer strategy, particularly in the Radix-2 FFT variant. By recursively decomposing the DFT into smaller sub-problems and utilizing symmetric properties of sinusoids, the FFT minimizes computational overhead while efficiently processing signals. Its core operation, the butterfly operation, merges frequency domain points at each stage of recursion, significantly speeding up the transformation process. Consequently, the FFT has become a cornerstone algorithm in fields such as signal processing, image processing, and data compression, facilitating real-time analysis of signals and data.

After getting the value of Frequency from FFT, we will be using an equation that will convert frequency into a number ranging from 0 to 88. This number corresponds to the number of notes inside the piano since the value of frequency for each note is fixed that is why we can create an equation to calculate the number and after that convert the number into a piano Notation. Here is the equation to convert from frequency into number notation

$$frequency_{to_{number}} = 69 + 12 * \log_2(freq/440)$$

3.3 Dynamic Time Warping(DTW)

Dynamic Time Warping(DTW) is a seminal time series comparison technique that has been used for speech and word recognition since the 1970s with sound waves as the source. DTW is an algorithm that compares two non-sync sequences to find optimal matching sequences between each other, by matching all the restrictions and the rules and that has the minimal cost, where the cost is computed as the sum of absolute differences, for each matched pair of indices, between their values.

$$d(i,j) = ||a_i - b_j||$$

$$g(i,j) = min\begin{cases} g(i,j-1) + d(i,j) \\ g(i-1,j-1) + 2d(i,j) \\ g(i-1,j) + d(i,j) \end{cases}$$

$$D(A,B) = \frac{1}{N}\sum_{i=0}^{I}\sum_{j=0}^{J} g(i,j)\,, where\ N = I + J$$

These equations are the basic equation of DTW. Here A and B are a set of data that has the size of I and J respectively. $d(i,j)$ is a measure of the difference/distance between two feature vectors of a_i and b_j. $g(i,j)$ is the adjusted value of distance that uses a window so that it will also consider the frame before and the frame after. Lastly, $D(A,B)$ is the distance between set data A and set data B.

4. EXPERIMENT RESULT

This research thus far doesn't have any setup. This research will use multiple videos from YouTube. The Videos this research will use one that is viewed from the top of the piano and shows clearly the hand movement. This study will be using Python 3.11, this research also uses these libraries:

- MediaPipe: MediaPipe is one of the Python libraries developed by Google. This Library has proven to be useful for detecting body pose landmarks. This research primarily uses the Hand Landmark detection provided by MediaPipe
- Dtaidistance: This library is used by many people to simplify programming Dynamic Time Warping.
- Numpy. FFT: This is a part of the Function library but this function is used to calculate the audio into a number using the Fast Fourier Transform algorithm

This research first will be used to input two desired videos, where one will be the student video and the other will be the teacher. Both of them will be processed by MediaPipe to create new videos with hand landmarks and Excel files that store the frame, hand landmark coordinates, and the note names of both videos.

After we get the Excel files, the study will continue to read the Excel files. The values inside the Excel files will be saved inside Variables. These Variables then will be sorted by frame, then the X coordinate. After that, we used Dtaidistance to calculate the Dynamic Time Warping distance from both the teacher and the student to compare the similarities. The first part of This research is the hand detection from MediaPipe. Here is what it looks like.

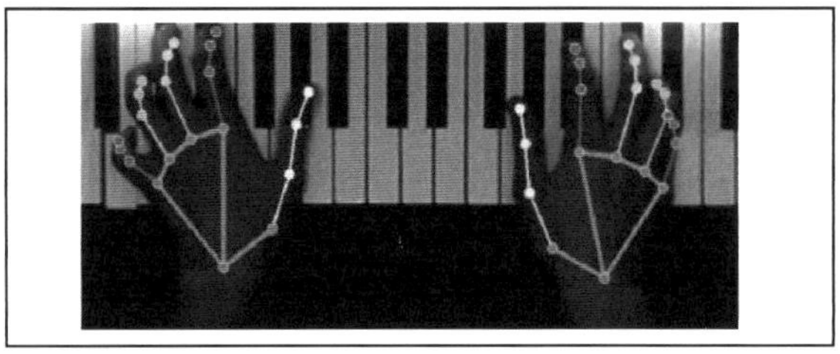

Figure 2. Hand Detection Using MediaPipe

After the use of Mediapipe on the Video the next part will be using Fast Fourier Transform to detect the audio of the video, first, we will convert the video file into a WAV, we choose WAV instead of MP4 so that we don't need to differentiate between the left ear and right ear sound. After we get the WAV file we will use the function from Numpy which is Numpy.FFT this function will create a numeric value that represents the frequency.

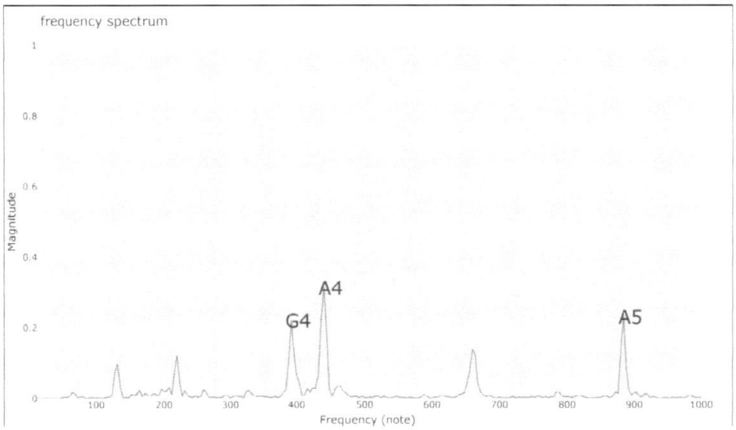

Figure 3. The result of transforming the audio into a note

While detecting the program will also save the hand landmarks and the notes into Excel. Each column will represent hand landmarks and audio notes. Every new frame that has both hand and audio notes in it, will be saved into a new row, each cell will save the frame, x coordinate, y coordinate, and audio notes.

Then the program will load the Excel file of the student and the teacher. It will save each hand landmark into a variable. After that, the variable will be sorted based on the frame and then the X coordinate. Next, it will calculate the DTW. Here is the result of DTW between the THUMB.

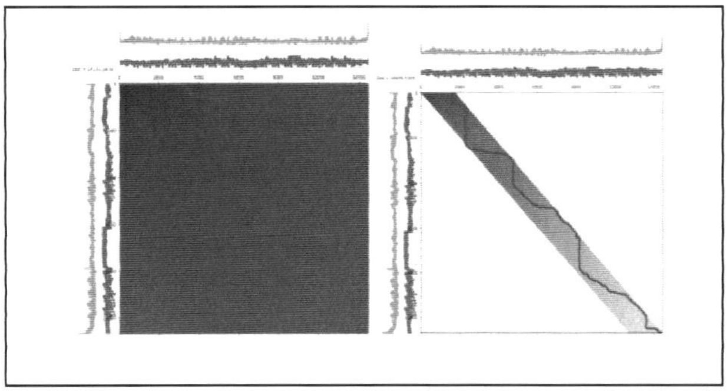

Figure 4. DTW with no window(Left) and window size= 1(Right)

After getting the DTW next will be getting the score of evaluation. From the DTW we will get the overall distance between the teacher and the student. This value then will be used for scoring evaluation. Here is the equation for scoring evaluation

$$S = 100 * 1.07 \exp(0.17 * Distance(Q, Q'))$$

The result of the equation is between 0 to 100. In the equation values, 1.07 and 0.17 are tuneable variables, right now I am using 1.07 and 0.17 because they produce the best result. Distance(Q, Q') is the result of DTW between the teacher and the student video.

5. CONCLUSION AND FUTURE WORKS

This study still can be extended into multiple implementations to create a better scoring evaluation, hand detection, and audio detection. It can implement Machine Learning or Deep Learning together with the DTW to calculate a better distance. This study can also limit the FPS for hand detection so that it can do a live scoring frame by frame where it will decrease the score every time the test makes a mistake.

This research identifies several areas for enhancement. The foremost aim is to amalgamate Dynamic Time Warping (DTW) with Hand detection to swiftly score ongoing sequences of a song. Furthermore, the intention is to integrate Hand detection with either pitch detection or keypress detection to streamline data processing within the DTW framework. Lastly, the objective is to synthesize these concepts to facilitate live scoring without dependence on pre-recorded video, enabling immediate functionality upon program initiation.

REFERENCES

Dmitry, O. G. et al. (2006). Detection and tracking of pianist hands and fingers, *Computer and Robot Vision, 2006*, doi: 10.1109/CRV.2006.26

Ibrahim, A. et al. (2015). Image Similarity Using Dynamic Time Warping of Fractal Features. *13th Australian Digital Forensics Conference*, pp. 111-122.

Lee, J. et al. (2019). Observing Pianist Accuracy and Form with Computer Vision, *2019 IEEE Winter Conference on Applications of Computer Vision*, doi: 10.1109/WACV.2019.00165

Liu, L. et al. (2021). Joint Multi-Pitch Detection and Score Transcription For Polyphonic Piano Music. *IEEE International Conference on Acoustics, Speech and Signal Processing (ICASSP)*, DOI: 10.1109/ICASSP39728.2021.9413601

Lugaresi, C. et al. (2019). MediaPipe: A Framework for Building Perception Pipelines, *IEEE Computer Vision and Pattern Recognition (CVPR) 2019*, doi: https://doi.org/10.48550/arXiv.2006.10214

Modi, D. (2022). Harmonium and Piano frequencies, *International Research Journal of Engineering and Technology (IRJET)*, Vol. 08, Issue. 02.

Osawa, R. et al. (2020). Pitching Motion Matching Based on Pose Similarity Using Dynamic Time Warping, *2020 IEEE 9th Global Conference on Consumer Electronics (GCCE)*, doi: 10.1109/GCCE50665.2020.9291730

Parmar, P. et al. (2021). Piano Skills Assessment, *IEEE 23rd International Workshop on Multimedia Signal Processing*, doi: 10.1109/MMSP53017.2021.9733638

Tsai, W. H. et al. (2012). Automatic Evaluation of Karaoke Singing Based on Pitch, Volume, and Rhythm Features. *IEEE Transactions on Audio, Speech, and Language Processing*, Vol. 20, NO. 4.

Wang, A. et al. (2021). An Efficient Piano Performance Evaluation Model Using DTW based on Deep Learning, *2021 IEEE 30th International Symposium on Industrial Electronics (ISIE)*, doi: 10.1109/ISIE45552.2021.9576338

Zhao, X. et al. (2023). A ResNet-Based Audio-Visual Fusion Model for Piano Skill Evaluation, *CC BY 4.0*, doi: 10.3390/app13137431

BONE POROSITY AND THICKNESS EVALUATION BY ULTRASONIC SIGNALS USING PATTERN RECOGNITION

Maksims Mamontovs[1], Aleksandrs Sisojevs[2] and Alexey Tatarinov[2]
[1]*Riga Technical University, 6A Ķīpsalas Str., Riga, Latvia*
[2]*Institute of Electronics and Computer Science, 14 Dzerbenes Str., Riga, Latvia*

ABSTRACT

The fragility of long bones in osteoporosis is linked to a decrease in cortical layer thickness (CTh) and the development of internal porosity (P) within the cortex. This study is dedicated to investigate whether it is possible and how accurately P and CTh can be determined using a pattern recognition methods, utilizing discrete Fourier transform (DFT) analysis of ultrasonic signals transmitted through a soft tissue layer. As input data, ultrasound scans of phantom of cortical bone with different grades of CTh and P were used. Each of the phantom scans was chosen in turn as a test object, while other specimens composed the training set. For analysis, three different existing approaches were applied firstly and the later one was developed by improving the existing ones. The analysis was carried out in three categories: P and CTh ratio, P only and CTh only. Based on the results of each analysis, a method was obtained that predicts P and CTh better than other applied ones. A comparison of the methods for P and CTh determining and choosing the most effective ones are shown.

KEYWORDS

Bone Phantom, KNN, DFT, Cortical Bone Thickness, Porosity

1. INTRODUCTION

To evaluate risk of brittle fractures in osteoporosis (degenerative bone disease in aging and some metabolic disorders), it is important to determine two factors of lowered bone quality: decrease of cortical thickness and increase of intracortical porosity. The current methods used to determine both factors are not perfect and have various limitations. The use of quantitative ultrasound may help solving the diagnostic task by the most effective way.

The main goal of the study was to examine whether it was possible to determine the degree of internal bone porosity using ultrasound signals processed by discrete Fourier transform (DFT), as well as to ascertain how accurately various methods can accomplish this. The study was inspired by the previous work of the team (Sisojevs et al., 2023), but considering a different approach. In this work, the authors relied on existing pattern recognition methods, adapting them to work with ultrasonic scanning data. A new method based on known approaches was also proposed. Methods differ both in their essence and in the way they interact with data. Additionally, some of the work is related to DFT as it serves as the transformation mechanism for all the data in our experiment. The analytical part is based on an evaluation study (Sisojevs et al., 2022). In this study, the analysis is divided into three subsections to determine P and CTh jointly and separately.

Three methods were used in the project: KNN, Taxicab, and the method of Correlation coefficient. A custom-designed improved method was developed based on the KNN method specifically for the dataset of the project. The enhanced KNN was based on the approaches approbated in (Mladenova et al., 2022) and (Okfalisa et al., 2017). The Taxicab method (Ghosh et al., 2017, Kemp et al., 2021) and the Correlation coefficient method (Meng et al., 2019, Li et al., 2020) for were used according the presented sources.

2. INITIAL DATA

Plate-shaped cortical bone phantoms (total number 25) composed of the solid bone part and porous bone part in different proportions and covering soft tissues of different layer thickness (Sisojevs et al., 2023) were produced. The thickness of cortical layer (entire thickness of the phantom) CTh varied in the range from 2 mm to 6 mm with a 1 mm step. Internal porosity P was simulated by thickness of the lower porous layer within CTh varying from 0 (P=0%) to the entire CTh (P=100%) also with a step of 1 mm. Three thicknesses of the soft tissue layer (0, 2, and 4 mm) were applied. The data was primarily categorized by the thickness of soft tissues.

Ultrasonic data were obtained by the surface scanning of the phantom through the layer of soft tissues. One scan contained 24 ultrasonic signals acquired by stepwise records moving the ultrasonic receiver apart from the emitter along the phantom. As a result, the dataset for each phantom type contained 72 signal files (24 steps of scanning at 3 grades of soft tissues layer). The signal files were frames 1 ms long that contained three ultrasound propagation signals at different ultrasonic frequencies separated by time.

The next step was data obtained after DFT processing. After analyzing the obtained DFT data, the most informative type of signals turned out to be the magnitude, further chosen as the main parameter for the analysis. In this study, all methods applied only the DFT magnitude data.

To categorize data by various ways, it was necessary to distinguish between bone phantoms simultaneously keeping the information about CTh and P of each phantom. To solve this, the following object naming system was created. The phantom name consisted of two digits. The first digit indicated CTh in millimeters and the second digit indicated P or the thickness of the porous layer in millimeters.

3. PROPOSED APPROACH

Since 24 tests (signal files) were done for each object, it was necessary to compare the objects. Therefore, it was decided to standardize 25 objects by using the average arithmetic values of all 24 tests. The same was done for each thickness of soft tissues, i.e. 0, 2, and 4 mm.

Implementation of the methods.

KNN. The method examined all magnitude values of bone phantoms from the database for each frequency value. Then, the difference in value of magnitude was considered as distance between the test object and the other bone phantoms in comparison. This distance was calculated using the KNN method formula for distance calculation. Then it was compared among all objects at a specific frequency.

A comparison was conducted for each frequency in the magnitude range of 1-750. The object with the smallest distance to the test object for a specific frequency received a point. At the end of the algorithm, the object with the highest score was considered as the most similar to the test object.

Enhanced KNN. This method was an enhanced version of the regular KNN method. Instead of comparing data at each frequency, a range of 5 frequencies was taken. The overall range was divided into intervals of 5 frequencies each. Comparison was done based on the average arithmetic values within each interval. Subsequently, points were assigned to the samples that have the smallest distance to the test sample. At the end of the algorithm, the object with the highest score was considered as the most similar to the test object.

Taxicab. In this method, the unified analysis was performed. Within the range from 1 to 750 different frequencies, each object was compared to the test object, calculating the distances. The distance value was calculated as the module of the difference between the magnitude values of the test object and the object from the database. The next step was the calculation of the sum of these distance values for each object in the database, i.e. the sum of modules.

By analyzing the sum of modules, which indicated the distance from the object in the database to the test object, a list of objects from the database was obtained, where each object was assigned a number reflecting its sum of module values depending on the test object. Since the list depends on the test object, the best results in it corresponded to the smallest distance values. The smaller the result, the more similar the database object was to the test object.

Correlation coefficient. The Correlation coefficient method was used to find matches between the test object and the database object. Objects had two values: magnitude and frequency. Since only the magnitude values differ at the same frequency, they were considered as separate values. From the test object and one object from the database, the magnitude value with the same frequency value was taken and added as a point to the correlation coefficient. Thus, the magnitude values of the test object were obtained as Y and the magnitude values of one object from the database as X. Then, for each frequency value, a point was added to the graph with the magnitude values of the test object and the magnitude values of one object from the database.

The correlation coefficient for the respective pair of objects was calculated using the graph obtained from the points. By performing this operation with each object in the database, a list was created where each object has its own correlation value. From the list data, it can be determined which objects were more similar to the test object because they had a higher correlation coefficient.

All methods were adapted to work with current data and to be able to compare the obtained results with each other. In all methods, the identical data obtained during scanning was used.

4. EXPERIMENTS

Since the available number of bone phantoms (samples) was limited, it significantly restricted the use of various testing methods. Therefore, to evaluate how methods could classify a test sample at the same thickness of soft tissue layer, one sample was chosen as the test object, while the remaining 24 were used as the database.

For the objectification of the experiment, the test object should not be present in the database. Therefore, to understand the classification results, it was necessary to determine which of the other objects in the database were the most similar to the test object. Firstly, all objects were graphically displayed on the diagram showing two analyzed parameters – CTh and P (Figure 1).

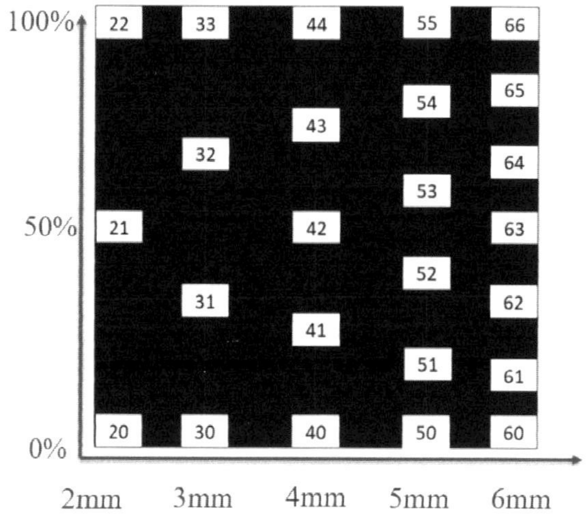

Figure 1. Structure of initial data (abscissa – CTh, ordinate P)

The goal of all methods was to find objects in the database that were closest to the selected test phantom on the diagram. Each method was used such that the result for each test object was a list of three other objects from the database that were most similar to the original object (the three nearest neighbors were selected). The results for each method (KNN / Enhanced KNN / Taxicab / Correlation coefficient) were obtained in the form of a test object and the result in the form of three other objects.

The next step after obtaining the results was their analysis. It was divided into 3 parts:

- Combined analysis of P and CTh
- Analysis of P
- Analysis of CTh

For each analysis, its own evaluation system was created, which also took into account the probability of error wherever possible.

The result of the analyses are presented in Tables 1-3, where the effectiveness of the methods in determination of P and CTh are compared in percentage terms.

Table 1. Combined analysis of P and CTh

Soft tissue type	Results match	KNN	Enhanced KNN	Taxicab	Correlation coefficient
0 mm	Perfect	44%	36%	56%	28%
2 mm	Perfect	60%	44%	52%	16%
4 mm	Perfect	56%	56%	56%	48%
Average	Perfect	53%	45%	54%	31%

Table 2. Analysis of P

Soft tissue type	Mistake	KNN	Enhanced KNN	Taxicab	Correlation coefficient
0 mm	<1%	40%	40%	32%	32%
0 mm	1%-17%	32%	36%	48%	48%
2 mm	<1%	24%	36%	28%	12%
2 mm	1%-17%	56%	44%	28%	40%
4 mm	<1%	16%	28%	24%	0%
4 mm	1%-17%	44%	36%	32%	48%
Average	<1%	27%	35%	28%	15%
Average	<17%	71%	73%	64%	60%

Table 3. Analysis of CTh

Soft tissue type	KNN	Enhanced KNN	Taxicab	Correlation coefficient
0 mm	52%	44%	60%	64%
2 mm	68%	76%	68%	72%
4 mm	72%	76%	76%	92%
Average	64%	65%	68%	76%

5. CONCLUSION

The results showed that the most precise methods for complex analysis of porosity P and cortical thickness CTh were Taxicab and KNN capable to determine the exact state of bone on average with 53% accuracy (KNN) and 54% accuracy (Taxicab). In P analysis, the enhanced KNN method performed the best being able to determine P on average with 35% (with <1% error) and 73% (with <17% error). In the analysis of CTh, the Correlation coefficient method performed the best on average with a success rate of 76%.

ACKNOWLEDGEMENT

The study was supported by the research project of the Latvian Council of Science lzp-2021/1-0290 "Comprehensive assessment of the condition of bone and muscle tissues using quantitative ultrasound" (BoMUS).

REFERENCES

Ghosh P., Goto T., Sen S., (2017). Computing Skyline Using Taxicab Geometry. *Proceedings of the 5th International Conference on Applied Computing and Information Technology/4th International Conference on Computational Science/Intelligence and Applied Informatics/2nd International Conference on Big Data, Cloud Computing, Data Science (ACIT-CSII-BCD'2017).* Hamamatsu, Japan, pp. 7-12.

Kemp A., Vidakovic D., (2021). Ways secondary mathematics teachers apply definitions in Taxicab geometry for a real-life situation: Midset. *The Journal of Mathematical Behavior,* Vol.62, p.100848.

Li, C., Yang, H., Bao, B., Guo, H., Jiang, Y., & Zhang, J., (2020). Spearman Correlation Coefficient Abnormal Behavior Monitoring Technology Based on RNN in 5G Network for Smart City. *Proceedings of the IEEE International Wireless Communications and Mobile Computing (IWCMC)*. Limassol, Cyprus, pp. 1440–1442.

Meng C., Jiang X.S., Wang J., Wei X.M., (2019). The Complex Network Model for Industrial Data Based on Spearman Correlation Coefficient. *Proceedings of the IEEE International Conference on Internet of Things (iThings) and IEEE Green Computing and Communications (GreenCom) and IEEE Cyber, Physical and Social Computing (CPSCom) and IEEE Smart Data (SmartData).* Atlanta, GA, USA, pp 28-33.

Mladenova T., Valova I. (2022). Comparative analysis between the traditional K-Nearest Neighbor and Modifications with Weight-Calculation. *Proceedings of the IEEE International Symposium on Multidisciplinary Studies and Innovative Technologies (ISMSIT'2022).* Ankara, Turkey, pp. 961-965.

Okfalisa, Ikbal G., Mustakim, Nurul G.I.R., (2017). Comparative analysis of k-nearest neighbor and modified k-nearest neighbor algorithm for data classification. *In Proceedings of the IEEE 2nd International conferences on Information Technology, Information Systems and Electrical Engineering (ICITISEE'2017),* Yogyakarta, Indonesia, pp. 294-298.

Sisojevs A., Tatarinov A. and Chaplinska A., (2023). Evaluation of Factors-of-Interest in Bone Mimicking Models Based on DFT Analysis of Ultrasonic Signals. *Proceedings of the 12th International Conference on Pattern Recognition Applications and Methods (ICPRAM'2023).* Lisbon, Portugal, pp. 914-919.

Sisojevs A., Tatarinov A., Kovalovs M., Krutikova O. and Chaplinska A., (2022). An Approach for Parameters Evaluation in Layered Structural Materials based on DFT Analysis of Ultrasonic Signals. *Proceedings of the 11th International Conference on Pattern Recognition Applications and Methods (ICPRAM'2022).* Online streaming, pp. 307-314.

Reflection Papers

EXPLORING THE INCORPORATION OF ARTIFICIAL INTELLIGENCE INTO DIGITAL TECHNOLOGIES FOR ART THERAPY

Augustina Ao Liu and Yuxi Ethan Cui
University of Washington, 1410 NE Campus Pkwy, Seattle, WA, USA 98195

ABSTRACT

This paper discusses how Artificial Intelligence (AI) can be integrated with digital technologies to achieve better treatment outcomes in art therapy, an effective complementary psychotherapy for mental health issues. AI tools can assist in the client's creation process, helping them to express more freely and imaginatively. It can also provide analytical insights into the reflective discussion between clients and art therapists. However, the integration of AI also raises concerns, such as potential distractions and over-reliance on technology, which can detract from the therapeutic benefits. The paper emphasizes the importance of balancing AI assistance to support therapeutic goals, leveraging AI for more objective analyses, and addressing data privacy concerns through informed consent and robust data protection measures. By integrating AI into both the creative and analytical phases, art therapy can offer clients a more nuanced understanding of their emotional and psychological states, leading to more effective and personalized sessions.

KEYWORDS

Art Therapy, Artificial Intelligence, Human-AI Interaction, Digital Technologies, Mental Health, User Experience

1. INTRODUCTION

Mental disorders are prevalent social issues worldwide, resulting in significant economic and social burdens on healthcare systems (Christensen et al., 2020; Zschucke et al., 2013). Art therapy has been effectively used to treat various mental health problems as a form of complementary psychotherapy (Joschko et al., 2022; Du et al., 2024). To enhance its efficacy, various forms of art therapy have been explored, including the use of digital technologies. Emerging digital technologies have gradually been adopted in art therapy practices, offering greater flexibility (Orr, 2012). The recent breakthrough in Artificial Intelligence (AI) presents a new opportunity at the intersection of digital technologies and art therapy. This reflective paper discusses how AI can be integrated with digital technologies to achieve better treatment outcomes in art therapy for mental health issues.

2. ART THERAPY

Art therapy is a form of psychotherapy to improve a person's overall mental well-being. It typically consists of two parts: the creative process and the reflective discussion. Both the self-expression during the creation of art and the subsequent discussions are critical for achieving effective treatment outcomes.

2.1 Art Therapy, Self-expression, and Reflective Discussion

The creative process involved in artistic self-expression is a key element in art therapy. Through the process of self-expression, clients can retrospectively examine their own emotional states, gaining self-awareness, self-reflection, and self-growth (Braus & Morton, 2020). Art therapy includes various formats of self-expression, such as drawing, painting, crafting, dancing, theater therapy, body psychotherapy, and music therapy (Priebe, 2016). Each format provides unique insights into the individual's emotions, mental state, and life experiences.

The subsequent discussions between clients and therapists about the artistic works help clients discover insights from new perspectives and achieve their therapeutic goals (Potash et al., 2020). The analysis of the artwork is not solely the therapist's responsibility but involves joint interpretation between clients and therapists (Du et al., 2024). Therapists need to incorporate the clients' self-interpretation into the analysis to gain a holistic and conceptual understanding of each client's mental state, rather than simply focusing on the content of the artwork (Loue, 2023; Pénzes, 2018). The goal is not to provide a simple diagnosis but to offer a conversational and interactive experience (Hu et al., 2021). Hence, the discussion between clients and therapists, along with active engagement from both sides, is essential for effective treatment.

2.2 Art Therapy, Digital Technologies and AI

Various digital technologies have been explored in art therapy. Early explorations focused on remote therapy by enhancing accessibility and supporting therapy-client relationships (Cubranic et al., 1998). By 2014, research expanded to investigate the properties required for drawing applications used in art therapy, including considerations for those with disabilities. However, most efforts centered on leveraging existing tools rather than developing new ones specifically for art therapy (Choe, 2014; Darewych et al., 2015).

In 2024, Du et al. proposed DeepThInk, an art-making tool specifically tailored for art therapy. DeepThInk incorporates AI to improve clients' creativity and expressivity in the creation process. It features a Human-AI co-creation brush to assist in the art-making process and an AI Styling tool that offers a variety of art styles.

Integrating digital technologies into the discussions after the art-making process is also crucial. In 2023, He and Liu proposed using Convolutional Neural Networks (CNNs), an AI-integrated image recognition and analysis tool, to understand the semantic and contextual information from the artwork, complementing human understanding in art therapy sessions.

3. OPPORTUNITIES AND CHALLENGES OF DESIGNING DIGITAL TECHNOLOGIES WITH AI FOR ART THERAPY

The emergence of AI brings new possibilities to digital technologies, assisting clients in expressing themselves during sessions and helping both clients and therapists in interpreting and discussing artwork.

3.1 Enhancing Self-Expression and Managing Challenges with AI Art-Making

With AI assistance in art-making, clients experience less mental burden and gain more confidence in the creative process, enhancing their self-expression. This allows clients to focus on the expression itself rather than fixating on the aesthetics of the artwork, which is especially beneficial for those who identify as "not art persons" (Du et al., 2024). AI not only makes art therapy more inclusive by lowering the threshold for art-making but also offers clients more ideas to explore and helps them visualize their imagination. The randomness of AI introduces a degree of uncertainty, inspiring clients, inducing creativity, and allowing them to generate new ideas in art therapy (Du et al., 2024).

However, therapists have raised concerns about potential compromises in the treatment due to the incorporation of AI. If the excessive power of AI is not well-controlled, it can distract clients' attention to the technical aspects of the artwork instead of the expression itself (Du et al., 2024), contradicting the intended benefits. In some cases, AI's rendering can go off track, hindering clients' expressivity. Additionally, some clients might overuse AI's content creation and stop pushing 1themselves further in the creative process, instead relying on AI to provide excessive hints, which undermines their self-expression and the overall treatment effect (Du et al., 2024).

3.2 Ensuring Objective Interpretation of Art Work through AI Integration

Another crucial aspect is the interpretation and analysis of the artwork created in the session. Artwork interpretations are often subjective because therapists bring different perspectives based on their academic, cultural, and work backgrounds (He & Liu, 2023). For example, some therapists may focus more on colors, lines, and compositions, while others may emphasize the meanings of symbols in the clients' artwork. Additionally, individual therapists may have different preferences when interpreting the same piece of art (He & Liu, 2023). AI integrated with Convolutional Neural Networks (CNNs) can analyze patterns, colors, and shapes to provide deeper insights into clients' emotional and psychological states. CNNs can offer references to therapists and help interpret artwork with less influence from personal preferences, leading to more objective and comprehensive analyses. Additionally, CNNs can leverage larger datasets to enhance the interpretation of clients' artworks (He & Liu, 2023).

3.3 Enhancing Art Therapy through Holistic Human-AI Integration

For better therapeutic efficacy, design efforts should explore the end-to-end integration of AI into art therapy sessions, rather than only focusing on individual parts of the therapy process separately. Art therapy is a deeply personal experience, with clients expressing themselves differently based on their backgrounds and cultures. The same element in the artwork can represent different things to different clients. Through the Human-AI co-creation process, digital tools should be able to record, consider, and analyze previous pieces created by the same clients, along with insights gained during the co-creation process, to generate a more holistic interpretation of the artwork. This comprehensive approach can be particularly useful in identifying subtle details that may be overlooked by human interpretation alone. By training AI to learn the associations between different art creations and the corresponding emotions in therapy for the same client, it can draw meaningful conclusions and provide recommendations based on historical data, thereby enhancing the overall therapeutic process. Moreover, integrating AI into both the creative and analytical phases ensures a seamless therapeutic experience, leveraging AI's strengths to support and enrich human expertise. This holistic integration promotes a more nuanced understanding of clients' emotional and psychological states, leading to more effective and personalized art therapy sessions.

3.4 Ensuring Data Privacy and Security in AI-Integrated Art Therapy

With the extensive involvement of AI in end-to-end therapy sessions, data privacy has become a legitimate concern. Clients should be able to make informed decisions about how their data is being used, with clear communication of the benefits and potential risks. Therapists should not use AI without obtaining informed consent from clients. Even if clients opt to use AI in their sessions, their identifiable personal data, such as names, dates of birth, and addresses, should be stored using robust anonymization techniques and encrypted to protect data both in transit and at rest. Providing clients with control over their data, including the ability to view, edit, or delete their information, helps maintain transparency about data usage and builds trust. Implementing strict access controls and regular audits can prevent unauthorized access while enforcing data minimization practices ensures that only necessary information is collected. Educating clients about AI use and securing clear, straightforward consent, along with a consent management system, is crucial. Regular security assessments and updates to AI systems, along with using tools that comply with recognized privacy and security standards (e.g., GDPR, HIPAA), can further safeguard data. These measures collectively ensure that AI integration in art therapy respects clients' privacy and maintains confidentiality.

4. CONCLUSION

Integrating AI into digital technologies for art therapy presents significant opportunities and challenges. AI has the potential to enhance the therapeutic process by reducing the mental burden on clients, fostering creativity, and providing comprehensive insights into clients' emotional and psychological states. AI tools like DeepThInk can assist in the creation process, helping clients express themselves more freely and imaginatively (Du et al., 2024). Furthermore, interpretation can be enhanced using CNNs, the AI-integrated image recognition and analysis tools, to provide more objective and comprehensive analyses. CNNs can analyze patterns, colors, and shapes in the artwork and leverage larger datasets to offer deeper insights (He & Liu, 2023). However, incorporating AI into art therapy raises concerns about potential distractions and over-reliance on technology (Du et al., 2024), which can detract from the therapeutic benefits. Therefore, it is important to balance AI's assistance to ensure it supports rather than undermines the therapy's goals.

Moreover, design efforts should explore combining the Human-AI co-creation process with AI integration in analysis sessions to achieve better therapeutic outcomes. This holistic approach considers clients' backgrounds and previous artworks, leading to more personalized and effective art therapy sessions.

Additionally, with the extensive involvement of AI, data privacy becomes a critical concern. Therapists must ensure that clients make informed decisions about AI use in their therapy, with clear communication of benefits and risks. Obtaining informed consent and implementing robust data protection measures, including anonymization techniques and advanced encryption, are essential. Providing clients control over their data and maintaining transparency about its use can build trust and ensure confidentiality.

In summary, while AI integration in art therapy holds promise for improving treatment efficacy, it requires careful implementation and ethical considerations. By addressing potential drawbacks and ensuring data privacy, AI can be effectively integrated into art therapy to support and enhance the therapeutic process.

REFERENCES

Braus, M., & Morton, B. (2020). Art therapy in the time of covid-19. *Psychological Trauma: Theory, Research, Practice, and Policy*. https://pubmed.ncbi.nlm.nih.gov/32478544/

Choe, S. N. (2014). An exploration of the qualities and features of art apps for art therapy. *The Arts in Psychotherapy, 41*(2), 145–154. https://doi.org/10.1016/j.aip.2014.01.002

Christensen, M. K., Lim, C. C., Saha, S., Plana-Ripoll, O., Cannon, D., Presley, F., Weye, N., Momen, N. C., Whiteford, H. A., Iburg, K. M., & McGrath, J. J. (2020). The cost of Mental Disorders: A systematic review. *Epidemiology and Psychiatric Sciences*, *29*. https://doi.org/10.1017/s204579602000075x

Cubranic, D., Booth, K. S., & Collie, K. (1998). Computer support for Distance Art therapy. *CHI 98 Conference Summary on Human Factors in Computing Systems*. https://doi.org/10.1145/286498.286758

Darewych, O. H., Carlton, N. R., & Farrugie, K. W. (2015). Digital technology use in art therapy with adults with developmental disabilities. *Journal of Developmental Disabilities, 21*(2), 95.

Du, X., An, P., Leung, J., Li, A., Chapman, L. E., & Zhao, J. (2024). Deepthink: Designing and probing human-ai co-creation in Digital Art therapy. *International Journal of Human-Computer Studies*, *181*, 103139. https://doi.org/10.1016/j.ijhcs.2023.103139

He, Y., & Liu, D. (2023). Application of artificial intelligence on painting therapy, *Frontiers in Art Research, 5(11)*. https://doi.org/10.25236/far.2023.051103

Hu, J., Zhang, J., Hu, L., Yu, H., & Xu, J. (2021). Art therapy: A complementary treatment for mental disorders. *Frontiers in Psychology*, *12*. https://doi.org/10.3389/fpsyg.2021.686005

Joschko, R., Roll, S., Willich, S. N., & Berghöfer, A. (2022). The effect of active visual art therapy on health outcomes: Protocol of a systematic review of randomised controlled trials. *Systematic Reviews, 11*(1). https://doi.org/10.1186/s13643-022-01976-7

Loue, S. (2023). Expressive therapies: Music, art, and sandplay. *Encyclopedia of Mental Health, 866–876*. https://doi.org/10.1016/b978-0-323-91497-0.00044-8

Orr, P. (2012). Technology use in Art therapy practice: 2004 and 2011 comparison. *The Arts in Psychotherapy*, *39*(4), 234–238. https://doi.org/10.1016/j.aip.2012.03.010

Pénzes, I., Hooren, S. van, Dokter, D., & Hutschemaekers, G. (2018). How art therapists observe mental health using formal elements in art products: Structure and variation as indicators for balance and adaptability. *Frontiers in Psychology*, *9*. https://doi.org/10.3389/fpsyg.2018.01611

Potash, J. S., Kalmanowitz, D., Fung, I., Anand, S. A., & Miller, G. M. (2020). Art therapy in pandemics: Lessons for covid-19. *Art Therapy*, *37*(2), 105–107. https://doi.org/10.1080/07421656.2020.1754047

Priebe, S., Savill, M., Wykes, T., Bentall, R. P., Reininghaus, U., Lauber, C., Bremner, S., Eldridge, S., Röhricht, F. (2016). Effectiveness of group body psychotherapy for negative symptoms of schizophrenia: Multicentre randomised controlled trial, *British Journal of Psychiatry*, *209*(1), pp. 54–61. https://doi.org/10.1192/bjp.bp.115.171397

Zschucke, E., Gaudlitz, K., & Ströhle, A. (2013). Exercise and physical activity in mental disorders: Clinical and experimental evidence. *Journal of Preventive Medicine & Public Health, 46*(Suppl 1). https://doi.org/10.3961/jpmph.2013.46.s.s12

CLARIFYING DEFINITIONS: A SCOPING REVIEW OF DATA PHYSICALIZATION IN HUMAN-COMPUTER INTERACTION

Giorgia Burzio and Venere Ferraro
Department of Design - Politecnico di Milano
Via Durando 10, Milan, Italy

ABSTRACT

This paper presents a targeted reflection on the evolving research area of Data Physicalization (DP) within the Human-Computer Interaction (HCI) domain. In recent years substantial works have been done to define this relevant research area and to address its opportunities and challenges. Nonetheless, literature shows that there is not an unequivocal agreement on a definition of DP, with scholars proposing closely related areas that approach the "physicalization" of data in varied ways. This work aims to clarify the many definitions appearing in literature. Authors chose to perform a scoping review to select, compare, and classify DP definitions. The proposed map classifies the definitions progressively, according to the ways data is integrated into the physical system or object: data rendered, data encoded, and data embodied. Finally, this work suggests an extended definition for DP including the dimensions of embodiment and dynamicity, to be further supported by empirical validation and through user-centered design experimentations.

KEYWORDS

Data Physicalization, Human-Data Interaction, Embodied Interaction, Datafication

1. INTRODUCTION

Humans have created representations of data since at least 12,000 BC to make sense of their surroundings. Making data tangible allowed, for instance, to understand abstract concepts, exchange gifts, and take part in collective decisions (Huron et al., 2023). Today our environments are imbued with data, to an extent where scholars talk about data-driven society (Pentland, 2013). The mathematician Clive Humby compares the relevance of data today to oil during the Industrial Revolution. As oil, raw data need to be refined and shaped to generate value. This process relates to what scholars define as datafication, meaning:
"The process by which subjects, objects, and practices are transformed into digital data" (Southerton, 2019).

On this regard, the academic community vocally raised concerns on the ethical implications of the extrapolation of personal data, such as privacy issues and a gender bias approach to data (Kovacs, 2022). Scholars in the computer science domain propose the concept of Human-Data Interaction (HDI) to make the human dimension explicit in the data ecosystem (Mortier et al., 2014). In this scenario, the data-interaction design space is expanding, challenging current conventions of data as unusable numbers, while experimenting with interactive and sensorial materials embedding data, allowed by advancements in digital fabrication, programmable and shape-changing materials (Dumičić et al., 2022). Placed in the Human-Computer Interaction (HCI) domain, *data physicalization* is widely defined as

"a physical artifact whose geometry or material properties encode data" (Jansen et al., 2015).

DP shifts the interaction with data from a bi-dimensional modality to a three-dimensional one. While DP is strongly related to the concept of Tangible Interaction, here the outputs are enabled by digital data. Scholars highlight how DP can support communication, learning, decision-making, and sensemaking in various contexts (Dragicevic et al., 2020).

The definition above is widely considered the foundational one for DP. Yet literature brought to light several related labels and definitions. The scope of this work is to clarify whether scholars uniformly adhere to this definition or, instead, advocate for an extension or an entirely new interpretation. Authors classified and mapped definitions according to the ways data are "integrated" into the system and how the system "behaves" to the human. The following methodology section depicts how authors conducted the scoping review. The next section portrays a synthesis of the findings, and finally, a conclusion section proposes considerations and limitations.

2. METHODOLOGY

The authors first adopted an explorative approach to get an overview of the topic, both on grey and scientific literature. The software Research Rabbit has been enquired to find foundational papers. Among the collected sources, authors analysed foundational (Zhao & Vande Moere, 2008; Jansen et al., 2013) and relevant (Hogan & Hornecker, 2012; Jansen et al., 2015; Bae et al., 2022) records. The explorative approach allowed authors to extract main concepts and similar nomenclatures of DP, which were then used as keywords to conduct a scoping review over Scopus. The scoping review was chosen as it allows to clarify working definitions and conceptual boundaries of a topic (Peters et al., 2015).

2.1 Scoping Review

Authors enquired the software Scopus. Since the goal of the study was very concise, the search was accurately filtered to get a reasonable number of results. The keywords included in the search were *data physi** (* to include physicalization, physicalisation, physical, physicality), OR *data manifestation*, OR *data materialization*, OR *data object* AND *design* OR *HCI*, all to be in the title, abstract or authors keywords. The search was limited to the following subject areas: computer science, arts and humanities, engineering, and social science. From the results authors included only full articles and conference papers belonging to ACM, IEEE and MCCSIS conferences. A total of 96 records resulted, from 2012 to 2024.

The Scopus string was exported in CSV (Comma-separated values) and organized on an Excel sheet. A first screening process checked for duplicates, but there were none. Then authors proceeded with the screening phase, including, or excluding records according to their eligibility. The criteria of inclusion were the following:

1) The paper had to be pertinent to the research area of DP (clearly stated in the abstract).
2) The paper had to refer to one or more definitions, extend a consolidate one or propose a new one.

Each abstract was red, and 11 records were immediately excluded, because they were found not eligible due to criteria 1. The remaining records were entirely red and ultimately a total of 19 was found eligible and included both for criteria 1 and 2. The analysis of the included records was performed through an open coding, where all the definitions of DP were extracted and reported on the Excel sheet. Next, authors performed an axial coding, where they draw connections between the definitions and build categories (table 1). Ultimately, a selective coding process narrowed down to the relevant, essential data to answer the research question, from which derived the conceptual scheme depicted in the next section.

Table 1. Categories derived from analysing the literature

Data (category)	Data (sub-category)	Human
Data rendered	Rendered on a physical shape (by designers)	Maker/observer (cognitive use)
	Rendered through materials (by data/phenomena themselves)	Observer (contemplative use)
Data encoded	Encoded through shape and materials (by designers)	User (active, affective use)
Data embodied	Embodied to shape behaviours and interactions (by designers and final users)	User (proactive, affective, and behavioural use)

3. RESULTS

This section elaborates the results, structuring the findings according to three main categories that emerged from the literature analysis, and presents a conceptual scheme of definitions and related areas to DP (figure 1).

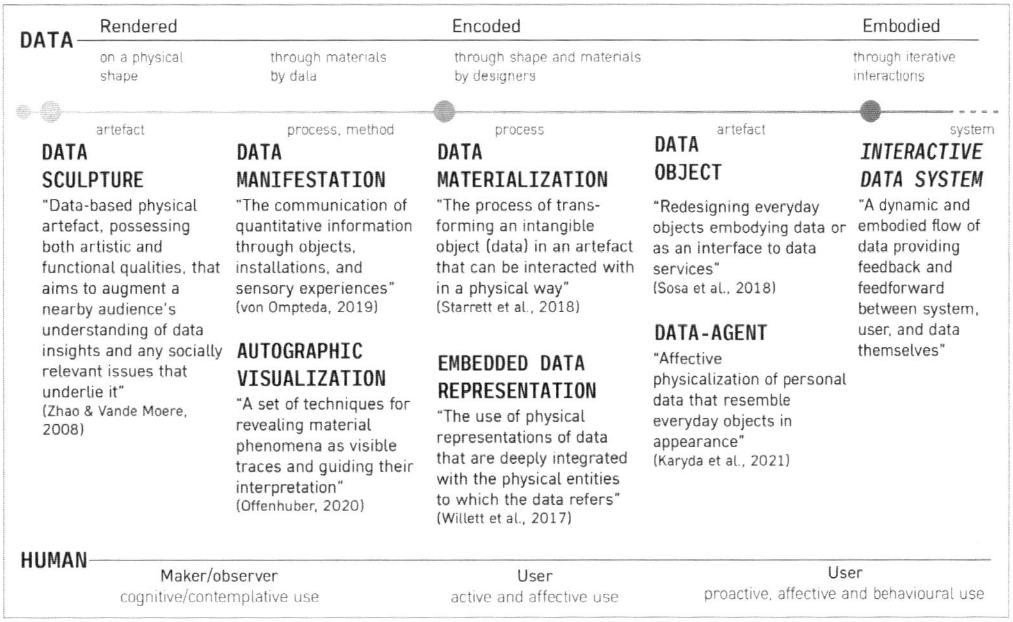

Figure 1. Definitions and related areas within DP are mapped according to how data is "integrated" in the object and how the object interacts with the human. Elaborated and produced by authors

3.1 Data Rendered

Most of the literature analysed cite the definition provided by Jansen et al. in 2015. Before that scholars already attempted to formalize a definition of "objects that physicalize data". Building from the rich foundation of information visualization, Zhao and Vande Moere defined *data sculpture* as data-based physical artefacts aiming at augment the audience understanding of datasets. Data sculpture could be effective to raise awareness over environmental phenomena and climate change events, since it moves numbers from a pixel-based representation to a tangible object acting as a metaphor for such numbers. An example is the data artwork Perpetual Plastic by Liina Klauss, Skye Morét and Moritz Stefaner, which investigates our global plastic waste stream and emphasizes how mismanaged waste ends up in the ocean. Data sculpture is considered a form of data physicalization, yet in this work authors intend it more as a passive visualization on a tangible object. Evolving from this concept, *data manifestation* (von Ompteda, 2019) and *autographic visualization* (Offenhuber, 2020) are defined respectively as a process and as a set of techniques, through which data manifest themselves onto a tangible object or material. These concepts are based on the premise that data is a material entity rather than an abstract representation (Offenhuber, 2020), inscribing material traces. These processes refer mostly to environmental data, such as sea level rise and air pollution: the project Solar Totems by Charles Sowers is an automated spherical lens system that use the sun to inscribe records of atmospheric conditions on a wood log. In this physicalization, data is not rendered by the designer, but it *inscribes* itself in real-time into the material.

3.2 Data Encoded

Here data are encoded in the shape of the object, shifting from a representational purpose of data towards the incorporation of data in the same structure of the object. *Data materialization* is defined as a process where datasets are transformed into physical objects that can be interacted with physically, such as furniture pieces and clothing (Starrett et al., 2018). This area is strongly connected to product design and digital fabrication tools since it transforms datasets in g-code for 3D printing objects to use and contemplate in daily life. While materialization interprets data encoding in the shape of the object, already in 2012 Hogan and Hornecker stated that data can be encoded not only in the shape but also in its behaviour. Scholars point out the importance of designing DP in relation to the context: this concept has been defined as *embedded data representation*, being the use of physical representations of data that are deeply integrated with the physical spaces, objects, and entities to which the data refers (Willett et al., 2017). Moreover, the concept of *data objects* and *data-agents* refers to the redesign of everyday, known objects encoding data, to foster an affective interaction between the users and personal data.

3.3 Data Embodied

Data objects and data-agents are not explicitly declaring whether the proposed DP is static or dynamic. Signer et al. already highlighted the potential limits of static DP by proposing a dynamic DP framework, useful as a starting point to envision design applications. Nonetheless, a proper extension of the DP definition which highlights the role of dynamic interaction is still missing. This work proposes the concept of embodiment to describe both the way data are "encoded" in the system and the types of interaction it enables. Embodiment is grounded in the phenomenological tradition, and it is often elaborated in tangible interfaces literature (Dourish, 2001). Embodied interactions leverage human skills in the interaction with technology, using bodily metaphors to engage with abstract concepts. Reasoning on this, authors propose an extension to the definition of DP as an *interactive data system*, where:

the interactive data system is defined as a dynamic and embodied flow of data providing feedback and feedforward between the system, the user, and the data themselves.

Embodiment within DP could enhance users' understanding and leverage affective experiences with data, as well as employing DP in other fields beyond HCI, such as education, data journalism and public exhibitions.

4. CONCLUSION, LIMITATIONS AND FURTHER DEVELOPMENT

The scoping review reveals a plethora of closely related areas to DP. This study maps such definitions from the concepts where data is "rendered", enabling a more passive engagement with data, to the concepts where data is encoded in the objects and the user has an active physical, cognitive and emotional role. Each definition highlight relevant aspects that lead to a comprehensive understanding of what DP are and could be. Considering this, authors identified a lack of focus on the dynamic interaction of such artefacts. Based on this ground, this paper proposes an extended definition integrating the dimensions of dynamicity of the system through embodiment. A limitation of this work concerns the narrow scope of the inquiry and the narrowed gaze toward the sole field of HCI. Further development of this work will verify the efficacy of the proposed extended definition through a deeper empirical validation, likewise through interviews, and/or through design experimentations aimed at crafting interactive data systems.

REFERENCES

Bae, S. S., Zheng, C., West, M. E., Do, E. Y. L., Huron, S., & Szafir, D. A. (2022, April). Making data tangible: A cross-disciplinary design space for data physicalization. In Proceedings of the 2022 CHI Conference on Human Factors in Computing Systems (pp. 1-18).

Dragicevic, P., Jansen, Y., & Vande Moere, A. (2020). Data physicalization. Handbook of human computer interaction, 1-51.

Dourish, P. (2001). Where the action is: the foundations of embodied interaction. MIT press.

Dumičić, Ž., Thoring, K., Klöckner, H. W., & Joost, G. (2022). Design elements in data physicalization: A systematic literature review.

Hogan, T., & Hornecker, E. (2012). How does representation modality affect user-experience of data artifacts?. In Haptic and Audio Interaction Design: 7th International Conference, HAID 2012, Lund, Sweden, August 23-24, 2012. Proceedings 7 (pp. 141-151). Springer Berlin Heidelberg.

Hornecker, E. (2005, September). A design theme for tangible interaction: embodied facilitation. In ECSCW 2005: Proceedings of the Ninth European Conference on Computer-Supported Cooperative Work, 18–22 September 2005, Paris, France (pp. 23-43). Dordrecht: Springer Netherlands.

Huron, S., Nagel, T., Oehlberg, L., & Willett, W. (Eds.). (2022). Making with Data: Physical Design and Craft in a Data-Driven World. CRC Press.

Jansen, Y., Dragicevic, P., Isenberg, P., Alexander, J., Karnik, A., Kildal, J., ... & Hornbæk, K. (2015, April). Opportunities and challenges for data physicalization. In proceedings of the 33rd annual acm conference on human factors in computing systems (pp. 3227-3236).

Jansen, Y., & Dragicevic, P. (2013). An interaction model for visualizations beyond the desktop. IEEE Transactions on Visualization and Computer Graphics, 19(12), 2396-2405.

Karyda, M., Mekler, E. D., & Lucero, A. (2021, May). Data agents: Promoting reflection through meaningful representations of personal data in everyday life. In Proceedings of the 2021 CHI Conference on Human Factors in Computing Systems (pp. 1-11).

Kovacs, A. (2022). Searching for a Room of One's Own in Cyberspace: Datafication and the Global Feminisation of Privacy. Emerging Trends in Data Governance. New Delhi: Centre for Communication Governance. Available at https://ccgdelhi.s3.ap-south-1.amazonaws.com/uploads/nlu-delhi-law-book-2022-ff-web-345.pdf.

Mortier, R., Haddadi, H., Henderson, T., McAuley, D., & Crowcroft, J. (2014). Human-data interaction: The human face of the data-driven society. arXiv preprint arXiv:1412.6159.

Offenhuber, D. (2019). Data by proxy—material traces as autographic visualizations. IEEE transactions on visualization and computer graphics, 26(1), 98-108.

Pentland, A. S. (2013). The data-driven society. Scientific American, 309(4), 78-83.

Peters, M. D., Godfrey, C. M., Khalil, H., McInerney, P., Parker, D., & Soares, C. B. (2015). Guidance for conducting systematic scoping reviews. JBI Evidence Implementation, 13(3), 141-146.

Signer, B., Ebrahimi, P., Curtin, T. J., & Abdullah, A. K. (2018, October). Towards a Framework for Dynamic Data Physicalisation. In *Proceedings of the International Workshop Toward a Design Language for Data Physicalization, Berlin, Germany*.

Southerton, C., Damkjaer, M. S., & Albrechtslund, A. (2019). Living Big Data: Datafication in everyday practices of participatory surveillance. In Big Data and the Power of Narrative.

Starrett, C., Reiser, S., & Pacio, T. (2018). Data materialization: a hybrid process of crafting a teapot. In ACM SIGGRAPH 2018 Art Gallery (pp. 381-385).

Sosa, R., Gerrard, V., Esparza, A., Torres, R., & Napper, R. (2018). Data objects: Design principles for data physicalisation. In International Design Conference 2018 (pp. 1685-1696). Faculty of Mechanical Engineering and Naval Architecture, Univ. of Zagreb.

von Ompteda, K. (2019, October). Data manifestation: merging the human world & global climate change. In 2019 IEEE VIS Arts Program (VISAP) (pp. 1-8). IEEE Computer Society.

Willett, W., Jansen, Y., & Dragicevic, P. (2016). Embedded data representations. IEEE transactions on visualization and computer graphics, 23(1), 461-470.

Zhao, J., & Vande Moere, A. (2008, September). Embodiment in data sculpture: a model of the physical visualization of information. In Proceedings of the 3rd international conference on Digital Interactive Media in Entertainment and Arts (pp. 343-350).

TRANSDISCIPLINARY FUTURES: ENHANCING GAME DESIGN AND INTERACTIVE MEDIA EDUCATION IN THE HIGHER EDUCATION LANDSCAPE

Bradley Young
Winthrop University
701 Oakland Ave, Rock Hill, SC 29733, USA

ABSTRACT

The purpose of this paper is to provide a conceptual framework to further stimulate and progress the ongoing discussion and innovation around the challenges and opportunities for educational programs in Game Design and Interactive/Immersive Media. As a reflective paper it provides a curated literature overview that illustrates key drivers in this conversation and thus highlights critical aspects of recent trends that have emerged. It then situates this within the curriculum contexts and realities that presently exists within the higher education (HE) sector specifically outlining mechanisms and approaches that can be infused/adopted to enhance the quality of the learning experience and graduate outcomes in the field and allied professions. Effectively addressing these issues further provides much added value to new proposals and evolving programs in Game Design. Indeed, when examining available data it could reasonably be theorized that interdisciplinary programs in Game Design and Interactive Media could become a ubiquitous feature of the higher and continuing education landscape not dissimilar to the rise of other major fields of endeavor in recent decades.

KEYWORDS

Game Design Education, Interdisciplinary, Transdisciplinary, Ludification

1. INTRODUCTION

"Play is the highest expression of human development in childhood for it alone is the free expression of what is in a child's soul." (Fröbel, 1899)

We have indeed come a long way since Neumann and Morgenstern (1944) published the "Theory of Games and Economic Behavior". By the end of the 20th century Game/Play Theory or Gamification and Edutainment in its myriad of forms had also significantly grown in popularity. Today, Esports has taken off exponentially. The multifaceted manner in which gaming has been and can be effectively applied to the field of education, as well as many others, is becoming an increasingly popular feature in the learning environment that shows no sign of slowing (Anastasiadis et al., 2018, Dichev and Dicheva, 2017, Miglino et al., 2011, Tori et al., 2022, Videnovik et al., 2023, Zhang and Shang, 2015). Notably, just the global gaming market size alone is a key driver that is expected to grow from USD 245.9 Billion 2022 - USD 682 Billion 2030 with a compound annual growth rate of 13.6% - 2023-2030 (Hancock, 2023). More generally creative workers are employed in sectors outside the creative industries often in greater numbers than within the creative field (Hearn et al., 2014). This often goes hidden and routinely overlooked by government statistics and it is not readily captured.

The general trend away from traditional public funding to a model more aligned with a private market-led one or other policy driven financial changes has resulted in increased competition within HE peer groups (Pietsch, 2020, Sengupta and Rossi, 2023). With the exception of China and parts of Asia the last two decades has seen significant changes in the mechanisms for funding allocation in HE (Sengupta and Rossi, 2023).This being the case emerging trends and opportunities around gaming do not escape an institutions radar. The exponential growth in popularity of gaming at HE institutions has been further fueled by technological advances (thanks to Moore's Law) that was a catalyst for increasingly interactive and immersive media experiences. This also encouraged further investment and program development in HE. With better communications technologies and the rise of flexible, blended, and online learning modes additional enhancements and opportunities were quickly adopted by institutions globally in an attempt to increase market share. Educational offerings in interactive multimedia and game design to date have usually either been siloed within a department or a partnership across two or more, with varying degrees of success. The author after conducting a cross-sectional search found that while espoused there was nevertheless limited treatment of the efficacy of interdisciplinary programs in game design.

2. BODY OF PAPER

Interactive media and game design programs in Australia, the United Arab Emirates, and the USA that the author has had direct experience with have been examined over 25 years and can provide some qualitative insights that aligns with assertions of the utility of interdisciplinary programs in enhancing student achievement on institutional learning outcomes. While not under controlled conditions, for example, an interdisciplinary program in Multimedia Design at Zayed University in the United Arab Emirates consistently evidenced students scores on institutional learning outcomes in teamwork, critical thinking, and technological literacy notably higher than institutional averages. It would be of value to determine the reason for this and whether it was due to some characteristic inherent in the students who chose the program, the interdisciplinary nature of the program, or some other factor(s).

In addition to the large body of literature on the expression of learning outcomes assessment and the evidence and processes utilized in their assessment Repko (2021) has made additional notable contributions in the development of learning outcomes for interdisciplinary studies (Repko and Szostak, 2021). Interdisciplinary programs in Game Design would naturally need the development of similarly focused learning outcomes. This would require additional development if considering a transdisciplinary approach, this being the border crossing between different knowledge domains and communities of practice (van Baalen et al., 2021). Indeed, van Baalen, Groot, and Noordegraaf-Eelens (2021) further cite the importance of the Arts as being a key enabler and citing Nicolescu's (2018) call for the reconciliation between the arts and science being critical to realize a new transdisciplinary culture. The embryonic form of this can be seen in trends such as Arts Integration, Arts-Based Methods, and STEAM education (van Baalen et al., 2021) that aligns very nicely with the area of Game Design. More specifically, the artefacts generated through such a transdisciplinary approach would likely provide rich research opportunities.

"...the diversity of the game studies discipline, [is] characterized by its multidisciplinary and dynamic nature. It also suggests a potential shift towards design orientation in game studies, emphasizing the instrumental utilization of game research through designed artefacts." (Annakaisa, 2015)

Keogh and Hardwick (2023) identified 30% of Australian HE institutions (119 programs) that teach Game Design in some capacity. These programs either included at least one of the terms game, interactivity, interactive media, or play in the program or major title or explicitly reference game development as a potential career outcome for graduates (Keogh and Hardwick, 2023). In this study they acknowledged the broad range of technical and creative skills required and the variance between disciplinary contexts that resulted in terms of "ideologies, cultures, skills, and graduate imaginaries that students are recruited into" (Keogh and Hardwick, 2023). Furthermore, these authors identified the epistemological tension between technical and creative skill sets illustrating that while the programs surveyed espoused technical and creative components, they were nevertheless positioned institutionally within either a technical or creative domain. One particularly noteworthy finding from this study however was that when housed in an Arts/Design based College the teaching of game development from a design perspective showed indications of being a potentially more inclusive pathway based on the enrollment trends observed.

2.1 Challenges

While some writers have describe the proliferation of the industry as a sign of a saturated market and for some frustration with financial realities in the industry (Wright, 2018, Zhang and Shang, 2015) others take a more dynamic view of the current situation. There is a transformation occurring according to Poell, Nieborg, and Duffy (2022) as a result of the "platformization across the cultural industries" that have impacted markets, infrastructure and governance (Poell et al., 2022). These authors assert that platformization provide "economic and material affordances to develop, disseminate, market, and/or monetize cultural content" pp 52.

Rapid technological advancements make remaining current and industry relevance for educational programs a constant challenge and so finding mechanisms that support this real cost is critical for the programs credibility and sustainability. Game design also involves various disciplines such as programming, art, storytelling, sound design, inter alia. and as indicated earlier a focus beyond merely an interdisciplinary delivery but with a move towards transdiscipinarity will likely yield a more effective program. Integrating rich and diverse fields into a cohesive curriculum while ensuring depth in each area can be complex. As game design education requires a balance between theoretical knowledge and practical skills finding the right balance to equip students with both conceptual understanding and hands-on applied experience is important. This balance can be even more challenging when there are multiple colleges/domains involved each with their own accreditation requirements along with institutional and/or government accreditation regimes requiring accommodation. Limited resource challenges often need to be addressed and in addition to questions of funding often discussions around faculty expertise, access to technology, student recruitment and retention along with other environmental factors take place. Constraints can have a deleterious impact on the effective development and delivery of comprehensive game design programs if not effectively mitigated.

2.2 Opportunities

Expanding beyond notions of gamification as a tool towards a curriculum that truly embraces a "Ludification of Culture" (Dippel and Fizek, 2016) provides a mechanism in developing curriculum in Game Design that has the potential to enhance student engagement, further enrich diverse and inclusive practices, and facilitate a pathway to more global educational opportunities. In this regard the opportunities are limitless, which could also be viewed as a very applied way to approach the placement of the learner at the center of the learning experience (Keogh, 2022).

Kerr (2021) stated that "while contemporary discourses and industry data seem to support the democratization of games production, contemporary software for game development and available learning spaces impose restrictions that continue to marginalize and impose a technicity that is gendered, classed, and raced." Harvey (2022) claims that while Games programs are assumed to be an avenue for diverse talent they have not been systematically examined in terms of the learning environment, in particular "how these environments require marginalized people to develop strategies for coping with exclusionary norms to 'stay in'" (Harvey, 2022). In 2019 he also noted that by addressing tensions that exist between team-based collaboration and individual competition could provide an avenue for intervention in terms of diversity and inclusivity (Harvey, 2019). Kennedy (2018) provided two case studies that gave insight into the challenges of diversifying games, game design/development, and the gaming culture more broadly. However in contrast to this, Penney et.al. (2020) has described that the "de-formalising" of games has increased access to the means to create digital interactive experiences and that these producers "are leaders in the discourses of gender diversity, non-binary representation and support for neurodiversity, despite perceptions of the field being to the contrary." This cultural shift has, according to Oakley (2014), opened doors to more inclusive opportunities. Encouraging diversity and inclusion in game design programs is essential for fostering creativity and representing diverse perspectives. Keogh (2022) endeavors to politicize the notion of agency in digital play and views this through the process of craft arguing that the "videogame maker" is a cultural producer. Oakley (2014) examined cultural entrepreneurship particularly with the increasing availability of digital technology coupled with small business support and the destabilization in the employment model (Oakley, 2014). McRobbie (2016) supports this notion, examining how the creative economy can be a model for labor reform (McRobbie, 2016). Videnovik (2024) identified 5 strategies for advancing inclusivity and thereby developing new markets: Diverse and Inclusive Development Teams; Intersectionality in Storytelling; Accessibility Features; Collaboration with Marginalized Communities; and Inclusive Marketing and Promotion.

One opportunity that institutions are increasingly looking towards is fostering industry linkages and partnerships, particularly with game development studios, hardware/software companies, and other industry professionals to provide the much need opportunities for students to gain applied experience, access up to date resources, and stay current with industry practices. This has also been leveraged in some institutions through focusing on undergraduate research initiatives, exploring grant and other novel financial opportunities to fund research to support the many needed resources required to support an effective and relevant game design program. Micro-credentialing, digital badges, and industry qualifications have also emerged as a feature in HE programs in Game Design in this regard.

2.3 Institutional Considerations

When attempting to design and develop systems and processes required to support some of the opportunities, curriculum planners are often immediately confronted with real structural realities and embedded practices that significantly augment the challenges in realizing a successful implementation. For many, these are so embedded and if not insurmountable are not easily circumvented. Therefore, the time and effort required to engage with these challenges, especially with limited or no scope for success, is in itself a key disincentive for many Faculty and Administrators. Innovative curriculum models can also be challenging not just for Faculty but for many support areas of an institution. An example of this would be dealing with entrepreneurial activities within a program that would require the finance area to adapt or develop new processes to support. Another is gaining Faculty buy-in to a truly transdisciplinary program when the funding model structurally favors the maintenance of academic silos. This would also require structural mechanisms to foster an equal partnership in practice, as described by Binder et al (2015) "Truly lived co-leadership and trust."

Creative industries and programs such as Game Design provide a venue for innovative expression that pushes boundaries and takes us to new places. This can be more easily accomplished when students feel comfortable and part of a community of practice and have a sense of academic home. Student clubs provide an important bridge between the curriculum and applied professional experience along with being a valuable vehicle for social experiences and development that reinforce a sense of self, purpose, and agency (Young, 2003). In addition to student clubs, establishing professional association chapters can provide a strong external link back into the local and international communities of practice. Strong alumni connections also provide a necessary academic belonging for students, particularly in interdisciplinary programs that perhaps are spread across multiple colleges in an institution. Additionally advising plays a role in supporting this sense. The physical spaces also influence this and so it could necessitate revisiting notions of spaces like computer labs and perhaps consider a shift to project/studio spaces that mirror more realistic work environments while at the same time still balancing the need for integrity of the hardware and software ecosystems and network infrastructure.

It is the authors belief that Interactive Media and Game Design programs go largely untapped in terms of design/development capacity for institutional and local/international projects. The reason for this is often due to the fact that this requires a coordinated approach and management overhead not dissimilar to the work involved in creating a realistic simulation experience for students to enhance their learning or having students work on a game design project as part of an international team. As with many new initiatives there is inherent a time commitment and management overhead that cannot be just overlooked or absorbed. So that practices are sustainable there should be inbuilt inducements that are systemic in nature, whether these be mechanisms like consultancy accounts for faculty, profit sharing structures for students, or any one of many vehicles that support entrepreneurial activities of faculty and students. These can provide valuable extrinsic inducements to further foster motivation, engagement, and success.

3. CONCLUSION

This paper has outlined a framework for developing interdisciplinary academic programs in game design and interactive media, advocating for a transdisciplinary approach enriched by ludification and community engagement. It posits that such programs not only offer a robust educational model but also contribute significantly to global education and research paradigms. Acknowledging the challenges in this evolving field, the potential for transformative change is underscored, suggesting these programs can substantially support institutional missions and visions for the future. Future research should explore the implementation of these strategies and their impact on educational outcomes and industry readiness.

REFERENCES

Anastasiadis, T. et al. (2018). Digital Game-based Learning and Serious Games in Education. *International Journal of Advances in Scientific Research and Engineering,* Vol. 4, No. 12, pp. 139-144.

Annakaisa, K. Game Design Research. Academic Mindtrek 2015, 2015 Tampere, Finland. Association for Computing Machinery, 18-25.

Binder, C. et al. (2015). The reality of transdisciplinarity: a framework-based self-reflection from science and practice leaders. *Sustainability Science,* Vol. 10, pp. 545–562.

Dichev, C. & Dicheva, D. (2017). Gamifying education: what is known, what is believed and what remains uncertain: a critical review. *International Journal of Educational Technology in Higher Education,* Vol. 14, No. 1, pp. 9.

Dippel, A. & Fizek, S. (2016). Ludification of Culture. The significance of play and games in everyday practices of the digital era. *In:* KOCH, G. (ed.) *Digitalisation, Theories and Concepts for the Empirical Cultural Analysis.* New York: Routledge. pp. 276-292.

FröBel, F. (1899). *Education by Development*, Arnold.

Hancock, A. (2023). *Global Gaming Market Size, Share & Trends Analysis Report by 2030* [Online]. Available: https://www.linkedin.com/pulse/global-gaming-market-size-share-trends-analysis-report-ashley-hancock-dbi3f#:~:text=Market%20Research&text=The%20Global%20Gaming%20Market%20is,13.6%25%20between%2020 23%20and%202030. [Accessed 24 February 2024].

Harvey, A. (2019). Becoming gamesworkers: Diversity, higher education, and the future of the game industry. *Television & New Media,* Vol. 20, No. 8, pp. 756-766.

Harvey, A. (2022). Making the grade: Feminine lack, inclusion, and coping strategies in digital games higher education. *New Media & Society,* Vol. 24, No. 9, pp. 1986-2002.

Hearn, G. et al, (2014). *Creative work beyond the creative industries*, Edward Elgar Publishing.

Kennedy, H. (2018). Game jam as feminist methodology: The affective labors of intervention in the ludic economy. Games and Culture. Vol. 13, No. 7, pp. 708-727.

Keogh, B. (2022). Situating the videogame maker's agency through craft. *The International Journal of Research into New Media Technologies,* Vol. 28, No. 2, pp. 374-388.

Keogh, B. & Hardwick, T. (2023). Creative, Technical, Entrepreneurial: Formative Tensions in Game Development Higher Education. *Games and Culture,* Vol. 0, No. 0, pp. 1-21.

Mcrobbie, A. (2016). *Be creative: Making a living in the new culture industries*, Polity Press.

Miglino, O. et al. (2011). *Role-Games, Computer Simulations, Robots And Augmented Reality As New Learning Technologies: A Guide For Teacher Educators And Trainers.*

Oakley, K. (2014). Good work? Rethinking cultural entrepreneurship. *In:* BILTON, C. & CUMMINGS, S. (eds.) *Handbook of management and creativity.* Edward Elgar.pp. 145–159.

Penney, T. et al. (2020). The resilience of game design education. Proceedings of the 2020 Australian Council of Art and Design Conference, 2020 Sydney. Australian Council of Art and Design Conference, 1-21.

Pietsch, T. (2020). A history of university income in the United Kingdom and Australia, 1922–2017. *History of Education Review,* Vol. 49, No. 2, pp. 229-248.

Poell, T. et al. (2022). *Platforms and cultural production*, Polity Press.

Repko, A. F. & Szostak, R. (2021). *Interdisciplinary research : process and theory,* Los Angeles, SAGE.

Sengupta, A. & Rossi, F. (2023). The relationship between universities' funding portfolios and their knowledge exchange profiles: A dynamic capabilities view. *Technovation,* Vol. 121, No. C, pp. 1.

Tori, A. et al. (2022). Serious Game Design in Health Education: A Systematic Review. *IEEE Transactions on Learning Technologies,* Vol. 4, No. 12, pp. 1-21.

Van Baalen, W. et al. (2021). Higher education, the arts, and transdisciplinarity: A systematic review of the literature. *Research in Education,* Vol. 111, No. 1, pp. 24-45.

Videnovik, M. (2024). Promoting Diversity in Video Game Design: Empowering underrepresented voices. Available from: https://moldstud.com/articles/p-promoting-diversity-in-video-game-design-empowering-underrepresented-voices [Accessed 1 Feb 2024].

Videnovik, M. et al. (2023). Game-based learning in computer science education: a scoping literature review. *International Journal of STEM Education,* Vol. 10, No. 54, pp. 23.

Von Neumann, J. & Morgenstern, O. 1944. *Theory of games and economic behavior,* Princeton,, Princeton university press.

Wright, S. (2018). *There are too many video games. Now what?* [Online]. Available: https://www.polygon.com/2018/9/28/17911372/there-are-too-many-video-games-what-now-indiepocalypse [Accessed 25 February 2024].

Young, B. (2003). Published. ZURadio – an example of a student club Initiative and its Impact at Zayed University. The 2nd Europe, Middle East, Africa, ThinkPad University Fly-In, 2003 of Conference Dubai Womens College, Dubai, UAE.

Zhang, L. & Shang, J. (2015). How Video Games Enhance Learning: A Discussion of James Paul Gee's Views in His Book What Video Games Have to Teach Us About Learning and Literacy. Vol. 0, No. 0, pp. 404-411.

ACHIEVING MOTIVATION-PSYCHOLOGICAL IMMERSION IN TECHNOLOGY-ASSISTED LEARNING, CONSIDERING EMOTIONAL STATES

Ehm Kannegieser[1] and Robert Külpmann[2]
[1]*Fraunhofer Institute of Optronics, System Technologies and Image Exploitation*
Fraunhoferstraße. 1, 76131, Karlsruhe, Germany
[2]*Karlsruhe Institute of Technology*
Kaiserstraße. 12, 76131, Karlsruhe, Germany

ABSTRACT

Learning activities are often perceived by many as a work task. To counter this perception, concepts such as Gamification and Game-Based-Learning have been introduced, to make learning activities more enjoyable. Deep Focus States, like Immersion and Flow, describe situations in which learners are highly concentrated and blot out the work aspect of the activity. In this context the presented study concept tries to to gain information about the correlation between reaching a Deep Focus State and the learner's current Emotional State. The paper focuses on the question of whether high Arousal/Valence values result in Deep Focus States or not. To explore this question a possible study will be presented, which includes the evaluation of Arousal/Valence Models, Flow and Immersion. In order to extend the applicability of this method, a concept of a minimal experimental setup will be envisioned where data regarding the emotional connection in different game genres should be recorded.

KEYWORDS

Learning, Flow, Arousal, Valence, Emotion

1. INTRODUCTION

The problem this research paper will tackle is based in the research field of Learning Application and Serious Games. The envisioned approach should help to measure and maximize the success of participants of learning activities. To achieve this goal it is desirable that a learner reaches a Deep Focus State, like the Flow State, where they are *learning by gaming* (Cheng et al., 2015) and therefore get a more enjoyable and productive experience because of a higher intrinsic motivation (Shiefele, 2001).

This research tries to gain knowledge about the question, how Deep Focus States can be measured more objectively, by investigate the hypothesis if Flow and Immersion are linked to the emotional state of a learner. Previous works in this field have been conducted (Kannegieser et al.. 2019; Kannegieser et al., 2021), exploring the connection between Flow and Arousal/Valence. A similar approach in a gaming scenario has been presented by Reuderink (Reuderink et al., 2013) using Self-Assessment Manikins developed by Bradley and Lang (Bradley & Lang, 1994).

The main object of this work is to explore possible a correlation between high Arousal/Valence values and a deepening of the Flow State. Additionally a concept for an experiment procedure should be discussed which could be useful to collect more data regarding Arousal and Valence in the future.

2. STUDY CONCEPT

2.1 Related Works

2.1.1 Flow

In 1975, the psychologist Csikzentmihalyi dealt with the phenomenon, that painters could immerse themselves deeply into their work, neglecting to meet basic needs. He called this phenomenon the Flow State. To reach this Flow State he defined several conditions. Those include claims, that the task should be tailored to the skills of the individual and direct feedback for the subject regarding their progress. For the Flow State itself Csikszentmihalyi defined characteristica, based on prior observations (Nakamura & Csikszentmihalyi, 2009). Foremost he observed an intensive focus on the task at hand. The participants were absorbed in the activity accompanied by a loss of external perception, sense of time and the inability to access a social situation accordingly. On the other hand, the participants felt able to cope with the task and found the work itself rewarding. For measuring the flow state several different questionnaires have been developed, for example by Ijsselsteijn, Poels and de Kort (Ijsselsteijn et al., 2013).

2.1.2 Immersion

There are various definitions and considerations of immersion, most of which stem from the gaming context. Coomans and Timmermann described Immersion as a feeling to immersively interact with a virtual world, as if she would be real (Coomans & Timmermann, 1997). Instead Brown and Cairns (Brown & Cairns, 2004) tried to find out, in which extend players saw themselves involved in the game, to make immersion tangible. To classify immersion, they set up three stages: Engagement, Engrossment and Total Immersion. This model was later extended by Cheng (Cheng et al., 2015). Works by Kannegieser (Kannegieser et al., 2021), discuss a model combining Flow, Immersion and Arousal/Valence, by carrying out experiments similar to studies done by Reuderink (Reuderink et al., 2013), were able to show a connection between Immersion and Flow.

2.1.3 Arousal, Valence and Dominance

To determine the Emotional State of a subject, Shu compiled a detailed list of different measurement methods (Shu et al., 2018). One multidimensional model is the Arousal/Valence Model which was derived from the Valence/Arousal/Dominance Model (VAD) based on theories by Wundt (Wundt, 1897) and Schlosberg (Schlosberg, 1954). In this model valence describes a person's emotional state, while Arousal represents their physiological activity level. For measuring Valence, Arousal and Dominance, Bradley and Lang developed a questionnaire with *Self-Assessment Manikins(SAM)* (Bradley & Lang, 1994). This model has been used in a modified version by Reuderink (Reuderink et al., 2013), to get a sense of Arousal and Valence in a gaming scenario. A version of the SAMs suitable for digital questionnaires the *Affective Slider* was developed by Batella and Verschure in 2015 (Batella & Verschure, 2015).

2.2 Methodology

The chosen approach is based on the proposed model of Arousal/Valence presented by Kannegieser (Kannegieser et. al. 2021) and a modification of their experiment concept, leaving out the gain of physiological data, to make the experiment more accessible and reduce technical hazards. As in the aforementioned study, Intensity could be used as a comprehensive alternative representation of Arousal. As Deep Focus States Flow and Immersion should be considered and compared to the Arousal/Valence Model. It is planned to use different Likert Scales (Likert, 1932) as well as *Self-Assessment Manikins* (Bradly & Lang, 1994), in these questionnaires to elicit results regarding Arousal, Valence or Intensity, Flow and Immersion. As in the study by Reuderink (Reuderink et al., 2013) the dominance part of the original VAD Model should be omitted, assuming the participants are capable of successfully completing the given task. The results should be compared at the end and analyzed regarding the question, whether there is a connection between the Emotional State of the Player and Immersion or not.

2.3 Experiment Procedure

In order to gain insights into arousal, valence, flow and immersion, the following experiment is envisioned:

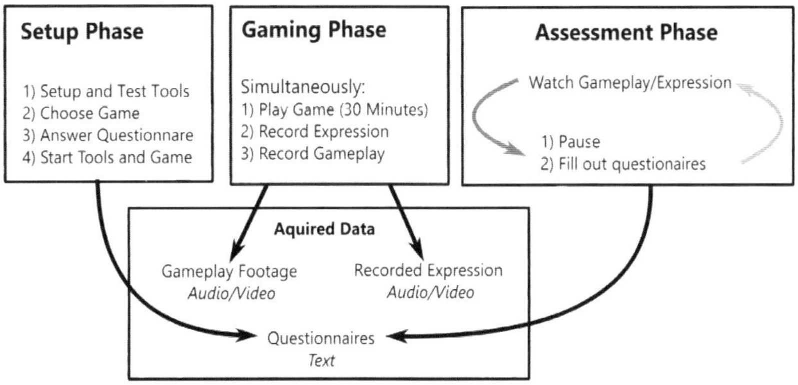

Figure 1. Phases of the Experiment and Acquired Data

At the beginning of the experiment the participant should be asked to choose one of a pre-selected pool of games. Afterwards a questionnaire should be filled out, to divide them into groups regarding their gaming experience and familiarity with the selected game or genre. The level of familiarity with the game might influence the outcome of the Arousal or Valence criteria. The selection of games should be the same for every experiment conducted and should include games from different genres, like action or story based games. One assumption is that different game genre will yield a different depth of immersion and a different emotional connection between participant and game, which might lead to different Arousal Levels. Other criteria for the game selection should be the length of one playthrough, Players/Cameras perspective, control mechanism and availability. In order to guarantee reusability, popular but freely accessible games should be used. A questionnaire regarding previous gaming experience should be filled out, including genre distinctions (compare: Green & Bavelier, 2022; Bediou et al., 2023).

After the participant chose the game and filled out the questionnaire, they should play the game for at least 30 minutes. Such a long period is important to improve chances for the participant to reach a state of Deep Focus. At the end the participants should watch their recorded video footage. While watching they should fill out the Immersion Questionnaire (Cheng et al., 2015) and the Flow Short Scale questionnaire (Rheinberg et al., 2003). To assess Arousal and Intensity the *Self-Assessment Manikins* (Bradley and Lang, 1994) as well as the *Affective Slider* (Batella & Verschure, 2015) should be used. Since creating a large data set difficult task in this field, it is planned to make the experiment as accessible as possible. For this purpose the experimental setup should fit on one laptop, including the necessary tools, for recording, video playback, the selected games, as well as interactive questionnaires. Using a minimal setup and making it portable should help to attract a broader audience and create a larger data set in the long run. To minimize the technical and human related risks, the concept still envisages a supervisor looking over the procedure.

3. CONCLUSION

The presented concept should be useful to measure Arousal/Valance values and determine if a high Arousal/Valence values are related to Deep Focus States or not. By choosing a pool of games, certain criteria and an expected player acceptance should be reached and lead to better comparability and an easier reproduction of the study. The simple setup of the experiment and the possibility to conduct it online, should help to reach broader audience. Using a virtual machine in this context should also reduce factors which would make the experiment unusable. Having a researcher observe the experiment will ensure the correct proceedings. If participants do not reach a Deep Focus State the experiment might fail. Outside factors may also interfere and invalidate the experiment. The questionnaires will be filled out with a delay in time, responses of the test persons might not be accurate or incomplete, because they have to answer from memory and no spontaneous tests are provided. Even though the experiment is envisioned to address a broad audience, the sample size of a particular game might be too low.

The envisioned experiment processes should be helpful to determine whereas higher Intensity of an Arousal State results in high Immersion. Insight into the question, if such a correlation exists or not, should be useful for measuring Arousal/Valence in a learning or gaming environment.

REFERENCES

Bediou, B., et al, 2023. Effects of Action Video Game Play on Cognitive Skills: A Meta-Analysis. *Technology, Mind, and Behavior, 4.* https://doi.org/10.1037/TMB0000102

Betella A, Verschure PFMJ 2016. The Affective Slider: A Digital Self-Assessment Scale for the Measurement of Human Emotions. *PLoS ONE 11(2): e0148037.* https://doi.org/10.1371/journal.pone.0148037

Brown, E. and Cairns, P. 2004. A grounded investigation of game immersion. *CHI'04 Extended Abstracts on Human Factors in Computing Systems*, pp. 1297–1300.

Cairns, P. et al. 2006. Quantifying the experience of immersion in games. *Cognitive Science of Games and Gameplay Workshop at Cognitive Science 2006, 7.* http://discovery.ucl.ac.uk/149051/

Cheng, M. T., et al. 2015. Game immersion experience: Its hierarchical structure and impact on game-based science learning. *Journal of Computer Assisted Learning, 31*(3), pp. 232–253. https://doi.org/10.1111/jcal.12066

Coomans, M.K.D., & Timmermanns, H.J.P. (1997). *Towards a Taxonomy of Virtual reality user interfaces.* International conference on information visualisation.

Csikszentmihalyi, M. 1975. *Beyond Boredom and Anxiety. The Experience of Play in Work and Games.*

Csikszentmihalyi, M. 2014. Flow and the Foundations of Positive Psychology. In *Flow and the Foundations of Positive Psychology.* https://doi.org/10.1007/978-94-017-9088-8

Green, C., Bavelier, D. 2022. *Video Game Questionnaire.*

IJsselsteijn, W. A., et al. 2013. *The Game Experience Questionnaire. 2013.*

Kannegieser, E., et al. 2019. Surveying Games With a Combined Model of Immersion and Flow. *In K. Blashki & P. Isaías (Eds.), Handbook of Research on Human-Computer Interfaces and New Modes of Interactivity,* pp. 59-70. https://doi.org/10.4018/978-1-5225-9069-9.ch004

Kannegieser, E., et. al. 2021. Measuring Flow, Immersion and Arousal/Valence for Application in Adaptive Learning Systems. *Lecture Notes in Computer Science (Including Subseries Lecture Notes in Artificial Intelligence and Lecture Notes in Bioinformatics), 12793 LNCS*, pp. 62–78. https://doi.org/10.1007/978-3-030-77873-6_5

Likert, R. 1932. A technique for the measurement of attitudes. *In: Archives of Psychology*, 22, 140. p. 55.

Nakamura, J., & Csikszentmihalyi, M. 2009. Flow Theory and Research. *In C. R. Snyder, & S. J. Lopez (Eds.), Oxford Handbook of Positive Psychology,* pp. 195-206. https://doi.org/10.1093/oxfordhb/9780195187243.013.0018

Pavlas, D. 2010. A Model of Flow and Play in Game-based Learning: The Impact of Game Characteristics, Player Traits, and Player States. *PhD Thesis*, 201. http://www.navistudios.net/Pavlas_Davin_A_201012_PhD.pdf

Reuderink, B., et al. 2013. Valence, arousal and dominance in the EEG during game play. *International Journal of Autonomous and Adaptive Communications Systems*, *6*(1), 45–62. https://doi.org/10.1504/IJAACS.2013.050691

Rheinberg, F., et al. 2003. *Die Erfassung des Flow-Erlebens.* https://doi.org/10.23668/psycharchives.8590

Schiefele, U. 2001. The role of interest in motivation and learning. *In J. M. Collis & S. Messick (Eds.), Intelligence and personality: Bridging the gap in theory and measurement*, pp. 163–194.

Schlosberg, H. 1941. A scale for the judgment of facial expressions. *Journal of Experimental Psychology,* *29*(6), pp. 497–510.

Schlosberg, H. 1954. Three dimensions of emotion. *Psychological Review, 61*(2), 81–88.

Shu, L., et al. 2018. A review of emotion recognition using physiological signals. *Sensors (Switzerland)*, *18*(7). https://doi.org/10.3390/s18072074

DEVELOPMENT OF A COMPETENCE MEASUREMENT TOOL WITHIN A CUSTOMIZABLE GAMIFICATION ENVIRONMENT

Manuela Sachse, Christoph Laroque and Lisa Strauch
Westsächsische Hochschule Zwickau, Germany

ABSTRACT

Gamification offers considerable potential in the context of HR marketing, especially for increasing employer attractiveness as part of employer branding or for supporting recruitment, skills assessment, training and team building measures in human resource management.

The aim of the research presented here is to develop a multi-user gaming platform that can be used to measure the professional, cognitive, and psychological-social skills of employees as well as the image-driving denotative and connotative characteristics of an employer brand. For this purpose, the diagnostics of the corresponding behavioral target variables must be developed as a pre-, in- and post-game analysis.

KEYWORDS

Gamification, Employer Branding, Employer Attractiveness, Recruiting, Team Building, Competence Measurement

1. OPPORTUNITIES OF GAMIFICATION AND ESPORTS FOR HR AND MARKETING

The clever integration of gamification elements in HR Marketing processes can represent an opportunity to recruit and retain specially qualified employees. A positive working environment can be created and employee motivation, commitment and development can be promoted.

In the context of digital transformation, young professionals with specific gaming experience fulfill many job profiles, for example in terms of IT skills, programming knowledge and general digital skills. Gamification engages professionals in their daily lives, can improve work culture, increases employee motivation and boosts overall productivity. The implementation of playful methods and elements in the areas of recruitment, onboarding, training and employer branding offers an opportunity to reach young target groups and solve the problem of unsuccessful recruitment of young professionals. The use of gamification has proven to be an effective tool in the recruitment process, in communicating company values to (potential) candidates or existing employees, as part of team building and retention activities, and in employer branding (Abuladze & Hasimi, 2023).

Companies can use gamification to create an engaging and interactive working environment that meets the growing preference of young employees for digital processes and gaming environments (Brademann & Piorr, 2019). Conventional games from major publishers can already be used for team-building measures. However, customized gamification solutions are needed that, depending on the area of application, either enable a comprehensive and detailed analysis of the skills of applicants or employees and thus support the assessment center or training process, or measure the image characteristics of the company among potential employees after contact with the game environment. The sociological-psychological results can be used to gain insights into the design of recruitment processes, which have traditionally been content-oriented. Employer branding strategies can also be monitored.

2. WORK IN PROGRESS REPORT

The goal of the research is to develop a multi-user gaming environment in which behavioral diagnostics can be used as competency assessment tool, training- or team-building tool. So far, "serious gaming" has been used to impart knowledge and skills in a playful and entertaining way. Initial meta-analyses of various recruitment procedures suggest a more effective use of gamification in the sense due to the weaknesses of static procedures (Sackett et al. 2022). The development of an individually configured gaming environment offers the opportunity for new forms of assessment centers, innovative (further) training formats, more efficient design of onboarding processes and new ways of measuring employee identification in the context of employer branding.

The focus of the research is on the interaction between the development and technical implementation of a multi-user game environment with data interfaces that can be used to measure behavioral science-oriented, i.e. cognitive and psychological-social skills of employees as well as image-driving denotative and connotative characteristics of an employer brand. The diagnostics of the corresponding behavioral science target variables are currently being determined using an experimental design. The development of the behavioral measurement scale for gaming software, which will later be customized to the needs of the company, will be done through qualitative experiments. The development of a behavioral scale for gaming software requires a detailed and iterative approach. By combining in-depth interviews, observations, and thematic analysis, a sound and valid scale can be developed that adequately captures player experiences and behaviors. The diagnostics will be carried out as a pre-, in- and post-game analysis.

3. APPLICATION OF THE RESULTS

The diagnostic components can be used to measure individual professional skills of (potential) employees (e.g., work samples) as well as social characteristics (communication skills, team spirit, cooperation behavior, resilience, integrity) and psychological states important for activities (e.g., activation, emotions, flow, reactance, attitude) (Drengner/Sachse/Furchheim 2009; Sackett et al. 2022) in a test environment adapted to the new consumer needs and output as a competence profile. For example, the diagnostics in the specially developed (serious) gaming approach can be used to determine how skillfully a (potential) employee really programs, whether the (potential) manager has proven leadership qualities, what characteristics a (potential) customer service employee has in stressful situations, whether a person tends to act strategically/intuitively, individually/as a team player, hectic/thoughtfully. As an additional use of eSports offers for breaks and leisure activities (e.g., team-building measures), the employer image can be influenced, which can also be measured in terms of the evaluation of employee retention, employee loyalty, recommendation behavior, the associated increase in work motivation and employer satisfaction.

The measured values obtained from the multi-user environment specially tailored to this diagnosis are to be made available for automated evaluation in near real time using big data approaches (in particular streaming analytics). The constantly growing volume of data generated by the application can be used in anonymized form by machine learning methods to identify patterns in the behavior of all test subjects. After an intensive test phase during the project, the behavior of individual subjects can later be matched to these behavioral profiles in real time to enable HR and marketing analysts to make a faster assessment. The agile process of conceptualizing and developing the platform as well as several concrete application scenarios ultimately leads to the abstraction of a general building block box for applications. This includes the generalization of (serious) game elements into configurable building blocks for the development of new scenes/games as well as the abstraction of measurement and analysis elements into flexible building blocks for pre-, in- and post-game analysis.

REFERENCES

Abolhassan, F. (2016). What drives digitalization, Wiesbaden: Springer Fachmedien.

Abuladze, L., & Hasimi, L. (2023). *The Effectiveness and Attractiveness of Employer Branding: The Effects and Role of Gamification in Recruitment Activities.* Conference Paper, Economics.

Brademann, I., & Piorr, R. (2019). Generation Z - Analysis of the needs of a generation on the move into working life. In

B. Hermeier, & T. Heupel, *Working worlds of the future - How digitalization is changing our jobs and ways of working.*

Wiesbaden: Springer Gabler.

Drengner, J.; Sachse, M.; Furchheim, P. (2009). Flow in consumer research: A novel approach. ACR North American Advances.

Eichhorst, W.; Buhlmann, F. (2015). Die Zukunft der Arbeit und der Wandel der Arbeitswelt, IZA-Standpunkte, No. 77, Institute for the Study of Labor (IZA), Bonn.

Kunz, R. E.; Roth, A. & Santomier, J. P. (2021). A perspective on value co-creation processes in eSports service ecosystems. Sport, Business and Management: An International Journal.

Reusch, H. (2021). Gamification in Recruitment: Self-Assessment and Matching in Talent Relationship Management, Dissertation.

Sackett, P. R.; Zhang, C.; Berry, C. M. & Lievens, F. (2022). Revisiting meta-analytic estimates of validity in personnel selection: Addressing systematic overcorrection for restriction of range. Journal of Applied Psychology, 107(11), 2040- 2068.

Vargo, S.L.; Lusch, R.F. (2016). Institutions and axioms: an extension and update of service-dominant logic, Journal of the Academy of Marketing Science, Vol. 44 No. 1, pp. 5-23.

Woratschek, H., Horbel, C. & Popp, B. (2014). The sport value framework-a new fundamental logic for analyses in sport management, European Sport Management Quarterly, Vol. 14 No. 1, pp. 6-24.